Teaching Seminar

with

Milton H. Erickson

Teaching Seminar with Milton H. Erickson, M.D.

✦✦

Edited with commentary

by

Jeffrey K. Zeig, Ph.D.

BRUNNER/MAZEL, *Publishers* • New York

All royalties from this book are property of the Milton H. Erickson Foundation, 1935 East Aurelius Avenue, Phoenix, Arizona 85020. Royalties will be
used to foster educational and scientific efforts that pertain to Ericksonian
Psychotherapy and Hypnosis. Directors of the Milton H. Erickson Foundation, Inc., are: Jeffrey K. Zeig, Ph.D., Sherron S. Peters, Ms. Elizabeth M.
Erickson and Kristina K. Erickson, M.D.

THIRD PRINTING

Library of Congress Cataloging in Publication Data

Erickson, Milton H.
  Teaching seminar with Milton H. Erickson, M.D.

  Includes bibliographies.
    1. Hypnotism—Therapeutic use.   I. Zeig, Jeffrey K., 1947-   II. Title.
RC495.E73   616.89'162   80-23804
ISBN 0-87630-247-9

Copyright © 1980 by THE MILTON H. ERICKSON FOUNDATION
Published by
BRUNNER/MAZEL, INC.
19 Union Square
New York, New York 10003

MANUFACTURED IN THE UNITED STATES OF AMERICA

To Mr. and Mrs. Martin J. Zeig

"Into each life some confusion should come . . . also some enlightenment."

"And my voice goes everywhere with you, and changes into the voice of your parents, your teachers, your playmates and the voices of the wind and of the rain. . . ."

MILTON H. ERICKSON, M.D.

FOREWORD

✦✦✦

Although there is already considerable literature on the late Milton H. Erickson, M.D., the present volume deserves a warm welcome. Not only does it offer an opportunity to learn more *about* Erickson, but through this transcript of one of his teaching seminars, one comes as close as one can to learning directly *from* him.

Upon reading this book, even those who had the privilege to actually participate in a seminar like this one will undoubtedly discover aspects of Erickson's teaching of which they previously had been unaware. This statement can be made with confidence because the teaching method of Milton Erickson was such that, in the student's mind, confusion always preceded enlightenment, and the first was not necessarily followed promptly by the second. In spite of the very clarifying introductory chapter by Jeffrey Zeig, and in spite of the appendix which offers valuable information on how to understand Erickson's handling of the interaction during the seminar, the reader of the present volume may find himself caught up in the same sequence of confusion and enlightenment.

Relying upon "unconscious learning" (as Erickson does during this seminar) is a very powerful and penetrating method. However, it must be admitted that intellectual understanding has its charms and merits, too. In order to obtain more overt understandings, the reader is referred to the works of Haley, Erickson and Rossi, Bandler and Grinder, and the other commentators who offer frames of reference for further analysis of important aspects of Erickson's methods. In fact, the reader will be in a far better position to appreciate this seminar if he is already familiar with these other works.

Apart from introducing a very valuable book, writing this foreword is a particular personal pleasure, because I met Milton Erickson through a seminar quite similar to the one recorded here. Prior to meeting Erickson, for quite some years, some colleagues and I in the Netherlands worked on the development of a type of brief therapy which we called "Directive Therapy." Our approach was strongly influenced by Erickson, although we only knew of him through his writings and through the writings of Jay Haley.

It was from Kay Thompson, a long-time associate of Dr. Erickson, who had been giving courses in hypnosis in the Netherlands, that I learned that Erickson still received visitors when his health permitted. Dr. Thompson wrote a letter of introduction, and it was not only with great curiosity, but also with a sense of great respect, bordering on awe, that I undertook the trip to Phoenix.

Apart from an abundance of the color purple, I was not sure what to expect when I arrived. What struck me most in the initial meeting with him was his simplicity, friendly interest, and total lack of self-importance. Erickson expressed his pleasure at having a visitor from the Netherlands and initiated discussion by telling a story which, as I figured out later, was intended to establish a common point of interest between us. The anecdote was about the breeding of cows of Frisian descent in the Arizona desert, and the concomitant irrigation that was necessary to raise them. He explained how long ago the Indians had dug canals for irrigation, and concluded, "You wonder how they did the prospecting that was necessary to dig the canals." I certainly did wonder, although at the same time I puzzled about how his remarks related to the purpose of my visit.

The seminar with Erickson gave me many more occasions to wonder. From an uncommon therapist, an uncommon way of teaching should be expected. Erickson hurled a rock at a student, which upon hitting him would turn out to be an imitation rock made of foam rubber. He then stated emphatically: "Things are not always what they seem to be." Subsequently, he told a story of a therapy which illustrated that point.

At superficial inspection, the case histories seemed merely entertaining. Some of us wanted to get down to the "real teaching" and would ask questions for clarification. Erickson would answer with another story. Further questions would be answered by more stories. Rather than allowing us to digest a story and ruminate upon its meaning, Erickson would start a new tale at once, sometimes using a few jokes to first catch our attention, and sometimes without using any clear transition at all.

Except for brief, one-sentence statements at the beginning or conclusion of the teaching tale, Erickson hardly gave any explanation about what he wanted us to learn. This method forced us to draw our own conclusions and was at times somewhat distressing. The feeling of confusion and mild discomfort which resulted was one of the elements that contributed to the regularly occurring shifts of attention that Erickson labeled as the "natural trances" which facilitated unconscious learning.

I entered the seminar with the intention of asking a number of questions. I never did ask them. To some, I got answers without asking. The others I did not ask because I felt I was already receiving more information than I could handle. Only gradually did I discover a structure to the seminar. It was not until I was back in Europe that I began to grasp what I may have learned.

One of the more immediate impressions I gained was that Erickson put far less emphasis on always being a successful therapist than might have been expected from reading the literature about him. He stressed that the gains which could be achieved were at times of a limited nature and could sometimes consists only of a change in the patient's appreciation of himself and his symptomatic behavior.

Direct improvement of symptoms might not always be possible. It was a relief to hear him state that for some people a therapist can do nothing. Also, it was comforting to learn that sometimes even Erickson himself saw fit not to meet the patient on his own ground (as is illustrated in his correspondence with the stutterer who applied for treatment p. 202).

Clearly, Erickson had no urge to pose as a mythical figure of any kind. Rather he presented himself as a competent craftsman with a strong desire to transmit his skills. Instead of trying to impress his audience (which occurred anyway), he made an effort to get us on the tracks that were important to us and so familiar to him.

His love for craftsmanship was obvious not only in the collections of art and souvenirs with which he surrounded himself, but also in the care with which he told us a tale about a therapy or performed an induction.

Erickson's ways reminded me of one senior neurologist, also a remarkable craftsman in his trade, whom I had known during my training years. Difficult diagnostic cases were usually saved for him. He watched patients very carefully from the moment they entered the examining room. Overtly, although perhaps only for our benefit, he seemed to perform the standard neurological examination in a somewhat absentminded, perfunctory manner. But he appeared to be *drawn* towards the specific areas of pathology, rather than having to discover them by the laborious and methodological search that others used. Of course, his vast clinical experience had taught him to recognize subtle signs of which we had not even heard, many of which were not in the textbooks, and some of which he may not even have been consciously aware of himself. His approach resulted in the same deceptive simplicity as was typical of Erickson. He reached his diagnosis as a matter of course with the same admirable ease that Erickson demonstrated in finding crucial elements in the way a patient presented himself.

It can be dangerous for students to misinterpret this type of simplicity. Noticing that the well established rules of data-gathering are not respected, students may assume that it is all right to just follow their intuition. In his teaching stories, Erickson appeared to hardly gather any data and to do practically no diagnostic work. However,

Erickson had skillfully developed ways to learn very much while asking little. He succeeded in gaining his information inconspicuously. Further elucidation about the Ericksonian diagnostic process will be very important in order to make his methods more available to others.

It is clear that Erickson was concerned with different data from those used in general psychiatry or pyschodynamic therapies. He appeared to rely more heavily upon a knowledge about living, which seems to be at the core of direct and everyday experience, but with which traditional psychology or psychopathology seems to be hesitant to get involved. Erickson's diagnostic approach included individual idiosyncrasies, personal values, and unique circumstances, all of which contribute little to science as a body of generalizable data, but which are crucial to the individual and his potential for change. Another element of Erickson's diagnostic approach was that he was not a neutral collector of facts, but a searcher for solutions. He developed a particular talent to discover, in all kinds of events from the past, a meaning which may point to a positive future. From all kinds of symptoms, he could envision a constructive opening to a better life.

Even more than for his exceptional personal skills, Erickson will be remembered because his approach will change the direction of psychotherapy. Where others concentrated on analyzing shortcomings and trying to find compensation for weaknesses, Erickson showed how to discover potential, and how to turn losses into assets. In traditional psychotherapeutic thinking, the typical approach is to formulate a general theory of dysfunction and then apply it in specific cases. Difficulties consistently arise at the point of application. Unexpected individual variations which cannot be controlled keep coming up.

Erickson did not contribute much to theory in this classical tradition, but he endowed the profession with a treasure of examples on how to adapt to unique circumstances and effect change. He left it to others to construct theories of change out of his numerous experiments. Unlike Freud and others since him, Erickson did not create a closely knit school of followers with an organization to conserve and guard his contributions. Many therapists of different orientations have been inspired by Erickson, and some of them became his close friends and associates. It is a testimony to the richness of Erickson's contributions that he attracted several gifted therapists who, like Jeffrey Zeig, have been inspired to devote a great deal of time and effort in close collaboration with Erickson. These colleagues continue to collect, analyze and clarify Erickson's work, thereby making it more available to other therapists. Rather than producing "orthodox Ericksonians," he stimulated developments that branched off in many different directions, which is an eloquent illustration of his profound respect for the freedom and individuality of his students as well as his patients.

Several of the above points can be recognized in the anecdotes in the book. The one I love most is about the suicidal nurse, Betty (p. 149). It is more than a psychotherapy; it is a work of art. It is meaningful in many ways. To the audience it was a demonstration of various hypnotic phenomena. To the subject it was a therapy, or rather an indirect but powerful invitation to return to the project of living. Change was achieved by offering her a guided visit to nature's cycle of dying and regenerating, which in itself is fascinating. Note the master's touch: He does not simply point out the value of life. Dying is described first, thereby meeting Betty at her immediate frame of thinking. This story is not only typical of Erickson's therapeutic techniques but also is important in a broader sense. He was doing something very unique and worthwhile. At the same time he was going against the usual professional reaction of instinctive withdrawal. What other therapist would have had the courage to allow Betty to make her own decision after involving himself so deeply and so publicly? Consequently, Erickson was blamed for Betty's seeming suicide. It was many years before it finally became clear that the course he had taken had been right and wise from the onset.

RICHARD VAN DYCK, M.D.
President of the Dutch Society
of Clinical Hypnosis,
Oegstgeest, The Netherlands
June 24, 1980

CONTENTS

✤✤✤

ACKNOWLEDGMENTS

✠✠

I feel very fortunate to be able to thank many friends for their assistance and support in helping me to complete this manuscript. Dick Heiman, Dale Fogelstrom and Marge Cattey provided invaluable technical assistance that made videotaping of Erickson possible. Trude Gruber and Bernd Schmid provided materials that made completion of the transcript much easier. Elizabeth Erickson, Edward Hancock, and Roy Cohen did proofreading and made editorial corrections. Barbara Bellamy, Sherron Peters and Barbara Curtis assisted in typing of the manuscript. I am grateful to Mrs. Bellamy for her insistence on perfection.

My thanks to the participants at Erickson's week-long seminar for their cooperation with the videotaping.

Although the people are too numerous to name individually, a special recognition is due to many participants in my training workshops in the United States and Europe who provided stimulating

xvii

ideas that eventually became incorporated in some form in this book.

I am very grateful to Sherron Peters for her love and support during the writing of this book.

And to the memory of my mentor, Milton H. Erickson . . . he gave me much knowledge to pass on to other people. Erickson also taught me about enjoying both enlightenment and confusion and enhanced my appreciation of the wonders of opening my eyes.

J. Z.

ABOUT MILTON H. ERICKSON, M.D.

✦✦

Milton H. Erickson was generally acknowledged as the world's foremost authority on hypnotherapy and brief strategic psychotherapy. He was one of the most creative, perceptive and ingenious psychotherapeutic personalities of all time. Erickson was called the world's greatest communicator. Alternately, it has been said that he was the premier psychotherapist of the century. It is not hyperbole to state that history will demonstrate that what Freud contributed to the theory of psychotherapy, Erickson will be known as contributing to the practice of psychotherapy.

Erickson received his Bachelor's, Master's in Psychology and M.D. degrees from the University of Wisconsin. Among his other professional accomplishments, he was founding President of the American Society of Clinical Hypnosis, founding editor of the *American Journal of Clinical Hypnosis,* and founding director of the Education and Research Foundation of the American Society of Clinical Hypnosis. Erickson was Associate Professor of Psychiatry at Wayne State

University, College of Medicine. He was a Life Fellow of the American Psychological Association and a Life Fellow of the American Psychiatric Association. Erickson authored over 140 scholarly articles, most of which were on the subject of hypnosis. He co-authored a number of books, including *Hypnotic Experience: Therapeutic Approaches to Altered States, Hypnotherapy: An Exploratory Casebook, Hypnotic Realities, Practical Applications of Medical and Dental Hypnosis,* and *Time Distortion in Hypnosis.* Erickson is also the subject of a number of other books, both in print and in progress.

In regard to Erickson's professional approach, it is important to note that, although he created many new permissive approaches to therapeutic hypnosis, he was quite adamant in being atheoretical. Erickson had no explicit theory of personality that he promoted. He was a firm believer that an explicit theory of personality would limit the psychotherapist and make the psychotherapist more rigid. Erickson was committed to the ideas of flexibility, uniqueness and individuality. He made that clear in his writings and in the way that he lived.

Erickson moved to Phoenix, Arizona, in 1948. He maintained an active private practice and traveled frequently to teach hypnotherapy. During the later years of his life, when he could no longer travel, students came from around the world to listen to him and learn his approach. As busy as he was with his work, he was very much a family man. He was very proud of and dedicated to his family.

Erickson surmounted a considerable number of health problems throughout his adult life. He was confined to a wheelchair since 1967 from the residuals of anterior poliomyelitis. Erickson explained that he thought that poliomyelitis was the best teacher he ever had about human behavior and its potentials. Erickson had a color-vision deficiency, but he appreciated the color purple and enjoyed having it around him and receiving special gifts in that color.

Erickson was a genius in the practice of psychotherapy. However, his genius at practicing psychotherapy was eclipsed by his genius at living. In his later life, when the videotapes which comprise the bulk of this book were recorded, Erickson suffered from many physical problems. He suffered from an enormous amount of pain due to the residuals of polio and a host of other physical illnesses. He was practically quadriplegic—having little use of his right arm and limited use of his left arm. He had no real use of his legs. Erickson had use of only half of his diaphragm, his lips were partially paralyzed, and his tongue was dislocated. He could not wear false teeth. Here we had a man who had developed his voice as a tool and who prided himself on his ability to manipulate language. Yet his speech became thick and difficult to understand. Perhaps because of this, he spoke in a slow and measured voice. One had the sense that he was weighing the impact of each word.

Although he had to work to retrain himself in so many ways and although he suffered so many physical problems, Erickson was consistently one of the most glad-to-be-alive human beings that one could ever expect to encounter. Almost everyone who met him was impressed by his personal qualities.

Erickson was a very alert and lively individual. Sitting with him, one got the sense of an individual who was very present and very alive to the now—to the immediate moment. Erickson really enjoyed life and he was a very good model of living "the good life." He was a kind, considerate, compassionate person. He laughed often and had a bright, delightful smile. He had an infectious way of chuckling to himself when something amused him.

Erickson also had a delightful attitude of amazement and awe. He was a very positive person, very much the kind of person who looked at the flowers rather than the weeds. He encouraged his patients to do the same. Erickson was pleased by the positive changes that people could make. Whenever his patient made a positive change or whenever a patient did an arm levitation (even though for him it was the thirty-thousandth arm levitation), he was still pleased and amazed and very proud that his patient had accomplished that task. Most of that sense of awe and pleasure was transmitted on a nonverbal level, and that made it difficult to discount.

Further, Erickson would not take a sense of personal credit for the positive changes that his patients and students made. Instead, Erickson would communicate his delight that the person got in touch with new potentials and new power in his own life.

Erickson was born on December 5, 1901. He grew up in rural communities in Nevada and Wisconsin. That rural attitude was very much part and parcel of Erickson's life. He was future-oriented and unpretentious.

On March 25, 1980, Erickson died of an acute infection. He had been active and in relatively good health up to the time of his death.

In many of his teaching stories about working with chronic pain patients, Erickson explained that, after he applied his technique, the patient lived an active life until suddenly lapsing into a coma and dying peacefully. In a similar fashion, Erickson suddenly lapsed into unconsciousness on Sunday, March 23, 1980. He remained semi-conscious for two days until the night of Tuesday, March 25, when he died restfully, surrounded by family members. Erickson was active to the end. He had had every intention of continuing his teaching schedule before he suddenly became ill.

During much of his professional life in Phoenix, Erickson had his students and patients climb Squaw Peak, the highest mountain in the Phoenix area. It is about 1,100 feet high and the path to the top is a mile and a half long. The path is well traveled; people climb regularly for health reasons and for the spectacular view of of the Phoenix valley. The climb is a strenuous one, but a healthy person can make the climb to the top in 45 to 60 minutes. The path up the mountain is winding and has many ups and downs. One gets a good lasting feeling of accomplishment when one reaches the top. Further, one gets a higher point of view and a vaster perspective on the world in which he lives.

It is rumored that Dr. Erickson's ashes were scattered on Squaw Peak. If so, it is quite fitting. Erickson made that activity so much a part of his therapy. Now, to pay respects, people will continue to climb Squaw Peak.

Books Co-authored by Milton H. Erickson, M.D.

Cooper, L. F. & Erickson, M. H. *Time Distortion in Hypnosis.* Baltimore: The Williams & Wilkins Company, 1959.

Erickson, M. H., Hershman, S., & Secter, I. I. *The Practical Application of Medical and Dental Hypnosis.* New York: The Julian Press, Inc., 1961.

Erickson, M. H., Rossi, E. L., & Rossi, S. I. *Hypnotic Realities.* New York: Irvington, 1976.

Erickson, M. H. & Rossi, E. L. *Hypnotherapy: An Exploratory Casebook.* New York: Irvington, 1979.
Erickson, M. H. & Rossi, E. L. *Hypnotic Experience: Therapeutic Approaches to Altered States.* New York: Irvington (in press).
Haley, J. (Ed.). *Advanced Techniques of Hypnosis in Therapy: Selected Papers of Milton H. Erickson, M.D.* New York: Grune & Stratton, 1967.
Rossi, E. L. (Ed.). *The Collected Papers of Milton H. Erickson, M.D.* (4 volumes). New York: Irvington (in press).

INTRODUCTION

✦✦✦

A friend of mine who is a Swiss physicist told me a story about the famous Danish physicist Niels Bohr. At a lecture, Dr. Bohr was discussing Heisenberg's Uncertainty Principle. This principle of "complementarity" suggests that when an observer discovers information about the location of a particle, he sacrifices information about the momentum of that particle. Conversely, when the observer discovers information about the momentum of a particle, he sacrifices information about location.

At the lecture a student asked Bohr, "What is complementary to clarity?" After a moment of thought Bohr replied, "Precision."

Though possibly apocryphal, this anecdote expresses an important understanding. When it comes to truths, in order to be clear, it is necessary to be simplistic, thereby sacrificing precision; in order to be precise, it is necessary to be lengthy, detailed and perhaps confusing, thereby sacrificing clarity.

The manuscript that follows is a transcript of a week's teaching seminar for health professionals that Milton H. Erickson, M.D., held in his home in Phoenix, Arizona. Erickson's communication is complex and the reader will note Erickson's consummate precision. However, in trying to understand Erickson's process, the reader may also note some confusion and lack of clarity.

A word of note about Erickson's teaching seminars is necessary. After his formal retirement from private practice, Erickson continued to be actively engaged in teaching. Groups of students from around the world contacted Erickson and asked to be included in his teaching seminars. The students who attended Erickson's groups included physicians, psychologists, psychiatrists and master's level psychotherapists. Erickson taught from approximately noon to 4:00 p.m. each weekday. As Erickson's popularity grew, it became increasingly difficult to arrange time to learn from him. By the end of 1979, Erickson's schedule for 1980 was completely filled.

In the summer of 1979 (July 30 to August 4), I arranged to videotape a one-week teaching seminar at Dr. Erickson's home. That teaching seminar constitutes the bulk of this book. No commentary has been added to describe Erickson's technique during this week. Rather, the opportunity is given for the reader to involve himself in the transcript and come to his own conclusions and understandings about Erickson's methods and techniques.

Other authors describe Erickson's technique in detail. Haley (1973) takes an interactional view to describe Erickson's method. Bandler and Grinder (1975) use a linguistic approach based on transformational grammar to microscopically analyze Erickson's patterns of communication. Rossi (Erickson, Rossi, & Rossi, 1976; Erickson & Rossi, 1979), as a Jungian-oriented analyst, uses an intrapsychic perspective to understand Erickson. One can speculate that Erickson did well in promoting the description of his work by theorists with three such widely divergent perspectives. By reading the analyses of these authors, one gets a balanced perspective on Erickson's technique.

Erickson's method was characterized by indirection. Throughout his life Erickson taught indirectly. His early lectures were marked by the use of indirect technique. It is interesting to note that Erickson's fame also spread indirectly. Erickson was popularized more by the people who wrote about him than he was by his own efforts.

This volume is not meant to provide a different way of understanding Erickson. The idea is not to present anything new about Erickson; rather the idea is to present Erickson in a new light. Through this volume, one can get a feeling for the flow of Erickson's teaching stories and one can get a perspective on Erickson's process.

For those who never saw Erickson, this manuscript provides an opportunity to visualize Erickson in action. For those who did get to see Erickson, the manuscript provides an opportunity to get a different view on Erickson and his work.

It is very difficult to get clarity on Erickson's communication while listening to him in person. People frequently commented that they felt "woozy" when they listened to Erickson. It is a different experience to read Erickson's anecdotes or watch them on videotape. Perceiving Erickson from such perspectives makes it easier to understand what he did. Being with Erickson in person, one easily became confused due to the multiplicity of verbal and nonverbal levels on which Erickson worked. For example, it was not unusual for people to leave Erickson's teaching seminars with each one saying, "He was talking to me today."

Although, on first reading, Erickson's teaching stories may seem easily understandable, that is not really the case. I have presented films and videotapes about Erickson at meetings of national professional associations. I have challenged groups of professionals with the statement, "If you get 50% of what Erickson is doing, you are a very astute observer and listener." Although it may be easier to comprehend what Erickson does in transcript form, I can still make a similar challenge to the reader.

To demonstrate this challenge, I have included an Appendix in this volume. The Appendix provides a commentary that Erickson and I made on one of the hypnotic inductions that Erickson did during the week. The discussion of that 50-minute induction lasted for almost five hours. It should be interesting for the reader to read that induction (which occurred early on Tuesday with Sally) and compare his/her understanding with the details that are provided in the Appendix.

There are a number of other things to keep in mind regarding Erickson's teaching stories. Erickson was a very consistent individual. He lived and worked by telling stories. This was true if he was talking to his family, colleagues, students or patients. If one asked him for advice, Erickson usually replied with an anecdote. Therefore, in this book, one gets a good impression of Erickson's therapeutic, as well as his educational, approach.

Additionally, Erickson was very involved in the telling of his teaching stories. One often got the impression that he was reliving the story as he told it. Erickson told his stories with a sense of drama; he orchestrated his stories in a lively manner. These nonverbal facets are, of course, missing in a written transcript. Erickson's nonverbal behavior, his intonations, his laugh and sense of aliveness unfortunately cannot be reproduced.

Erickson told and retold these anecdotes many times. Because he was so conversant with the stories, he could add a lot of muscle into the communication and make the messages more powerful with the use of additional verbal and nonverbal techniques. Erickson knew what would come next, while his students didn't. Besides the content of the story, Erickson used his anecdotes to communicate on other therapeutic levels at the same time. In fact, Erickson never seemed to be satisfied with communicating on only one level. Perhaps he did not like the single-mindedness that came with doing only one thing at a time.

In regard to multilevel communication, most psychotherapists are trained to note that their patients will communicate on one level and to realize that the meaning of their patients' communication will lie on other levels, including historical and symbolic and other "psychological" levels. It is to Erickson's credit that he demonstrated that if the patient can communicate on a number of levels, the therapist can also communicate on a number of levels. Therapeutic communication does not need to be clear, concise and direct. Focused multilevel therapeutic communication can be a powerful technique. Erickson used multilevel communication consistently. For example, as one reads this manuscript, one realizes that many times Erickson described a principle, illustrated it with an anecdote and also demonstrated the use of the principle with the people in the room, all at the same time.

In this manuscript, effort was made to preserve as much of the original communication as possible. Minimal changes were made in order to preserve Erickson's style while still providing a readable transcript. Because of the extra precision that Erickson put into his hypnotic inductions, the inductions in the transcript were kept precisely as they were said. Editing Erickson's stories was not really difficult. For the most part, Erickson spoke in complete and grammatically correct sentences.

Erickson's use of stories depended very much upon the composition of the group that he was teaching. If Erickson was talking with a group that was interested in children, he would talk more about children. If Erickson was talking with a group that was more interested in pain control, then he would center on pain control. The group that was in attendance in the week transcribed was a mixed basic group; therefore, Erickson's approach was general. However, he did spend each day talking about a theme or two. Also, with some of the anecdotes, Erickson was definitely therapeutically working on expanding the flexibility of individual members of the group.

Erickson's nonverbal behavior during his teaching seminars was very interesting. He usually looked down at the floor while he told his stories. However, he would watch his students' and patients' responses from his peripheral vision. He had limited control of his body. When he wanted to mark out a therapeutic message to a particular student, he would do so by altering the locus of his voice.

Erickson did not have to use formal inductions to fixate his students' attention. People listening to him often had their eyes closed as they went in and out of trances spontaneously during the session. Erickson, himself, seemed to go in and out of trances. It was as if he used the opportunity to teach to get more outside of himself and thereby decrease the chronic pain that he suffered from the residuals of poliomyelitis.

REFERENCES

Haley, J. *Uncommon Therapy.* New York: Norton, 1973.
Bandler, R. & Grinder, J. *Patterns of the Hypnotic Techniques of Milton H. Erickson, M.D.,* Volume 1. California: Meta Publications, 1975.
Erickson, M. H., Rossi, E. L., & Rossi, S. I. *Hypnotic Realities.* New York: Irvington, 1976.
Erickson, M. H. & Rossi, E. L. *Hypnotherapy: An Exploratory Casebook.* New York: Irvington, 1979.

Teaching Seminar

with

Milton H. Erickson

❖❖❖

ERICKSON'S USE OF ANECDOTES

❖❖❖

One of the hallmarks of Erickson's approach was his use of anecdotes as a teaching device and as a therapeutic tool. Erickson was
known for his precise, focused communication which was geared to
the individual patient. His use of anecdotes represented a most highly
developed and effective use of verbal communication. In order to
supply the reader with a general framework that can be used to
understand the transcript that follows, some uses of anecdotes are
described. Additionally, my initial introduction to Erickson in 1973
is presented as an example of Erickson's use of anecdotes for powerful
multiple-level therapeutic communication.

Using Anecdotes in Psychotherapy

A dictionary definition of "anecdote" is a short narrative concerning an interesting or amusing incident or event. Anecdotes can be

---

Portions of this section were presented at the October 14, 1978 scientific meeting of
the American Society of Clinical Hypnosis.

3

fictional. For example, they can be fairy tales, fables, parables or allegories. However, anecdotes can also be narratives that chronicle true life experiences and adventures. The overwhelming majority of anecdotes that Erickson told were nonfictional descriptions of events from his own life and from the lives of his family and patients.

Anecdotes can be used in any type of psychotherapy and they can be used in any phase of the treatment process. There are no known contraindications for their use.

Certain operations are common to all psychotherapies, notably, diagnosis, establishing empathic rapport, and carrying out a treatment plan. Anecdotes can be used during any of these therapeutic operations.

Diagnosis

The astute observer can use anecdotes diagnostically. An anecdote can be used projectively somewhat similarly to the way that a Rorschach is used. In this sense, stimuli are provided that lead to a response that has diagnostic significance.

For example, a patient can be told a story that has multiple components, and the therapist can notice to what part of the anecdote the patient responds. The therapist can tell a story about a person having relationship problems with a spouse that stem from problems that the person had getting along with his parents when he was a child. Further, these problems have ramifications for the person's present sexual functioning and also lead to the abuse of alcohol.

This condensed story has a number of components. The observant therapist will notice to what parts of the anecdote the patient reacts nonverbally. Moreover, the observant therapist will also note what particular part of the anecdote is responded to verbally by the patient. Diagnostic information can then be followed up by the therapist.

A clinical example from the author's own practice can be cited to illustrate additional diagnostic use of anecdotes. A patient presented with a phobia of 13 years' duration and requested treatment by hypnosis. In the initial interview she was told a series of anecdotes about other patients who got over their problems in various lengths of time. Some patients got over their problems immediately and unexpectedly. These patients got over their problems quickly and needed little insight. Other patients got over their problems slowly and laboriously and enjoyed getting insight into their problems. This particular patient had a style of nodding her head affirmatively that was outside of her conscious awareness. She consistently nodded her head to the parts of the anecdotes that had to do with getting over problems slowly. Equally consistently, she refrained from nodding her head during the parts of the anecdotes that had to do with getting over problems immediately. This pattern was confirmed through the use of similar anecdotes told in varying orders.

(Because her head nod confirmed that she was going to get over her problem slowly, no therapy was attempted in the initial session. Instead, detailed questions were asked that concerned the etiology and pattern of her symptomatology. During the ensuing month, the patient was seen for two additional sessions and achieved relief of her phobia. There was no need to have more closely spaced sessions because the patient had already indicated that she was going to change slowly.)

While he told his stories, Erickson consistently kept track of the behavioral responses of his patients. Erickson often did not look directly at his patients when he told his stories. However, he did keep track of his patients' behavioral responses by watching them in his well-developed peripheral vision.

Erickson's perceptiveness was legendary. He diligently trained himself to notice and understand subtle nuances in human behavior. His ability to respond therapeutically was predicated on his acute diagnostic acumen. It is beyond the scope of the present work to delve into Erickson's diagnostic approach. However, the importance of Erickson's developed ability to quickly perceive core issues for individual patients cannot be emphasized enough.

Establishing Rapport

Establishing a sense of relatedness and empathic rapport is generally considered to be one of the cornerstones of psychotherapy. Some theoreticians (e.g., Carkhuff & Berenson, 1967) consider empathic responses to be one of the main tools of psychotherapy. However, there are drawbacks to the empathic approach. The patient can learn a self-diagnostic type of empathy that entails an ongoing scrutiny of his feeling states. Such scrutiny can be disruptive to the process of enjoying and utilizing the flow of feeling. In some cases, a direct empathic approach may be contraindicated or unnecessary. For example, it is not in some people's style to attune themselves to their feelings. Also, some patients object to or are embarrassed by having their feelings directly pointed out to them.

(Erickson's approach speaks to the idea that things function best when they function automatically or unconsciously, i.e., without interference or hindrance from the conscious mind. Erickson made much use of indirection in order to make unconscious change as quickly as possible.)

In line with Erickson's use of indirection, anecdotes can also be used to empathize with a patient and with processes that are either inside or outside of the patient's immediate conscious awareness. The patient does not need conscious realization that an empathic response was made by the therapist. Anecdotes can be used to establish empathic rapport with the unconscious. Although the fact that an empathic response has been made remains outside the patient's conscious awareness, the client still often acknowledges, on the verbal or nonverbal level, that an "unconscious" empathic response was made by the therapist.

To illustrate the use of empathic anecdotes, a case can be presented from an earlier teaching seminar with Erickson. In 1975, three students were present in Erickson's office to learn about his approach.

Erickson told an anecdote about a competitive patient who came to him and wanted to be put into a trance. Erickson stated that he established a trance with this patient by telling the patient to watch his own hands to see which one rose first and which hand touched his face first. In this way, Erickson utilized the patient's competitiveness to help the patient achieve his own goals. This was an engaging anecdote for the students because Erickson was teaching an interesting aspect of his technique.

However, it immediately became aparent that there was an additional purpose to this story. Some of the students at the session were themselves competitive for Erickson's time and attention. When the multiple purpose of the anecdote was pointed out, Erickson discussed this additional aspect of his technique. He stated that he recognized the students' competition and that he indicated to the students through his story that he recognized the ongoing competition.

The students could then respond by recognizing the competition consciously (which they did). Also, the students could have responded by making a nonverbal indication that they recognized the competition and that they were not ready to bring that information to conscious awareness. Lastly, the students could have failed to recognize the implied meaning of the story as it applied to the immediate situation.

Any of the aforementioned three responses would have been satisfactory responses to Erickson because they would have been in keeping with the students' own needs and personalities. Erickson was prepared to follow up on whatever direction was indicated. Erickson's own remark in that situation was that he was willing to discuss the anecdote consciously because it was a teaching situation.

Additionally, the anecdote had a third message. It was geared to suggest or "corner" the students into a particular behavioral response. After discussing the anecdote, Erickson added that he did not know how much competition there was among the students but that he certainly did not want them competing against *him*.

Treatment Process

Anecdotes can be used during any phase of the treatment process to achieve the goals of the therapy. For example, consider the following eight nonmutually exclusive categories.

1) *To make or illustrate a point*

Anecdotes can be used to make or illustrate a point. Through the use of anecdotes, a point can be made in a memorable and powerful way. In consideration of the structure of human memory, it is easier to remember the theme of an anecdote than it is to remember the same material in the form of a simple sentence. Anecdotes can be used to "tag" a person's memory; they make simple ideas come alive. Consider the following example:

Early in 1980, I was involved in my first case regarding the forensic use of hypnosis. Erickson was quizzed for some advice. He initiated the following story with the phrase, "Know the opposing attorney."

Erickson explained that he was testifying in a child custody case on behalf of the husband. He stated that the wife was clearly suffering from severe psychological problems and that the husband was the best person to have custody. Erickson then went on to say that he was familiar with the opposing attorney and knew her to be a very thorough individual. He explained that when the day came for him to give his testimony, the opposing attorney came well prepared. Erickson said that she had 14 typewritten pages of questions to ask him. Erickson said that when he got on the stand the lawyer asked, "Dr. Erickson, you say that you're an expert in psychiatry. Who is your authority?" Erickson responded by saying, "I am my own authority." Erickson knew that if he named someone, this well prepared lawyer would begin to undermine his expertise by citing conflicting authorities.

The lawyer then asked, "Dr. Erickson, you say that you are an expert in psychiatry. What is psychiatry?" Erickson said that he provided the following response: "I can give you this example. If I were an expert in American history, I would certainly know something about Simon Girty, also called 'Dirty Girty.' Anyone who is not an expert on American history would not know about Simon Girty, also called 'Dirty Girty.' "

Erickson explained that when he looked up at the judge, the judge was sitting with his head buried in his hands. The clerk of the court was underneath the table trying to find his pencil. The lawyer for his side was trying to suppress an uncontrollable laugh.

Erickson stated that after he gave that analogy the lawyer put aside her papers and said, "No further questions, Dr. Erickson." Then Erickson looked at me and said, "And the lawyer's name . . . was Gertie." Erickson went on to explain that whenever his lawyer faced that other lawyer in opposition, he always found some way of sneaking in a reference in his arguments to "Dirty Girty."

Erickson's anecdote was very amusing and engaging. It was a delightful way to make a point. If Erickson had told me, "Don't be intimidated by the situation," the impact would have been minimal. However, told in this engaging and illustrative manner, the impact of the message was enhanced.

2) *To suggest solutions*

Erickson often used anecdotes to directly or indirectly suggest a solution to his patient. Commonly this was accomplished by telling a *parallel anecdote* and/or by telling *multiple anecdotes* with the same theme. The conclusions of these anecdotes could provide either a new perspective or a previously overlooked solution.

Erickson would often tell a patient an anecdote that *paralleled* his problem but that provided a new perspective. For example, if a patient describes multiple failures in his life, he can be told stories about someone who experienced multiple failures. However, the therapeutic stories can be carefully constructed so that the final outcome is success. In this way, each of the failures in the therapeutic stories is constructed to eventually become a "building block" for success.

There is a good example of a parallel anecdote with a new perspective in the transcript of the week's session. On Tuesday, Erickson does an induction with Sally. He has her live through some difficult and embarrassing circumstances. Then he follows this up by telling Sally a story about a patient who lived through embarrassing circumstances and in the process became more successful and flexible in his life.

Erickson might also suggest an overlooked solution to his patient by telling a story. This particular use of anecdotes can be more therapeutically effective than giving direct advice which patients can be prone to resist. The patient is presented with a story about someone with a similar problem who used a solution successfully. Then it is up to the patient to actually make the connection and apply a similar solution in his/her own life.

Anecdotes can be used to indirectly suggest solutions. When the solution is suggested indirectly, the patient is the one who "gets the idea" of the solution. Thereby, the patient can make the change to his/her credit rather than to the credit of the therapist.

Erickson often used an indirect teaching style of telling *multiple anecdotes* with the same theme. For example, Erickson might have introduced an idea such as the importance of "meeting the patient within his own frame of reference." Erickson would then tell multiple anecdotes with the same theme threaded through each one of these stories. (Additionally, at the same time, Erickson would invariably demonstrate the principle by meeting the students at their frame of reference.) Erickson might have preceded the anecdotes by generally mentioning the theme or he might have mentioned the theme at the end of the series of anecdotes. If he realized that the patient or students had unconsciously (or consciously) gotten the point, he might not have mentioned the theme directly at all.

3) *To get people to recognize themselves*

One of the common tools that therapists use is confronting the patient so that he can see himself as he is in reality. Then the patient can change accordingly. Anecdotes can be used to supply such understanding in a more or less indirect manner.

For example, in the transcript of the week with Erickson, toward the end of Wednesday, Erickson tells stories about symbolic psychotherapy. He describes a case of a couple's therapy where he sends a psychiatrist and his wife out to do tasks alone. These tasks include climbing Squaw Peak and going to the Botanical Gardens.

In this case, Erickson used an activity to get patients to symbolically recognize themselves and take appropriate action. However, Erickson is also providing an example to the therapists in the room listening to him. The therapists in the audience can use the opportunity to recognize themselves.

Erickson follows the anecdote about the psychiatrist with another anecdote about a psychoanalyst and his wife. When one reads through these two anecdotes, one realizes that the anecdotes guide the audience's (and reader's) associations. It is very difficult to listen to Erickson telling these stories or to read those two stories without thinking about one's own relationships. Erickson could use anecdotes to guide associations and get people to recognize themselves so they could take appropriate action.

This use of anecdotes to guide and elicit associations was quite important in Erickson's approach. He was fond of providing this illustration: "If you want a person to talk about his brother, all you need to do is tell him or her a story about your own brother."

Erickson reminds us that the power to change is something that lies dormant within the patient and needs to be reawakened. Anecdotes can be used to guide people's associations, but it's really the patient who makes the change. "The therapist just provides the climate, the weather."

4) To seed ideas and increase motivation

In the case that was cited earlier about the phobic patient, it should be noted that the anecdotes that she was told were all about successful psychotherapy. Therefore, the anecdotes also served the purpose of increasing her positive expectancy. Further, the anecdotes would diagnose her motivation to change. It was clear from that patient's pattern of nodding her head that she was motivated to make the necessary change in her previously phobic pattern. The only question was in regard to how much time the change would take.

Erickson was quite capable of telling an anecdote that would stimulate a basic idea in a patient or student. Then, because he knew the sequence of his anecdotes, he could build on that idea with a story told later that day, or even days or weeks later.

This idea of "seeding" is very important in hypnotic technique. If the hypnotist is going to suggest an arm levitation, he does it by "chaining" small steps or seeds. For example, the operator will bring the person's attention to his/her hand; then bring attention to the possibility of sensation in the hand; then bring attention to the potential of movement; then bring attention to the desirability of movement; then bring attention to the fact of movement; and then suggest the actual movement. When the therapist knows the desired outcome, he can seed the idea of this outcome early in the therapy. Seeding technique was very common in Erickson's approach. It was one of the techniques that added much power to his communication.

5) *To therapeutically control the relationship*

Patients often learn maladaptive, manipulative and self-defeating relationship patterns. Anecdotes are an effective tool that can be used in controlling the relationship so that the patient is kept in a "one-down" complementary position (cf., Haley, 1963). Such a tactic by the therapist can be therapeutic for some patients who are rigid and who have problems being comfortable and effective when in a one-down position. Through the use of anecdotes, they can learn something about being secure although in a one-down position in a relationship. Anecdotes can keep a patient "off balance," so he/she cannot use habitual methods to control relationships. Through the use of anecdotes, patients can become secure in the knowledge that there is someone that they cannot manipulate with their symptomatology.

6) *To embed directives*

Anecdotes can be used to give embedded directives (cf., Bandler and Grinder, 1975). This technique entails taking an important phrase out of the context of a story and delivering that phrase directly or indirectly to the patient. An embedded directive can be presented to the patient or student indirectly, as, for example, by underemphasis or by the therapist's redirecting the locus of his voice.

For example, on Friday of the week's transcript, Erickson is discussing human sexual development. In the midst of that discussion of human sexual development, he tells a story about Dr. A. who was his supervisor at Wooster State Hospital. The anecdote appears to be out of context. However, imagine the effect of the last sentence of that anecdote were it directed to a resistant student. In that last sentence, it is suggested that the person maintain "a blank face, your mouth shut, your eyes open and your ears open, and you wait to form your judgments until you have some actual evidence to support your inference and your judgments."

7) *To decrease resistance*

Anecdotes are indirect and for that very reason they are helpful in decreasing resistance to ideas. An anecdote stimulates an association inside the patient. The patient can then act on the association that was stimulated. It is difficult to resist an association that one has oneself.)

Also, an anecdote can present an idea indirectly. Many ideas are presented in one anecdote and the patient has to become actively involved in the process of making sense of the anecdote and deciding what portion of the anecdote relates to him. Thereby, the energy for change is stimulated to come from within the patient.

Anecdotal messages, because of their structure, can become unconscious quickly. The patient cannot consciously absorb and understand all of the messages contained in a complex anecdote. The patient can experience a behavior change occurring outside of his/her conscious awareness because he/she can respond to part of an anecdote even though that part was not registered consciously. It is often reported that patients saw Erickson and found themselves changing on their own without realizing the effect of Erickson's own therapeutic communication.

In general, Erickson used anecdotes when an increased amount of indirection was called for. The more resistance there was to ideas, the more indirect and anecdotal Erickson became. This follows from the principle that the amount of indirection used is directly proportional to the amount of perceived resistance (Zeig, in press, b).

Additionally, anecdotes can be used in technical ways to defuse resistance. For example, an idea can be seeded in one anecdote and then the therapist can quickly switch to a second anecdote that has a different theme. This type of therapeutic maneuver makes it more difficult for the patient to resist the idea presented in the initial anecdote. Additionally, in using this maneuver, there is an increased chance that the idea presented in the first anecdote will become "unconscious" more quickly. The patient can have an amnesia for the first story.

Anecdotes can also be used to distract the patient. Erickson has suggested that he used anecdotes at times to therapeutically bore the patient. Such technique can be a set-up for presenting the therapeutic idea at a time when the patient is less resistant and more responsive.

8) *To reframe and redefine a problem*

Anecdotes can also be used to "reframe" a problem. The art of reframing has been described by a number of authors (e.g., Watzlawick, Weakland, & Fisch, 1974). Reframing is a technique for supplying an alternative and positive attitude for the symptomatic situation. Reframing works on the level of attitudes. Patients have attitudes about their symptoms. Reframing can change the person's attitude about his symptoms.

Changing attitudes about the symptom is therapeutic. Erickson was a proponent of the idea that therapy is anything that changes the habitual pattern of behavior. Change could happen in a positive direction or it could initially occur in a negative direction. Changing a person's attitude about his symptom can often change the symptom complex itself (cf., Zeig, in press, b).

Redefinition is a technique of defining the problem in a slightly different way than the patient defines the problem. After defining the problem in a different way, therapy can be supplied that will correct the new definition of the problem, thereby correcting the problem. Erickson used anecdotes to do both reframing and redefining.

A good example of using anecdotes to provide reframing and redefinition of the problem is found in the beginning of the day on Thursday when Erickson talks with Christine and tells her anecdotes about headaches. When you read those anecdotes, note how Erickson reframes and redefines Christine's headache.

The categories presented above are by no means exhaustive. A number of additional uses of anecdotes can be listed:

1) Anecdotes can be used for ego-building techniques, i.e. to build up a person's emotion, behavior and/or thinking, thereby helping the patient to get more balance in his life.

2) Anecdotes themselves are a creative and unusual way of communicating. In that sense, they serve to "model" the good life. The therapist encourages the patient to live more creatively and flexibly by being creative and flexible in his own communication.

3) Anecdotes can be used to stimulate and reawaken patterns of

feeling, thinking and behaving. Anecdotes can be used to help a person get in touch with a resource in his personal life that he had not previously realized. Erickson reminds us that patients have the resources in their own history to resolve the problem that they bring to the therapist. Anecdotes can be used to help remind a patient of his own resources.

4) Anecdotes can be used to desensitize a patient from his fears. In working with phobics, one may tell a series of anecdotes and alternately increase and decrease tension, thereby desensitizing the fear.

Anecdotes can be used for a variety of technical reasons in any psychotherapy. Anecdotes can also be used during formal and naturalistic induction and utilization of hypnosis.

USING ANECDOTES IN HYPNOSIS

Anecdotes and formal hypnosis have three basic structural similarities: 1) In both, the therapist basically speaks to a passive subject. The therapist attempts to elicit the power inside the patient and demonstrate to the patient that he or she has the power to change. 2) In the use of hypnosis and in the use of anecdotes, the subject is defined to be in a one-down complementary role. 3) In both techniques, the operator works from the patient's minimal behavioral cues.

Because of the structural similarities, anecdotes can be very effectively applied in both formal and naturalistic hypnosis. Anecdotes are applied in hypnosis in a way similar to the way that they are used in psychotherapy. Anecdotes can be used to diagnose hypnotizability and to create rapport. Anecdotes can also be used in the induction and utilization phases of hypnotic treatment.

Diagnostic Use

Anecdotes can be used diagnostically to assess the hypnotizability and the style of trance utilization that the subject will manifest. The diagnostic process is similar to the diagnostic use of anecdotes in psychotherapy that was described above. However, additional factors go into diagnosing hypnotizability.

Four factors—absorption, responsiveness, attentiveness and control —are especially relevant.

1) (When telling an anecdote, the therapist can notice the degree of absorption that the listener manifests. Those subjects who manifest the most rapt attention and who seem the most absorbed in the story usually tend to be the classically better hypnotic subjects.)

2) One can assess something about the responsive style of the particular subject by using anecdotes. Some people respond more to direct suggestion and others respond best to indirect suggestion. One can use anecdotes to learn what type of suggestion the patient responds to best.(For example, if, in telling an anecdote, the operator mentions that the protagonist of the anecdote suddenly looks up to notice what the time is, one can determine something about the responsiveness of the patient by noting his reaction to this particular type of suggestion.)

3) Anecdotes can be used to diagnose the style of attentiveness of the patient, whether it is focused or diffuse, and whether it is internal or external. As the patient listens to an anecdote, the therapist can note whether the patient is focused or diffuse in his style of attentiveness. A more focused person will show limited movement and will focus on one thing for extended periods of time. A more diffuse person will move more often and shift his/her attention from one thing to the next.

(Attentiveness can also be diagnosed as to whether the focus is internal or external. Internal people are preoccupied with their own inner life—their own feelings and thoughts and movement. External people are more attentive to what is going on around them. (Erickson was like a cat. He enjoyed watching, and was very external in his orientation.)

4) (By telling an anecdote, the therapist can also learn something about the patient's flexibility in regard to control in relationships. Some patients need to be one-up, some need to be one-down and some need to be equal. These needs come out in the verbal and nonverbal response to "prehypnotic" anecdotes.)

While many other factors can be used to diagnose hypnotic style, the above four factors of absorption, responsiveness, attentiveness and control are especially amenable to be diagnosed while the therapist is casually telling the patient a story. In consideration of this diagnostic approach (and without straying too far beyond the scope of this book), implications for composing a therapeutic strategy are clear. (The anecdotes and directives that a therapist tells are most powerful when they closely match the patient's experience. For example, the hypnotic and psychotherapeutic techniques that one applies to a one-down, externally oriented person who is highly responsive to direct suggestion should be different from the therapeutic techniques one applies to a one-up, internally absorbed person who is more responsive to indirect suggestion.)

At first, until one really learns how to do it, using anecdotes diagnostically can be quite taxing for the therapist. The therapist needs to compose his story and pay attention to his patient's responses at the same time.

Use in the Induction Phase of Hypnosis

Anecdotes can be used in formal hypnosis. Charles Tart (1975) has aptly described the induction of hypnosis as consisting of disruption of the basic state of consciousness and patterning of a new hypnotic state of consciousness. Anecdotes can be used in either of these two phases.

Disruption

(Confusion technique can be used to facilitate disruption of the subject's conscious set in the early phase of formal hypnotic induction. Anecdotes, in themselves, are confusing in that they keep the listener off balance. The listener is challenged to make sense out of the content of the anecdote and realize and apply the relevance of the message to his/her situation. Moreover, anecdotes are confusing in that they have multiple meanings and are ambiguous. Listening to Erickson, even an astute listener could not possibly be aware of all of the component messages and their possible referents. Anecdotes can "set up" an induction by distracting and depotentiating the conscious set (cf., Erickson, Rossi & Rossi, 1976). Thereby, the subject can become more open and more responsive to concurrent and subsequent suggestions.)

Erickson often naturalistically used anecdotes as an entrée into hypnotic induction. I have seen a number of Erickson's ex-patients who explained that they would listen to Erickson's stories and all of a sudden find themselves in a trance. One patient explained that she was listening to Erickson's stories and found herself getting sleepy. She said she was quite embarrassed about getting sleepy listening to her doctor. Then she stated she realized that was what Erickson wanted and so she closed her eyes and drifted into a trance!

Patterning

Anecdotes can be used to pattern the hypnotic state (i.e., to establish experiential parameters of what the hypnotic state can be for the particular individual). An operator can use anecdotes to describe and suggest to the patient what hypnosis can be like for him or her. A possible example of this technique would be to tell an inexperienced subject about the hypnotic experience of another, more experienced subject. This could be done in such a way that the behavior of the experienced subject discussed in the anecdote matched and overlapped with the actual behavior of the inexperienced subject. The effect would be to give the inexperienced subject suggestions in an indirect manner.

Another way of patterning the hypnotic state is to have subjects demonstrate to themselves (in or outside of conscious awareness) that they can do some of the classical hypnotic phenomena. Any of the classical hypnotic phenomena can be suggested through the use of directed anecdotes. For example, one of Erickson's favorite inductions entails anecdotal discussion of early school learnings, including how people learn the letters of the alphabet and how they learn to form mental and visual pictures of the letters of the alphabet without consciously realizing that process. This anecdote suggests and can elicit many classical hypnotic phenomena, including age regression, hyperamnesia, dissociation and hallucination. Moreover, it simultaneously fosters an internal absorption and internal fixation of attention.

Use in the Utilization Phase of Hypnosis

In the utilization phase of hypnotherapy (i.e., after induction), anecdotes can be used in the same way that they can be used in the treatment phase of psychotherapy, e.g., to make a point, increase motivation, etc. Anecdotes can be told to remind a person of previously unused potentials in learning. For example, in work with pain control, one can remind the hypnotic subject, through use of an anecdote, about a time when he/she had a minor injury and didn't realize the pain until a considerable amount of time had passed. Such a story implies that the subject already has experience in controlling pain that can be reawakened.

Anecdotes are engaging and can promote dissociation as the patient involves him/herself in the story. Thereby, anecdotes can also be used to set the patient on a train of thought that excludes his/her symptomatic problem. Such use of anecdotes is also very effective in pain control work.

<h2 style="text-align:center">COMBINING USES OF ANECDOTES—MULTIPLE
LEVEL COMMUNICATION</h2>

Psychotherapists learn to take a small sample of social level communication and interpret additional meaning in regard to what is "really" happening on the patient's psychological level. It is interesting to note that, although therapists are aware of multiple-level communication and use it diagnostically, most therapists are not trained to use multiple-level communication as a therapeutic tool. It may be one of Erickson's major contributions to psychology that he demonstrates therapeutic use of multiple-level communication. Erickson demonstrates how much muscle can be packed into therapeutic communication and how much of the fat can be stripped away.

To demonstrate powerful, multilevel therapeutic communication, discussion of my initial introduction to Erickson in December of 1973 is presented. The anecdotes Erickson told me demonstrate a complex combining of some of the aforementioned simple uses of anecdotes. Before describing these anecdotes in detail, and to set the stage, I will describe my intial meeting with Erickson from the beginning.

I started studying hypnosis in 1972 and became quite impressed by Erickson's work. Serendipitously, I wrote to my cousin, who was studying nursing in Tucson. I told her that I was studying hypnosis and suggested that if she should ever go to Phoenix, she should visit Erickson because he was a genius at doing psychotherapy.

My cousin wrote back and she told me that I had met Erickson's second-to-the-youngest daughter. My cousin and Roxanna Erickson had been roommates years earlier in San Francisco.

Subsequently, I wrote to Roxanna and wrote to Erickson and asked if I could study with him. He explained that he would take me as a student. In December 1973, I drove to Phoenix for the first time to learn from him.

My initial introduction was quite unusual. At about ten-thirty at night, I arrived at Erickson's home. I was to stay in his guesthouse. I was greeted at the door by Roxanna. She introduced me to her father, gesturing to Dr. Erickson, who was seated to the immediate left of the door watching television. She stated, "This is my father, Dr. Erickson." Erickson slowly, mechanically moved his head upward, in small stepwise movements. When his head reached the horizontal, he slowly, mechanically, using the same stepwise movements, twisted his neck toward me. When he caught my visual attention and looked in my eyes, he again started the same mechanical, slow stepwise movements and looked down the midline of my body. To say that I was quite shocked and surprised by this "Hello" would be an understatement. Nobody had ever said "Hello" to me like that before. Roxanna took me into the other room and explained that her father was a practical joker.

However, Erickson's behavior was an excellent nonverbal hypnotic induction. All of the parts necessary to induce hypnosis were presented in Erickson's nonverbal behavior. He was confusing and he disrupted my conscious set. My conscious expectation was that he would shake hands and say "Hello." Further, Erickson modeled hypnotic phenomena. He modeled the stepwise cataleptic movement that patients show when they do an arm levitation. Moreover, his behavior focused my attention. Then, when he looked down the midline of my body, he was suggesting for me to "go down inside." Basically, Erickson was using nonverbal technique to disrupt my conscious set and to pattern a new unconscious pattern set.

Erickson had provided me with an example of the power that he could put into communication.

The next morning, Erickson was wheeled into his guesthouse by Mrs. Erickson. Without saying a word or making any visual contact, he painfully transferred himself from his wheelchair to his office chair. I asked him if I could set up my tape recorder and without making any visual contact he nodded yes. Then he began to speak to the floor in a slow, measured way:

E: To aid you over the *shock* of all the purple . . .
Z: Uh-huh.
E: I am partially color-blind.
Z: I realize that.
E: And the purple telephone . . . was a gift from four graduate students.
Z: Uh-huh.
E: Two of whom *knew* they would fail their majors . . . and two of whom knew they would fail . . . their minors. The two who knew they would fail their majors, but *pass* . . . their minors . . . passed all. The two who knew they would pass their majors and flunk their minors . . . flunked their majors and passed their minors. In other words, they selected the help I offered. (E. looks at Z. for the first time and fixes his gaze.) Concerning psychotherapy . . . (Here Erickson went on to introduce and discuss his therapeutic approach. To read how Erickson continued, see Zeig, in press a.)

This brief anecdote is an elegant piece of communication. It contains many levels of message. It is an excellent example of how many messages can be condensed into a relatively short communication. What follows is a listing of the messages that Erickson was directing to me in that brief anecdote:

1) The anecdote was a confusion induction of hypnosis. No mention was made of hypnosis, but the anecdote with its references to majors and minors was, in fact, confusing. Also, it did fix my attention hypnotically. I had already studied Erickson's confusion induction (Erickson, 1964) and had incorporated the use of confusion induction in my technique. However, Erickson's approach was so casual and

so unusual that I did not realize that he was using confusion technique on me.

2) Erickson's first sentence contained the word "shock," which was emphasized in a peculiar fashion. Actually, as Erickson was well aware, seeing all the purple was as no shock to me. I had already been in Erickson's office and guesthouse (which was decorated in purple) and I had already met Erickson (whose clothing was all purple-colored). I had already gotten over the shock of all the purple color. Erickson's emphasis on the word "shock" was done to focus my attention and to alert my unconscious to the shock that was already happening, and the shock that was about to come.

3) Erickson's nonverbal behavior was also confusing. He did not look at me. He spoke while looking at the floor. I had a lifetime of learning that indicated, "When you speak with somebody, look at them." Erickson's nonverbal behavior disrupted my habitual pattern. Then, when he did look at me, it supplied additional confusion and shock. This had the further effect of fixing my behavior and attention.

4) One of the effects of this communication was that I was amnesic for the entire anecdote. It was not until I returned home and played the tape at a hypnosis seminar I was attending that I heard what was said. It was then that I realized that Erickson had supplied a confusion induction of hypnosis. It was a wonderful experiential learning for me and an excellent demonstration of my own capacity to experience amnesia.

5) There were a number of things inside the story that had meaning. The content of the story was about graduate students. Erickson met me within my own immediately understood frame of reference. He established some relatedness by talking about graduate students, a subject to which I could well relate and understand.

6) The anecdote had a message in its immediate content. The graduate students who were there to learn from Erickson had some unexpected things happen. I could relate the anecdote to my own situation. Some unexpected things could happen to me. Actually, some unexpected things were already happening to me, not the least of which was that never before had anyone introduced himself in such an unusual fashion or talked to me in such an unusual fashion.

7) Moreover, the anecdote was about students who selected the help that Erickson offered. In a parallel form, he was also

implying that I, as a student, would also select (although perhaps unexpectedly) from the help and teaching that he offered me.

8) There was an additional message contained in the anecdote. These students came to learn from Erickson. In return, they presented him with a gift. Erickson never charged me anything for his teaching because I could not really afford to pay him for his time. Erickson's policy was that if you could pay for your visit you did. If you did not have the financial resources, he refused to charge for his time.

However, I could repay Erickson for his time by presenting him with a gift. I gave him a wood carving that sat on his desk (as did the purple telephone). I cannot be sure that one of the "seeds" for my presenting Erickson with a gift wasn't contained in that anecdote. It is possible that my presentation of that gift was partially due to responsive behavior.

9) Erickson's anecdote had the effect of structuring what kind of relationship we would have. Erickson stopped me from speaking and introducing myself. He made it clear that the relationship was going to be a complementary relationship where Erickson would be doing the talking and I would be one-down and doing the listening.

10) I am quite certain that Erickson was also evaluating my responsiveness. Out of his peripheral vision he was noting my response to the concepts that he mentioned. For example, when he mentioned the purple telephone, I may or may not have glanced at the purple telephone on his desk. Thereby, he learned something about my style of responding to suggestions.

11) There is an additional aspect to this anecdote. In 1980, a psychologist from Phoenix named Don came to me and asked for individual supervision in the Ericksonian approach to psychotherapy. I agreed to see him and provide that supervision. In our conversation, he explained to me that in 1972 he and some other graduate students went to see Erickson. In return for his time, they wanted to give Erickson the gift of a purple telephone. Don explained that they had much difficulty in getting a purple telephone from the telephone company, but that eventually they were successful.

Subsequently, during one of our individual teaching sessions, I played the tape for Don of my initial meeting with Erickson. Don explained that he and three other graduate students went to learn from Erickson and that Erickson was tutoring them through their preliminary examinations. In fact, two of the students passed their examinations and two failed.

The anecdote Erickson told me was absolutely true!

After his introduction, the next case that Erickson discussed with me was an example of Erickson's early work with a psychotic patient (reported in Zeig, in press, a). This was also very effective in establishing rapport because he was talking with someone who was a novice psychotherapist about an example of therapy that he had done in the 1930s, when Erickson himself was just a beginner. Additionally, he was discussing a case of working with a psychotic patient and I had worked for many years with psychotic patients. Erickson used the few facts that he knew about me very well.

The next two cases that Erickson discussed with me were both examples of patients that Erickson was not effective with in psychotherapy. In fact, Erickson did not do much work with either of these patients. One patient was used as an example that to assume anything about a patient was very wrong. The other patient was used as an example of the importance of making a quick and accurate diagnosis. However, there was also another message involved. Erickson was speaking to the importance of understanding the fact that some patients are not amenable to psychotherapy and that it does not pay to invest therapeutic energy in such patients. That message took on an added dimension, considering the fact that it was given by someone who was known for his overwhelming successfulness in doing psychotherapy.

These anecdotes of my initial meeting with Erickson present an example of some of the complex and powerful communications that characterized Erickson's style. Erickson's teaching method was enhanced by his ability to use multi-level communication.

WHY USE ANECDOTES

To review and summarize, there are a number of reasons for using anecdotes. They can be illustrated in the following way:

THE WIND AND THE SUN

The North Wind and the Sun once fell into a dispute as to which was stronger of the two. They related their most famous exploits, and each ended as he began, by thinking he had the greater power.

Just then a traveler came in sight, and they agreed to test the matter by trying to see which of them could soonest make the traveler remove his cloak.

The boastful North Wind was the first to try, the Sun meanwhile watching behind a gray cloud. He blew a furious blast and nearly tore the cloak from its fastenings; but the Man only held his cloak more closely, and old Boreas spent his strength in vain.

Mortified by his failure to do so simple a thing, the Wind withdrew at last in despair. "I don't believe you can do it, either," he said.

Then out came the kindly Sun in all his splendor, dispelling the clouds that had gathered and sending his warmest rays down upon the traveler's head.

The Man looked up gratefully, but growing faint with sudden heat, he quickly flung aside his cloak, and hastened for comfort to the nearest shade (Stickney, 1915).

In summary, anecdotes have the following uses and characteristics:

1) Anecdotes are nonthreatening.
2) Anecdotes are engaging.
3) Anecdotes foster independence. The individual needs to make sense out of the message, and then come to a self-initiated action. In this way, anecdotes foster a sense of self-determined mastery. The patient takes credit and responsibility for change. The change comes from inside the patient rather than being due to the therapist's direction.
4) Anecdotes can be used to bypass natural resistance to change. Anecdotes can be used to present directives and suggestions in such a way as to maximize the possibility that they will be accepted. When a patient has a symptom, his/her neurotic defenses are built up. Through use of anecdotes, his/her defenses can be breached indirectly. If a patient is going to follow suggestions, then indirection is not necessary. In general, the amount of indirection necessary is directly proportional to the anticipated resistance. In Erickson's style of doing hypnotic inductions, he seemed to be more direct with

subjects who were more classically responsive. With subjects who were more resistant, Erickson was more prone to present ideas through his anecdotal method.

5) Anecdotes can be used to control the relationship. The listener needs to work to make sense of the anecdote. When listening to an anecdote, the listener is kept off balance. The listener cannot use habitual ways of controlling relationships when he/she is forced to listen to an anecdote.

6) Anecdotes model flexibility. Erickson was devoted to creativity. He used anecdotes as a way of expressing his interest in subtlety and creativity. Margaret Mead (1977) wrote that one of the hallmarks of Erickson as a person was his desire to be creative.

7) Erickson used anecdotes to create confusion and promote hypnotic responsiveness.

8) Anecdotes tag the memory; they make the presented idea more memorable.

Conclusions

Anecdotes are best used when they are carefully geared and individualized to the respective patient. Anecdotes should be constructed so that they meet the patient within the patient's frame of reference. They are best used to establish changes that are consistent with and follow from the patient's own behavior and understandings. In this way, a cure that has previously been dormant is elicited. The best use of anecdotes is not to trick the person out of his symptom but to get him to change under his own power and to his own credit (cf., Zeig, in press, a).

Anecdotes have the further effect of modeling to the patient a creative and flexible way of being in the world. Thereby, patients learn experientially that they can confront their own rigidities and confining habits and become more flexible and effective in their living.

With these ideas in mind, pay attention to your associations and realize the effect that the teaching anecdotes that Erickson presents have on you.

REFERENCES

Bandler, R. & Grinder, J. *Patterns of the Hypnotic Techniques of Milton H. Erickson, M.D.*, Volume 1. California: Meta Publications, 1975.

Carkhuff, R. R. & Berenson, B. G. *Beyond Counseling and Therapy*. New York: Holt, Rinehart and Winston, 1967.
Erickson, M. H. The Confusion Technique in Hypnosis. *American Journal of Clinical Hypnosis*, 1964, 6, 183-207.
Erickson, M. H., Rossi, E. L., & Rossi, S. I. *Hypnotic Realities*. New York: Irvington, 1976.
Haley, J. *Strategies of Psychotherapy*. New York: Grune & Stratton, Inc., 1963.
Mead, M. The Originality of Milton Erickson. *American Journal of Clinical Hypnosis*, 1977, 20, 4-5.
Stickney, J. H. *Aesop's Fables*. Boston: Ginn and Co., 1915.
Tart, Charles T. *States of Consciousness*. New York: E. P. Dutton, 1975.
Watzlawick, P., Weakland, J., & Fisch, R. *Change: Principles of Problem Formation and Problem Resolution*. New York: Norton, 1974.
Zeig, J. K. Symptom Prescription and Ericksonian Principles of Hypnosis and Psychotherapy. *American Journal of Clinical Hypnosis*, in press. (a)
Zeig, J. K. Symptom Prescription Techniques: Clinical Applications Using Elements of Communication. *American Journal of Clinical Hypnosis*, in press. (b)

The
Seminar

MONDAY

❖◆

The session takes place in Dr. Erickson's guesthouse, a small three-room house containing a bedroom, waiting room (with an adjoining kitchen) and Dr. Erickson's office. Sessions are held in the larger waiting room due to the fact that Dr. Erickson's office is too small to accommodate the groups which sometimes consist of as many as 15 people. There are three bookcases in the room. The waiting room is decorated with diplomas, pictures and memorabilia.

The students sit in a circle on a couch and on cushioned folding chairs. To the left of the spot where Erickson sits in his wheelchair is a green stuffed armchair which often is "the subject's chair."

Erickson is wheeled into the waiting room by Mrs. Erickson. Erickson allows a number of students to clip lapel microphones to his jacket. He then holds up a pencil that has an ornamental top. The ornamental top consists of a head with purple fiber hair. The fibers are neatly lined up in a pointed shape on top of the pencil. As he

31

displays the pencil Erickson says to the group, "People come here like this." Then he twirls the pencil vigorously between his palms, disrupting the fibered hair, and states, "And they leave here like this."

Erickson then indicates to people that they should fill out some data sheets. He requests that they write the following information on a sheet of bond paper: the present date; their name, address, zip code and telephone number; their marital status and number of children; their education and where their degrees were earned; their age and birthdate; siblings and their sexes and ages; and whether they were brought up in a rural or urban environment.

Erickson waits while people fill out the requested information. Then he carefully reads each sheet, making comments to some of the participants. He corrects some students who did not supply all of the requested information.

We begin the session as Jan, a psychologist from New York, replies to a comment from Dr. Erickson by stating that she had a number of years of experiences being an only child. Erickson then responds to her:

E: Now how much sympathy does a 15-year-old girl have for a seven-year-old brother?

Jan: Things started to turn around after that.

E: Poor brother.

Jan: He survived.

E: You have no siblings? (Dr. Erickson addresses Anna, a social worker from Switzerland.)

Anna: Yes, I do have. I didn't hear clearly what to fill in. What do you want me to fill in?

E: Siblings, their ages and their sex.

Sande: Hello, Dr. Erickson, I am Sande. (Sande is a therapist from New York who just entered the room.)

E: (Acknowledges Sande with a nod.)
    Carol, your degree and the date. (Carol is a doctoral student in clinical psychology from Massachusetts.)

Carol: Date of degree?

E: No, today's date. Your name, address, telephone number, your

zip code, your degree, where you got it, your siblings and their
sex and ages, your marital state, children, urban or rural background.

Siegfried: I am Siegfried from Heidelberg, Germany. (Siegfried is a
Ph.D. clinical psychologist.)

E: Pleased to meet you.

Siegfried: Is it OK if I put an additional microphone on you?

E: Any number of bugs will be all right.

Siegfried: Thank you.

Sande: Can you tolerate one more?

E: I have a soft voice. I had polio twice, my tongue is dislocated
and my lips are partially paralyzed. I have only half a diaphragm
and I can't speak too loudly. Your tape recorders will record
what I say all right, but you may have difficulty understanding
my speech. If you don't understand, why not tell me about it.
And then another precaution—all of you who are hard of hearing, sit up closer. Usually the people with hearing difficulties
sit way back. (Erickson laughs.)

Now, in teaching psychotherapy I emphasize a state of conscious awareness and a state of unconscious awareness. For convenience sake I speak about the conscious mind and the unconscious mind.

Now the conscious mind is your state of immediate awareness.
Consciously, you are aware of the wheelchair, the rug on the
floor, the other people present, the lights, the bookcases, the
night-blooming cacti flowers, the pictures on the wall, Count
Dracula on the wall right behind you. ("Count Dracula" is a
dried skate that hangs on one wall.) In other words, you are
dividing your attention between what I say and everything
around you.

The unconscious mind is made up of all your learnings over a
lifetime, many of which you have completely forgotten, but
which serve you in your automatic functioning. Now, a great
deal of your behavior is the automatic functioning of these
forgotten memories.

For example . . . I will pick on you. (Erickson smiles and
addresses Christine, a physician from California, who has a

strong German accent.) Do you know how to walk? How to stand up? Will you please tell me how you stand up?

Christine: By probably shifting my center of gravity and at the same time . . .

E: Now how did you move your center of gravity?

Christine: Making many unconscious adjustments, I am sure.

E: Well, what are they?

Christine: I don't think I am aware of it.

E. Do you think you could walk six blocks down a street with no traffic of any kind at a steady pace? And can you walk in a straight line at a steady pace?

Christine: Probably not accurately at a steady pace. And I think the more attention I pay to it the less I would succeed.

E: Now, how would you walk down the street?

Christine: If I made an effort? . . . Worse than if I didn't make an effort.

E: What?

Christine: Much worse than if I didn't make an effort.

E: How would you walk down the street naturally . . . in a hurry?

Christine: Setting one foot in front of the other and not paying attention to it.

E: And how straight a line would you walk?

Christine: I don't know. Maybe reasonably straight.

E: And where would you stop and where would you pause?

Christine: Where circumstances make it appropriate.

E: Now that's what I call an evasive answer. (Erickson laughs.) Where would you pause and where would you stop?

Christine: If there were a red light I would stop.

E: Where?

Christine: At the curb.

E: Not until you got to the curb?

Christine: Maybe just before the curb.

E: How far before the curb?

Christine: A few steps, maybe one step.

E: Well, suppose instead of a stoplight, there is just a stop sign, and suppose there is no sign?

Christine: If there were traffic, I would stop.

E: I said there is no traffic of any kind.

Christine: Then I might continue.

E: Well, say this is the intersection (Erickson gestures) and if there was a stoplight and you walk along here, you look up and then you move your head to see how far it is to the curb. And if there is a stop sign you slow down to read that. And when you got to the curb, what would be the next thing you did?

Christine: After I stopped?

E: After you reach the curb.

Christine: I would stop and look around.

E: Look around where?

Christine: In the directions where I anticipate traffic might be approaching.

E: I said there was no traffic.

Christine: Then I would continue. Then I would look across the street and assess how big a step I have to take down.

E: You have to stop and see how far down you have to step, and you look right and left and up the street automatically. And when you get to the opposite curb, you pause and measure the height of the curb there and you wouldn't have to look right or left. And what would cause you to slow down?

Christine: Oncoming traffic?

E: Well, if you were hungry, you would slow down passing a restaurant. After looking at your necklace, you would veer towards the jewelry store. (Christine laughs.) And a man who likes hunting and fishing could veer from a straight line toward a sporting goods store window.

And, where would all of you *all slow down?* At what building? ... As if you were walking through an invisible barrier? Didn't any of you try to walk past a bakery? You always slow down passing a bakery—man, woman or child.

(Addresses Christine.) Now, since you are a doctor, how did you learn to stand up? The same question applies to all of you. You know how you learned to stand up. What was your first bit of learning?

Christine: Making the effort and trying.

E: You didn't even know what "stand up" meant. How did you learn to stand up?

Christine: Maybe by accident.

E: Not everybody has the same accident. (Laughter.)

Rosa: 'Cause I wanted to reach something. (She is a therapist from Italy.)

E: Well, what was it you reached for?

Rosa: What I was reaching for?

E: Don't try to answer that question.

Anna: Probably by wanting. By wanting to do the way other people do. As a little baby reaching to the grownups coming up.

E: Yes, but how did you do it?

Anna: Physiologically, pushing my feet down, I imagine . . . and then helping myself with my hands.

E: (Speaking to the group, but looking at a particular spot on the floor in front of him.) I had to learn to stand up twice—once as an infant and once as an 18-year-old boy. I was totally paralyzed at 17. I had a baby sister. I watched her creeping around and I watched her to see how she stood up. And I learned from my baby sister, 17 years younger than me, how to stand up.

First you reach up and pull yourself up. Then accidentally, sooner or later (you all make the same accident), you discover that you put some weight on your foot. And then you discover that your knee bends and you sit down. (Erickson laughs.) Then you haul yourself up and you try the other foot and the knee bends again. It takes a long time to learn to put your weight on your feet and to keep your knees straight. You have to learn to keep your feet far apart and never get them crossed, because if you get your feet crossed you can't stand up. You have to learn to keep your feet as far apart as you can. Then you keep your knees straight and then your body betrays you again—you bend at the hips.

After awhile, after many efforts, you manage to keep your knees straight, your feet far apart, your hips straight and you hang on the side of the playpen. You have four bases—two of your feet and two of your hands.

And then what happens when you lift this arm? (Erickson

lifts his left hand.) You sit down. It is quite a job to learn to lift this hand and a bigger job to put your hand out because your body goes over that way. (Erickson gestures to the right and to the left.) And then it goes that way, and that way. And you have to learn to keep your balance no matter how you move this hand. And then you have to learn how to move the other hand. And then you have to learn to coordinate it with the movement of your head, your shoulders and your body. And finally you can stand up with both hands free.

Now, how do you shift from two feet to one foot? It is an awfully big job because the first time you try to do it, you forget to hold your knees straight and your hips straight, and you sit down. After awhile you learn to put all your weight on one foot and then you move one foot forward and that alters your center of gravity, so you fall down. It takes a long time to learn how to put one foot forward. So, you finally take your first step and it seems to be pretty good. Then you take the second one with the same foot and that doesn't seem so good. You take a third one and sit down. It takes a long time to go right, left, right, left, right, left.

You all can walk, yet you really don't know the movements or the processes.

(Erickson addresses Christine) Now, you speak German, do you not?

Christine: Yes.

E: How much more easily did you learn English than German?

Christine: Not any more easily. It was more difficult to learn English.

E: Why?

Christine: German was natural and came effortless because I heard it being spoken. English I learned . . .

E: You had to learn an entirely new set of vocal movements. You had to coordinate those with your ears. Can you say "The bird flies high?"

Christine: The bird flies high.

E: Now say it in German.

Christine: Der Vogel fliegt hoch.

E: Can you say it in Plattdeutsch?

Christine: No.

E: Why not?

Christine: I never learned it. I don't think I could even understand it. It's quite different.

E: Do you know this: "It's nice to be Preiss (pronounced 'price'), but higher to be Bayer (pronounced 'buyer')?"

Christine: I don't think I quite understood.

E: It's nice to be Preiss, but higher to be Bayer.

Christine: I've never heard that.

E: I can't speak German. My accent may be wrong. It's good to be Prussian, but it's better to be Bavarian. (Laughter)

Siegfried: Would you please speak louder.

E: Now, I want to make the accusation of all of you that you talk too softly. I think the truth is, I can't hear so well. (Erickson laughs.)

(Erickson speaks while looking down.) All right. In psychotherapy you teach a patient to use a great many of the things that they learned, and learned a long time ago, and don't remember learning.

The next thing I want to say is that we all have billions of brain cells. Billions and billions of brain cells. And brain cells are highly specialized. You learn German with one set of brain cells, and you use another set of brain cells to learn English and another set of brain cells to learn Spanish.

The illustration I can give you of that is this: I had two patients on a ward that I used to illustrate things for one of my medical students. Both patients had a minor hemorrhage of the brain—a very minor hemorrhage. One patient could name anything. But if you asked him what you do with these things, he didn't know. He could name a key, and the door, the doorknob, the keyhole. He could name anything, but he didn't know any verbs.

The other patient didn't know the names of things, but he could illustrate their use. He couldn't name a key; he couldn't point out a keyhole or a doorknob or a door. And if you handed him a key and told him "Unlock the door," he didn't know what you were talking about. But if you indicated to put it in the keyhole, he'd unlock the door. If you told him "Turn the doorknob," he didn't know what you were talking about. If you showed him this (Erickson gestures to indicate turning the doorknob), he understood. If you pulled the door open he understood that.

In other words, your brain cells are so specialized that you have literally a brain cell for every item of knowledge, and they are all connected.

Now, another thing I want to call your attention to is the matter of hypnosis. Hypnosis is the ceasing to use your conscious awareness; in hypnosis you begin to use your unconscious awareness. Because unconsciously you know as much and a lot more than you do consciously. (Addresses Sande, who is sitting in the green chair.) I am going to ask you to change seats with . . . (Addresses Christine.) What is your first name?

Christine: Christine.

E: Kristie?

Christine: Christine. (Christine moves to the green chair.)

E: Has Joe Barber put you in a trance?

Christine: Yes.

E: Many times?

Christine: A few times.

E: All right. Lean back in your chair and look at that horse. (Erickson indicates that she look at a plaster horse on the bookcase across the room. Christine adjusts her posture and puts a note pad aside. Her legs are uncrossed and she puts her hands on her thighs.) Do you see it?

Christine: Yes.

E: Just look in that general direction. I want all of you to listen to me and note what I am saying.

Now, Christine, just look at that horse. (Christine readjusts the note pad and puts it on her left side, between her and the chair.) You don't need to move. You don't need to talk. I am going to remind you of something that you learned a long time ago. When you first went to school and the teacher asked you to learn to write the letters of the alphabet, that seemed to be a terribly difficult job. All those letters. All those different shapes and forms. And what made it worse, there were printed letters and small letters. (Christine blinks slowly.) And while I've been talking to you, your respiration has changed. Your heart rate has changed. Your blood pressure has changed. Your muscle tonus has changed. Your motor reflexes have changed. And now (Christine closes her eyes), I would like to have you keep your eyes closed, and I would like to have you feel very comfortable. And the more comfortable you feel, the deeper into trance you'll go. I would like to have you go so deeply into a trance that it will seem to you that you don't even have a body. You'll feel yourself to be just a mind without a body. A mind floating in space. Floating in time. And memories of long ago will come back to you. Memories that you had long ago forgotten.

And my voice will go with you everywhere, and my voice can become the voice of your parents, your teachers. It can become a German voice. It can be the voice of your playmates, your schoolmates, your teacher.

And next, I want you to learn something else very important. I want your body to keep sleeping deeply, soundly, in a very deep trance, and after awhile I want just your head to awaken. Just your head. For your body, sleep. From above the neck you will be wide awake. Now it will be difficult for you to do so, but you can awaken from the neck up. It will be hard, it will be difficult, but you can do it. And let your body sleep soundly. You can make more effort than that; even though you don't want to awaken, you are *going* to awaken from the neck up. (Christine opens her eyes.)

How do you feel?

Christine: Fine. (Christine smiles. Initially as she speaks to Erickson her body is rigid and her visual attention is focused solely on Erickson.)

E: And, what memories would you like to share with us?

Christine: The only thing I experienced was what you were saying.

E: Yes . . . How about school?

Christine: I don't believe I had a memory of school.

E: You don't believe you had a memory of your school days?

Christine: I could recount something consciously now, but I did not experience anything.

E: You are sure of that?

Christine: (Looking up.) I think so.

E: You feel that you are awake.

Christine: As you said, I am awake from the neck up. (Smiling.) I think that if I made an effort I could probably move my hands, but I just don't feel like doing it.

E: One of the important things you learn when you are first born (Christine looks to the camera) is that you don't know you've got a body. You don't know, "This is my hand (Erickson gestures with his left hand), and this is my foot."

And you cry when you are hungry (Christine looks to the group) and your mother can pick you up and pat you on the tummy and put you back. Your thinking is not sufficiently advanced, but your emotions are. And when the next hunger contraction hits (Christine looks to the group as her right hand slowly rises) you say emotionally to yourself, "That dinner didn't stick to my ribs very long." Your mother can pick you up and pat you on the back and it feels like a good dinner until the next hunger pangs hit you and you again react emotionally to the fact that the poor dinner didn't last very long.

And sometime after you've learned to pick up and play with a rattle or some other toy, you happen to notice this hand. (Christine's hand stops moving. It is at a level just below her shoulder.) It looks interesting so you reach for it and you have a terrible problem figuring out why does that "toy" go away when you try to pick it up. Someday you accidentally try to pick up this "toy" and you look as puzzled as can be because toys feel one way and don't feel . . . on both sides of you. Here you get palmar and dorsal stimulation, and to learn this is more easily done.

How come your hand is lifted?

Christine: I noticed that it wanted to begin to levitate before I opened my eyes. I know where it is.

E: Is that the important thing, or is the important thing that your hand levitated and you don't know why?

Christine: (Smiling.) That's right. I always rationalize it because it has happened before.

E: What's that?

Christine: I always rationalize it and I always observe it because it's happened before. It is usually this hand that will do it.

E: Well, what caused it to levitate?

Christine: (Shaking her head.) I don't know.

E: There is a lot of your behavior you don't know about. You always use your right-hand direction and levitate up to your face. (Christine's hand begins to move up to her face. Shortly, the back of her hand touches her face. The palm of her hand faces the group and her thumb and little finger are extended.) And you know that you are not doing it and it will stick to your face and you can't move it away from your face. Now, the harder you try to take it away, the more it will stick to your face. So try hard to put it away. Because you can't. (Christine smiles.) The only way you can get that hand down . . . (Erickson has his left hand up.)

And you are very responsive. I made a hand movement and you started to copy it.

Christine: Pardon.

E: I made a hand movement. You started to copy it. Now, the only way that you can get that hand down to your lap is to have the other hand lift up and shove it down.

Christine: At this point I am always in a tremendous conflict because I think that I could do it, but I also am trying to be polite. And I'm not sure whether I am role playing, in order to be polite, or whether I really can't do it.

E: I know. You are letting your intellect interfere with your learning.

Christine: It always does.

E: Now I'll call the attention of everybody. Did you ever see anybody sit that still, that quietly. And she didn't turn her head to look at me first. She turned her *eyes* to look at me first. Ordinarily, when you want to look at somebody, you turn your face. (Addresses Christine.) And you turned your *eyes*. You separated your eyes from your head and your neck.

Christine: My arm is getting tired.

E: What's that?

Christine: My arm is getting tired.

E: I'm very glad to hear that. When you *really* want your right hand to go down, your left hand will lift up and push it down. And you think you're awake, don't you?

Christine: (Weakly.) Yes.

E: You really do, don't you. And you really don't know that you are asleep. How long do you think you will be able to keep your eyes open?

Christine: I don't know.

E: Will they close *now*? (Christine's eyes blink.) And stay closed? (Christine's eyes close.) Now you want to rationalize that? (Christine opens her eyes.)

Christine: I wish I could eliminate that silly conscious mind of mine. It always rationalizes everything.

E: Are you aware of the fact, you can't stand up?

Christine: No.

E: Are you beginning to have doubts that you could stand up?

Christine: Uh-huh.

E: Aren't you behaving like a sacral block?

Christine: Like a what?

E: Sacral block. A sacral anesthesia . . .

Christine: Oh, I see what you mean. Oh, yes.

E: Aren't you behaving that way?

Christine: Almost.

E: She didn't watch her wiggle (Erickson points to another woman) and watch all the others wiggle. Now all of you understand what I mean when I say "watch the others wiggle." You're staying awfully still for somebody who is awake. (Christine moves her right elbow slightly.) Now let your arm get more and more tired until you *want* to . . . (Christine closes her eyes) use your left hand to push it down. . . . (Christine smiles, opens her eyes, and lifts her left hand and gently pulls her right arm down.)

You feel more awake in your arms, don't you?

Christine: In my hands? Yes.

E: Can you move them? Your fingers aren't your hands.

Christine: It's so much effort. (Smiling.)

E: Can you rationalize that effort? The doctor here is an anesthesiologist and she is interested in hypnosis. Now to produce a sacral block in a pregnant woman, I would many times put her in a trance like this and never mention anything else. And I tell her, "When you go into the delivery room, think about the sex of the baby, its weight, its appearance and features, whether or not it will have hair. After awhile, the obstetrician, who is in full charge of the lower half of your body, will tell you to look and see what your baby is. He will hold it up. You have a complete sacral block—a total anesthesia."

When my daughter, Betty Alice, had her first baby, the doctor was very worried. He was a student of mine. And she said, "Don't worry, Doctor, you are an obstetrician, you know your business. In the delivery room you own the lower half of my body, I only own the upper half." And she started telling the nurses and delivery room personnel about teaching school in Australia. After awhile the doctor said, "Betty Alice, don't you want to know what it is?" And he was holding up a baby boy. She said, "Oh, it's a boy. Hand it to me. I'm like any other mother, I've got to count its fingers and toes." She should know what was going on, except she was talking about school teaching in Australia.

I notice that all of you are constantly changing your posture. (Christine smiles.)

(Erickson looks to the floor.) I had a patient once, who came to me for therapy. She had been coming for several months. And one day she said, "I'm going to go into a trance, Dr. Erickson." And when she was in a trance she said, "I feel so comfortable, I'll stay here all day." And I said, "Unfortunately, there are other patients coming in. You can't stay here all day." She said, "I don't care about the other patients." I said that I make my living seeing patients. She said, "That's all right, I'll pay you for every hour. I'm going to stay here all day." (Erickson looks at Christine.) How would I get rid of her? I told her to enjoy her sleep and "I *do* hope you don't have to go to the bathroom."

(Addresses Christine.) Your shoulders are waking up.

Christine: Do you want the rest of me to wake up?

E: I think it will save you some embarrassment. (Erickson laughs and Christine smiles.)

Christine: I just didn't know what I was supposed to do.

E: Well, I do hope you don't have to go to the bathroom too suddenly. . . . (Christine laughs and moves her hand.) You are
getting better acquainted with yourself now. (Christine adjusts
her body and hands.)

Christine: Yes.

E: You don't have to go to the bathroom. (Laughter.)

(Addresses the group.) Who among you have never been in a
trance?

(Addresses Carol.) You haven't. (Addresses Siegfried.) And
you haven't. Well, doctor, a pretty girl is easier to look at in a
trance than a man. Isn't that your experience?

Siegfried: Would you please repeat, I didn't get it.

E: A pretty girl is easier to look at.

Siegfried: Now I got it. (Laughter.)

E: (Addresses Carol.) So, will you change seats with . . . (Christine
and Carol change seats.)

And did all of you notice, I didn't ask anything of Christine.

Rosa: Did you ask if we were ever in a trance before, and she was
never in a trance? Oh, I was never in a trance before. I thought
you asked a different question, that's why I didn't. . . .

E: (Addresses Christine). Your name is Kristie, isn't it?

Christine: No. Christine.

E: Christine. Did I ask you to sit over there?

Christine: I thought you asked me to change places with her.

E: No, I asked her. (Indicating Carol.)

Christine: Oh, what would you like me to do.

E: Well, you have already done it. I didn't ask you to wake up.
(Laughter) I let your conscious mind take over. I only asked
her if she would sit *here*. You did all the rest.

(Addresses Carol.) You've never been in a trance? (Carol is
sitting with her arms on the arm rests.)

Carol: I'm not really sure. (Carol shakes her head "no.") Maybe one
time, maybe not. (Carol adjusts her hands slightly.)

E: Your name?

Carol: Carol.

E: Carol. (Erickson lifts Carol's left hand by the wrist and leaves it
suspended cataleptically. Carol looks at her hand and then looks

at Erickson. Her wrist is bent and her fingers are spread widely.) Is it your common experience to let a strange man lift your hand and leave it in midair? (Carol looks away, then looks back at Erickson.)

Carol: It's never happened to me before. (Carol laughs.) But I'll wait and see what happens.

E: Do you think you are in a trance?

Carol: No.

E: You really don't?

Carol: No.

E: You're sure?

Carol: After watching that, I'm not sure. (Carol laughs.)

E: You're not sure. Do you think your eyes will soon close? (At this point Carol is looking at Erickson. Erickson continues to look directly at her.)

Carol: I don't know.

E: You don't know.

Carol: It feels like I will.

E: Are you really sure your eyes won't close and stay closed?

Carol: I'm not sure. They feel blinky. (Smiling.)

E: Do you suppose that soon they'll blink shut and stay shut?

Carol: The chances are getting better. (Laughter from the group. Carol smiles.)

E: You're not really sure at all are you, Carol?

Carol: No.

E: But you're beginning to get sure your eyes will close. (Carol's eyes blink.) Pretty soon now . . . and stayed closed. (Carol's eyes close.)

In psychotherapy, you ought to know that your patient knows more about his past learnings than you can ever know. You don't know how you go to sleep. You don't know how you let loose your awareness, your conscious awareness. And so when a patient comes to me, I have all the doubts. I doubt in the right direction. The patient doubts in the wrong direction. (Erickson addresses Carol as he slowly moves her arm back down to her lap.) More and more comfortable. And go so deeply asleep, that it will seem to you as if you had no body at all. It will seem to you as if you were just a mind, an intellect, floating in space, in time.

Maybe you are a little girl playing at home, or maybe you are a little girl in school. I would like to have many memories you have forgotten a long time ago come forth. I want you to have the *feelings* of a little girl. *All* the feelings. And whatever feelings you had, sometime later, you might choose to tell us some of them.

You might be playing a game on the school grounds. You might be eating your lunch, or you might be interested in your teacher's dress, and what you see on the blackboard, or the pictures in a picture book . . . things you have forgotten a long time ago.

And the year is not 1979—it's a long way off. It's not even 1977—It's not even *1970*. And I don't know if the year is 1959 or 1960. I don't know whether you are looking at a Christmas tree or a church or playing with a dog or a cat.

After awhile you will awaken and tell us about the little girl named Carol. And really be that nice little girl, Carol, in the year of 1959 or 1960. Maybe you'll wonder what you will be when you're a big girl. I would like you to have the experience of letting your body sleep deeply while you awaken only from the neck up. (Erickson waits for a moment. Then Carol turns her head and looks at him.)

E: Hi. (Erickson looks directly at Carol. During most of the induction, Erickson was looking at the floor in front of Carol.) What would you like to say to me?

Carol: You look like a nice man. (Carol's voice sounds young.)

E: I do?

Carol: Uh-huh.

E: Thank you. Where are we?

Carol: I think in a park. (As Carol speaks her attention is focused on Erickson.)

E: In a little park.

What are you going to do when you are a big girl?

Carol: I don't know, that's a long time away.

E: It is a very long time away. What do you like to do now?

Carol: Games.

E: What kind of games?

Carol: Ball.

E: Ball?

Carol: Hopscotch.

E: Hopscotch. Where do you live? Near this park?

Carol: No.

E: Where?

Carol: I live far away. I'm just visiting here.

E: Where do you live far away?

Carol: In Reading.

E: Where is that?

Carol: Pennsylvania.

E: Pennsylvania. (In a lilting voice.) How old are you?

Carol: Five.

E: You're five years old.

Carol: Maybe three, I think. Or four.

E: Three or four. And what do you like best about this park?

Carol: Well, I like to come here with my Grandfather and look at his friends.

E: Do you wish they were here now?

Carol: No.

E: And are there lots of trees?

Carol: Trees and benches and a store.

E: Any people around?

Carol: Then?

E: Now.

Carol: Now, Yeah. Uh-huh.

E: Who are these people?

Carol: Professionals.

E: You are only three or four or five years old. Where did you learn to say such a big word as "professional"? (Carol smiles.)

Carol: Well, I know the difference between now and then.

E: How do you feel right now that you can't stand up?

Carol: I wasn't aware that I *can't* stand up.

E: Now you are aware.

Carol: Very strange.

E: It is.

Would you like to have me tell you a secret?

Carol: I'd love that.

E: Now, all the people around here have forgotten to hear the traffic sounds. (Erickson smiles.) And I never once told them to be deaf. And all of a sudden they begin to hear the traffic noise. And how many of *you* are in a trance? (A number of people have their eyes closed.) If some of you look around you will see a lot of immobility.

(Addresses Carol.) Close your eyes. (Carol closes her eyes.) Just close them. And enjoy sleeping soundly . . . in a very comfortable trance, and (Erickson addresses others) you too, and you too. Close your eyes *now*. All the way *now* . . . and go into a deep trance because you have got billions of brain cells that will function and you will learn all that there is to learn.

In teaching psychiatry to residents in psychiatry I would give them each a book to review at home. I told them, "Someday, three or four months from now, I'm going to call a meeting of all of you. Every one of you better have your book read and be ready to give a total review of the book." And they knew I meant it. Now some of my residents were good hypnotic subjects and about four months later I'd call the residents together in the conference room and say, "Remember . . . I assigned some books to each of you to review. The time has now come for the review." And those who were not hypnotic subjects were feeling very happy because they knew they had already read the book I assigned. And they would one by one give their report on the book.

The residents who were good hypnotic subjects would look unhappy and distressed. When I would call them one by one, they would say unhappily, "I'm sorry, Dr. Erickson, I forgot to read that book." I would tell them, "I do not accept excuses. You were assigned the book to read and were told in three or four months to be ready with your report. And you tell me you haven't even read it. Do you know the title and the author?" They would tell me the title and author, and apologize again. And I would tell them "Get out some paper and take your pen and each of you summarize what you *think* the author should have put in the third chapter; summarize what you think he should have put in the seventh chapter, and in the ninth chapter." And they wildly looked and said, "But how would we know that?" "Well, you know the name and the title of the book. That is all there is to it. Sit down and summarize those three chapters each one of you." They would sit down and start writing: "I think that the author in chapter three would discuss a,b,c,d,e,f,g and a whole list of things." "In chapter seven I think the author discussed. . . ." And then they listed the things. "And in chapter nine, I think that the author discussed. . . ." Then I got out the books and asked them to read chapter three and look at their written report and they would ask, "How did I know that?" They had read the books in a hypnotic trance and had no recollection of it. But they had a far better book review that just came out of their head. They didn't recall reading the book. And after a couple of times when that happened, they no longer got frightened when we came into the conference room to report on the books. They knew they must have. (Erickson laughs and looks at Carol.)

And shortly, Carol, I would like to have you awaken all over. Gently, comfortably.

What do you think about that Count Dracula hanging there? (Erickson points.) During the day, that is where he lives. But at night he comes alive and feeds on blood. (Carol smiles.) Now all of you have seen Count Dracula. You see, this way he doesn't need a coffin, and nobody suspects who he is. (Carol moves her arms.)

(Addresses Carol.) Would you like to have me tell your fortune?

Carol: Yes.

E: (Erickson looks at Carol's outstretched palm.) See this line—do you see the letters "R, e, a, d, i, n, g"? It's the name of a park.

Carol: Name of what?

E: Name of a park.

Carol: Park.

E: In Pennsylvania. Over here you see your Grandfather? Do you really enjoy going to that small park in Reading, Pennsylvania? How am I at palm reading?

Carol: What?

E: How am I at palm reading?

Carol: Not bad. (Carol laughs and lets her hand drop.)

E: Now why did I talk about Count Dracula? Why did I speak about Count Dracula?

Count Dracula has an appeal for childhood.

Siegfried: Has a what?

E: Appeal—an interest for childhood.

Anna: Appeal for what?

Siegfried: An influence on children?

E: No, an interest.

Siegfried: An interest.

E: (Addresses the group.) So I am saying something that children think about. And palm reading is another useful thing. And the fact that Count Dracula is a long, long way from Reading Park allowed for amnesia and directed her attention away from this chair to Reading Park, to her childhood, to the past, and I didn't tell her to have an amnesia.

(Addresses Carol.) What am I talking about?

Carol: I haven't been able to follow it very well. (Laughs.)

E: So, she hasn't been able to follow it very well. (Laughs.) And all of you were taught by your teachers and your parents, "Look at me when I speak to you, and you look at me when you talk to me." And she came here and listened to me and I've evoked a pattern of behavior that belonged to long ago.

(Addresses Christine.) She was unable to follow me even when I was talking about her.

(Addresses Carol.) When did you leave that place in Pennsylvania that had Reading Park?

Carol: After high school.

E: Well, how did I know that you and your grandfather went to Reading Park?

Carol: (Whispering.) I told you.

E: (Overlapping.) He did, didn't he? And you liked to look at his friends. Any other dark secrets of yours that you don't want me to know? (Laughter.)

(In therapy, the patient actually does the therapy, you only furnish a favorable climate. Then you let them bring forth the things they have repressed and the things they have forgotten for one reason or another.)

Isn't it funny how all the traffic sounds stopped again? (Erickson smiles.) Now you hear them again.

All right. Now we move in three different ways. It may be intellectually, it may be emotionally and we move motorically by moving around. Some move more than others.

Now, the ability to move from one place to another . . . A polar bear can live in the Arctic, but not in the Antarctic. Penguins can live in the Antarctic, but not in the Arctic. Animals are restricted. They live above sea level, below sea level, on the desert, in the tropical forest. We can live anywhere. That's characteristic of the human animal.

We have our affective, or our emotional life, and we have our cognitive, or intellectual life. And we are taught from the very beginning to emphasize our intelligence as if that were really the important thing. But, the important thing is the person on all those levels.

Now, one year I was teaching hypnosis to dentists, doctors and psychologists at Phoenix College. I taught in the evening from 7:00 to 10:30, and people came from Yuma, Flagstaff, Mesa and Phoenix to attend my classes. And after class they would go home.

In the first semester I taught, there was a psychologist from Flagstaff named Mary. The first class, as soon as I started lecturing, she went into a deep trance right away. I awakened her and she said she had never studied about hypnosis, had never been a hypnotic subject, and was surprised that she went into a trance. She was in her mid-thirties. She was a doctoral candidate for a Ph.D. in psychology. I awakened her, and told her to stay awake. I started my lecture. She promptly went into a trance. A deep trance. I awakened her again and told her to "stay awake." She went into a deep trance as soon as I began lecturing. All during the first class she was in a deep trance, all the time. So, I gave up trying to awaken her.

Now, in mid-semester, I thought I'd use her as a demonstration subject, so I told Mary to come out of her deep trance and bring some childhood memories with her. And Mary awakened and said the only thing she could remember about her childhood was butterfly sleeves and a bamboo clump. I asked what that meant and she didn't know. I tried again and again, but that's all the childhood memories I got—butterfly sleeves and bamboo clump.

She repeated the course the next semester and again she went into a trance and stayed in a trance throughout every lecture. She repeated the course for a third time. And I thought "Well, since I can't get anything out of her, I will create a situation in which Mary can really teach us all a great deal."

I told Mary, "I want you to go into a deep, deep trance." First I explained that you live intellectually, emotionally and by movement. I told her to "go into a deep trance, a very deep trance and find some emotion. An emotion you didn't dare to know the meaning of." I told her it would be a very strong emotion and that she would bring it out. "And no knowledge, no intellectual comprehension, just bring emotion and only the emotion."

And Mary awakened, sitting very rigid and hanging on to the arms of the chair. She was perspiring. Perspiration was running down her face and dripping from her chin and nose. And she was pale. I asked her "What is the trouble, Mary?" And Mary said "I'm awful scared!" But she only moved her eyeballs. She didn't move any other part of her body, except, of course, the organs of speech. "I'm awful scared, awful scared!" And she was pale. I asked her if she could take my hand and she said, "Yes." I asked her if she would take my hand, and she said, "No." I asked why. She said "I'm awful scared!"

I invited the rest of the class to look Mary over and talk to her. Some of the class got sick at seeing Mary so scared. And Mary was scared. And the class could see the perspiration running down her face, dripping, and her pallor, and the limitation of her eyeball movements. And she talked out of the corner of her mouth. She hung on to the arms of the chair so rigidly. She breathed very slowly and very carefully.

And when all my class was satisfied that Mary had come out of the trance with a very strong emotion, I told Mary "Go back into the trance, way deep in the trance and bring out the intellectual side." And Mary awakened and mopped her face and said, "I'm so glad that happened 30 years ago." And, of course, we were all interested in what happened 30 years ago.

She said, "We lived on a mountainside and there was a deep gorge, a crevice, on the side of the mountain, and my mother always warned me, 'Don't go near that gorge.' And one morning I went out to play and I forgot about my mother's warning and I wandered over to that deep gorge and I saw that there was an iron pipe across it. The iron pipe was 15″ in diameter. I forgot all about my mother's warning, and I thought it would be a wonderful idea if I got down on my hands and knees, kept my eyes on the pipe and totally crawled across the gorge on that pipe.

"When I thought I was almost there, I took my eyes off the pipe and I look up to see how far away I was from the other side. When I did, I could see how deep the gorge was. It was awful deep. And I was only halfway across and I froze in terror. I stayed frozen for half an hour and wondered how to get out of my predicament. And finally, I figured out how to get out of my predicament. Very carefully, keeping my eyes on the pipe, I crawled backwards until my feet were on solid ground. And then I turned and ran and hid in a clump of bamboo, and stayed there a long time."

I said, "What is the rest of the story, Mary?" And she said, "That's all the story. There isn't anymore." I said, "There is still something more." Mary said, "I can't remember." I said, "The next class meeting bring in the next installment."

The next meeting of the class, Mary came blushing furiously. She said, "It's embarrassing to tell you this. When I got back to Flagstaff it was past 1:00 a.m. I went across town. I awakened my mother and told her how I had climbed out on that iron pipe across the gorge and would she spank me. My mother said, 'I'm not going to spank you for something you did 30 years ago!' "

And Mary said, "And when I tried to sleep my bottom hurt all night long, and my bottom still hurts. I wanted that spanking so bad and mother wouldn't give it to me. I wish she had. My bottom hurts."

And I said, "Anything else, Mary?" Mary said, "No, that aching bottom of mine is enough." I said, "At the next meeting of the class, you bring in another installment of the story." She said, "That's it, nothing more." I said, "All right."

At the next class meeting Mary appeared and said, "My bottom doesn't hurt anymore, and that's the only other part I can tell you." I said, "No, Mary, you can tell us the next part of the story." Mary said, "I don't remember any other part."

I said, "I'll ask you a question and then you can tell us the next part." Mary said, "What question could you ask me?" I said, "It's very simple. How did you explain it to your mother that you were late for lunch?" Mary said, "Oh, that! I was late for lunch and I told my mother a band of bandits had captured me and locked me up in a great big cave with a thick wooden door and it took me hours and hours to beat down that door with my hands. And then I knew there was no blood on my hands so I had to put my hands under the table. And I hoped my mother would believe that story. I desperately hoped. She only seemed to be mildly amused that a band of bandits had locked me up in a cave."

I said, "Anything more?" Mary said, "No, that's all." I said, "All right, bring in the next installment the next meeting of the class." Mary said, "There isn't any more to the story." I said, "Oh, yes there is."

Mary came in the next class meeting and said, "I've thought and thought and there is no more to that story." I said, "Well, I will have to ask you a question again." I said, "Now, tell me, Mary, when you went in the house, did you go in the front door or the back door?" Mary flushed and said, "I sneaked in the back door feeling very guilty." Then she straightened up and said, "Now I know some more about that! Shortly after my escapade of crossing the gorge, my mother had a heart attack and was taken to the hospital and there was a bamboo screen placed around her bed. I sat there looking at my mother in bed and I knew that my trying to cross that gorge had caused my mother to have a heart attack, and that I was guilty of killing my mother. I felt horribly guilty, awfully, awfully guilty. I wonder if that's why I have been working on my doctorate in psychology —in sort of a desperate search of this deeply repressed memory."

I said, "Is there anything else, Mary?" And Mary said, "No."

The next meeting of the class Mary said, "Dr. Erickson, there is another part of the story. When I got back to Flagstaff, I felt so guilty about having caused my mother's heart attack that I had to tell her about the guilt that I had forgotten all about— that gorge and the iron pipe, and when she came home from the hospital. It was past 1:00 a.m., and I went across town and awakened my mother and told her all about it. My mother said, 'You know, Mary, I was always taking snapshots of you as a little girl. Let's go to the attic and get out that great big pasteboard box in which I keep those snapshots, always intending to put them in order in an album.' "

They went to the attic and here is the picture of little Mary wearing butterfly sleeves and standing beside that bamboo clump. (Erickson shows the picture to Carol who looks at it and then passes it to the person to her left.)

Now when patients have deeply repressed memories, that doesn't mean they haven't got them. And sometimes the best way to dig out those repressions, those horrible memories, is to have them bring out the emotion, or the intellectual part, or the motoric part. Because emotions alone don't tell the story. The intellectual part alone is like reading something in a storybook, and the memory reactions don't mean anything at all.

So, Mary gave me that picture. And Mary said, "I took up psychology in an effort to find out about that memory. I'm not interested in psychology. I'm a married woman. I have a happy husband, happy home and happy children. I don't want a Ph.D." Right up to the age of almost 37, she had been governed for 30 years by that deeply repressed emotion.

And in doing psychotherapy, don't try to dig up everything all at once. Dig up the safe thing when it's a deep repression.

Now, a dentist's wife asked me to put her in a trance and regress her to early childhood. I asked her, "Suggest to me what year or what event." She said, "Why not regress me to my third birthday."

I regressed her in time till she said that she was three years old. She was having a party and I asked her all about the party and what she did. She told about birthday cake and her little friends and she told me that she was wearing an appliquéd dress and she was riding her horsey in the backyard.

When she awakened from the trance and heard the tape recording of her third birthday, she laughed and said, "That's not a true memory. No three-year-old child knows the word 'appliqué' and I certainly didn't know the word appliqué when I was three years old. As for riding a horse in the backyard—our backyard was so small, you couldn't get a horse in it. That was pure fantasy."

About a month later she was visiting her mother and her mother said, "Of course you knew the word 'appliqué' when you were three years old. I made all your dresses, and every dress I made for you, I appliquéd it. Now, let's go to the attic. I took pictures of you at every birthday and a lot more pictures."

They finally dug out her picture at the age of three wearing an appliquéd dress, and riding her horsey in the backyard. They found pictures and the dentist's wife had a copy made of them and she gave me copies of the snapshots. (Erickson shows them to the group.) There's the appliquéd dress and there is her horsey.

But, being adult, she and I both heard the word "horsey" and thought she meant "horse." She had a tricycle that looked like a horse. (Erickson laughs.) And she was riding her "horsey" in the backyard. (Erickson laughs.) And despite her adult convictions, a three-year-old does know the word "appliqué." Here is the proof that a three-year-old does know "appliquéd" dress.

When one of your patients speaks to you in their language, don't translate it into your language. Her three-year-old mind recalled a "horsey," and we translate it as adults into "horse." So, I warn all of you, don't ever, when you are listening to a patient, think you understand the patient, because you're listening with your ears and thinking with your own vocabulary. The patient's vocabulary is something entirely different. To a three-year-old, a "horsey" is a "horsey," and to a 60-year-old, a "horsey" is a "horse."

What time is it please?

Stu: 2:05. (Stu is a psychoanalyst from Arizona.)

E: Now I'm going to give you a case record. I think I'll give you two. The first one will show you how completely unimportant the therapist is.

A young lawyer from Wisconsin came into my office Wednesday afternoon. He said, "I have a law practice in Wisconsin. My wife and I don't like Wisconsin weather. My wife and I want to move to Arizona and begin a family here. So I have taken the Arizona bar examination. I've taken it five times and I've failed it five times. I have a good law practice in Wisconsin, and for five times I've failed the Arizona bar examination. And I've got to go to Tucson tomorrow early in the morning to take the bar examination again."

So, he came in on Wednesday afternoon to leave the next morning for Tucson where he had failed the bar examination five times. "Yet you say you and your wife want to move to Arizona and start a family?" He said, "That's right." I said, "Well, I don't know anything about Arizona law; I'm only a psychiatrist, and I don't know the law. I do know how the bar examinations are conducted. I know that the lawyers seeking a legal license gather in a certain building in Tucson. It is an essay examination. The examination questions are mimeographed and there will be a stack of the questions and blue books. Each applicant picks up a copy of the questions and blue books and finds a comfortable seat, sits down and writes all day from 9:00 in the morning to 5:00 at night. And then on Friday he starts in the same way at 9:00 and finishes at 5:00. On Saturday, he gets another new set of questions, and he writes to five o'clock.

Then the examination is done. Each day is an essay examination
and each day a different set of questions is presented."

Now, I put him in a deep trance and said, "You've got to go to
Tucson tomorrow morning and you say that you and your wife
want to move to Arizona, that you like Arizona, that you don't
like Wisconsin. Therefore, when you are driving to Tucson, and
it is well over 150 miles, you'll start early in the morning and
you'll watch the scenery on the left-hand side of the highway
and the right-hand side of the highway. And you will *enjoy* the
Arizona scenery all the way to Tucson. (The new roads make it
125 miles now.) You will enjoy the scenery in the early morning
light.

"When you get to Tucson, you'll absentmindedly find a parking lot and park your car and you look around and you will
see a building. You will wonder what that building is and yet
you'll walk in. You'll see a lot of people, young and old, male
and female. They really won't interest you. You will see a stack
of mimeographed sheets of papers with questions, and you will
pick up one of the bunch and a blue book. Find a comfortable
chair or seat.

"You will read all the questions and they won't make any
sense to you at all. Then you will read the first question a second
time and it will seem to make a little bit of sense. And so, a little
bit of information will trickle out of your pen on to the blue
book. And before that little trickle of information dries up there
will be another little trickle, followed by another little trickle.
After awhile the little trickles dry up and you will read the
second question. And it seems to make a bit of sense, and a little
bit of information will trickle out of your pen onto the paper
followed by another trickle and another trickle. And finally that
trickle will dry up. You'll move on to the next question, and
so on for all the questions.

"And that evening you will walk around Tucson and admire
the scenery, near and far. You will work up a good appetite and
you will enjoy the food you eat. You will go for a walk before
you go to bed. You will enjoy the Arizona blue skies. And you
will go to bed and you will sleep soundly. Wake up feeling

refreshed. You will eat a good breakfast. You will wander over to that building for a repeat of yesterday, a repeat of Thursday.

"And Friday evening you will walk around Tucson, working up an appetite enjoying the scenery far and near, and you will eat a wonderful dinner. And you go out for another walk and enjoy the blue sky and the mountains that rim around Tucson, and go to bed and sleep soundly.

"The same thing will happen Saturday."

About a year later a very pregnant woman entered my office. She gave me her name, and I recognized the lawyer's name. She said, "I am on my way to the hospital to have a baby. After what you did for my husband, I would like a hypnotic delivery of my baby." So, I hinted gently about the value of a little more time.

I told her to go into a trance. She went into a very nice trance, and I told her, "Go to the hospital, cooperate in every way, except you explain that you want no medication of any sort, and you won't take any anesthesia. You just want to go into the delivery room and have your baby. And while you are lying on the delivery table think about the baby. Is it going to be a boy, or a girl? How much will it weigh? How long will it be? What color hair will it have, or will it be bald? And what color will its eyes be? And will you really name it the name you and your husband picked out? And while you are lying there waiting for your baby, enjoy all the happy thoughts about having a baby. And wait patiently and gladly to hear its first cry. Think of all the happiness that you hope to derive from having a baby. And think about how happy your husband will be, and how nice it is to live in Arizona."

She was enjoying her thoughts and suddenly the obstetrician said, "Mrs. X., here is your baby." And he held up a baby boy.

Two years later she came in and said, "I remembered what you said about more time. I'm not going into the hospital for three whole days. I would like to have another hypnotic delivery."

I said, "All right, just close your eyes. Go into a trance very deeply and do a repetition of what you did the first time." I awakened her and she left.

The time before she had told me about how her husband had driven home that Saturday evening so he could see the Arizona scenery from the opposite point of view. He viewed it on the way there and he could view it on the way back. (Erickson laughs.)

Siegfried: Please repeat the last sentence, I didn't get it.

E: When her husband finished the law examination, he returned that evening so that he could see the Arizona scenery from the opposite point of view. He viewed it in the evening light.

And he didn't think it was at all necessary to tell me that he had passed the law examination. Because my attitude towards patients is: You are going to accomplish your purpose, your goal. And I am very confident. I look confident. I act confident. I speak in a confident way, and my patient tends to believe me.

And too many therapists say, "I hope I can help you," and express a doubt. I had no doubt when I told her to go into a trance. I had no doubts about her. (Erickson points to Carol.) I had no doubt about those two either. (Erickson points to two women on the couch.) I was utterly confident. A good therapist should be utterly confident.

(Erickson looks at the floor.) Now, after the first baby, the lawyer came to see me and said, "That was a very nice thing you did for my wife. We really enjoyed giving birth to the boy. But something is troubling me. When my grandfather on my father's side was my age, he developed back trouble, and it hindered him, hampered him all his life. He suffered from chronic backache. And his brother had that kind of a backache all his life, beginning at about my age. My father, when he was my age developed a chronic backache. It handicaps him in his work and my older brother, when he reached my age, developed a chronic backache. And now I am beginning to have a backache.

I said, "All right, I'll take care of that. Go into a deep trance." When he was in a deep trance, I told him, "If your backache is of organic basis, or if something is wrong in the spine, nothing I say will help it. But if it is a psychological, a psychosomatic pattern that you learned from your grandfather, granduncle, from your father, from your brother, then you can know you don't need that backache. It is just psychosomatic patterns of behavior."

And nine years later he returned to me and said, "Remember that backache you treated me for, I never had it again until a few weeks ago when my back began to feel a little bit tender. I've been afraid of all those backaches my granduncle, grandfather, father and brother had, and now my back is a little bit tender."

I said, "Nine years is a long time. I'm not able to give you an x-ray and the kind of physical examination that I would like. I'll send you to a friend of mine and he will report to me his findings and recommendations."

My friend, Frank, said to the man, "You are practicing law, corporation law. You sit at your desk all day long. You don't get enough exercise. Now here are some exercises I want you to do everyday for your general good health and you won't have a backache."

He came to me and told me what Frank had said, I put him in a trance and said, "And now you do those exercises and live a well-balanced life of activity and inactivity."

A year later he called me up and said, "You know, I feel a lot younger, a lot healthier than I did a year ago. Those exercises made me feel much younger and I don't have any backache."

But now, there is something you ought to know. A secretary who was a good hypnotic subject called me up on the telephone and said, "Sometimes when I menstruate I get very severe menstrual cramps. And I am just beginning my menstruation and I've got very severe cramps located somewhat to the right side of my lower abdomen. Now, will you give me an anesthesia for my menstrual cramps?"

I put her into a trance over the phone. I told her, "You just told me in a waking state about menstrual cramps and you want relief from them. So, understand this, your menstruation will cause you no *further* pain. You will have no more menstrual cramps." And I emphasized menstrual pain, menstrual cramps. "Now you wake up." She awakened, and said, "Thank you, the pain is all gone." I said, "Fine."

About 20 minutes later she called and said, "The anesthesia

has worn off. The menstrual cramps are back again." I said, "Go into a trance and listen carefully. I want you to develop a hypnotic anesthesia for menstrual cramps, for menstrual pains of all kinds. Now wake up free of your pain." She awakened and said, "This time you gave me a good anesthesia. Thanks very much."

A half-hour later she called me up and said, "My menstrual cramps are back again." I said, "Your body is a lot wiser than you are. You haven't got menstrual cramps. I gave you a hypnotic anesthesia, and any doctor knows an acute appendicitis can give pain like menstrual cramps. I produced an anesthesia for menstrual cramps and I didn't mention your appendix. Call your surgeon." She did. He put her in the hospital and operated for an acute appendicitis the next morning.

Your body knows more about you than you do. So when you do therapy with a patient, know what you are talking about. Don't give general instructions. If I treat a headache, I may give the suggestion "for a *harmless* headache." Then, if the headache is from a brain tumor, the hypnotic anesthesia won't work. Now, with appendicitis pain, give them hypnotic anesthesia and it disappears, but the real diagnosis is menstrual cramps or some other alternative diagnosis. So when you treat an organic illness, know what you are talking about.

Now, as for the lawyer, all I did for him was to make him think Arizona was a nice place to live, and that the law examination was awfully unimportant; so he had no anxiety, no fear. He only had to write one little trickle of information at a time. Anybody can do that. And I've treated quite a number of lawyers in the same way—and medical men in the same way—by giving them a feeling of mental peace, of confidence and of self-assurance.

A woman had flunked her Ph.D. examination over and over again. Her committee knew that she could pass, and yet she always went into a panic and blanked out everything. So I had her sit in with a class where I told about the lawyer and she went into a trance listening to the case about the lawyer. After I finished the report she awakened. I dismissed her and she went back to her home state. A month later she wrote to me: "I passed my Ph.D. exam with flying colors. What did you do to me?" (Erickson laughs.) I didn't do anything to her except tell her about that lawyer.

Now all of you will listen to things I say. All of you will apply what I say in accordance with your own specific understandings. When I talk about how the lawyers appreciate the wonderful scenery of Arizona, (to Christine) you will think about the "wunderbar" scenery of Germany and those are two different things.

And how do you get information from patients? You talk socially with them. You start talking about the college you went to. I went to the U. of Wisconsin. And all of you begin thinking about your *own* university. If I speak about the Mississippi River, our German friend will think about the Rhine.

We always translate the other person's language into our own language.

And now, in 1972, a 35-year-old woman, married, very pretty, rang the doorbell. Her statement to me when she came in was, "Dr. Erickson, I have an airplane phobia. And this morning my boss told me, 'On Thursday you fly to Dallas, Texas and you fly back on Saturday.' And he said, 'Either you fly both ways or you lose your job.' Dr. Erickson I am a computer programmer, and I have programmed computers all over the United States.

"In 1962, ten years ago, a plane I was on crashed. There was no real damage done to the plane and nobody on board the plane was hurt. And for the next five years I rode planes, Phoenix to Boston, New York, New Orleans, Dallas, everywhere. Each time I was on a plane and riding through the air, I got more and more fearful. And finally my fears were so great that I would shake visibly all over my body. (Erickson demonstrates.) And I'd have my eyes shut. I couldn't hear my husband speaking to me and my phobia is so strong that by the time I got to the place where I would do my work, even my dress was wet with perspiration. It got so bad that I had to go to bed for eight hours and sleep before I could do my work. So, I began going to my different jobs by train, by bus, and by automobile. My airplane phobia is so peculiar. I walk on the plane all right. I can taxi to the end of the runway. But the moment the plane lifts off the ground I start my shuddering, and I am so full of fear. But when the plane lands at an intermediate stop, as soon as the plane is on the ground, I am very comfortable. I taxi to the airport, and back to the runway.   .

"So, I began using cars, buses and trains. Finally my boss got tired of me using my vacation time, my sick time, and my allowable absentee time in order to travel by bus, or car, or train. This morning he said, 'You fly to Dallas or you lose your job.' I don't want to lose my job. I like it."

I said, "Well, how do you want your phobia treated?" She said, "By hypnosis." I said, "I don't know if you are a good hypnotic subject." She said, "I was in college." I said, "That was a long time ago. How good are you now?" She said, "An awfully good one." I said, "I'll have to test you."

She was a good hypnotic subject. I awakened her and said, "You are a good hypnotic subject. I really don't know how you *behave* on a plane, so I want to put you in a hypnotic trance and have you hallucinate being on a jet plane 35,000 feet up in the air." So she went into a trance and hallucinated being on a jet plane at an elevation of 35,000 feet. The way she bobbed up and down, trembling all over, was a horrible sight to see. And I had her hallucinate landing the plane.

I said, "Before I can help you, I want you to understand something. You are a rather beautiful woman in your mid-thirties. Now, I am a man. And, while I'm in a wheelchair, you don't know how much I am handicapped. Now, I want a promise from you that you will do anything, good or bad, that I can ask of you. And, bear in mind that you are an attractive woman, and I am a man whose handicap you don't know. I want an absolute promise that you will do anything and everything, good or bad, that I suggest."

She thought it over for about five minutes and then said, "Nothing you could ask of me or do to me could be worse than my airplane phobia." I said, "Now that you've given me that promise, I'm going to put you in a trance and ask for a similar promise." In the trance state, she gave me the promise right away. I awakened her and told her, "You promised both in a trance state and in a waking state—your absolute promise."

I said, "Now, I can treat you for your airplane phobia. Go into a trance and hallucinate being 35,000 feet up in the air, traveling 650 miles per hour ground speed." She was shuddering frightfully, bent over, her forehead touching her knees. I said, "And *now*, I want you to have the plane descend and by the time it reaches the ground all your fears and phobias, anxiety and devils of torture will slide off your body and into the seat beside you." And so she hallucinated landing the plane, awakened from the trance and suddenly leapt out of the chair with a scream and came rushing to the other side of room saying, "They are there. They are there!" (Erickson points to the green chair.)

I called Mrs. Erickson into the room and said, "Betty, sit in that chair." (Erickson points.) And the patient said, "Please Mrs. Erickson, don't sit in that chair." Mrs. Erickson continued walking toward the chair and the patient rushed forward and physically prevented Betty from sitting in the chair. So, I dismissed Betty, and turned to the patient and said, "Your therapy is complete. Have a good time flying to Dallas and flying back to Phoenix, and call me from the airport and tell me how much you enjoyed the plane trips."

After she left, I had my daughter take an overexposed picture of that chair (Erickson points), and an underexposed picture, and a properly exposed picture. I put them into three separate envelopes. I labeled the overexposed picture: "The eternal resting place of your phobias, fears, anxieties and devils of torture slowly descending into the oblivion of eternal gloom." The underexposed picture, I labeled: "The eternal resting place of your fears, wholly dissipating into outer space." And the properly exposed picture, I labeled: "The eternal resting place of your phobias, fears and anxieties."

I mailed the envelopes to her. She got them Wednesday morning. Saturday I got an excited phone call from the airport: "It was magnificent. It was utterly wonderful, the most beautiful experience of my life." I said, "Would you be willing to tell your story to four students of mine whom I am tutoring for their

Ph.D. examinations?" She said, "Yes." I told her to come at
8:00.

At 8:00 she and her husband walked into the house. She
walked around that chair, skirting it as far as she could, and she
sat in a seat furthest from that chair. The students came about
five minutes later and one of them started to sit in that chair.
My patient said, "Please, please, don't sit in that chair!"

The student said, "I've sat there before. It's a comfortable
chair and I'll sit there again." The patient said, "Please, please
don't!" The student said, "Well, I've sat on the floor before
and I'll sit there now if it will satisfy you." The patient said,
"Thank you very much."

And she told the students the story, including the story about
the pictures I sent to her. She said, "I took those pictures with
me in the way you carry a good luck charm and a good luck
piece, a rabbit's foot, a Saint Christopher's medal. They were
part of my traveling kit. The first leg of the trip was to El Paso.
I was comfortable and I kept wondering when the air turbulence
would begin. There was a 20-minute layover in El Paso. I dis-
embarked and went to a quiet place in the airport and went into
a trance and said, 'Dr. Erickson told you to enjoy it. Now you do
what Dr. Erickson *told* you to do.' I went back to the flight and
the trip from El Paso to Dallas was wonderful. On the trip back
from Dallas, high up, all we could see below was a bank of clouds
with holes here and there. We could look through those holes
and see the earth far below. It was a fantastically beautiful trip."

I said, "Now, I would like to have you go into a trance, right
here and now." So she did. I said, "Now, in this trance I want
you to go down to the airport in Phoenix, buy a ticket to San
Francisco, and enjoy the scenery all the way there, especially the
mountain scenery. When you get to San Francisco, disembark,
rent a car and drive out to the Golden Gate bridge. Park your
car and walk out to the middle of the bridge and look down.

"Now, I will tell you a bit about the history of that bridge.
The pylons supporting the bridge were 740 feet high. When the
bridge was completed, one of the workmen who painted the
bridge had a fish net on the end of a long pole and he caught

seagulls and painted their heads red. One day an enterprising reporter published a story in the newspaper about a new breed of redheaded seagulls. His name was Jake. All that is factual.

"Then, you watch the waves down below, the foam on top of the waves, and you watch the seagulls. Then the fog will roll in. You won't be able to see anything. So you go back to your car and go back to the airport, and use your return ticket to Phoenix, and come from the airport directly here."

Very promptly she awakened from her trance and said to the students, "I must tell you about my trip to San Francisco, and about that nasty Jake." Her husband said, "I knew she wouldn't like that." She was an ecology freak. (Erickson laughs.) And when she finished telling the story, she said, "And I came directly here from the airport. Oh my goodness, I was in a trance when I did all that. I didn't really go to San Francisco. I was in a trance and I thought I went there."

But then I asked her an important question. "What other problem did you get over on your trip to Dallas?" She said, "I had no other problem, just my airplane phobia." I said, "Yes, you had another problem, a very troublesome problem. I don't know how long you've had it. Now you are over it. But tell the students what your other problem was." She said honestly, "I didn't have any other problem. I don't have any other problem." I said, "I know you don't have any other problem now, but what was the other problem you solved in Dallas?" She said, "You'll have to tell me." I said, "No. I will just ask you one question and then you will know what your problem was."

Now, I'm going to ask you as a group, what were her problems? (Pause.) And I'll say in advance she had three main problems. They were serious handicapping problems. What were they? (Pause.)

I'll help you in your thinking. She didn't have an airplane phobia. (Erickson laughs.) She just thought she had an airplane phobia. I heard every word she said. I said all the important words to you that I heard her say. (Pause.)

I let the students study awhile. They couldn't figure out the

MONDAY   **69**

problems. I've had a few of my students make fairly good guesses
about one of her problems. (Pause.)
     You all don't need to shout the answers at once. Take your
turns. (Erickson laughs. Pause.)
Sande: She is afraid of men.
E: Speak for yourself, John.
Anna: Did she have a problem with her boss with work?
E: (Shakes his head no.)
Siegfried: My guess is that she is scared of getting too successful.
E: (Shakes his head no.) I told her, "You had another problem you
    corrected. Now, what was that problem? I'll ask you a simple
    question: What was the first thing you did in Dallas?"
        She said, "Oh, that? I went to that 40-story building and I
    rode the elevator from the ground floor clear to the top." I said,
    "How did you used to ride an elevator?" She said, "I rode from
    the first floor to the second floor, got off, took another elevator
    and rode to the third floor, got off, waited for another elevator
    and went to the fifth floor. All the way up on the elevator, one
    flight at a time. I'm so used to doing that that I didn't look
    upon it as a problem."
Anna: Fear of heights?
E: (Shakes his head no.) She said, "I can go aboard an airplane. I can
    ride to the runway comfortably. I can taxi back to the end of
    the runway. The moment the airplane lifts off, I go into my
    phobic shuddering." She was afraid of enclosed spaces where
    there were no visible means of support. An airplane is enclosed
    space with no visible means of support; so is an elevator.
        I said, "Now what was the other problem?" She said, "I don't
    know of any other problem. If you say so, I must have had an-
    other problem." I said, "You did have another problem. Now it's
    corrected. Now when you weren't flying, you were in a car, buses
    and trains. You had no trouble on the train. And in the car or a
    bus, what happened when you came to a suspension bridge—a
    long one?" She said, "Oh, that. I used to get down flat on the
    floor, keep my eyes shut and shudder. I'd have to ask some
    stranger, 'Is the bus over the bridge?' " My students knew that

I knew about it because I had her make that hypnotic trip to San Francisco and had her walk out on the bridge.

And now, the patient lives aboard a plane. She and her husband took their vacation flying all over Australia. She goes to Rome regularly, to London, to Paris. And she doesn't like staying in hotels. She prefers sleeping onboard a plane, eating onboard a plane. And she still has those three pictures. And she is still afraid of that chair. (Erickson points and laughs.)

You see, you didn't listen. She didn't have a phobia for airplanes. She said, "I'm comfortable in a plane, and when it lifts off, I begin shuddering." And I know that when a plane lifts off, it's an enclosed space with no visible means of support. The same with an elevator. The same with a bus on a suspension bridge. You can't see the support at either end; you look to the right and look to the left. (Erickson gestures to the right and to the left.) You are up in the air. Onboard a train, she had proof of support, auditory proof—the clicking of the wheels on the rails, so she didn't have any phobia in the compartment of a train. She could hear the outside support.

And I can wonder a year later how each of you will remember that story. Because I have told it many times, and a year later one of my students will tell me about that case and I hear variations of my case. (Erickson laughs.) Mary sometimes is a man.

Because when you talk to people, they hear you in their language.

I can get any one of you to think about your school by saying "University of Wisconsin." I can tell you I was born in the Sierra Nevada Mountains, and all of you will know where you were born. You think about that. I speak about my sisters, and you think about yours if you have some—or you think about not having sisters, if you don't have sisters. We respond to the spoken word in terms of our own learnings. Therapists ought to keep that in mind.

Now, how many of you have been here before? Any of you been here before? (One woman raises her hand.)

E: You have? How long ago?

Sande: Seven months.

E: Don't tell on me. How many of you believe in Aladdin's lamp?
Anna: Aladdin's lamp?
E: How many of you believe in Aladdin's lamp? I have an Aladdin's lamp. Aladdin would stroke the lamp and a genie came out. I have a modernized Aladdin's lamp. I put the plug into the wall socket and the genie comes out. I'm willing to let you see my genie. She is very friendly. She likes to smile and wink and kiss. But remember, she belongs to me.

I just happen to remember that Mrs. Erickson is not home this afternoon. Otherwise I would invite you in to see my genie. (Erickson addresses Anna.) I know you doubt me. You doubt that that is Count Dracula too.
Anna: I don't doubt it.
E: Then don't be around here at midnight; you are going to lose some blood.

And, that is the other point I make. In teaching, in therapy, you are very careful to use humor, because your patients bring in enough grief, and they don't need all that grief and sorrow. You better get them into a more pleasant frame of mind right away.

Would you find a card there for me please. (Erickson points to a series of papers to his immediate right. Christine helps him pick out the card that he wants.) There is a black card there.

I am going to pass this around for all of you to read. It was sent to me by my daughter, Betty Alice. She was in college. Usually an Erickson will receive a nice card, and cross off the name of the sender and send it on to someone else. For example, my sister sent my wife a birthday card. My wife crossed off my sister's name, signed it herself and sent it to somebody else in the family. My sister was the 35th person to get that card.

(Erickson gives the card to Carol, seated to his left.) Read the outside seriously and then open it and read the inside. (Carol smiles.) (Erickson takes the card from Carol and passes it to the next woman.) Consider the effect on a depressed patient and read that card. It's a very beneficial card for them to read. (The card is passed around the group. The front of the card says:

"When you stop to think of all the unexplained mysteries in the universe. . . . Doesn't it make you feel humble and insignificant?" The inside of the card reads: ". . . me neither.")

(Erickson addresses Christine.) I give my depressed patients that card to read. (Erickson laughs.) I remind all my other students that if you are interested in buying Indian jewelry, one place that you can be sure of your value is at the Heard Museum on Central Avenue. You will be sold true Indian jewelry. In all the stores, you get plastic turquoise, turquoise mixed with plastic, reconstituted turquoise and fake silver, fake gold. At the Heard Museum, which is the museum of the Southwest, you can buy the genuine stuff. The Heard Museum is worthwhile visiting.

And, go down here three-quarters of a mile to Glendale Avenue, and go East to Lincoln Drive. Glendale Avenue turns into Lincoln Drive. The street leaves Phoenix and becomes part of Scottsdale. Very shortly, around 24th Street, you'll find a park labeled Squaw Peak Park. Drive in there, park your car, climb to the top of Squaw Peak.

Because I believe that patients and students should do things. They learn better, remember better. Besides, the climb is worth it.

The best time is not in the heat of the day. Go at sunrise, after dark, midnight—gives you a wonderful view. It is 1,100 feet high and the walk up is a mile and a half. The record for climbing it is 15 minutes and 10 seconds. And one of my students who had a boyhood ambition to climb a 10,000 foot mountain climbed it ten times in one day. His average time going up was 23 minutes. My wife takes an hour and a half. My son takes a comfortable 43 minutes. I would suggest that you start a little bit before sunrise. It's worth it.

The other place you should visit is the Botanical Gardens. .

Anna: In Phoenix?

E: In Phoenix. It is a magnificent Botanical Garden, and there are two particular things to see in the Botanical Gardens. There is a Boojum Tree. Do you remember reading "The Hunting of the

Snark"? A Boojum Tree—there is a genuine Boojum Tree there.*

Anna: I saw it in Tucson in the Botanical Gardens.

E: And the Boojum Tree will give you a problem. When you see it you will know intellectually that it is a tree, but you won't want to believe it.

Anna: Its an upside-down turnip.

E: Let them find out for themselves. And there are Creeping Devils. You will find them near the Boojum Trees. You will recognize them. You won't have to ask directions. You'll find them. You will recognize them right away. And you will have a great deal of respect for Creeping Devils.

And, tomorrow, I will see you at noon.

Now, I am going to go into the house, drink some water and go to bed. I'll wake up tomorrow morning and get dressed and go back to sleep until noon. I don't have much strength. Now, if you'd decontaminate me. (Laughter.) (Erickson indicates to group members to take the "bugs" off him.)

---

* *Editor's Note*: The term "Boojum" was first applied to the tree in 1922. The British botanist, Godfrey Sykes, obviously knew the reference to the mythical Boojum in Lewis Carroll's epic nonsense poem "The Hunting of the Snark." When he first spied the tree through his telescope Sykes reportedly said, "Ho, Ho, a Boojum. Definitely a Boojum."

TUESDAY

❖❖

E: (Erickson begins the session by having a new student fill out a data sheet. He then mentions to Christine that he has two granddaughters named "Christine.")

Christine: That is unusual to have two that have the same name.

E: So, now I am going to change the seating arrangement. (Addresses Rosa.) See how she tries not to look at me. (Speaking directly to Rosa.) Because you're it.

(Erickson has Rosa move to the green chair. She has some difficulty speaking English.) You kept avoiding my glance.

Rosa: No, I couldn't see you very well. I am farsighted. (Pause.)

E: (Erickson puts a toy, a purple octopus made of yarn, on his wheelchair seat just to the left of his body.) When we were very young, we were willing to learn. And the older we grow, the more restrictions we put on ourselves. Now I'm going to give you an example of that. (Erickson leans to his left. Rosa leans closer to Erickson.)

75

Seven. Ten. One. Five. Two. Four. Six. Three. Eight. Nine. (Erickson addresses group.) What did I just do?

Anna: You counted backwards.

Siegfried: You said numbers.

E: I will do it again. Nine. Five. Three. Six. Two. One. Seven. Ten. Eight. (Pause.) How many of you have heard a child count the fingers from one to ten? Four. Seven. Ten. Nine. Eight. Three. Five. Two. One. Seven. (Erickson sequentially points to the fingers on his hands as he says the numbers.) It takes a lot more time to learn to count from one to ten. The child first learns the numbers. He has a concept of counting to ten, but he doesn't know the right order.

    (Addresses Rosa.) Now, how many fingers do you have?

Rosa: Twenty. Ten up and ten down.

E: Uncross your legs. Hold your hands on your knees. Does it make any difference if you count from here to there? (Erickson points to her fingers from left to right.)

Rosa: Me?

E: Does it make any difference?

Rosa: No.

E: If you count from there to here (Erickson points from right to left) will the answer be the same?

Rosa: Yes. (Tentative.) There are always ten.

E: If you add the fingers on this hand to the fingers on this hand (Erickson points to her right and her left hand), will you get the correct number?

Rosa: Five plus five?

E: I just asked a question. If you add these fingers to these fingers (he points to his left hand and his right hand), will you get the correct number?

Rosa: You asked me if I add these fingers to these fingers, which would be the correct number? Ten. (She points to her left hand and her right hand.)

E: You sure?

Rosa: I'm not sure, but I think. . . . That's what I thought, until now. (Laughs.)

E: (Laughs.) And you say you've got ten fingers.

Rosa: Yes.

E: I think you've got eleven.

Rosa: Eleven. OK, I believe it. (Shakes her head no.)

E: You believe it? (Laughter.)

Rosa: Sure. I can see only ten of them.

E: Can you move your chair closer?

Rosa: (Moves her chair closer to Erickson.)

E: Now you count them.

Rosa: One. Two. Three. . . .

E: No, I'll point to them, you count them. (Erickson points.)

Rosa: One, two, three, four, five, six, seven, eight, nine, ten.

E: That's the way *you* count them. You already agreed that you can count them from this way, or this way. (Erickson points from the left hand to the right hand, and then from the right hand to the left hand.) You already have agreed that these added to these (Erickson points to his left hand and right hand) give you the correct number.

Rosa: Correct number.

E: Now, I'm going to count them. Ten, nine, eight, seven, six (he counts the fingers on her left hand and then points to her right hand), and five is eleven. (Everyone laughs.)

Rosa: That's right. I can tell my friends I have eleven fingers.

E: And now do you know your right hand from your left hand?

Rosa: They told me that this is the right one. (She moves her right hand.)

E: And do you believe it?

Rosa: Yes, I did.

E: Put that hand behind you. (She puts her left hand behind her.) Now, which hand is left? (Erickson laughs.)

Rosa: That's a joke.

E: But, it's a marvelous technique for working with children.

Rosa: It works in English, but in Italian it wouldn't work.

E: Why?

Rosa: Because "left" doesn't mean two things. It doesn't mean the one who remains here. You say two different words, so it wouldn't work in another language. That's too bad.

E: You mean the English have a right hand that's left.

Rosa: What?

E: You mean the English have a right hand that can be a left hand. (Laughter.)

Rosa: Yes.

E: (Shakes his head and smiles.) These national differences are astonishing.

All right, yesterday I emphasized the importance of understanding the patient's words and really understanding them. You don't interpret your patient's words in *your* language. And she just demonstrated that the right hand in English can be the left hand. But it can't be the left hand in Italian.

Now, every word in any language has usually a lot of different meanings. Now, the word "run" has about 142 meanings.

Siegfried: Run?

E: Yes, "run." The government can run. A run of luck in cards. The girl can run. A run of fish. A run in a lady's stocking. A road runs uphill and downhill, and still stands still. A hundred and forty-two meanings for one word.

In German you say, "Machen Sie das Pferd los." Is that right? (Addresses Siegfried and Christine. Both indicate it is correct.) In English, you say, "Untie the horse." The Germans put their verbs one way, the English use their verbs a different way. And so, you ought to be acquainted with the linguistic patterns of your patients. And we all have our own linguistic patterns, our own personal understandings.

I was invited to speak to the Medical Society in St. Louis. The president and his wife were to be my hosts, and the president's wife said, "Dr. Erickson, I would like to prepare a very nice dinner for you and I would like to prepare your favorite foods." And I told her, "I'm a meat and potatoes man. Any kind of meat, any kind of potatoes. And you can boil the potatoes. But if you want to give me a special treat, I would like some milk gravy."

(To the group) You all know what milk gravy is? (Everybody says, "no.") Flour mixed with milk and boiled. Milk gravy is very tasty.

And when I said, "If you want to give me a treat, give me milk gravy," her husband collapsed on the couch and roared with laughter. And the wife stood transfixed as if frozen, her face very, very red. Her husband kept on roaring with laughter. Finally, he got control of his laughter and said, "For 25 years I've been asking my wife, begging her, to make milk gravy and she has always told me, 'Milk gravy is for poor, white trash.' And tonight I'm going to have milk gravy." (Group laughter.)

Her husband had lived on a farm and so had I. We both knew how good milk gravy was. She was a city girl, and that was only for poor white trash.

Now your patients come to you and tell you their problems. But do they tell you their problems or do they tell you what they *think* are problems? And are they problems only because they *think* that the things are problems?

Now, a mother brought her 11-year-old daughter in to see me. As soon as I heard the word "bedwetting," I sent the mother out of the room and took the history from the little girl—a tall blond, a very pretty girl.

Her story was that within a month of her birth she had developed a bladder infection. That infection had been treated by urologists. She had been cystoscoped, day after day, week after week, month after month, year after year. Finally the pelvis and each kidney were examined with a lucite lamp inserted through the bladder and up into the pelvis and the kidney. The focus of the infection was found in one kidney so she was operated on and was freed of the infection. But she had been cystoscoped . . . I hope you all know that word. Do you? (To Rosa.) Do you know what a cystoscope is? . . . so many times that her bladder sphincter was so dilated that as soon as she relaxed in sleep she wet the bed. While she could forcibly control her urination in the waking state, it was an all-day job. And as soon as she laughed at something, bodily relaxation would cause her to wet her pants.

Since she was now 11, had been free of the infection for several years, her parents were impatient. She ought to learn to control herself and not have a wet bed every night. She had three younger sisters who ridiculed her and called her bad names.

All of the neighbors knew that she wet the bed and wet her pants. All of the two or three thousand children at school knew that she was a bedwetter, and took pleasure in making her laugh so that she would wet her pants. And life was not very pleasant for her. I asked her if she had been to see any other doctor and she said that she had seen a lot of them and swallowed a barrel full of pills and barrels full of medicine. Nothing helped. And finally her mother brought her to me for me to help her.

Now, how would you treat that case? (Erickson looks at Rosa.)

Rosa: How would I? (Erickson nods.) I would have seen the entire family together, the father, the mother and the sisters. I would have seen the family.

E: Family therapy. (Looks at Carol directly opposite from him.) How would you. (Pause.) In fact, how would all of you . . . and don't shout all at once.

Anna: I would have checked the physiological things first. See if there were damage on a physiological level. And once I had information, I would have gone along with family therapy and individual therapy and what's her investment in not controlling.

E: How long would you expect to treat her?

Anna: How long? Probably once I had dealt with the whole family and seen what was going on, I could tell. . . . It might be more the family than her.

E: Another?

Carol: I'd try hypnosis.

E: And what would you tell her?

Carol: Well, maybe I would try working with her around her laughing and consciously letting go, then trying to gain control, and approach it that way.

E: What do you think she has been doing for the last four years?

Dan: How about getting her back to the age when she was originally trained and retraining her. I haven't used hypnosis myself, but my first thought was I would send her to you. (Laughter.)

Jane: (Jane is a therapist from New York.) Finding out if the sphincter muscle could be tightened up.

E: How would you do that?

Jane: I would ask a physician who knew about muscles and I would ask him if it were possible. Maybe I could teach her through exercises or send her to a physiotherapist who could teach her to retrain that muscle.

E: How long would you anticipate treating her?

Jane: I don't know how long it takes a muscle to get back into shape.

Christine: I can think of one other approach which may be similar to hers. Maybe in hypnosis to get her motivated and teach her to um . . .

E: (Interrupts.) Don't you think being called a bedwetter for 11 years would motivate her enough?

Christine: OK. I should start differently then. To have her practice before she empties her bladder to contract and not allow herself to empty the bladder completely which would train her to increase the muscle tone.

E: How long would it take you?

Christine: I think without hypnosis it would take a long time. But I think with hypnotic training, with hypnotic suggestions, it would be rather fast that the child would be able to do it. And she would be able to understand better what you were trying to tell her, also.

E: All right.

Christine: (Continuing over Erickson.) I think you did mention that there was some damage to the muscle.

E: Yes.

Christine: And she needs to have some retraining about strengthening the sphincter muscles.

E: Don't you think that she has been trying to exercise those muscles in 11 years?

Christine: I'm sure that she has, but I'm not sure that she knows how to do it.

E: How would you explain to her how to do it?

Christine: To try to hold her urine as much as she can before going to the bathroom voluntarily. To try to do that off and on.

E: All right. Now all of you know the answer, but you don't know that you know the answer. I told her, "I'm like all other doctors. I can't help you either. But there is something that you know, but you don't know that you know it. As soon as you find out what it is that you already know, but don't know you know, you can begin having dry beds." Now what did she already know, but didn't know she knew?

Christine: She could hold her urine during the day voluntarily most of the time.

E: By "most of the time" you mean she could hold it some of the time but not all of the time. That isn't very helpful knowing that you can't hold it some of the time.

Now all of us grow up and we learn that when we empty the bladder we empty it completely. We have grown up with that knowledge. We take it for granted, and practice that knowledge every day.

So I told the girl, "Look at the paperweight on my desk," not to move, not to talk, "Just keep your eyes open and look at the paperweight." I would remind her of the time that she first went to school to learn to write the letters of the alphabet, how hard it was—all those different shapes and forms—and printed letters and written letters and capital letters and small letters. But eventually she had formed a visual-mental image, located somewhere in her brain and located there permanently. Even though she didn't know that she had a mental image, it was there permanently.

And then I told her, "Now keep looking at that paperweight, so don't move, don't talk, your heart rate is changed, your respiration is changed, your blood pressure is changed, your motor tone and muscle tone are changed, and your reflexes have changed. Now that is not an important thing—I'm just telling you that.

"And now, I am going to ask you a very simple question and I want a very simple answer. Suppose you were in the bathroom, sitting down and urinating and a strange man pokes his head in the doorway. What would you do?"

She said, "I'd freeze."

I said, "That's right, you would freeze and stop urinating. And as soon as that strange man went away you could start all over again. Now all you need to do is practice starting and stopping, starting and stopping. You don't need a strange man to look at

you. You can start and stop all by yourself. Some days you will
forget to practice. That's all right. Your body will be good to
you, and always give you more opportunities to practice. And
some days you may forget to practice. That's all right. Your body
will be good to you.

"And now, to get the first dry bed it may take you two weeks.
That's all right. You need to practice starting and stopping. To
get two dry beds in succession, that's much harder. To get three
dry beds in succession, that's still harder. To get four in succession, that's still harder. After that it becomes easier. And the fifth,
the sixth and the seventh will give you a whole week of dry
beds. After you have had one week of dry beds, you get another
week of dry beds.

"Now, it would surprise me very much if you had a permanent
dry bed within three months. It also would surprise me very
much if you didn't have a permanent dry bed in six months."

And six months later she was staying overnight with friends,
going to slumber parties. All she needed to know was that she
could stop, at any time, her urination, with the right stimulus.
And all of you know this truth. And that's what we all overlook.

We grow up thinking that we have got to finish. That isn't
true. And so . . .

Anna: We all overlook what?

E: That we must continue until we are finished. That isn't true. We
can always interrupt ourselves given the proper stimulus. And
all of you know what happens when you are sitting on the toilet
urinating and a strange man or woman looks in on you. You
stop. (Erickson laughs.) So, since she was only a little girl, 11
year old, I spent a whole hour and a half . . . and that was all.

As for treating the family, well, I figured it would be a task for
the father and the mother to get used to a dry bed. (Laughter.)
I thought it would be the hard luck of the sister to get used to her
big sister having a dry bed. I thought it would be the hard luck
of the school children to lose a very valuable way of teasing. I
thought the patient was the only one who needed treatment.

And so, about 10 days later she brought me this toy to sym-
bolize the first time in her life that she ever gave a present to

anybody knowing that she had a dry bed. (Erickson laughs and shows the group a purple yarn octopus that the girl had made for him.) And the first dry bed occurred within two weeks.

Why should I bother to see her a second time? Would there be any purpose for seeing her again?

Why are you hiding back there? (Erickson turns and addresses a woman who comes into the waiting room from the office behind Erickson. She did not attend the session yesterday. She is obviously late for today's meeting. She is an attractive tall blond wearing jeans and a blouse that loosely covers a tube top. She has completed all her Ph.D. requirements in psychology except for her dissertation.)

Sally: I was waiting for a good time to interrupt. Let's see if I can find a seat.

E: I can pick up at any point, so come in and find a seat.

Sally: Is there a seat back there?

E: (Speaking to Rosa in the green chair.) Can't that seat be shoved over. You can put another chair right here. (Points to a space directly to his left.) Hand her a chair. (A man sets up a folding chair just to the left of Erickson. Sally sits down next to Erickson and crosses her legs toward him.)

E: You don't need to cross your legs.

Sally: (Laughs.) I thought you might comment on that. OK. (She uncrosses her legs.)

E: Our foreign visitors may not know, "A dillar, a dollar, a ten o'clock scholar," but you know that rhyme, don't you?

Sally: No.

E: (Incredulous.) You never learned about a dillar, a dollar, a ten o'clock scholar?

Sally: I don't know the rest of it.

E: Frankly, I don't either. (She laughs.) Are you feeling comfortable?

Sally: No. Actually, I walked in in the middle of things and I'm . . . I ah. . . .

E: And I never met you before.

Sally: Mmm. . . I did see you one time last summer. I came with a group.

E: Did you go into a trance?

Sally: I believe so, yeah. (Nods head.)

E: You don't know?

Sally: I believe so. (Nods head.)

E: Just a belief?

Sally: Um-hum.

E: A belief and not a reality?

Sally: It's sort of the same.

E: (Incredulous.) A belief is a reality?

Sally: Sometimes.

E: Sometimes. Is this belief of yours that you went into a trance a reality or a belief? (Sally laughs and clears her throat. She seems embarrassed and self-conscious.)

Sally: Does it matter? (Group laughter.)

E: That's another question. My question is, is your belief a belief or a reality?

Sally: I think that it is probably both.

E: Now a belief may be an unreality and it can be a reality and your belief is both an unreality and a reality?

Sally: No. It's both a belief and a reality. (She shakes and holds her head.)

E: You mean it's both a belief which could be a reality, or an unreality? And it's also a reality? Now which is it? (Sally laughs.)

Sally: I really don't know right now.

E: Well, why did you take so long to tell me that. (Sally laughs.)

Sally: I don't know that either.

E: Are you feeling comfortable?

Sally: Oh, I'm feeling better, yeah. (She speaks softly.) I hope that the people here are not bothered by my interruption.

E: You are not feeling self-conscious?

Sally: Mm . . . I would probably feel better sitting in the back, but . . .

E: Out of sight?

Sally: Out of sight? Well, maybe.

E: What's that?

Sally: Inconspicuous.

E: So you don't like being conspicuous.

Sally: Oh, geez. (Laughs and again seems self-conscious. She puts her

left hand over her mouth as she clears her throat.) No . . . not
. . . no . . . uh . . . hmm.

E: You don't like what I'm doing to you right now?

Sally: Mmm . . . No. Well, I have mixed feelings. I am flattered by
the attention and I am curious about what you are saying.

E: (Overlapping.) And you wish the *hell* I'd stop. (General laughter.)

Sally: Um, mixed feelings (nods her head yes). If I was just talking
to you and hadn't interrupted that would be one thing, but . . .

E: So you are concerned about these people?

Sally: Well, yes, I. . . .

E: Mm-hmm.

Sally: . . . their time here . . . and I walked in on their time.

E: (Looking to the floor in front of him.) Now let's lay to rest another firm belief, that in doing psychotherapy you should make
your patients feel at ease and comfortable. I have done my best
to make her feel ill at ease, conspicuous and embarrassed and (to
the group) that's hardly a way to begin a good therapeutic relationship, is it? (Erickson looks at Sally, takes hold of her right
hand by the wrist and lifts it up slowly.) Close your eyes. (She
looks at him, smiles, then looks down at her right hand and closes
her eyes.) And keep them closed. (Erickson takes his fingers off
her wrist and leaves her right hand suspended cataleptically.) Go
deeply into a trance. (Erickson has his fingers around her wrist.
Her arm drops slightly. Then Erickson slowly pushes her hand
down. Erickson speaks slowly and methodically.) And feel very
comfortable, very much at ease, and really enjoy feeling very
comfortable . . . so comfortable . . . you can forget about everything except that wonderful feeling of comfort.

And after a while it will seem as if your mind leaves your
body and floats in space—goes back in time. (Pause.) It's no
longer 1979 or even '78. And 1975 is in the future (Erickson
leans close to Sally), and so is 1970 and time is rolling back. Soon
it will be 1960 and soon 1955 . . . and then you will know it's
1953 . . . and you will know that you are a little girl. It's nice
being a little girl. And maybe you are looking forward to your
birthday party or going somewhere—going to visit Grandma . . .

or going to go to school . . . Maybe right *now* you're sitting in the school watching your teacher, or maybe you're playing in the school yard, or maybe it's vacation time. (Erickson sits back.) And you're really having a good time. I want you to enjoy being a little girl who someday is going to grow up. (Erickson leans close to Sally.) And maybe you might like to wonder what you will be when you grow up. Maybe you would like to wonder about what you will be doing when you are a big girl. I wonder if you will like high school. And you can wonder the same thing.

And my voice goes everywhere with you, and changes into the voice of your parents, your teachers, your playmates, and the voices of the wind, and of the rain.

Maybe you are out in the garden picking flowers. And sometime when you are a great big girl you are going to meet a lot of people and you will tell them some happy things about when you were a little girl. And the more comfortable you feel, the more like a little girl you feel, because you *are* a little girl.

(Lilting voice.) Now I don't know where you live, but you might like to go barefoot. You might like to sit in your swimming pool and dangle your feet in the water and wish you could swim. (Sally smiles a little.) Would you like your favorite candy to eat right now? (Sally smiles and nods slowly.) And here it is and now you *feel* it in your mouth and enjoy it. (Erickson touches her hand. Long pause. Erickson sits back.) Now sometime when you are a big girl, you will tell a lot of strangers about your favorite candy when you were a little girl.

And there's lots of things to learn. A great many things to learn. I'm going to show you one of them right now. I'm going to take hold of your hand. (Erickson lifts her left hand.) I'm going to lift it up. I'm going to put it on your shoulder. (Erickson slowly lifts up her hand by the wrist and then puts it on her upper right arm.) Right there. I want your arm to be paralyzed, so you *can't* move it. You can't move it until I tell you to move it. Not even when you are a big girl, not even when you are grown up. You can't move your left hand and arm until I tell you so.

Now, first of all, I want you to awaken from the neck up while your body goes sounder and sounder asleep . . . you'll wake up from the neck up. It's hard, but you can do it. (Pause.) It's a nice feeling to have your body sound asleep, your arm, paralyzed. (Sally smiles and her eyelids flutter.) And be awake from the neck up. And how old are you? (Pause. Sally smiles.) How old are you? . . . How old are you? (Erickson leans close to Sally.)

Sally: Um . . . 34.

E: (Nods head.) All right. (Erickson sits back in his chair.) You're 35 and why are you keeping your eyes shut?

Sally: It feels nice.

E: Well, I *think* your eyes are going to open. (Sally smiles, and keeps her eyes shut.)

E: They are, aren't they? (Sally clears her throat.) They are going to open and stay open. (Sally smiles, moistens her lips with her tongue and opens her eyes and blinks.) I was right. (Sally keeps staring ahead.) Where are you?

Sally: I think I'm here.

E: You're here?

Sally: Uh-hum.

E: And what are some of your memories when you were a little girl? Something you can tell to strangers. (Erickson leans toward Sally.)

Sally: Mmm, well.

E: Louder.

Sally: (Clears throat.) I, uh, I remember, uh, a tree and a backyard and umm.

E: Did you climb some of those trees?

Sally: (Speaking softly.) No, they were small plants. Um, and an alleyway.

E: Where?

Sally: An alleyway between the rows of houses. And all the kids played in the backyard and the back alley. Played, uh . . .

E: Who were those kids?

Sally: Their names? You mean their names?

E: Uh-huh.

Sally: Oh, well, um . . . (Sally just continues to stare to her right, or look at Erickson. Erickson is leaning close to her. Her hand is still on her shoulder and she is not making visual contact with people in the room.) Well, I remember Maria and Eileen and David and Giuseppe.

E: Becky?

Sally: (Speaking louder.) Giuseppe.

E: And what did you think, when you were a little girl, you would grow up to be when you are a big girl.

Sally: I thought, um, an astronomer or a writer. (She grimaces.)

E: Do you think that will happen?

Sally: I think one of them will happen. (Pause.) I'm—my left hand didn't move. (Smiles.) I'm real surprised about that. (She laughs.)

E: You are a little bit surprised about your left hand?

Sally: I recall that you said that it wouldn't move and uh . . .

E: Did you believe me?

Sally: I guess I did. (Smiles.)

E: You're just guessing. (Sally laughs.)

Sally: I, uh . . . it seems like it didn't move to me.

E: It's more than a guess then? (Sally laughs.)

Sally: Umm . . . yes. (Softly.) I . . . it's very surprising too that you can wake up from the neck up and not the neck down.

E: It's surprising that you what?

Sally: That you can um . . . that your body can be asleep from the neck down and you can be talking—you know and be awake— your body can feel so numb. (Laughs.)

E: In other words, you can't walk.

Sally: Well, not right this minute. (Shakes her head.)

E: Not just now.

Sally: (Sighs.) Uh, um, not just now.

E: Any obstetrician in this group now knows how to produce anesthesia . . . of the body. (Erickson looks expectantly toward Sally.) (Sally nods her head yes and then shakes her head no. She continues to stare blankly to her right. She clears her throat.) How does it feel to be 35 years old unable to walk?

Sally: (Correcting Erickson.) 34.

E: 34 (Smiles.)

Sally: Uh ... It feels ... uh ... right now it feels pleasant.

E: Very pleasant.

Sally: Uh-hum.

E: Now when you first came in, did you like the joking attitude that I took toward you?

Sally: I probably did.

E: You probably did?

Sally: Yes.

E: Or you probably didn't?

Sally: Yes, it's probably so. (Sally laughs.)

E: (Smiling.) Now is the moment of truth.

Sally: Huh? (Laughs.)

E: Now is the moment for truth.

Sally: Well, yeah, I had mixed feelings. (Laughs.)

E: You say "mixed feelings." Very mixed feelings?

Sally: Well, yeah, I liked it and I didn't.

E: Very, very mixed feelings?

Sally: Uh, I don't know if I can make that distinction.

E: Did you wish to hell you hadn't come?

Sally: Oh, no, I'm very glad that I came. (Bites her bottom lip.)

E: And so, in coming here, you've learned how not to walk.

Sally: (Laughs.) Yeah, not to move from my neck down. (Nodding.)

E: How did that candy taste?

Sally: (Softly.) Oh, real good, but .. uh .. I had .. there were several different kinds.

E: (Smiles.) Then you have been eating candy.

Sally: Uh-huh. (Smiles.)

E: Who gave it to you?

Sally: You did.

E: (Nods yes.) Generous of me, wasn't it?

Sally: Yes, it was really nice. (Smiling.)

E: Did you enjoy the candy?

Sally: Uh-hum, yes.

E: And all philosophers say, reality is all in the head. (Smiles.) Who are all these people? (Sally looks around. Erickson leans close to her.)

Sally: I have no idea.

E: Now, tell me your frank opinion of them.

Sally: Well, they all . . . look different.

E: They look different.

Sally: Yeah, they all look different. (She clears her throat.) They all look nice. They all look different . . . from each other.

E: All people are different from each other. (Sally laughs self-consciously and clears her throat and sighs.) Where is Eileen now?

Sally: Oh, I don't know. Um . . .

E: How long since you have thought about Eileen?

Sally: Oh, well, um . . . a fairly long time. Um, her, uh, Maria was her sister. She was closer to my age and, uh, she was the younger sister and, uh, I recall them—you know; they're people I remember in my youth, but I seldom think about them.

E: Where was your home?

Sally: Oh, um, in Philadelphia.

E: And you were in the backyard.

Sally: Uh-huh.

E: In Philadelphia.

Sally: Uh-huh.

E: How did you get here?

Sally: Oh, maybe I just, um, thought about being here.

E: Just notice. He is moving his leg, he is moving his feet and toes and she is moving hers. (Points to people in the room.) How come you are sitting so still?

Sally: Well, I recall you said something about that . . . um . . .

E: Do you always do what I say?

Sally: (Shaking her head no.) It's very unusual that I take directions.

E: (Interrupting.) And you would say you are an unusual girl?

Sally: No, it's unusual for me to follow directions. I never follow directions.

E: You never do?

Sally: I can't say never—seldom. (Smiles.)

E: You're sure you never follow directions?

Sally: No, I think I just did. (Laughs and clears her throat.)

E: You follow ridiculous suggestions?

Sally: (Laughs.) Um . . . well, I could probably move.

E: Hmm?

Sally: I could probably move if I really decided to.

E: As you look around at each person, *who* is the next one you *think* will go into a trance. Look at every one of them.

Sally: (Looks around the room.) Umm . . . maybe this woman down here with the ring on her finger. (Points at Anna.)

E: Which one?

Sally: (Softly.) Umm . . . the woman facing us with the ring on her left finger. She has her glasses on her head. (Erickson leans very close.)

E: And what else?

Sally: What else? I think she is probably the next person who will be in a trance.

E: You sure that you didn't overlook somebody?

Sally: Well, there were a couple of people that I had the feeling—the man next to her.

E: Anybody else?

Sally: Uh . . . yes, anybody else.

E: Huh?

Sally: Anybody else. (Smiles.)

E: How about the girl sitting to your left? (Indicating Rosa.)

Sally: Yeah.

E: How long do you think it would take *her* to uncross her legs and close her eyes. (Rosa has her arms and legs crossed. She is sitting on the far side of the green chair from Erickson.)

Sally: Um, not very long.

E: Well, watch her. (Rosa doesn't uncross her legs. She looks back at Erickson, then she looks down. Next she looks up and smiles, and then she looks around.)

Rosa: I don't feel like uncrossing them. (Rosa shrugs her shoulders.)

E: I didn't tell you to be uncomfortable. Nobody told you to be uncomfortable. (Rosa nods her head.) I just asked this girl how long is it going to take you to uncross your legs and close your eyes and go into a trance. (Rosa nods her head yes. Pause. Erickson looks expectantly. Speaking to Sally to his immediate left.) Watch her. (Pause. Rosa closes and opens her eyes.) She closed her eyes, and she opened them. How long will it be before you closes (sic) them and keep them closed? (Pause. Erickson looks

at Rosa. Rosa blinks.) She is having harder work opening her
eyes. (Then Rosa closes her eyes, bites her lip and then opens
her eyes. Pause. Sally closes her eyes.) She is trying hard to play
a game with me, but she is losing. (Pause.) And she doesn't know
how close she is to being in a trance. So, close your eyes, *now*.
And keep them closed, *now*. (Rosa blinks her eyes once and
blinks them again longer.) That's all right, you can take your
time. (Rosa blinks again.) But you'll close them. (Rosa blinks
again.) And next time they close, let them stay closed. (Pause.
Rosa closes her eyes and opens them, closes them again and
opens them again.) And you are beginning to know that they
will close. You are fighting hard to keep them open and you
don't know why I'm picking on you. (Rosa closes her eyes and
opens them, closes her eyes and opens them.) That's right.
(Closes her eyes and they stay shut.) *That's* right. Now what I
wanted you to see was her cooperation. Now then, patients can
resist and they will resist. And I thought she would resist and
illustrate resistance very nicely. She doesn't know it yet, but she
is going to uncross her legs. But, she wants to show that she
doesn't have to. That's all right. When you deal with patients,
they always want to hang onto something. And as a therapist
you should let them. (Pause. Rosa moves around in her chair and
leans forward, but still has her legs crossed.) Because the patient
is not your slave. You are trying to help him. You're asking him
to do things and we all grow up with the feeling, "I'm nobody's
slave; I don't have to do things." And you use hypnosis for the
patient to discover, he can do things. Even things that he thinks
are against his wishes. (Rosa opens her eyes. Sally coughs. Addressing Rosa.) Now, how do you feel about me picking on you?
Rosa: I just wanted to see if I could resist what you were saying.
E: Yes. (Sally coughs.)
Rosa: I mean, I could uncross my legs. (She uncrosses them and then
    crosses them again. Sally is laughing and coughing. Erickson
    pauses.)
E: And I told you, you would uncross your legs.
Rosa: Hmm?
E: I told you that you *would* uncross your legs.

Rosa: Yes, I can.

Sally: (Coughs. The coughing caused her to move her left arm. A man gives her a cough drop or a mint and she puts it in her mouth. Then she opens her arms and shrugs at Erickson.) Did you tell me that I was going to cough? (Laughs and touches Erickson and coughs again.)

E: Now, wasn't that a nice, *devious* way . . . (Sally coughs and covers her mouth.) A nice, intelligent, *devious* way to get control . . . of her left hand. (Sally laughs and shakes her head yes.)

Sally: Develop a symptom.

E: You got rid of that paralyzed arm and you did it by coughing. (Sally nods and coughs.) And it worked too, didn't it? (Sally laughs and coughs.) You're not really a slave.

Sally: Guess not.

E: Because you got tired of keeping your left hand up there, so how could you get it down—just cough enough . . . (Sally laughs.) . . . and you get it down. (Sally sighs and laughs.)

Christine: Could I ask a question about this getting tired of having her arm up. I thought that in a trance one usually doesn't get tired no matter what awkward position one is in. Is that a misconception? Did your arm really get tired . . . being up there? Or were you so awake that you felt awkward sitting in that position?

Sally: Um, I felt, um . . . I experienced it as kind of . . . maybe . . . just a different feeling and an awareness of tension, but, um . . . I probably . . . I could have sat there a lot longer.

Christine: You could have?

Sally: I felt as if I could have. Yeah . . . sat there a lot longer . . . um. It was kind of strange, you know, I . . . (Erickson interrupts and addresses Rosa.)

E: Your name is Carol, isn't it?

Rosa: What's that?

E: Your name is Carol.

Rosa: My name, no.

E: What is it?

Rosa: Do you want to know my name? (Erickson nods.) Rosa.

E: (Quizzically.) Rosa?

Rosa: Like Rose.

E: All right. Now I had Rose show resistance, and Rose did a beautiful job of showing resistance. Rose showed resistance and also showed an acquiescence, because her eyes did close. What's your name? (Addresses Sally.)

Sally: Sally.

E: Sally. Now I was having Rose show resistance and yet yielding (Sally smiles.) Sally here developed a cough so she could free herself and show resistance *too*. (To Rosa.) And you set the example for Sally to get her arm free.

Rosa: Well, I closed my eyes because I thought it was easier at that point to close them. Otherwise you were going on telling me just to close them, so, I said, OK, I'll just close them so that you would stop asking me to close them.

E: Uh-huh. But you closed them, and Sally followed your example of resistance. She did it indirectly by coughing. (Sally smiles.) Clever girl. (Sally coughs and clears throat.)

(To Sally.) Now how are you going to get your legs free? (Sally laughs.)

Sally: Um, I'll just make them. (Erickson waits.) OK, watch. (Sally looks around before moving her legs. Erickson looks at her legs and waits.)

E: And what did she do? She first made use of visual clues. She looked for a different place to put her foot. She went through another sensory process in order to get a muscle response. (To Sally.) Now, how are you going to stand up?

Sally: Well, I'll just stand up. (She looks down first, laughs, then pushes herself forward and stands up.)

E: Does it ordinarily take that much effort? (Sally coughs and clears her throat.) You sure you ate some candy?

Sally: Just now, yeah, or before?

E: Before.

Sally: Well, yeah. But I remembered that it was a suggestion.

E: (Moves forward and closer to Sally.) Do you think you are wide awake now?

Sally: (Laughs.) Yeah, I think I'm pretty much awake.

E: Pretty much awake. *Are* you awake?

Sally: Yes, I'm awake.

E: You're sure of it?

Sally: (Laughs.) Yeah.

E: (Lifts her left hand, slowly. Her hands were clasped and he slowly separates them and lifts her left arm by the wrist.)

Sally: It doesn't look like it belongs to me.

E: What?

Sally: It doesn't look like it belongs to me . . . when you do that. (Erickson leaves Sally's arm suspended cataleptically. He laughs. Sally laughs.)

E: You are less sure about being awake.

Sally: (Smiles.) Less sure, yes. I don't experience any, uh, sense of weight in my right arm, my right arm having no sense of weight.

E: Experiences no sense of weight. That answers your question, doesn't it? (Addresses Christine, who asked the question about a person keeping her arm in an uncomfortable position in hypnosis. To Sally.) Can you *keep it there,* or will it lift up to your face? (Erickson gestures up with his left hand.)

Sally: Umm. I can probably keep it there.

E: Watch it. I think it's going to move up.

Sally: Uh-uh, no. (Shakes her head no.)

E: It will move up in little jerks. (Pause. Sally looks blankly forward, then looks at Erickson. She shakes her head no.) Maybe you felt that jerk. It's coming up. (Sally looks at her hand.) See that jerk?

Sally: When you mention it, I do feel it.

E: Hmm?

Sally: When you mention a jerk, I do feel it.

E: You don't feel all the jerks.

Sally: Hmm.

E: (Erickson pushes her hand down in slow stepwise movements by resting his fingers on her wrist. Then he takes his hand away.) You resisted having it lowered, didn't you?

Sally: Um-hum.

E: Why?

Sally: I was OK with it the way it was. (Laughing.)

E: (Smiles.) It was OK . . . the way it was.

(Looking to the floor.) A young man, 30 years old, who had been a member of the Marine Corps and had fought in World War II in the South Pacific, came home. Despite the battles he had been in, he had never been injured.

His mother and father were glad to see him. And mother decided to be very good to her boy, and father decided to be very good to him too. So, mother began telling him what to eat for breakfast and what to eat for lunch, and what to eat for dinner. Mother began telling him what clothes he had to wear each day. Father felt the son worked very hard and should have some recreation and so father picked out the stories in the *Saturday Evening Post* for Will to read.

Will was a very good boy. He ate and wore as his mother told him to do. He read the stories that his father told him to read. He was his parents' good little boy. But Will got sick and tired of doing only the things father and mother told him to do. And they really told him everything. The only freedom he had was working on a secondhand car lot.

And he discovered that he couldn't cross Van Buren street. The car lot was on Van Buren. He also discovered that he could not drive down North Central Avenue to work. There was a restaurant called the Golden Drumstick; it had a lot of windows, and he was afraid when he would drive past that restaurant, so he would go several blocks out of his way. And then he found out that he couldn't ride in an elevator; he couldn't ride in an escalator; and there were a lot of streets that he was afraid to cross.

Not liking his home situation, he came to me for therapy. When I found out that Will couldn't drive past the Golden Drumstick, I told Will: "Will, you are going to take Mrs. Erickson and me out to dinner, and I'm going to choose the restaurant." He said, "You're not going to choose the Golden Drumstick." I said, "Will, Mrs. Erickson and I will be your guests. And you will naturally want to please your guests, and you won't tell your guests where they can't go; you'll want to take your guests where they'd like to go."

Then I told him, "And you are afraid of women. Even selling

secondhand cars, you are very careful to look at the ground, but you never look at the women. You are afraid of women. And since you are taking Mrs. Erickson and me out to dinner, I think it would be very nice if you had a woman companion. Now, I don't know what kind of companion you would like, so tell me what kind of a woman you wouldn't want to take out." He said, "I wouldn't like to take out a pretty girl who is single." I said, "Is there anybody worse than a pretty girl who is single?" He said, "Oh, yes, a divorcee who is pretty—that would be much worse than taking out a single girl." I said, "Well, what other women would you prefer not to take out?" He said, "I don't want to take out any young widows." I finally came to the question: "If you are going to take a female companion, what kind are you willing to take out?" He said, "Oh, if I had to take out a woman, I'd want one who was at least 86 years old." I said, "All right, you come to my home next Tuesday evening at six o'clock, prepared to take Mrs. Erickson and me and some other woman out to dinner." Will said (fearfully), "I don't think I can." I said, "Will, be here at six o'clock next Tuesday, you *can* do that."

Will came in promptly at six the next Tuesday, all dressed up, perspiration rolling down his face. He found it hard work to sit down on the couch. I said, "The woman I have invited for you has not yet arrived so we can have a very pleasant time waiting for her." Will didn't have a very pleasant time. He fidgeted on the couch; he kept eyeing the front door, looking hopefully at Mrs. Erickson and hopefully at me. We had ordinary social conversation and finally a very beautiful girl came in 20 minutes late. Will looked shocked and horrified. I introduced them and said, "Will, meet Keech. Keech, Will is taking all four of us out to dinner." And Keech clapped her hands happily and smiled happily. I said, "By the way, Keech, how many times have you been married?" Keech replied, "Oh, six times." I asked, "How many times divorced?" She replied, "Six times." (Erickson laughs.) Will looked very pale.

I said, "Will, ask Keech where she would like to have dinner." Keech said, "Oh, Will, I would like to go to the Golden Drumstick on North Central." Mrs. Erickson said, "I would like that too." I said, "That is a good restaurant, Will." And Will shuddered. I said, "Let's go. Do I need to take hold of your arm, Will?" He said, "No, I can walk, I'm afraid I'm going to faint." I said, "There are three steps down from the front porch. Don't faint on the steps. You will hurt yourself on the pavement. Wait until you are on the lawn. Then you can faint there." Will said, "I don't want to faint. Maybe I can get all the way to the car."

When he reached the car—it was my car, and I knew I was going to do the driving—Will said, "I better hang on to the car, I'm going to faint." I said, "It's perfectly safe to faint here." And Keech said, "Oh Will, come in and sit in the back seat with me." So Will climbed in shuddering.

We got to the parking place at the Golden Drumstick, and I parked at the far side of the parking lot. I said, "Will, after you get out of the car, you can faint on the parking lot ground." Will said, "I don't want to faint here."

Keech and Mrs. Erickson got out and so did I. We started walking toward the restaurant. All the way I pointed (Erickson gestures): "There is a nice place to faint, there is a nice place to faint, there is another nice place to faint, there is another. . . ." He got to the restaurant door and I said, "Do you want to faint inside or outside the door?" He said, "I don't want to faint outside." I said, "All right, let's go in and you can faint there." And when we got inside, I said, "What table do you want, Will?" He said, "One close to the door." I said, "There is a raised balcony on the far side of the restaurant and they have nice booths there. Let's dine there, that way we can look over the whole restaurant." And Will said, "I'll faint before I get there." I said, "That's all right. You can (Erickson gestures) faint beside this table, or that table, or that table." Will kept walking past table after table.

Mrs. Erickson sat in the booth on one side and Keech said, "Now you go in there, Will," and she sat down beside him. Mrs. Erickson sat beside him and I was on the outside seat. Will was in that booth, hemmed in by a woman on each side of him.

The waitress came. She asked for our orders and something

she said offended me. I spoke sharply to her, and she spoke angrily to me. The first thing you know, we had a yelling, screaming fight. All the restaurant turned and looked at us, and Will was trying to hide under the table. Mrs. Erickson held him by the arm and said, "Now we better watch this." Finally, the waitress very angrily walked away and the manager came, and wanted to know what the trouble was. So I picked a fight with him and pretty soon he and I were yelling at each other. Finally, he left.

The waitress came back and said, "What do you wish to order?" So Mrs. Erickson gave her order and I gave mine. The waitress turned to Keech and said, "Your order, please." Keech said, "My gentleman friend there will have chicken and all white chicken meat. He wants a baked potato, not too large, not too small. He wants sour cream and chives. Now as for the vegetable, I think it is best for him to have a dish of cooked carrots, and I want those hard-topped rolls for Will." And then she ordered what she wanted.

All through the meal Keech kept telling Will what to eat, what to take a bite of next, and she supervised every mouthful he took. Betty and I enjoyed our dinner; Keech enjoyed her dinner. It was plain hell for Will.

And when he walked out, Keech said, "Of course, Will, you are going to pay for this dinner and, Will, I think you ought to give the waitress a nice tip. It was a very nice dinner and give her . . ." and she specified the amount of the tip.

I kept on advising Will as we walked out, "Here is a nice table to faint by." I pointed out all the spots he could faint till we got to the car and he climbed in.

We returned home, and Keech said, "Will, let's go inside and visit with Dr. Erickson and Mrs. Erickson." And she took hold of his arm and practically dragged him in. And then after a few social remarks, Keech said, "I'd love to dance." Will said triumphantly, "I don't know how." And Keech said, "That's wonderful. There is nothing I like more than teaching a man how to dance. And even though the carpet is wall-to-wall . . . you've got a record player, Dr. Erickson, play some dance records

and I'll teach Will how to dance." She got Will on the floor and
finally Keech said, "Really, Will, you are a natural born dancer.
Let's go to a dance hall and have a nice evening dancing." So
Will left unwillingly and they danced until about three o'clock
in the morning and then he took her home.

The next morning his mother started giving him breakfast and
Will said, "I don't want any soft boiled eggs. I want a fried egg,
and I want three slices of bacon and I want two slices of toast. I
want a glass of orange juice." His mother (softly) said, "But,
Will . . ." He said, "Don't 'but' me, mother, I know what I
want."

He came home that night and his father said, "I found a nice
story for you in the *Saturday Evening Post*." Will said, "I
brought home the *Police Gazette*. I'm going to read that." (To
group.) The *Police Gazette* for the foreigners is—how would you
describe the *Police Gazette*? It's pretty raw. The thrillers in the
Police Gazette concern crimes of every sort, especialy sex crimes.
His father was horrified and Will said, "And next week, I'm
moving out of here. I'm going to live in my own apartment. I'm
going to do what I want to do."

He called up Keech, took her out to dinner that Sunday, and
went dancing with her. And they continued seeing each other
for three months. Then, Will came to see me and said, "What
will happen if I stop dating Keech?" I said, "She has been
divorced six times. She will be able to take it if you walk out
of her life, too." He said, "I'm going to." He stopped seeing
Keech, and began dating other girls. He sent his sister and his
brother-in-law and a cousin to me as patients.

One day, Will showed up with a young girl and he said, "Miss
M is afraid to talk, she is afraid to go places. She just lives at
home and comes to work and she doesn't want to talk. I want to
take Miss M to a party next week that all of my friends are
giving, and she doesn't want to go. I want *you* to make her go,"
and Will left.

And I said, "Miss M, apparently Will likes you." She said,
"Yes, but I'm afraid of men. I'm afraid of people. I don't want
to go to that party. I don't know anything to say. I just can't talk

to strangers." I said, "Miss M, I know all the people who are going to be at that party. They all like to talk, and they all do talk. And there isn't going to be a single good listener at that party. So you are going to be the most valuable guest there, because everybody will have a listener."

Now Will and Miss M are married. Will has flown to Yuma, and took Miss M there. He flew to Tucson with Miss M; he flew to Flagstaff with Miss M to have dinner. He rode all the escalators, all the elevators in Phoenix. He is now the head of a new automobile dealership. That one trip to the Golden Drumstick taught Will that he could walk into a restaurant, drugstore, a building where there was an elevator or escalator. It taught him that he could go out with a woman and that he couldn't faint anywhere. (Erickson chuckles.) And it was *Will* who told his mother what he was going to eat and *Will* who told his father what he preferred to read . . . and Will who told his parents where he was going to live.

All I did was arrange a restaurant trip and make arrangements with the waitress and manager for a beautiful quarrel. And the manager, waitress and I had a good time, and Will found he could live through it. (Erickson smiles.) He could live through a divorcee, six times divorced. He could learn to dance from that pretty, six-times-divorced girl. And it didn't take many weeks of psychotherapy. Family therapy was needed, but I let Will do that. All I did was to prove to Will that he wouldn't die. (Erickson laughs.) And I had a good time doing it too.

But so many therapists read books and they undertake therapy: This week we will do so much this way; next week we will do so much this different way. And they follow all the rules . . . so much this week, so much next week, so much this month, so much next month. All Will needed was to find out he could cross the street, go into a restaurant. He would drive several blocks out of his way so he couldn't see it. I showed him all the good places to faint. He couldn't do it. I gave him every opportunity to faint, to die. . . . (Erickson laughs.) But he found out life was too good. And he did all the rest of the therapy. And

Miss M is now the mother of several children and she has a good social life. Because everybody needs a good listener.

(You see, I don't believe in Freudian psychoanalysis. Freud did contribute a lot of good ideas to psychiatry and psychology. A lot of ideas that psychiatrists and psychologists should have found out for themselves and not waited for Freud to tell them. And he also invented that religion called "psychoanalysis"—wherein that religion or therapy fits all people, of both sexes, at all ages, in all cultures, in all situations. And situations where Freud himself didn't know what those situations were.)

Psychoanalysis fits all problems in all times. Freud analyzed Moses. And I am willing to bet anything that Freud never had any contact of any sort with Moses. He didn't even know what Moses looked like, yet Freud analyzed him. And life in the time of Moses was far different from life in the time of Freud. And Freud analyzed Edgar Allen Poe from his writings, his letters and newspaper stories. I think any doctor who tries to diagnose appendicitis from an author's stories and his letters to his friends and newspaper stories about him ought to be committed. (Erickson laughs.) Yet Freud analyzed Edgar Allen Poe on gossip, hearsay and Poe's writings. He didn't know a thing about the man. And Freudian disciples have analyzed Alice in Wonderland. And Alice in Wonderland is entirely fictional. The analysts analyzed it, though.

And in Freudian psychology, whether you are an only child or one of 11, the only child has as many sibling rivalries as a child with 10 brothers and sisters. There is the father fixation and the mother fixation, even if the child never knows who his father was. There is always an oral fixation, anal fixation, Oedipus complex, Electra complex. The mere truth doesn't really mean anything. It's a religion. And I am very grateful to Freud for the concepts he contributed to psychiatry and psychology. And he also discovered that cocaine was an anesthetic for the eyes. (Erickson looks at a woman to his left.)

Now, Adlerian psychotherapy teaches that all left-handed people write better than right-handed people. You see, he based a lot of his theory on organ inferiority and the dominance of the male over the female. He never once looked at the writing of a lot of right-handed and left-handed people or had their writing analyzed to see who wrote better. I can think of many right-handed doctors . . . I wouldn't say many—doctors' writing is terrible. I think that the left-handed doctors write just as terribly as do the right-handed.

Adolph Meyer, whom I admired very greatly, had a general theory of mental disease. It was merely a question of energy. Well, I admit that every mental patient has a certain amount of energy and that energy can be expressed in a great number of ways, but you can't use energy to classify mental patients.

I think we all should know that every individual is unique. (Sally opens her eyes and then closes them.) There are no duplicates. In the three and one-half million years that man has lived on earth, I think I am quite safe in saying there are no duplicate fingerprints, no duplicate individuals. Fraternal twins are very, very different in their fingerprints, their resistance to disease, their psychological structure and personality.

And I do wish that Rogerian therapists, Gestalt therapists, transactional analysts, group analysts, and all the other offspring of various theories would recognize that not one of them really recognizes that psychotherapy for person #1 is not psychotherapy for person #2. I've treated many conditions, and I always invent a new treatment in accord with the individual personality. I know that when I take guests out to dinner, I let the guests choose what to eat, because I don't *know* what they like. I think people should dress the way they *want* to. I am very certain that all of you know that I dress the way I want to. (Erickson laughs.) I think that psychotherapy is an individual procedure.

Now I told you how I corrected that bedwetter. Because I didn't have much to do that day, I saw her for an hour and a half. That was really more time than she needed. I know that a lot of my fellow therapists could have spent two, or three, or four, or five years. A psychoanalyst could have spent ten years on her.

I remember a very bright resident in psychiatry that I had. He got it in his head that he wanted to learn psychoanalysis, so he went to Dr. S, a Freudian disciple. There were two leading psychoanalysts in Detroit. Dr. B and Dr. S. Those of us who didn't like psychoanalysis called Dr. B, "The Pope," and Dr. S, "Little Jesus." And my very bright resident went to "Little Jesus." In fact three of my residents did so.

And Dr. S. told my brightest resident in the very first meeting that he would have to be therapeutically analyzed for six years. Five days a week for six years. And then he explained that he would have to be analyzed for six more years in a didactic analysis. The first meeting, he said 12 years for Alex. And he told Alex, his wife, who "Little Jesus" had never seen, would also have to have six years of therapeutic analysis. And my resident underwent 12 years of psychoanalysis; his wife underwent six years. "Little Jesus" said that they couldn't have a baby until *he* said so. And I thought that Alex was a very, very bright young psychiatrist.

Now Dr. S said he did orthodox analysis the same way Freud did. And he had the three residents, A, B, and C. A had to park his car in parking lot A; B had to park his car in parking lot B; and C had to park his car in parking lot C. A came in at one o'clock and left at 1:50. He came in one door, "Little Jesus" shook hands with him. He lay down on the couch and "Little Jesus" moved his chair to the left side of the couch, 18 inches beyond Alex's head and 14 inches off to one side. When analysand B came in, he came in this door and left by another door. He laid down on the couch and "Little Jesus" was 14 and 18 inches to the left.

All three analysands were treated the same way—Alex for six years, B for five years and C for five years. And I think of what a crime it was, because Alex and his wife were very much in love, and to have "Little Jesus" tell them to wait 12 years for parenthood is an outrage.

Now here is another case: A 12-year-old boy came in for bedwetting—12 years old, six feet tall, a very big boy. His parents came with him, and told me how they had punished him for bedwetting. They rubbed his face in the wet bed, and deprived him of desserts; deprived him of playing with his playmates.

They scolded him. They spanked him. They made him wash his own bed linen, make his own bed, and deprived him of water beginning at 12 noon. And Joe went to bed every night for 12 years and Joe wet his bed every night for 12 years.

Finally his parents brought him to me in the first week of January. I said, "Joe, you are a big boy now. I want you to hear what I have to say to your parents. Parents, Joe is my patient and nobody interferes with my patient. And, mother, you are going to wash Joe's bed. You are not going to scold him. You are not going to deprive him of anything. You are not going to say anything about his wet bed. And you, father, you are not going to punish him or deprive him. You treat him as if he didn't wet the bed, as if he is a model son. I have everything to say about Joe."

I put Joe in a light trance and said, "Joe, listen to me. You've been wetting beds for 12 years, and learning to have a dry bed takes time for everybody. In your case it's taking more time than usual. That's all right. You're entitled to *take your time* in learning to have a dry bed. Now this is the first week in January. I don't think it would be reasonable for you to have a dry bed in less than a month, and February is a very short month, so I don't know whether you want to quit wetting the bed on April Fool's Day."

Now to a 12-year-old the first week of January is a long, long time before St. Patrick's Day, before April Fool's Day. That is, to a childish mind. And I said, "Joe, it's nobody's business whether you quit wetting the bed on St. Patrick's day or on April Fool's Day. It's not even my business. That is a secret that belongs to you."

In June his mother came to me and said, "Joe has had a dry bed for I don't know how long. I just happened to notice today that his bed has been dry every morning for quite a long time." She didn't know when the dry beds began. Neither did I. It might have been on St. Patrick's Day. It might have been on April Fool's Day. That's Joe secret. His mother and father didn't know about the dry bed until June.

Now another 12-year-old boy who wet the bed every night for

12 long years. His father rejected the boy, wouldn't even speak to the boy. And when mother brought him in to tell me, I had Jim sit in the waiting room while mother told me the story. She gave me two valuable items of information. Father had wet the bed until he was 19. Mother's brother had wet the bed until he was about 18.

Mother felt very sympathetic toward the son. She thought that his bedwetting might be inherited. So I told the mother, "I will talk to Jim in your presence. You listen carefully to everything I say. And you do everything that I tell you to do. Jim will do everything that I tell him to do."

I called Jim in and said, "Jim, I found out all about your bedwetting from your mother and I know you want to have a dry bed. That is something that you have got to learn. And I know a sure way for you to have a dry bed. Of course, like all other learning, it's hard work. I know you will want a dry bed enough to work for it, just like you had to do hard work to learn how to write. Now this is what I am going to ask you and your family to do. Your mother says that seven o'clock in the morning is the time the family gets up. All right, I've told your mother to set the clock for five o'clock in the morning and she is to come into your bedroom and feel your bed. If she feels wetness, she is to awaken you and the two of you will go to the kitchen, turn on the lights, and you will start copying some book. You can choose the book." He chose *The Prince and the Pauper*.

"And, mother, you like to sew, knit and crochet, and make patchwork quilts. You will sit in the kitchen with Jim while Jim copies this book he has chosen. You will sit silently sewing or knitting or crocheting, from five in the morning until seven. That's giving enough time so that Jim will dress and father will dress. Then, you will prepare breakfast, and a regular day will take place. And each morning at five o'clock you will feel Jim's bed. If it is wet you will awaken Jim and take him out to the kitchen without a word and start your sewing, and Jim starts his copying of the book. And each Saturday you bring over the copy work to me."

I sent Jim out and said, "Now, mother, you've heard what I

said. Here is one thing that I didn't say. Jim heard me say you are to feel his bed and if it is wet he is to be awakened and taken to the kitchen to do his copy work. Some morning, Jim's bed will be dry. You go back quietly to bed and sleep till seven o'clock. You wake up, then wake up Jim and apologize for having overslept.

Within a week, Mother found the bed dry, so she went back to bed and apologized at seven o'clock for oversleeping. I saw him the first of July; by the last of July, Jim had a dry bed every night. And his mother kept on oversleeping and not awakening him.

Because I had made my message that mother would check the bed, and if she finds it wet, "You will get up and copy." And if you look at that sentence carefully, it means, "Your mother will touch your bed and if it is wet, you will get up and copy." The opposite implication is, "If it is dry, you won't wake up." So a month later, Jim had his dry bed. And his father took him fishing, his father's favorite sport.

Now there was family therapy there to be done. I had mother do some sewing. She was sympathetic. And as she sat there in the kitchen sewing, Jim couldn't look upon being awakened and asked to copy a book as punishment. He was learning something.

And in the office, I had Jim come over and see me. I took out all his copy work, arranged chronologically. And Jim looked at the first page and said, "That's awful. I missed some words, and I misspelled some. I missed whole lines. That writing is awful." And as we turned the pages in chronological order, Jim looked more and more pleased. His writing improved and his spelling improved. He didn't miss words or sentences. By the time he got to the end of his writing he was very pleased.

After he went back to school for a couple of weeks—three weeks —I called him over and asked him how he was getting along in school. He said, "You know, it's funny. Nobody ever liked me at school before. Nobody would play with me. I was very unhappy in school, and I got poor grades. Now this year, I am the captain of the baseball team and I am getting A's and B's instead of D's and F's." All I had done was reorient Jim about Jim.

And Jim's father, whom I had never met, took Jim out fishing after disowning the boy for years and years. His poor work at school—he found out that he could really write well, copy well. So he took that knowledge to school with him. He knew he was good in writing, thus he was able to find out that he was good at playing and socializing. That was therapy for *Jim*.

Now another boy in the first year of high school: Two years earlier, he had a pimple on his forehead and he squeezed it. Like all kids with pimples—they have to squeeze their pimples. And Kenny, for two years, had been picking away at that pimple and it turned into a big ulcer. His parents were angry at him and took him to a doctor. The doctor put on a very tight bandage with collodion and Kenny absentmindedly would slip his fingers under the bandage and pick at it. The doctor threatened him with cancer. His parents punished him in every way they could think of: by slapping him, by whipping him, by depriving him of his toys and grounding him so he couldn't leave the yard. And Kenny had been getting D's and F's in school and the teachers were scolding him. And finally his parents threatened him that they would take him to a crazy doctor, and that made Kenny angrier than ever. And sometimes for dinner he had bread and water; he never had ice cream, dessert or cake. He had a can of cold pork and beans. He didn't eat like his sister, his mother or father. They told him that he had to stop picking at that ulcer. And Kenny said he did it absentmindedly; he didn't intend to.

Now he wouldn't let his parents bring him to me, so I made a house call and Kenny was there. He glared at me when I entered the house. I said, "Kenny, you don't want me to be your doctor, do you?" Kenny said, "I sure don't." I said, "I agree with you that you don't want me as a doctor. Yet you listen to what I say to your parents."

I told the father and mother, "You treat Kenny like his sister. Kenny eats the same foods as the rest of the family. You are going to return his football to him, his baseball, his bat, his bow and arrows, and BB gun, his drum, and all the things you took away from him. Kenny is now my patient and I will do all the treating. And you treat Kenny like parents should treat their son.

Now, Kenny, do you want to be my patient?" Kenny said, "I sure do." (Laughter.)

I said, "Now, Kenny, you don't like that sore on your forehead, neither do I. In fact, nobody likes it. So I am going to treat it in my way. It means hard work. Now you, I think, are willing to do the hard work. And the hard work is this: Every week for a thousand times you will copy this sentence: 'I fully agree with Dr. Erickson and I understand that it is neither wise nor good, nor desirable to keep picking at that sore on my forehead.' And you will do that for four weeks, a thousand times each week." The sore was healed up in two weeks' time. (Erickson smiles.)

And his parents said, "Thank goodness, now you won't have to copy that sentence." And Kenny said, "Dr. Erickson said you are not to interfere. Dr. Erickson told me to do it for four weeks, and I am going to do it for four weeks." So he did. Each week he would bring me over his copy work.

After four weeks, I said, "That is very nice, Kenny. I want you to call me on Saturday about a month from now." Kenny said, "Sure." And he came over. I had all the sheets he had written in chronological order. He looked at sheet number one. And he said, "That's awful writing, I misspelled words. I forgot to write all the words. I wrote very crooked lines." And we turned page after page. Kenny's eyes widened and he said, "My writing is getting better and better. No misspellings, no oversights." I said, "One thing more, Kenny. How are your grades in school?" He said, "Well for the last month I have been getting A's and B's. I never got A's and B's before."

(Erickson looks up at Carol and some other group members.) When you get that wrongly directed energy turned in another direction, the patient heals and, of course, his family improved a great deal. (Erickson laughs.) And so did his teachers.

Now another bedwetter: Ten-year-old Jerry had been wetting the bed every night for ten years. He had a younger brother, eight years old, who was bigger and stronger than he was, and the eight-year-old brother never wet the bed.

And 10-year-old Jerry was ridiculed. His parents whipped

him and he would go without his dinner. They belonged to a very narrow church. They had the congregation of the church pray aloud that Jerry would quit wetting the bed. They humiliated Jerry in every way. He had to wear a shield that covered his front and back and was held together by straps saying, "I am a bedwetter." Jerry had been given every punishment that his parents could think of and he still wet the bed.

I questioned them very carefully. I found out that they were extremely religious and belonged to a narrow church. I told the parents to bring Jerry over to my office. They did. The father had him by one hand and the mother had him by the other hand and they dragged him into my office and made him lie face down on the floor. I sent them out of the room and closed the door, and Jerry was yelling and screaming.

Now when you yell, you eventually run out of breath. I waited there patiently, and when Jerry paused his screaming and took another deep breath, I screamed. Jerry looked surprised. I said, "It was my turn. Now it is your turn." So Jerry screamed again. He paused for another breath and I took my turn screaming. He and I took turns screaming and finally I said, "Now it is my turn to sit in the chair." And Jerry took his turn sitting in the other chair. And then I talked to Jerry.

I said, "I know that you would like to play baseball. And do you know something about baseball? You have to coordinate your eyesight and your arm movements and your hand movements and have your body balanced. It's really a scientific game. You have to play it by coordinating, working together—your eyesight, your hearing. And you have to get your muscles set just exactly right. In football, all you have to have is bone and muscle and you just crash your way." His eight-year-old brother played football. (Erickson laughs.) We talked about the science of playing baseball and Jerry was delighted with the way I described the complicated things involved in playing baseball.

And Jerry also, I knew, played with a bow and arrow. I showed him how, in playing with a bow and arrow, you had to use your strength exactly right. You had to use your eyesight exactly right. You had to pay attention to the wind, to the distance, the right elevation in order to make a bullseye. "It's a scientific game," I told him. "A regular name for a bow and arrow is archery, a scientific name for bow and arrow shooting is toxophily." And I praised Jerry for being so good in baseball and in shooting the bow and arrow.

And the next Saturday, Jerry, without an appointment, came in and had another talk with me about baseball and archery. He came in the next Saturday voluntarily without an appointment. On the fourth Saturday that he came in, he said triumphantly, "Ma can't break her habit of smoking." That's all that was ever said. Jerry had broken his habit. (Erickson laughs.)

And throughout the rest of his years in grade school and high school, Jerry usually dropped around to have a weekly visit with me. We discussed various things and I never once said the word "bedwetting" to him. I just talked about what he could do.

I knew Jerry wanted to have a dry bed. I gave him praise on muscular coordination, visual coordination, sensory coordination and he applied it elsewhere too. (Erickson smiles.)
(You treat patients as individuals.)

One doctor, married to a nurse, became very concerned about their six-year-old son. He sucked this thumb. When he wasn't sucking his thumb, he was chewing his fingernails. They punished him, they spanked him, whipped him, deprived him of food, made him sit in a chair while his sister played. Finally they told little Jackie that they were going to call in a nut doctor who treated crazy people.

And when I made the house call, Jackie stood there with his fists clenched, glaring at me. And I said, "Jackie, your father and mother want me to treat you—for your thumbsucking and chewing your fingernails. Your father and mother have asked me to be your doctor. Now I know you don't want me to be your doctor and you just listen because I'm going to tell your parents something. And you listen carefully."

I turned to the doctor and his wife, the nurse, and said, "Some parents don't understand what a little boy needs to do. Every little six-year-old *needs* to suck his thumb and he *needs* to chew his fingernails. And, Jackie, I want you to suck your thumb and chew your fingernails all you want to. And your parents are not going to find fault. Your father is a doctor and he knows that one doctor never interferes with another doctor's patients. And you are my patient, and he can't interfere with how I handle you. And a nurse never interferes with a doctor. So, don't worry, Jackie. You can suck your thumb and chew your nails because every little six-year-old boy needs to. Of course, when you are a big kid, seven years old, you will be too big and too old to suck your thumb or chew your nails."

Now Jackie had a birthday coming up in two months. Two months' time to a six-year-old is forever. His birthday was far, far into the future. Jackie agreed with me. And every little six-year-old kid wants to be a great big seven-year-old kid. And Jackie quit chewing his nails and sucking his thumb a couple of weeks before his birthday. I had just appealed to a little boy's understanding.

You individualize your therapy to meet the needs of the individual patient.

(To Sally.) You are pretty immobile for a young woman who is awake. I think you have been listening to me as if you were in a trance. And I notice that all the others were doing the same, even in good company. (To Anna.) And you are the one most conscious of it.

What time is it?

Jane: Ten to three.

E: Ten to three. I asked you yesterday if you believed in Aladdin's lamp out of which a genie would come. Now how many of you believe that a genie can come out of a lamp? (To Stu.) You know that childhood story, don't you, about Aladdin and his magic lamp? I have an Aladdin's lamp and it is modernized. I don't have to stroke it. I just plug it in the wall socket and the genie comes forth—a real genie. You think I am telling you a tale or telling you the truth? Huh?

Stu: It depends on what your genie is like.

E: Well, she kisses, she smiles, she winks. Would you like to meet that kind of beautiful genie?

Stu: I'm sorry.

E: Would you like to meet that kind of beautiful genie?

Stu: I certainly would, but I think it is your wife. (Laughter.)

E: No. It isn't my wife.

Stu: I would like to meet her.

E: It is a real genie that comes out of a light. (Addresses Anna.) Now are you sure that you would like to see her?

Anna: Yes.

E: Do you believe that I am telling the truth? Or telling a fancy story?

Anna: I believe that you are telling the truth, and I believe there is a gimmick.

E: A gimmick? You wouldn't call a beautiful girl a gimmick, would you?

Anna: Yes, well, coming out of Aladdin's Lamp, yes.

E: But remember. She is my genie and I don't want anybody to try to take her away from me. And my wife is not jealous of her.

So will you decontaminate me? (Erickson indicates that the lapel microphones should be removed.)

Erickson takes the group into the house to see Aladdin's lamp and his collections. Aladdin's lamp was a gift from one of Erickson's students. It is a hologram of a woman. When the light inside is turned on, one can see a three-dimensional picture of a woman. As one moves around the holographic picture, the woman winks, smiles and blows a kiss toward the viewer.

Erickson was quite proud of showing visitors his collection of ironwood carvings and assorted memorabilia. His collection of Seri Indian ironwood carvings was extensive and filled his living room. Erickson had many interesting gifts that he would show to students. He would use these gifts to continue demonstrating some of the psychological principles that he discussed in his teaching seminars.

WEDNESDAY

❖❖

(Blinky is the sacrum of a cow that one of Erickson's sons fixed up to look like a cow's head. Two small lights have been put in for eyes. Electrical equipment was put inside so that after the plug is removed, stored electricity is discharged.)

E: (To Mrs. Erickson.) Betty, is there any way of turning on Blinky?
Mrs. E: Yes.
E: How do you like my friend Blinky back there?
Stu: It seems to be a curious observer.
Mrs. E: OK. Should I disconnect it now, Milton?
E: While everybody looks on?
    Start looking. She's going to unblink Blinky. (Blinky keeps blinking even though disconnected.) And Blinky is predominantly right-eyed. (Pause.)
    Now Christine gave me some information this morning. She

115

had a headache after being in a trance. I like to have that information come out later, and I am glad that you didn't tell it right away, because when you undertake to change the thinking of a person—whenever you upset their usual habitual patterns of thought—you very often have a headache resulting.

And now, none of you probably noticed it, but, in inducing trances I give the suggestions in such a way that *if* it's their natural response to have a headache, I let them have it. But I also intersperse suggestions that they will not become alarmed, or unduly frightened.

(Erickson addresses Christine directly.) How did you feel about your headache?

Christine: I was very puzzled when it occurred, but I recognized when it did happen, that it had happened before. I related it to my first experience with hypnosis, at which time I was very disappointed during the training session by the fact that the instructors seemed to permit the students to give post-hypnotic suggestions which were not in keeping with their training, and not in keeping with the knowledge that the trainees had of the one to whom they gave the suggestions.

E: I know. When I was on the teaching staff of the American Society of Clinical Hypnosis, I always took care to give suggestions to everybody . . . so that anybody who took the seminar or workshop did not suffer unduly, and did not suffer a headache, thereafter.

Christine: But—my interpretation may have been wrong—but it seemed to me that the trainees who were giving suggestions to another trainee were really overstepping their competence.

E: (Nods head. He is smiling and looking at Christine.)

Christine: And I . . . I was very disillusioned maybe, or upset with the instructors for permitting that. On the other hand, since I am not a psychologist myself, I just was also confused and really didn't know if I judged the situation correctly. And I had first observed everybody else working with everybody else and I stayed to be the last one to be used, and I felt that the person who was working with me was particularly insensitive, maybe, and really gave such absurd suggestions that I really just couldn't accept it. And yet I was trying to go along and be polite and not destroy her learning experience. And maybe that is why I have a headache and maybe this is what I relive every time I have an induction. I don't know.

E: Well, you don't need to relive it anymore.

Now, out of my farm boy experience, I studied agriculture in grade school and learned about the importance of rotating crops. I explained it in great detail to an old farmer, who made every effort he could to understand what I was talking about in regard to the importance of growing corn in one field one year, oats another year, alfalfa another year and so on. I found out that he always complained I gave him a headache. (Laughs.) Because he learned to change his ideas.

And, later, when I was in college, I sold books one year in a certain ethnic farming community. And there I learned another thing: You did not rotate your crops on your own responsibility. Now a father of a family would call in his married sons and his neighbors and they would all discuss the importance of rotating crops. Then, on the responsibility of the entire community, the farmer could rotate his crops. But if he did it all on his own, he got a headache. (Smiles.)

And for human behavior—we start from childhood to become rigid, very rigid in our behavior, only we don't know that. We think that we are being free, but we are not. And we ought to recognize it.

(Looking down.) Now, in this ethnic neighborhood—I won't tell you the ethnic group involved, but they were all farmers. In selling books, I would stay overnight with some farm family. I always was charged for my meals.

And with one family, I arrived at noon and so I asked for dinner. The young man was harvesting hay and his father had come to help him. Before we ate, a long chapter of the Bible was read and then a long, long grace was said, and then we ate. And then, a long grace was said, and another chapter of the Bible was read.

As his father got up to leave the table, he reached into his pocket, took out his wallet and said, "I had two medium-sized potatoes, I had some gravy, I had two slices of bread, I had two pieces of meat." He named the other food that he had eaten, and he added up the cost and paid his son the cost of the meal. I asked him, "Why, since you were putting in a day's work helping your son harvest the hay, do you pay him for your dinner?" And the father said, "I am helping my son, but it is my responsibility to feed myself; therefore, I pay."

And once I saw a young man in a car driving past an old man toward a certain town. I recognized the young man in the car, and I hastened myself and caught up with the old man. And I asked the old man, "Your son is going to town in a car. It is 10 miles distance, and you are walking. Now, why didn't your son stop to pick you up and give you a ride to town?" And the father said, "He is a good son. Stopping a car uses extra gas; starting up again uses extra gas, and that is not good. You do not waste things." (Smiles.)

And then, one morning I stayed with people from that group, and I ate breakfast with the family. After eating a good-sized breakfast, the man of the house went to the back porch. I curiously went with him. I saw the chickens come running. The man vomited up his breakfast, and the chickens ate it. So I inquired why, and the man explained to me, as many others did, "Now when you get married your life changes and a married man always vomits his breakfast."

And I knew there was a wedding coming up. It was going to take place at 10:30 in the morning, so I arranged my trip down the highway to arrive at that place where the wedding took place at 11:00 o'clock. I found the bride in the barn wearing some old shoes and an old dress. She was cleaning the barn, and her husband was in the back 40 acres cultivating corn. They were married on Wednesday, and you don't take time off frivolously. (Smiles.)

And once, at the induction board, I had one of my residents in psychiatry and medical students watch me do psychiatric examinations on the selectees for the Army. And my resident came to me and said, "Am I crazy? I've just rejected 12 young farmers. They are healthy. They all complained of a severe backache once a week. They stay in bed all day and six different neighbors come to assist them in the day's work because the man of the house is confined to bed with a severe backache." I said, "You are not crazy, you just ran into an ethnic culture, a specific one."

Now, men do vomit their breakfast every morning as he found out. And they spent one day in bed and six neighbors helped with the work. I did inquire enough to know that that young man helps all six of those neighbors one day a week, because each of them has a certain day of the week when he has a backache.

And the resident looked at me, and I explained that in that ethnic group, when you get married, you call on six of your neighbors and they have a very thoughtful, earnest discussion. Since the young man is getting married, that means after having intercourse with his wife he will be confined to bed with a severe backache the next day, as will each of his neighbors. So they each decide on which day of the week they each have intercourse (laughs), because it disables them. (Erickson shakes his head and laughs.)

I found that very amusing and it certainly caused that young resident who was very much in love with his wife to have the strangest kind of wild thinking. (Erickson laughs.)

Everything was done by routine. As his grandfather did, so did grandson do. I learned a lot of anthropology that summer from that group. I had always been interested in anthropology, and I think anthropology should be something all psychotherapists should read and know about, because different ethnic groups have different ways of thinking about things.

Now, for example, in Erie, Pennsylvania, the State engaged me to teach the state psychiatrists—give them a course in psychiatry. I arrived on Sunday, stayed at the Erie State Hospital in Pennsylvania. And when we went in to dinner, I liked the entire staff. I enjoyed meeting them and all the others that were there.

We went to the staff dining room and one of them who worked there at the hospital said to another colleague on the staff, "Is it Friday, today?" That colleague groaned and said, "Take it" (Erickson holds out his hand) and handed over his steak to his colleague and told the waitress, "Bring me a can of salmon."

If you said, "Is it Friday?" any day of the week, he couldn't eat meat. He was a good Catholic and he was so conditioned that he couldn't eat meat if you raised the question, "Is it Friday?" So his colleague wanted to demonstrate that to me.

And people are so very, very rigid. And each ethnic group has its do's and don'ts. When I went to Venezuela, South America, to lecture, I was curious about what would happen to me. So at the airport, through my interpreter, I explained that my wife and I were North Americans who had not had the advantages of the niceties of Venezuelan culture, that we would make many mistakes, and we hoped that they would forgive us because we were North Americans and not really trained in the niceties of their social behavior.

One of the first things I learned was you don't talk face-to-face with a Venezuelan. Because his idea of talking face-to-face is talking with his chest pressing against yours. As Groucho Marx said, "If you get any closer to me, you will be behind me." (Laughter.) So, I carefully held my cane here (Erickson gestures as if holding a cane in front of him), because I never learned to walk backwards after I had polio. And I knew that if they pushed my chest I would go over, so I held my cane where they couldn't get close to me.

Then I told my host through the interpreter that my wife and I would make very many errors in social adjustments. I would tell them what my wife and I would like to experience. So I told them that my wife and I would like to attend a party where we would meet men and women in a home with their children.

Later, I found out that in Venezuela, when a party is given, only men attend; when women give a party, only women attend; and when the children give a party, only one chaperone attends. And here was a mixed group being very sociable with us, with children, wives and husbands present.

Then Mrs. Erickson did an awful thing. She knew enough Spanish so she listened to the high school students discussing the genetic chain—how many chromosomes in each cell—45, 46, or 47? And she joined in the conversation in Spanish with the children, and she told them the correct number. And a lot of the doctors there didn't know the correct number, and the male population is supposed to be much better informed than the female population. And here was a North American woman telling their children things that their mothers and fathers didn't even know about. And that was a horrible thing for her to do.

A rigidity. But all of your patients have their own rigidities. (Pause. A new woman comes into the room with Sally. They are about 20 minutes late.) And you are a newcomer are you not? And you will fill out a sheet for my records. (There are now eleven people attending today's session.)

Now I am going to give you a case record and it shows you the importance of the knowledge of anthropology. (Erickson asks Stu to draw out a folder. Stu hands it to Erickson.)

(To new woman.) And, stranger, what is your first name?

Woman: Sarah.

E: Sarah Lee?

Sarah: No. (Laughs.)

E: (To Siegfried.) All right, my German friend, I just asked her if her middle name was Lee. Sarah Lee. Do you know why?

Siegfried: No. It must be a play with the language. I didn't get it.

E: And would you explain to him? (Erickson asks Christine to give the explanation.)

And my son calls his dog Sarah Lee (laughs), because nobody doesn't like her. (General laughter. To Sarah.) And that has been your experience, hasn't it?

Sarah: Maybe. (Erickson laughs.)

E: All right. Some years ago I got a long distance call from Worcester, Mass. A psychologist said, "I have a 16-year-old boy in my office. He is a very intelligent boy and he gets excellent grades in school. He has just graduated from the third year of high school, but he has stuttered since he first began to speak. His father is very wealthy, and his father has hired psychoanalysts, psychiatrists, speech therapists, psychologists, and tutors for 15 years to teach the boy how to talk. And he stutters worse now than ever. Would you take the boy as a patient?" I said, "I haven't got the energy to take on that kind of job."

A year later he called me up again and said, "Rick is now 17 years old, his stuttering is worse than ever, and won't you please take him as a patient?" I said, "That sounds like too much work, I haven't got the strength.

A few days later he called me again and said, "I've talked it over with his parents and they are willing to send Rick out to you if you will see Rick for just one hour." I asked, "Do they understand that a consultation of one hour does not place me under *any* obligation to see him another minute. He said, "I explained to the parents that one hour is one hour and they have no claim on you." I said, "If they want to go to the expense of bringing Rick out here from Massachusetts and paying my consultation fee of one hour, that's their problem, not mine. I'll see the boy for exactly *one hour only.*"

A few days later the boy, Rick, and his mother walked in. I took one look at the mother and Rick and I recognized the ethnic group. And Rick, in trying to talk, made a mish-mash of noises and I couldn't understand anything he said. So I turned to the mother, who I recognized as a Lebanese woman, and I asked her to give me the family history.

She told me that she and her husband had grown up in a certain community in Lebanon. I inquired about the Lebanese culture of that small community, and she told me about it.

They had grown up there and then emigrated to Massachusetts, decided to get married in Massachusetts, and then decided to become naturalized citizens. Now, in that culture, man is a lot higher than God, and woman is a lot lower than low. Now, a man's children live with him, and as long as they live with him, he is an absolute dictator. And girls are a nuisance. You try to get them married and off your hands, because girls and women are fit for only two things—hard work and breeding.

And the first child of the marriage should be a boy. If it isn't a boy, the man says, "I divorce you," three times, and even if his bride brought a million dollars in dowry, her husband confiscates it. She is allowed to take the clothes she is wearing and her female infant, and she has to go out on the street and make her own living any way she can. Because the first child *should* be a boy.

But being a naturalized citizen of Massachusetts, he couldn't tell his wife, "I divorce you," and so he had to put up with that horrible insult, that unbearable insult, of his first child being a girl. The second child was also a girl. Now that was carrying the insult far too far. There was nothing that he could do about it—he was a naturalized American citizen.

Rick was the third child. Now the very least that Rick could have done was to look like his father and grow up to be a tall, slender, willowy man, closely resembling the father. Instead, Rick was broad shouldered, sturdy, about 5'10". His father was a slender 6'. So Rick was an insult also, not only because he was the third child, but because he didn't resemble his father.

And father's word is law. And the children, as they grow up, work in the home or in the store, and father will now and then give them a penny, sometimes a dime. His children work for literally nothing, and they do things in a good, old Lebanese way of that particular area in Lebanon.

And Rick began stuttering when he first began to talk. He stuttered in spite of those 16 years of attendance with psychoanalysts, psychologists, speech therapists, tutors and any other kind of aid that the father, who was very wealthy, could buy. And so I got that information from mother.

I told mother, "I am willing to see Rick for a few more hours on two conditions: You may rent a car and drive it around Phoenix, Arizona, and see all the sights you want to see. Now remember, I am a man." And when I told her she "might do that," she was *under absolute orders to do that.* (Erickson points to Christine with his left hand and changes his inflection slightly.) "But in driving around, you must never, under any circumstances, talk to another Lebanese person because there is a Lebanese colony in Phoenix." So they agreed . . . to that.

And I said, "Now I have another condition. I have a friend who owns a florist shop and a nursery. I am going to call my friend up and I want you to listen to my conversation over the phone with her." That way, they knew the friend was a woman.

So I called my friend, Minnie, and I said, "Minnie, I have a 17-year-old boy in my office. He is my patient. Every day, at any time you wish, this boy is to come into your florist shop or your nursery. And, Minnie, I want you to give him the dirtiest, dirtiest work you can. You will recognize him when he comes in."

Minnie was Lebanese and I had treated two of her brothers, so Minnie knew what I meant. "And he is to work for two hours and he is not to be paid anything, not even a wilted flower. And I want the dirtiest work possible. When he comes in you will recognize him. You don't have to say hello. You don't have to say anything, just point to the dirty work." And no self-respecting Lebanese from that community would ever think of working for a woman—it is beneath his dignity. And as for dirty work, that's only fit for females.

I checked up later. Rick was showing up. Minnie pointed to his work, much of it was mixing manure with soil by hand. Because Minnie knew what I meant. She never spoke to him. Rick always showed up at the right hour, worked two full hours and left. Nobody said goodbye to him. Nobody spoke to him. And it is the duty of every Lebanese woman to make a courteous bow or say something very courteous to any male. And here Rick was being treated as the scum of the earth. I checked up on Rick and he was working two hours per day, seven days per week, and they didn't visit any Lebanese people.

During that time, I saw Rick from time to time. I questioned mother about him very carefully, about the sisters, where they lived in Worcester and so on, just to be sure of my general background. And after I had seen Rick on rare occasions, for an hour each time, I told mother, "Mother, I want you to rent a temporary apartment for Rick. I want you to give him a checking account. And then you get the first plane back to Worcester."

And mother said, "I do not think his father will approve."
(Erickson looks to Christine.) I said, "Woman, I never allow
anybody to interfere with my patients. Now go and do as I say."
So she knew she was speaking to a man. She rented an apartment, gave him a checking account and left for Massachusetts
that same day.

Rick came in to see me and I said, "Rick, I've been listening
to you. I am very puzzled about the noises you make when you
try to talk. I will see you a couple of times, because I'm beginning to think I know what is wrong." After I had seen him alto-
gether a total of 14 hours, I said, "Rick, I have listened to you
carefully. You have been told since you were one year old that
you stuttered. You have heard that from psychoanalysts, from
psychiatrists, medical men in general, from your teachers, from
speech therapists, psychologists, tutors and everybody else." I
said, "Rick, I have listened to you carefully. I don't believe you
stutter. And tomorrow, I want you to bring in two sheets of
paper. On the sheets of paper, you will write the numbers from
one to ten, and you will write the alphabet. And then you will
write a composition on any subject you wish and bring it in
tomorrow. And that will prove that you don't have a stutter."
He looked surprised when I told him that he didn't have a
stutter.

He showed up the next day with two pages. I will only show
you one. The underlining, I did. I did the underlining here to
help students understand why it was proof that he didn't have a
stutter. You only need to take a look, no longer than this (looks
at the paper for a few seconds and then passes it to Anna, who
is immediately to his left in the green chair), and then you
will know Rick didn't stutter.

Yet, I have the ambition to find somebody, someday who will
look at that sheet and say, "That's right, Rick didn't stutter."

(To Anna.) You are holding that long enough to write a
dissertation on it and you still don't understand it, so pass it on.

(To Sande, the next person.) You are not going to write a
dissertation on that.
Anna: Yes, I think I understand.

E: (Nods his head.) Pass it along. (The sheet is passed to each member of the group. To Anna.) Now you say you know why there is proof that he didn't stutter.

Rick's Assignment

9 8 7 6 5 4 3 2 1 0

z y x w v u t s r q p o n m l k j i h
g f e d c b a

Life Histoyr

I fele that theer is anothre reason fro my stuttergin, which ew have ton yet discussde. I fele, however, thta this reanos is onvl a minro one. Yte, you mya feel thta this reanos did ton contribute ot my stuttergin at lla.

During my childhood, untli around teh fourth graed, I saw very taf. Even won my wiegth goes pu and donw. I lliw gain net or twenyt pounds, thne I wlli go no a deit, and tyr to loes some weigth. Even won, I hvea decided ot go no a deit. I notcie that whne I ma nervous ro upset, ym weight (~~increases~~) (~~increasaes~~) increasaes because thne I

Anna: I am willing to tell you what my thinking is. His way of writing is from right to left, rather than from left to right. So probably in his thinking and in his learning, he mixed the two somehow in the brain, so that there was some confusion. Does that make sense?

E: That is *your* thinking?

Anna: Yes.

E: And it's wrong.

Anna: It's wrong?

Christine: Does it have something to do with his Arabic background? That they write from right to left?

E: No.

Siegfried: Did you say that you told him to write two pages to prove that he doesn't need to stutter?

E: He was to write the numbers from one to ten, the alphabet, and two pages of composition on any subject he wished. I took one

look at it and said, "That's right, Rick, you do not have a
stutter. Now I will show you, Rick, what is wrong." (Erickson
takes a book and begins reading from that book.) "Life," "love,"
"is," "an," "work," "is," "of," "both," "advantage," "the,"
"to," "responsibility," "facing," "my," "it," "to," "reacted,"
"he." You heard every word I said, but I didn't communicate
anything to you, did I?"

(Erickson looks at the page Rick wrote.) Let's see what he
put on this page. My communication to him was: Write the
numbers from one to ten. And he communicated back what?
"Nine, eight, seven, six, five, four, three, two, one, zero." Those
are numerical symbols. They are not the numbers from one to
ten. So he didn't get my communication and didn't communicate back that which I asked. I asked him to write the alphabet.
He wrote all the letters, but not the alphabet. So again, he
didn't get my communication and didn't communicate back.
Then in the composition every other (*other* is the important
word), word is misspelled. How is it misspelled? The last two
letters are reversed.

He came from Lebanese parentage. That is the first part of
the family, and they are all right. And he had two sisters who
were born before he was and there should be two reversals in
that family. But you can't reverse them.

I explained that to Rick and then said, "Now your therapy
is this, Rick. I want you to get hold of any book you wish and
read it aloud backwards from the last word to the first word.
That will give you practice at saying words without communicating. Just as I read without communicating, you need practice
saying words. So read the book backwards, word by word, the
last word to the first word. You'll have practice in saying words.

"Now the next thing, Rick. You come from a home where
the dominant culture is Lebanese. There is nothing wrong or
bad about Lebanese culture. It is all right for Lebanese people.
But you and your sisters are native-born Americans. Your culture is American. You are first class citizens of America; your
parents are second class. This is not to disparage them because

they did the best they could. So you can respect the Lebanese culture, but it isn't your culture. Your culture is American.

"You are a 17-year-old American boy. You work in your father's store. He gives you a penny, a nickel, maybe a dime once in a while. Lebanese children work for nothing, and they do everything as their father says. But you are not a Lebanese boy, *you* are an American boy. Your sisters are American girls. In American culture, you are a big boy, a big 17-year-old American boy. You know your father's store better than any of his clerks. You tell your father you'll be glad to work in his store but you expect an American worker's salary.

"And, your parents have the right to ask you to live at home, and you have the right to pay for your room rent, pay for your board and pay for your laundry. That is what an American does. I want you to explain it to your sisters.

"Now your parents from the Lebanese culture think that the American law says that you don't have to go to school after the age of 16. And every young American girl has the right, if her parents have the money, to go on and finish high school, and go to college if she wants to. That is their American right, their cultural right. You explain this very carefully to your sisters and make them understand *they are* American citizens, native American citizens, in a native American culture.

"Now, Rick, living in a Lebanese home, you've been taught how to think, when to think, and in what direction to think. But you are an American." (Erickson seems to be looking at Christine.) "Americans can think any way they please. Now I want you to get a good book, a good novel. I want you to read the last chapter first and then you sit down and try to think, wonder and speculate on what was in the preceding chapter. Think in all directions, and read that second to last chapter and see in how many ways you were wrong; and you will be wrong in a lot of ways. Then you read that second to the last chapter and wonder about the preceding chapter and by the time you read a good book from the last chapter to the first chapter, wondering and speculating, imagining, and figuring out, you'll learn to think freely in all directions.

"And then, Rick, there is some more education you ought to have. That is this: A good author has a plot to his story and he reports faithfully and correctly upon human thinking and human behavior. Now I will tell you my own experience. I read *The Magic Mountain* by Thomas Mann. By the time I got to page 50 I knew that Hans Castorp, the main character in the book, was going to commit suicide. The further I read in the book, the more certain I was that Hans would commit suicide. But I knew that he would try to commit suicide in many different ways and would fail. And finally I realized, yes, he is going to commit suicide, but he is going to commit suicide with social approval. And, Rick, I had to read the entire book before I knew how to commit suicide with social approval.

"Another thing about reading books—Ernest Hemingway is a good author. When I read *For Whom the Bell Tolls,* very shortly in that story, a very minor character wandered across one page against a certain psychological background. Right then I knew that Hemingway, as a good author, would have that minor character again enter the story against the same psychological background, thus making a neatly tied-up package.

"Now, Rick, your therapy is to respect your parents; to know what American culture is for you, for your sisters; and learn to think freely in all directions."

Rick looked very thoughtful and left. A day or so later I got a phone call from the psychologist who referred him. He was the first person Rick came to see. The psychologist called me and told me that Rick was 90% better.

Rick wrote me many letters. He wrote them as if he were writing to his father. I answered them avoiding any semblance of the role of the father. I just answered the letters as if I were a high school friend.

And a year ago last Christmas, Rick came to me. His speech was clear, easy, comfortable. His father had wanted him to go to Yale or Harvard, but he chose a different college, as any American boy would do. The father wanted him to study business administration. Rick said, "I knew a business administrator wouldn't hire me. I took it for one semester and didn't like it so I dropped it. I am more interested in chemistry or psychology."

After going to college for three years, he got to thinking, "Any good American boy ought to earn at least a part of his way through college." "Well, this year, I have been to college for three years. I dropped out of college. The employment situation in Massachusetts was very poor. I am going to take a regular job with my father's store. I know that store better than the other employees do and I am going to get an American salary. I am going to pay my board and rent and laundry. I am going to buy my own clothes and I am going to save money and help pay for my fourth year in college. Then maybe I will drop out and earn money to go to graduate school."

I said, "All right, Rick. What about your sisters?" He said, "I talked things over with my sisters and they agreed with me that they were native-born Americans and they were going to live like Americans. So my sisters didn't drop out of school at the age of 16. One sister has graduated from the University and she is living alone and teaching school. I know that the Lebanese way is for unmarried children to live with their parents. My sister is an American girl and she is living alone and she likes teaching. My other sister went through the University, was dissatisfied with her University education, so she entered law school. She is practicing law."

(Speaking to the group.) I don't know what the parents think about me, but I do know that they have three children to be proud of. You might call it family therapy.

The therapy on the mother was: "Woman, you heard what I said. Now do it." (Smiles and gestures toward Christine.) Now, I knew Lebanese culture. There are various cultures in Lebanon, various groups, Christians, Muslims, Zoroastrians, and so on.

But the important thing is: Deal with your patient and don't substitute your ideas.

And the Lebanese may write from right to left, but Rick was born in the United States. In the United States you write from left to right. And in America, you speak your own mind; you do your own thinking. And that is the important thing . . . to recognize everything there is about the patient.

Of course, having Minnie's two brothers as patients taught me an awful lot more about the Lebanese. Her two Lebanese brothers now respect their sister, Minnie. They regard her as a competent businesswoman and their equal American citizen.

Now, how many of you have tried to read backwards, trying to outguess the author? I think everybody ought to do that. In *The Caine Mutiny*, after the first few chapters, I remarked to my wife, "I know how Captain Queeg is going to end up." Now it is a big book to read, *The Caine Mutiny*.

There is a book called *Nightmare Alley* which describes the American carnival—the cheap carnivals that travel around the country. My daughter, Betty Alice, read the book, recommended it to her mother, and they both recommended it to me. I read the first page and I asked my wife and my daughter, "When did you know how the book would end?" And both said, "When we got to the end." I said, "Read that first page." That first page is the end of the book. And *Nightmare Alley* is a really good exposition of what carnivals are like and how swindles are done. I hope all of you will someday read *Nightmare Alley,* just for your general education. I think every therapist ought to read that book.

(Here Erickson discusses the shortcomings of several recent fads in psychotherapy. He then continues.) I think any theoretically based psychotherapy is mistaken because each person is different.

You wouldn't think of inviting someone to dinner at a hotel and telling him what he should eat. You want your guest to *choose* what he wishes to eat, if you really want to give him a dinner. And if you wanted to entertain your guest, and if you didn't like music, would you forbid him to attend music, and force him to see a Western show? If you really want to entertain your guest, you find out what he would like to see.

Now when you consider the psychotherapy, consider the patient.

Rick was American born of Lebanese people, who were Lebanese until they were adults. They got married in Massachusetts and they were naturalized. And Massachusetts culture is very different than that in Lebanon. They were adults.

All right, that is the story of Rick. (Erickson asks a student to put the file back on the shelf for him.)

Now another case I want to report. Yesterday, I pointed out that apple dolly on top of the clock in my living room (on the tour of the house after yesterday's session).

I got a phone call from Canada. A woman's voice said, "I am an M.D.; my husband is an M.D.; we have five children. The middle one is 14 years old, a girl. She is in the hospital with anorexia nervosa. During the last month she lost five pounds and she weighs 61 pounds. My husband and I know that she will soon die of starvation. She has had intravenous feeding, tubal feeding, rectal feeding, persuasion, nothing does any good."

Anorexia nervosa usually occurs in young teenage girls and can occur in adult men and women. And it is a disease, a psychological disease, in which the person identifies with religion, with God, with Jesus, with Mary, with some Saint or with religion in general and they voluntarily starve themselves to death. And they think that a soda cracker and a glass of water a day is all the nourishment they need.

Now I have seen in the hospital at least 50 anorexia nervosa cases that died. Yet the doctors made every effort, with proper medical dignity and proper professional behavior, to save their lives.

I remember a case where a 14-year-old girl weighing 59 pounds so angered the clinical director that he became unprofessional. He thought he would provoke the girl into eating and change her behavior. He had that nurse undress her completely. He asked the staff to walk around looking her over carefully and the girl stood there, unblushing, not blinking an eye, as if she were in total darkness a hundred miles away from any living person, and not the least bit embarrassed. She was totally unconcerned.

The emotional relationship with the family—I don't know how to describe it. They are meek, mild. They never do a wrong thing. They are apologetic, but they won't eat. And they can't see that they are skin and bones.

A 14-year-old girl, of normal stature, weighing 59 pounds is something horrible to look at. But major professional societies have, in general, looked the other way and let the anorexia patients die while they try to treat them with professional dignity, proper courtesy.

Mother had read *Uncommon Therapy*, that book about my techniques by Jay Haley, and she said, "Both my husband and I think that if anybody can save our daughter's life it will be you." I told her, "Let me think it over for a couple of days and phone again." I thought the matter over and I told the mother, when she called, to bring her daughter to Phoenix to see me.

And Mother and Barbie came in. Barbie was a very nice, bright, intelligent girl, except she only ate an oyster cracker and a glass of ginger ale daily. That's all. I started questioning Barbie. I asked her the street number of her home in Toronto, and mother answered. I asked Barbie the name of the street, and mother answered. I asked Barbie what school she went to, and mother answered. I asked Barbie on what street the school was located, and mother answered. I let that go on for two days, mother answering every question.

On the third day, the mother came in with a complaint. She said, "I haven't slept much the last three nights because Barbie softly whimpers all night long and I don't get any sleep." I turned to Barbie and said, "Is that true, Barbie?" The mother looked at Barbie and Barbie said, "Yes, I didn't know it kept mother awake. I'm sorry." And I said, "Now, Barbie, just being sorry isn't enough. Even though you didn't intend to keep your mother awake, you did keep her awake and I think you should be punished for keeping your mother awake." And Barbie said, "I think so too."

So I privately told the mother how to punish Barbie. I told mother, "Scramble an egg and feed it to Barbie as punishment." The mother scrambled two eggs and punished Barbie by having her swallow two scrambled eggs. Now Barbie thought that was punishment, but I think her digestive track thought it was food. (Erickson smiles.) So I upset her physiology and Barbie willingly took her punishment.

Now, in the first two weeks, Barbie gained three pounds, lost one and gained it back.

Oh, on that third day when I told mother how to punish Barbie privately, I told mother, "Every time I ask Barbie a question, you answer it for her. For example, this last question I asked Barbie, you answered. Now I want you to understand something. I asked that question to Barbie and I want Barbie's answer and from now on, Mother, you'll keep your trap shut." (Erickson gestures strongly with his left hand.)

Can you imagine what kind of effect that had emotionally on Barbie for a total stranger to tell her mother to keep her trap shut? Because that had to provoke an emotional reaction in Barbie and she had to view her mother in a totally different emotional fashion when talking to mother thereafter. When I asked Barbie a question, before mother learned to keep her mouth really shut, it was a hard struggle.

My treatment for Barbie was to tell her short stories, metaphors, suspenseful stories, intriguing stories, boring stories. I told her all kinds of stories, little stories. For example, I told Barbie my mother was born in a super-deluxe log cabin. Barbie came from a wealthy family. She had never seen or heard of anybody intimately who had been born in a super-deluxe log cabin. (To group.) Although you all have university educations, I don't think you know what a super-deluxe log cabin is.

A super-deluxe log cabin is a log cabin with four walls made out of logs and the floor is a board floor—a wooden floor. And then I sadly told Barbie that I had been born in a log cabin too. It was just a plain, ordinary log cabin. It was in a mining camp in the Sierra Nevada Mountains. It had three sides of logs and the fourth side was the side of a mountain, and it had a dirt floor.

And I told her how my mother ran a boarding house for that mining camp and that the number of miners staying at the mine was constantly changing. My mother arrived there from Wisconsin. Because my father was part owner of the mine, he invited my mother to leave Wisconsin and come to Nevada and take charge of the boarding house. My mother found out what her first duty was: To get ready the order for the grocers—the salt, the pepper, the cinnamon, the baking soda, the flour, number of pounds of dried apples, salt beef, salt pork, everything you need for the next six months because the trader bringing groceries came in on a 20-mule-team freight wagon just twice a year. And when you run a boarding house, you can't run out of supplies.

(To group.) Now you can imagine how hard it would be for any one of you who cooks for yourself to figure how much of this and that you will need for even one week. And that impressed Barbie very much because her mother had taught her a great deal about cooking before she began to get sick. Barbie was very greatly interested in that story.

And then I told her another true story about how my mother, married to my father for 73 years before she died, was left a widow for three long hours. That really absorbed Barbie's attention because how could you be married for 73 years to one man, and be a widow for three hours. I told her that story:

In the mining crew where my father was a foreman, one of the miners was called "Bad Man" Sawyer. In those days, everybody carried a six shooter and a gun belt. "Bad Man" Sawyer had the reputation of killing men from ambush and making a notch on the revolver handle. And he was never found guilty because there were never any witnesses to the actual murder . . . just the dead body was found.

And one Monday morning, "Bad Man" Sawyer came to work drunk. My father said, "Sawyer, you've got no business coming to work in a mine, drunk. Go and sleep it off." Sawyer tried to pull his gun on my father, but my father was quicker. He said, "Sawyer, you are too drunk to shoot it out with me." And Sawyer offered to fistfight. My father said, "You are too drunk to fight with your fists. Go and sleep it off. And if you ever show up drunk again, you are fired."

The next Monday, Sawyer showed up drunk again. All the miners were standing around to see what my father would do.

My father said, "Sawyer, I told you last Monday, if you ever got drunk again, you are fired. Go to the timekeeper, draw your pay and vamoose." (To Christine.) "Vamoose" means get the hell out of here (laughs) and as far as you can go too.

Sawyer tried to draw his gun and my father said, "You are too drunk to shoot it out with me. You are too drunk to fight me. Go and draw your pay and vamoose."

The mine was quite away from the cabin where my mother, my older sister, and my younger sister lived. Now, Sawyer wandered over the mountains and anybody who has done mountain climbing knows it is a lot of work. By the time Sawyer got to the cabin, he was pretty well sobered up. He asked my mother, "Mrs. Erickson, where will your husband be at six o'clock tonight?" My mother innocently said, "Well, Albert has to go down to Davis Canyon on some business there, and he will be coming home at six o'clock." Sawyer said, "You will be a widow at six o'clock."

My mother ran into the house and got the rifle to shoot it out with Sawyer. As she stepped out of the cabin, she felt very embarrassed because Sawyer could be hiding behind any of the big boulders there (Erickson gestures), and he could pick her off with ease and she wouldn't even be able to see him. So she went back into the cabin, and hung up the rifle.

At six o'clock, my mother had the food on the stove, keeping it warm. Six o'clock came and went, so did six-thirty, quarter to seven, seven o'clock, seven-thirty, eight o'clock, eight-fifteen, eight-thirty, eight-thirty-five, eight-forty, eight-forty-five, eight-fifty, eight-fifty-five, nine o'clock. But a few minutes after nine o'clock, my father came in. My mother set the warm food on the table, and my mother said, "How did it happen that you are late, Albert?" My father said, "I got lost and had to come home by way of Florence Canyon." My mother burst into tears and said, "I'm so glad you got lost."

And my father said, "Woman, why are you glad I got lost in the mountains. What are you crying about?" So she told him about "Bad Man" Sawyer. My father said, "Put the grub back on the stove and keep it warm." He took the six gun and went

out to go down to Davis Canyon in the dark to shoot it out with
"Bad Man" Sawyer. He returned to the cabin a few minutes
later, very much ashamed of himself. He said, "I am a damn fool
if I think Sawyer waited around to shoot it out with me. He is
probably outside the state already." (Erickson laughs.)

That interested Barbie very much. And I told her how my
mother ordered supplies six months in advance. Of course, pie
was served every meal and the miners got sick and tired of
dried apple pie and one day my mother decided to give the
miners a treat and made a cornstarch custard and dumped in
enough cinnamon to make it brown. She served them cinnamon
pie and they all liked it. And it is still my favorite pie. Now my
wife and my daughters have made alterations of the original
recipe.

Now mother got awfully tired of listening to me and my stories
to Barbie. Bob Pearson, a Michigan psychiatrist, sat in and said
at the end of the hour, "I wouldn't like to sit in and listen to you
telling her the stories. You ran that poor girl up and down the
whole gamut of emotions over and over again. And I'm sweating
as a result." I said, "That girl's emotions need exercising."

The family is very wealthy. They often vacation in Acapulco
and Mexico City, the Bahamas or Puerto Rico or London, or
Vienna or Paris. They liked to travel.

After about two weeks—I didn't see Barbie everyday, too much
work—her mother said, "Barbie has never seen the Grand Canyon. Would it be all right if we took a few days off and went to
see the Grand Canyon?" I said, "It sounds like an excellent idea."

And I asked Barbie if she were interested. I told Barbie that
I'm a doctor and supposed to look after her health. "That's why
your mother brought you to me. And I want you to understand
my medical authority. So far as I can see, there is nothing wrong
with your health. Nevertheless, I am an M.D. and I am obligated
to look after your health in every way. And the only thing I can
think of that I can do for you medically is to make sure you
brush your teeth twice a day, and brush your gums twice a day."
And Barbie promised to brush her teeth twice a day.

I said, "Now, you should use a mouthwash to rinse the toothpaste out of your mouth so you won't swallow it. And mouth-wash is a mouth rinse, and you are not supposed to swallow that either. Now I want you to promise me that you will brush your teeth twice a day and use a mouthwash twice a day." And Barbie gave me her absolute promise that she would brush her teeth twice a day and use a mouthwash twice a day. I told Barbie, "As for the toothpaste, any floride toothpaste will be all right. For mouthwash, it should be raw cod liver oil." (Smiles.)

(To group.) If any of you have tasted raw cod liver oil, you don't even want to look in that direction. And here was Barbie, very religiously rinsing out her mouth with raw cod liver oil. And I think all of you know that after rinsing your mouth out with raw cod liver oil, you'd try to wash out your mouth with street dirt, because it is so awful tasting.

Here was Barbie, identified with religion. She had given me an absolute promise and she was caught. She had promised. Being very religious, she had to keep her promise. I told her mother to buy an 8 oz. bottle of raw cod liver oil. And since her mother mentioned visiting Grand Canyon, I approved and mentioned Meteor Crater, the Petrified Forest, Painted Desert, Sunset Crater and various other scenes. And I told Barbie to be sure to take her mouthwash with her. I told the mother to be sure and remind Barbie to take her mouthwash with her. I told the mother, "And that is the last time you ever mention mouthwash to her. You will never notice that the mouthwash is gone." Because I know about 14-year-olds. I knew that Barbie would not remember to bring her mouthwash back with her.

So Barbie came back after touring Arizona with a huge burden of guilt. She had purposely left the mouthwash behind and yet she had made an absolute promise to me. So she had a terrible burden of guilt. And that doesn't mix well with religion. (Laughs.) And Barbie couldn't tell her mother. She couldn't tell me. She could just feel guilty. And that certainly doesn't mix well with religious identification.

I didn't see Barbie everyday. One day I said to the mother, "Mother, would you please stand up? How tall are you?" Mother said, "Five feet six." Actually, I think the mother lied. She looked to me as if she were five feet nine. When you ask some women personal questions, they often modify the answers.

Siegfried: I don't get it.

E: They modify the answers. She said she was five feet six, and I think she was five feet nine or five feet ten, because women may modify the answers to personal questions.

Then I said, "How much do you weigh?" And she said very proudly, "One hundred and eighteen pounds, the same weight I weighed when I was first married." (Erickson, incredulous.) I said, "One hundred and eighteen pounds? And in your mid-forties, and the mother of five children—and you weigh only 118 pounds? Mother, you are underweight, *seriously*. You ought to weigh, at the very least, 130 pounds—more probably 140 to 145 pounds. Mother, you are undernourished, underweight, and you had the nerve to bring Barbie here because you *thought* she was underweight? Barbie, I want you to see to it that your mother cleans up her plate every day, every meal." And Barbie got a new kind of a look at her mother. "And, Barbie, if your mother doesn't clean up her plate, I want you to tell me the next day."

So Barbie accepted her job. One day Barbie said, "I forgot to tell you yesterday that the day before Mother saved half of her hamburger at lunch, wrapped it up in a napkin and kept it for a midnight snack." I said, "Is that true, Mother?" Mother blushed and said, "Yes." I said, "Mother, you have offended against my orders and you are to be punished. And I am going to punish you for offending against me. And, Barbie, you too have offended against me. You were supposed to tell me that about your mother yesterday, but you didn't. You waited until today. So, you have offended against me and I am going to punish both of you. So, tomorrow morning at nine o'clock, I want both of you to show up in my kitchen with a loaf of bread and some cheese, some plain American cheese."

When they showed up, I had them take out two slices of bread and layer a slice of bread very heavily with cheese and put it under the broiler and melt the cheese, take it out, turn it over and put on another heavy layer of cheese, and put it in the broiler and melt it. I had them eat every crumb of their cheese sandwiches . . . or bread sandwiches. And they were very nourishing. And it was punishment.

Then I took up with them, "I don't think either of you like me very much. I don't think you like the way I treat you, and so I think that the time has come for you to choose at what weight you will be when you will go home." Mother chose 125 pounds. "And, Barbie, you might want to choose 75 pounds. I might want you to choose 85 pounds. We might compromise on 80 pounds." Barbie said, "Seventy-five pounds." I said, "All right, you can go home when you weigh 75 pounds, but if you don't gain five pounds the first month you are at home, your mother has my orders to bring you back here to be my patient as long as I want you to be. And I don't think you will enjoy that."

So both Barbie and her mother started gaining weight. And mother kept in touch with father by telephone. When Barbie weighed 75 pounds, and Mother weighed 125 pounds, Father brought the rest of the family down by plane to meet me.

I interviewed the father first. "Father, how old are you? How tall are you? How much do you weigh?" He told me and I said, "But, Doctor, you're five pounds under the average weight for a man of your age and height." He said, "It is merely a preventive measure." I said, "Is there any history of diabetes in your family?" He said, "No." I said, "Doctor, you ought to be ashamed of yourself for setting an example to your daughter of being five pounds underweight and gambling on your daughter's life just by being five pounds underweight." And I read him the riot act and I read it very thoroughly and Father was embarrassed and ashamed.

I sent him out of the room and called in the two older siblings and said, "When did Barbie first begin to get sick?" They said about a year ago. "How did she show it?" They said, "When any of us tried to give her any food, a fruit or candy or a present, she always said, 'I don't deserve it, keep it for yourselves.' And so we did." So, I read them the riot act for depriving their sister of her constitutional rights. I pointed out to them that Barbie had the right to *receive* the present regardless of what use she made of it. Even if she threw it away, she had the right to receive. "You selfish people kept the gift for yourselves just because she said she didn't deserve it. You robbed your sister of her right to receive gifts." And they were duly rebuked. I sent them out and had Barbie come in.

I said, "When did you first begin to get sick, Barbie?" She said, "Last March." I asked, "How did you show your sickness?" She said, "Well, when anybody offered me food, fruit or candy or presents, I always said, 'I don't deserve it. Keep it for yourself.'" I said, "I am ashamed of you, Barbie. You robbed your siblings and your parents of their right to give you something. It didn't make any difference what you did with them, with the gifts, but they did have the right to give the gift to you, and you robbed them of their right to give you gifts and I am ashamed of you. You ought to be ashamed of yourself."

(Erickson to Stu.) Will you get this record out for me, please? (Stu gets Erickson the folder he requested.)

And Barbie agreed that she should have allowed her parents and siblings to give her gifts. Not that she had to use them, but that they had the right to give them to her no matter what she did with them.

It was the 12th of March when this happened. Barbie had come to me on February 11th. I saw her for a total of 20 hours. My daughter was married March 12th. I didn't watch, but my daughters did. They saw Barbie eat a piece of wedding cake. The last day before they said goodbye to me, Barbie asked me if it would be all right if her brother took her picture while she sat in my lap in the wheelchair.

Here's the picture of the 75-pound Barbie sitting in my lap in the wheelchair. Now pass it along. (Erickson passes around the picture of Barbie sitting on his lap.)

At Christmas time, Barbie sent me from the Bahamas a picture of her standing beside Santa Claus. (Erickson passes around the new picture of Barbie. Her weight now appears near normal for her stature.)

Now, Barbie took home with her the recipe for cinnamon pie.

She wrote back that she had made a cinnamon pie for the family and they all liked it.

We kept on corresponding. I knew Barbie was far from being well. And Barbie wrote me detailed letters, and in every letter she made an indirect mention of food. For example, "Tomorrow we are going to plant the garden. The tomato plants are growing nicely. Soon we will be eating stuff from our garden."

And just recently, Barbie sent me this picture of herself. She is now 18 years old and she apologized because the picture is not a full-length picture. (Erickson passes the picture around.) She had promised to send me a full-length picture of herself.

In her last couple of letters she wrote me a very complete description of anorexia nervosa, because I treated only the first stage. And usually the first stage is the last stage. The first stage is self-starvation. I prevented that. Now during the starvation stage, they feel unworthy, inadequate, inferior, and unliked by everybody. They quietly identify with religion and literally say goodbye emotionally to their parents, and slowly starve themselves to death, not believing that they are starving themselves to death.

Once you get them past the starvation stage, they begin overeating and become very obese. And during that obese stage, they feel inadequate, ashamed of themselves, disliked, unlovable, lonesome and depressed. She went to a Canadian psychiatrist and had him help her get through that stage. She really didn't need me.

And then a third stage is a vacillating stage. Sudden increase in weight, dropping down to normal, going up, dropping down to normal. Then comes the final stage.

Barbie said, "I have gone through all the stages and still feel inadequate. This last picture shows you how I look now. And my next step is to build up enough courage to date a boy." I wrote back to her that I really would like to see her and why didn't she come and visit me. And I am going to send her up Squaw Peak, to the Botanical Gardens, the Heard Museum, the Art Gallery. I am going to see to it that she gets a date. (Erickson laughs.) Then she will be over it.

She wrote to me about two other girls suffering from anorexia nervosa. She wrote and told me how sympathetic she felt for those girls, and would it be all right for her to talk to the girls about her own case. I wrote back and said, "Barbie, when I first saw you I wanted to be sympathetic toward you. I knew if I were, it would lead to your death. So, I was just as hard and cruel on you as I could be. So please don't give those other girls any sympathy. You will only cause them to die sooner." And Barbie wrote back, "You are very right, Dr. Erickson. If you had given me any sympathy, I would have thought you were a liar and I would have killed myself. But the way you treated me was so unkind that I had to get well." (To group.) And yet, medical doctors are so damned professional, so dignified, that they treat anorexia nervosa "properly" in a dignified fashion with medication, tubal feedings, and intravenous feedings, and the body rejects all food. I just turned food into punishment and that she could accept. (Erickson smiles.)

You see, I think the important thing in working with a patient is do the thing that is going to help the patient. As for my dignity . . . the hell with my dignity. (Laughs.) I will get along all right in this world. I don't have to be dignified, professional. I do the thing that stirs the patient into doing the right thing.

Now I would like that box, please. (Erickson points to a box on the shelf to his right. Stu hands it to him.) Now here is an example of something very important.

One of my students explained to me that she was doing family therapy with a father and mother who had a retarded 20-year-old daughter. In every therapeutic hour, she got along all right with the father and mother, but the retarded daughter just had one temper tantrum after another. I told my student, "That's because you are being proper, dignified, and professional. The thing to do is to get your patient, any way you wish, any way you can, to do something."

And so my student went back to Michigan and continued her therapy. This is what that 20-year-old girl with temper tantrums finally made. (It is a small, stuffed purple cow.) I think that is a work of art. I don't believe any of you have enough talent to do the same thing.

Now I don't know why it turned out to be a purple cow (laughs), but maybe my student told her something about my wearing purple . . . (To Zeig.) Did you get a good picture, Jeff? And now that mentally retarded girl has no more temper tantrums. She knows she can do things. Things that others can admire. And a lot of energy goes into temper tantrums. A lot of energy went into this purple cow. (Erickson puts the purple cow away.)

Now, how many of you climbed Squaw Peak?

Anna: Not yet.

(Half the people raise their hand.)

E: And your name, Arizona? You are going to ASU, aren't you? (To Sally.)

Sally: I just finished.

E: Have you climbed Squaw Peak?

Sally: Yes.

E: Good. And you? (To Sarah.)

Sarah: I haven't.

E: How long have you lived in Arizona?

Sarah: Seven years.

E: Say it louder.

Sarah: Seven years.

E: (Incredulous.) And you *haven't* climbed Squaw Peak? When are you going to?

Sarah: Well, I've caught some of the other peaks. (She laughs.)

E: I wasn't asking about other peaks.

Sarah: (Laughs.) I will climb Squaw Peak.

E: When?

Sarah: (Laughs.) A definite date? At the end of the summer when it is a little cooler.

E: It is cool at sunrise.

Sarah: (Laughs.) That's true. It is.

E: Have you been to the Botanical Gardens?

Sarah: Yes, I have. (Sally shakes her head no.)

E: (Addresses Sally.) You haven't. (To the group.) How many of the rest of you have been to the Botanical Gardens? (Addresses Sally.) What is your excuse?

Sally: I don't know where they are.

E: You have something to learn, haven't you?

All right. Now, you've been trained to think that psychotherapy is an orderly process of taking a history, finding out all the person's problems, then teaching the patient something about the correct way to behave. (To the group.) Is that correct? All right.

(Talking to the floor.) A Pennsylvania psychiatrist who had been practicing psychiatry for 30 years had not yet built up a good practice. In fact, he neglected his practice; he didn't keep his records up-to-date. He was analyzed three times a week and had been for 13 years. He was married six years. His wife had a job she didn't like, but she had to work to help support herself and her husband. And she had been analyzed three times a week for six years. And they heard about me, and came out for marital therapy.

When they arrived, I got that much information from them. Then I asked, "Is this your first trip West?" They said, "Yes." I said, "There is a lot of scenery in Phoenix you ought to see. And since this is your first trip, I am going to suggest to you, doctor, that you climb Squaw Peak. Spend three hours doing it. And, wife, I suggest you go to the Botanical Gardens and spend three hours there. Come in tomorrow and report to me."

They came the next day and the doctor was very happy. He said that climbing Squaw Peak was the most wonderful thing he had done all his life. "My view, perspective upon life, has been changed so greatly." He never realized that the desert could be like Phoenix's and he was rapturous about it. In fact, he said he was going to climb it again.

I asked the wife about the Botanical Gardens. She said, "I spent three hours there as you told me to—the most boresome three hours of my life. Just more and more and more of the same old thing, same old thing. And I swore I'd never go back to the Botanical Gardens again. I was just bored to death the whole time. I spent the three hours just being bored to death."

I said, "All right." Now this afternoon, doctor, you will go to the Botanical Gardens, and wife, you will climb Squaw Peak. And come in tomorrow and report to me."

So the next day, before noon, they showed up. The doctor said, "I really enjoyed the Botanical Gardens. It was wonderful. It was awe-inspiring. So marvelous to see all those different living plants living in spite of the adversities of the weather—going without rain for three years, and all that heat." (They called in July.) "I am going back to visit the Botanical Gardens again and again."

I turned to the wife and she said, "I climbed that God damned mountain. (Laughter.) I swore at that mountain, I swore at myself, but mostly I swore at you all the way up with every step. I wonder why I was such a damn fool that I would climb that mountain. Boring. I hated myself for doing it. But, because you said I should, I did. I got to the top. For a few minutes, I felt a feeling of satisfaction, but it didn't last very long. And I cursed at you and myself more thoroughly every step of the way down. I swore I would never, never again climb a mountain like that and make such a fool of myself."

I said, "All right. To date I have assigned the tasks you were to do. Well, this afternoon, you each choose a task for yourself and do it separately and come in tomorrow and report to me."

They came in the next morning and the doctor said, "I went back to the Botanical Gardens. I want to go back there again and again. It's an absolutely wonderful place. I enjoyed myself every second. I hated to leave. I am going back again someday."

I turned to the wife and she said, "Believe it or not, I climbed Squaw Peak again. Only this time I cursed you more fluently. I cursed myself for being such a damn fool. I cursed and cursed every step of the way up. I admit, at the very top I had a momentary sense of satisfaction. Now I really turned the air blue coming down cursing you and the mountain and myself."

I said, "All right. Glad to hear your reports. Now I can tell you your marital therapy is complete. Go down to the airport and return to Pennsylvania."

And they did. A few days later I got a long distance telephone call from the doctor. He said, "My wife is on the extension line. She has filed for divorce. I want you to talk her out of it."

I said, "Divorce was never mentioned in my office and I am not going to discuss it over the long distance telephone line. I would like to have some questions answered: How did the two of you *feel* on your plane trip back to Pennsylvania?" And they both said, "We were very, very puzzled, confused and bewildered. We wondered why we had ever come out to see you. All you had us do was climb Squaw Peak and visit the Botanical Gardens." And when they got home the wife said, "I told my husband I was going to get in my car and go for a drive to get the cobwebs out of my mind." And he said, "That's a good idea." The doctor said, "So I did the same thing. I went for a drive to clear my mind." The wife said, "I went directly to the psychoanalyst and fired him, then went to my lawyer and filed for divorce." The husband said, "I drove around a while and I went to my psychoanalyst and fired him, then I went to my office and started tidying it up, putting the records in order and filling in the records completely." I said, "Well, thanks for the information."

Now they are divorced. She's got a different job that she likes. She got tired of climbing that mountain of marital distress day after day and feeling that brief sense that "Alas that day is over." Her whole story was a symbolic report.

And the final outcome of it was: their psychoanalyst and *his* wife came to see me. They had the same psychoanalyst. They talked with me for a while and now *they* are divorced and they are both happy.

And the analyst's ex-wife said, "This is the first time in my life that I have been able to live my own life. My ex-husband had bullied me into making my home his office, and making me his office girl. He was just interested in his patients and not really interested in me. We just believed we had a happy marriage, but when I got back from Arizona, after what you did to that other doctor and his wife, I knew what I had to do. My divorce was very difficult because I found out how very selfish my husband was. He didn't want to settle anything on me. He was willing for me to take my clothes and go out and find a job and a boarding house. He didn't think I owned anything in that house. My lawyer had a hard time, and my ex-husband wanted to keep that home for his office and his patients. He wanted all the furniture for himself.

"Now that we are divorced, I have my home and my husband has his fair share of the property, and I've got a job I like. I can go out to dinner if I want to. I can go to the movies if I want to. I can go to a concert if I want to. All those years of my marriage, I just wished for those things, instead of taking them. As for my husband, he has changed a lot himself. He goes out for dinners now and then. We are still friends, and neither of us wants to be married to the other."

Siegfried: How did you find out that so early? Did you have an idea before that this would have this effect?

E: That was the first that I saw of them or heard of them.

When he told me he had been in psychoanalysis for 13 years and still had a poor psychiatric practice, a poorly kept office— that was enough. And when his wife told me she was unhappy every day of her life and had been in analysis for six years, didn't like her job, there was no joy in her life . . . What more did I need to know? So, I did symbolic psychotherapy just as they told me, symbolically, their whole story. I didn't have to ask if the doctor had brothers, I knew he had wasted 13 years of his life and I knew she had wasted six years of her life. And I had them do something. And he got a new perspective upon life and she got a new perspective upon the boresomeness of something she didn't like.

It is the patient who does the therapy. The therapist only furnishes the climate, the weather. That's all. The patient has to do all the work.

Now there is another case: In October, 1956, I was invited to address a national meeting of psychiatrists on the subject of hypnosis at Boston State Hospital in Boston.

Dr. L. Alex was on the staff and he was the chairman of the program committee. When I arrived, he asked me if I would not only lecture on hypnosis, but would I demonstrate.

I asked him whom I should use for a subject and he said,
"Members of the audience." I said, "That won't be entirely
satisfactory." He said, "Well, why don't you walk around the
wards and find a subject that you think would be satisfactory."

I went around the wards until I saw a couple of nurses talking.
I watched one of the couple and noted all of her behavior. After
they finished talking, I went to the one nurse, introduced myself,
and told her I was lecturing before the meeting on hypnosis and
would she be willing to be my hypnotic subject. She said she
didn't know anything about hypnosis, had never read about it,
had never seen it. I told her that was fine, it would make her
an even better subject. She said, "If you think I could do it, I
will be very happy to do it." I thanked her and said, "That's an
agreed upon promise." She said, "Certainly."

Then I went and told Dr. Alex about the nurse named Betty
who was going to be my subject. And he reacted very violently.
He said, "You can't use that nurse. She has been in psychoanalytic therapy for two years. She is a compensated depression."
("Compensated depression" means a patient who is very seriously depressed, but who has resolved to continue. No matter
how bad they feel, how unhappy they feel, they are going to do
their work.)

Dr. Alex added, "And she is suicidal. She has already given
away her personal jewelry. She is an orphan. She has no siblings,
and her friends are the other nurses at the hospital. She has
given away her personal property, and a lot of her clothes. She
has already sent in her letter of resignation." (I don't remember
the date of her resignation. I think it was October 20th and this
was October 6th.) "After she resigns on the 20th, she is going
to commit suicide. You can't use her."

The analyst, Dr. Alex, all the staff and the nurses pleaded with
me not to use Betty. I said, "Unfortunately, I accepted Betty's
promise, giving her mine in return. Now if I go back on my
promise and don't use her, being depressed, she may consider
that the final rejection and commit suicide this evening and
not wait until the 20th." I held my ground and they yielded.

I told Betty where to sit in the audience in the auditorium. I gave my lecture. I called on various members of the audience to demonstrate a little something about hypnosis here and there —various phenomena. And then I said, "Betty, please stand up. Now walk slowly up to the stage. Continue on directly in front of me. Now don't walk too fast or too slowly but go a little bit deeper into a trance with each step you take."

When Betty finally arrived on the stage in front of me, she was already in a very, very deep hypnotic trance. I asked her, "Where are you, Betty?" She said, "Here." I said, "Where is here?" She said, "With you." I said, "Where are we?" She said, "Here." I said, "What's there?" (Erickson points out to an imaginary audience.) She said, "Nothing." I said, "What's there?" (Erickson gestures behind him.) She said, "Nothing." In other words, she had a total negative hallucination for all of her surroundings. I was the only visible thing to her. So I demonstrated catalepsy and glove anesthesia. (Erickson pinches his hand.)

Then I said to Betty, "I think it would be nice if we went out to the Boston Arboretum and made a visit there. We can do it very easily." I explained all about time distortion—how you could shorten time or expand time. So, I said, "Time has expanded and each second is a day long."

So, she hallucinated being in the aboretum with me. I pointed out that the annuals were dying now since it was October. The perennials were dying since it was October. I pointed out that the change of colors of the leaves was taking place, since the leaves turn color in October in Massachusetts. I pointed out the shrubs, bushes and the vines of various trees, and pointed out how each bush, each shrub, each tree had a differently shaped leaf. I spoke about the perennials coming back to life next spring. The annuals being planted next spring. I talked about the trees and their blossoms. The kind of fruit on the trees. The kind of seed and how the birds would eat the fruit and distribute the seed which might sprout under favorable conditions and grow to be another tree. I discussed the arboretum thoroughly.

Then I suggested we might like to go to the Boston Zoo. I explained I knew there was a baby kangaroo there and that we could hope it would be out of it's mother's pouch so that we could *see* the baby kangaroo. I explained to her that baby kangaroos are called "joeys." They are about an inch long when born. They climb into the mother's pouch and attach themselves to the nipple. Then a physical change occurs in the mouth of the inch-long baby kangaroo and it can't let loose of the nipple again. And so it nurses and nurses and nurses and grows. I think it spends about three months in the mother's pouch before it looks out. We looked at the kangaroos. We saw the baby kangaroo was looking out of the pouch. We looked at the tigers and their cubs, the lions and their cubs, the bears, the monkeys, the wolves, all of the animals.

Then we went to the aviary and looked at all the birds there. I spoke about the migration of birds—how the Arctic tern spends a short summer in the arctic zone and then flies to the southernmost tip of South America—a trip of 10,000 miles. The bird spends the winter, which is summer in South America, and does it by a guidance system no man can understand. The Arctic tern and various birds instinctively knew how to migrate thousands of miles without a compass—a thing men couldn't do.

Then we went back to the State Hospital and I had her see the audience and talk to Dr. Alex. I didn't awaken her. I had her in the trance state. I had her discuss that feeling of heaviness that Christine mentioned and others mentioned feeling. And she answered questions for them. Then I suggested that we really ought to walk down the street to the Boston Beach.

I spoke about the Boston Beach being there long before the Puritans settled Massachusetts. How the Indians had enjoyed it. How the early colonials had enjoyed the beach. How it was a place of pleasure today and had been in the past for countless generations—how it would be a place of pleasure and happiness far into the future.

I had her look at the ocean and see the ocean very quiet, and then there were storm waves on it, then huge storm waves on it, and then I had her watch the ocean quiet down. I had her watch the tide come in and go out. Then I suggested we go back to the Boston State Hospital.

I demonstrated a few more things about hypnosis and then I

thanked her very profoundly in the trance for having helped me
so much—having taught the audience so much. I awakened her
and did my thank you all over again, and sent her back to the
ward.

The next day Betty did not show up at the hospital. Her
friends were alarmed. They went to her apartment. There was
no note, no sign of Betty, no uniform there . . . just ordinary
clothes. Finally, the police were called in, and Betty's body could
not be found anywhere. She had completely disappeared and
Dr. Alex and I were blamed for Betty's suicide.

The next year I lectured in Boston. I still got a lot of blame
for Betty's suicide. So did Dr. Alex.

Five years later almost everybody had forgotten about Betty
except Dr. Alex and me. Ten years later, never a word about
Betty. Sixteen years later in July, 1972, I got a long distance
call from Florida. A woman's voice said, "You probably won't
remember me, but I am Betty, the nurse you used to demonstrate hypnosis at the Boston State Hospital in 1956. I just happened to think today that you might like to know what happened
to me." I said, "I certainly would." (Group laughter.)

She said, "After I left the hospital that night, I went down
to the Naval Recruiting Station and I demanded immediate
induction into the Nursing Corps of the Navy. I served two
enlistments. I was discharged in Florida. I got a job in a hospital.
I met a retired Air Force officer and we were married. I now have
five children and I'm working in the hospital. And the thought
came to me today that you might like to know what happened
to me." So I asked if I could tell Dr. Alex. She said, "If you wish.
It makes no difference to me." We have carried on an active
correspondence ever since.

Now then I went to the aboretum and had her hallucinate
the aboretum, what was I talking about? Patterns of life: life
today; life in the future; blossoms; fruit; seeds; the different
pattern of each leaf for each plant. We went to the zoo and I
was again discussing life with her—youthful life, mature life,
the wonders of life—migration patterns. And then we went to
the seashore where countless generations in the past had found

pleasure, where countless generations in the future would find pleasure, and where the current generation was finding pleasure. And the mysteries of the ocean: the migration of whales; sea turtles, like the migration of birds, something that man can't understand, but fascinating.

I named all the things worthwhile living for. And nobody knew I was doing psychotherapy except me. They heard all the things I said, but they just thought I was demonstrating time distortion, hallucinations—visual and auditory. They thought I was demonstrating hypnotic phenomena. They never realized I was intentionally doing psychotherapy.

So, the patient doesn't have to know that psychotherapy is being done. And it illustrates that the therapist doesn't have to know why the patient needs psychotherapy. I knew she was depressed and suicidal, but that was just general information.

At that same meeting, when it closed, a grey-haired woman stepped up to me and said, "Do you know me?" I said, "No, but your question implies I should." She said, "Well, you ought to know me. I am a grandmother now." I said, "There are a lot of grandmothers I don't know." (Group laughter.) And she said, "You wrote a paper about me." I said, "I've written a lot of papers." And she said, "I will give you one more clue. Jack is practicing internal medicine. And I am still practicing psychiatry." I said, "I am happy to meet you again, Barbara."

I worked at Worcester State Hospital on the research service. I was the first psychiatrist hired on the research service and I was very busy. I learned that on the general service there was a young girl, very good looking, very intelligent, who was taking her residency in psychiatry.

I joined the staff in April and I learned from the other members of the staff that this resident had suddenly become very, very neurotic in January. She began losing weight, developed some ulcers, colitis, insomnia; a pattern of fear, uncertainty, and doubt. She spent her time up on the ward working with patients from early in the morning until late at night because that was the only place she felt comfortable. She didn't eat very much; she avoided contact with people, except patients.

In June, that resident came to me and said, "Dr. Erickson, I've listened to your lectures on hypnosis, I've seen what you do with normal subjects and patients who are subjects. And I want you to come to my apartment tonight at seven o'clock. I will tell you what I want after you get there and don't be alarmed if I prove to have forgotten I invited you to my apartment." And then she vanished.

And at seven o'clock that night, I rapped on her apartment door. She opened it and looked surprised. I said, "May I come in?" She said, dubiously, "If you wish."

So I explained how it was my first spring in New England. I knew all about spring in Wisconsin and Colorado, but it was my first experience with spring in New England. We got to talking about that, and all of a sudden I noticed that she was in a deep trance. So I asked her, "Are you in trance?" She said, "Yes." I said, "You want to tell me something?" She said, "Yes." I said, "Tell it to me."

She said, "I am very neurotic. I don't know why. I'm afraid to know why. So will you tell me to go into my bedroom and lie down on the bed and go to work on my problem? You can come in, in an hour's time, and ask me if I am through. I will tell you." So I told her to go into her bedroom and lie down and go to work on her problem.

At eight o'clock, I went in and asked her if she were through. She said, "No." I told her I would come in at nine o'clock. At nine o'clock, she wasn't through. At ten o'clock, she wasn't through, but she did say, "Come back in half of an hour, I'll be through then."

At ten-thirty, she told me that she was through. She told me to take her out into the livingroom and sit down and let her awaken. Before she came out of the bedroom she said, "Give me an amnesia for everything that happened in the trance. I don't want to know what happened in the trance. But before you leave you tell me, 'It is all right to know *just* the answer.' "

I continued our conversation I had begun previously. I talked with her about the spring in New England and how much I looked forward to the seasons. She awakened, looked puzzled, and replied to my remarks about New England. She jumped up and said, "Dr. Erickson, you have no right to be in my apartment at 11:00 p.m. Will you please leave." I said, "Certainly." She opened the door. I stepped out and I said, "It's all right to know *just* the answer." She flushed and said, "A thought just came to me. I can't understand it, would you please leave. Hurry up. Hurry up. Get out of here." So I left.

At the end of June her residency was up. I was busy on the research service. I had no particular interest in her. I didn't even know where she went to. July passed. August passed. In the last week of September she came rushing into my office about 10:00 or 11:00 o'clock. She said, "Dr. Erickson, I am working with Northhampton State Hospital. Obviously, today is my day off. I am working there on the psychiatric service and my husband, Jack, is working on the medical service. He is an internist. I was lying in bed reveling in the fact that I was married to Jack and Jack loved me. I was thinking like a new bride, being very happy, just reveling with the happiness of knowing that Jack loved me and I loved Jack. I was thinking how wonderful Jack was, and how wonderful it was to be married to him.

"All of a sudden, I remembered early last June, and I knew I ought to tell *you*. I didn't wait to eat breakfast. I dressed and got into my car and drove here as fast as I could. You should know what happened. You remember I asked you last June to come to my apartment and told you not to be surprised if I forgot that I invited you. And you came into my apartment and you started talking about springtime, summertime, and the seasons in New England.

"I went into trance and you noticed it. You asked me if I were in a trance and I told you, 'Yes,' and I told you I wanted you to do something for me. Then I told you I was neurotic and I didn't know why, and would you please send me to my bedroom, and tell me to lie down and work on my problem. I told you to return in an hour's time and ask me if I were through. You asked me if I were through at eight o'clock and I told you I wasn't; you asked me at nine o'clock and I told you I wasn't; you asked me at ten o'clock and I told you I wasn't, but that I would be at ten-thirty.

"I told you when you came in to get me at ten-thirty that I wanted a total amnesia for everything that I had worked on in the trance, and would you take me out in the livingroom.

"Finally, I woke up and you talked about springtime in New England. I was so surprised when I saw you there and I noticed the clock said eleven. I had a total amnesia of why you were there. I knew you had no right to be in my apartment at eleven at night. So, I asked you to leave.

"And this morning, while I was feeling so happy, I remembered everything. I went in and laid down on my bed in a trance state and a long parchment unrolled. There was a line down the middle. On one side were the 'pros' and on the other side were the 'cons' and the whole question arose around the young man I had met last December.

"Jack worked his way through high school. His family was very poor, poverty-stricken and uninformed. Jack had to work his way through high school, through college, through medical school. Between work and the fact that he isn't the most brilliant man in the world, he only got C's and D's.

"I come from a very wealthy family, from the upper crust, a very snobbish family. In December, I suddenly found myself thinking about Jack, thinking about marrying him. That shocked me because Jack came from the other side of the tracks, and I belonged to the high society. I had the benefit of wealth. I am much brighter than Jack. I always got A's without any trouble. I saw the operas in New York City, went to the concerts there, stage plays, traveled in Europe. I had every advantage of wealth, and my whole background is snobbery. It struck me *hard* that I was falling in love with someone who came from poverty, who wasn't as bright as I am.

"In the trance state, I read all the pros in favor of marrying Jack and all the cons against marrying him. I read them all through. I took a long time. And then I started canceling out the cons with the pros, and answered the cons. It took a little time because there were so many pros and so many cons. I went through them very thoughtfully and very carefully. When all the cons were cancelled out, there were a whole lot of pros left. But I knew that I couldn't face it all at once, so I told you to give me a total amnesia. Before you left I had you tell me, 'It's all right to know *just* the answer.'

"You stepped outside of the apartment and you said, 'It's all right to know *just* the answer,' Then a thought flashed in my mind. 'Now I can marry Jack.' I didn't know where that thought came from. I was confused. I was bewildered. I couldn't think. I just stood there and you closed the door. I forgot about everything.

"After I completed my residency, I met Jack and our acquaintanceship blossomed into a romance. We got married in July and got a job in Northhampton together—I on the psychiatric service, Jack on the medical service. And this morning I was lying in bed, on my day off, thinking how fortunate I was to have Jack as my husband, to be loved by Jack, and to love him. And then I remembered last June, and I thought you ought to know." (Erickson chuckles.)

In 1956, she said, "Do you know me, Dr. Erickson?" Well, I didn't. As soon as she told me Jack was still in internal medicine, I remembered. I didn't know what her problem was. She didn't know what her problem was. I didn't know what kind of psychotherapy I was doing. All I was was a source of a weather or a garden in which her own thoughts could grow and mature and do so without her knowledge. (Erickson chuckles.)

The therapist is really unimportant. It is his ability to get his patients to do their own thinking, their own understanding. And now she is a grandmother. Jack is still practicing internal medicine and she is still practicing psychiatry. It's a long and happy marriage.

All the books on psychotherapy stress rules. Yesterday . . . what's your first name? (To Sally.)

Sally: Sally.

E: Sally came in late. I laughingly made fun of her, embarrassed her, made her uncomfortable. I don't know if I irritated you. Certainly, it wasn't the type of treatment you expected. And yet she went into a trance because she came here to learn something. And I think you learned something.

Sally: (Nods yes.)

E: And in psychotherapy you listen to your patient, knowing that you don't understand the personal meanings of his vocabulary. I can tell a German that something is wonderful. He can tell me, it is "wonderful" or he can tell me it's "wunderbar." And I can wonder what's the difference between "wunderbar" and "wonderful." And there is a difference. So you listen to your patient knowing he has personal meanings for his words and you don't know his personal meaning. And he doesn't know your personal meanings for words. You try to understand the patient's words as *he* understands them.

Now the patient with the airplane phobia—I don't have to believe anything that anybody tells me. I don't believe it until I understand her words—when she talked about her airplane phobia and she told me she could walk aboard a plane, and ride it comfortably out to the end of the runway, but as soon as the plane left the ground, she had a phobia, I could understand that she didn't have an airplane phobia. She had a phobia for closed space where someone else was in charge of her very life, and that someone else was a stranger to her—the pilot.

I had to wait until I understood *her* words. I made her promise she would do everything good or bad. I got that promise very carefully because it duplicated her life in the hands of a strange pilot. Then I told her, "Enjoy your trip to Dallas. Enjoy your trip back, and tell me how much you enjoyed it." She didn't know that she was keeping her promise, but she was. I knew what I intended by that promise. She didn't know. And it was said so gently, "Enjoy the trip there and back." And she had promised to do whatever I asked of her. She didn't notice that I asked that of her. (Erickson smiles.) And neither did you. (To Jane.)

I hope I've taught you something about psychotherapy. The importance of seeing and hearing and understanding, and getting your patient to do something.

And Barbara—she unrolled in her mind a long parchment. She read the pros and the cons. She discovered that she had a lot of pros left over. She knew that she was not ready to know more than the answer. So the thought came to her, "Now I can get married to Jack." And she didn't know where that thought came from, so she got rid of me in a hurry. (Erickson smiles.) I didn't know until months later what telling her, "It is all right to know the answer," really meant.

When you get the patient to do the main work, all the rest of it falls in place.

The bedwetting girl—her family had to adjust to that. There was nothing else for them to do. Her sisters, neighbors and the schoolchildren had to adjust to it.

Now another observation: When I joined the staff at Worcester State Hospital, Dr. A., the Clinical Director, took me around the hospital to see the wards and the patients. Then he invited me into his office and said, "Take a seat, Erickson."

He said, "Erickson, you have got a very bad limp. I don't know how you got it. It's none of my business. I got mine in World War I. I've had 29 operations on my leg for osteomyelitis. I will always have a bad limp. Now, Erickson, if you are interested in psychiatry, you can be a success. That limp of yours will evoke the maternal feelings of all female patients. And that limp of yours will tell all the male patients that you are nobody to be afraid of, you are just a cripple and a no-account. So they won't mind talking to you, because you don't amount to much. You are a cripple.

"So, you walk around with a blank face, your eyes open, your ears open." I took that advice but added something to it. Whenever I made an observation, I wrote it down, sealed it in an envelope and put it in a drawer. Sometime later, when I made another observation, I'd write it down, and then compare it with the first observation I made.

I can illustrate that in this way: In Michigan, there was a secretary who was very, very shy. She kept her desk in the far corner of the room. She never looked up at you. She kept her head down to take your dictation, and never looked at you.

On the average she came to work five minutes early—five minutes to eight o'clock. Starting time was eight o'clock. She was already at work at eight o'clock. She worked until about five minutes past twelve o'clock. Then she went to lunch and resumed work about five minutes to one o'clock. Quitting time was four o'clock and she would always work about five minutes past quitting time.

The hospital gave the employees a two-week vacation with pay. The work week was from eight o'clock Monday morning until Saturday noon. But Debbie, when her vacation came up, waited until five minutes past eight o'clock on Monday morning before she began packing, thus wasting her weekend of Saturday afternoon and Sunday. And she returned the second weekend about five minutes to twelve, losing a second weekend of her vacation. She was very conscientious, obsessionally so.

And one summer, I saw a strange girl walking down the corridor about 60 feet in front of me. I knew everybody there. I was in charge of personnel. I knew their walk, the way they swung their arms, the way they carried their head. I could recognize any of them. And I saw this strange girl. I didn't know her. I wondered how it was possible. I was in charge of personnel. And when the girl turned to go into the bookkeeping office, I saw Debbie's profile.

I went to my office, took out a sheet of paper and wrote down my observation. I put it in an envelope and sealed it, and handed it to my secretary. I told her, "Initial it, date it and lock it up."

She kept the only key to a certain drawer I had, so I couldn't sneak a look at my observations. I don't trust myself, either. (Erickson smiles and he looks directly at a student, perhaps Sally.)

A month later my secretary came back from lunch and said, "I know something you don't know." I said, "Don't bet on it." And she said, "This I can bet on. Debbie didn't go on her vacation this summer. She got secretly married. She told us at the lunch table today." I said, "Ms. X, look up that envelope dated about a month ago." And the secretary said, "Oh, no. No." (Laughter.) She located the envelope, opened it, and took out my observation. My observation read, "Either Debbie is having a torrid love affair, or she is secretly married and making a good sexual adjustment."

And that brings up another point. For a man, sex is a local phenomenon. He doesn't grow another extra whisker. It is just a purely local phenomenon.

When a woman begins her sex life, it's a biological function of her body, and all of her body becomes involved. As soon as she begins having sex regularly, her hairline is likely to change slightly, her eyebrow ridges become just a little more prominent, her nose becomes a millimeter longer, her chin gets a little bit heavier, her lips a little bit thicker, the angle of the jaw changes, the calcium content of the spine changes, the center of gravity changes, breasts and fat pads of the hips become either larger or denser. (Erickson points to his body as he mentions the various changes.) She walks differently because her center of gravity is lower. She moves her arms differently. And if you observe a large number of people carefully, you will learn to recognize that.

Don't look at your peers or your family. That's an unwarranted intrusion into the privacy of others. But feel free to look at your patients, the nurses, your medical students, your residents in surgery, because you've got a job of looking after patients and the people who look after patients. You are teaching medical students and you ought to know what their problems are, because they are going out to practice medicine. You watch your residents. But when it comes to watching your peers or your family, that's an unwarranted intrusion into privacy. I never knew when my daughters menstruated. I always knew when a patient came in menstruating or was going to or had just completed it.

There was one secretary in Michigan who, one day, told my friend Louie and me, "You damned psychiatrists think you know everything." And I said modestly, "Well, practically." (Erickson smiles.)

That secretary, Mary, was married and her husband was a salesman. His sales territory sometimes kept him away from home for two days, a week, two weeks, three weeks—nothing certain about him. One morning I came to work and Mary was in her office with the door closed, typing. I listened, opened the door, struck my head in and said, "Mary, you began menstruating this morning," and closed the door. Mary knew I was right. Some months later, I listened to Mary typing in her office. I opened the door and said, "Mary, your husband came home last night." (Erickson chuckles.) Mary never doubted what I knew.

And some of the nurses and secretaries would come to me in advance. One day a secretary walked into my office and said, "Will you send your secretary out? I want to tell you something." I did. She said, "Last night I began a love affair and I wanted to tell you before you noticed it." (Group laughs.)

When you look at your peers or your family, your own innate sense of courtesy and privacy will stop you from learning. But patients are another thing, and the nurses in charge of my patients are another thing. As for medical students, they are going to go out and practice on people and you better know what is wrong with them.

You are adults and my peers. I won't look at you. I will read faces and if any of you dislikes me, I'll know it. And you two know it too, don't you? That I can read faces? (To Sally and Sarah.)

Sally: That you can read faces, yes.

E: Now I will tell you another case history. A Yale professor had been analyzed two years in this country and his wife was analyzed for one year. They went to Europe and he had a year's analysis for five days a week with Freud and she had a year's analysis with one of Freud's disciples. They returned next summer and they volunteered to do some work at Worcester State Hospital.

The professor told me about his two years of psychoanalysis, interview with Freud, and his wife's two years of psychoanalysis. He said he wanted psychotherapy from me and for his wife too. Now I was newly engaged in the research service and I was very busy. I told them it would take some time for me to rearrange my program.

During the first week, there was a book sale downtown in Worcester. I always liked to go to book sales, especially for publishers' remainders. I went downtown and the professor accompanied me. He liked to buy books too. And as we were walking down the street, an extremely obese woman, about five by five, came out of the store and walked down the street about 20 feet in front of us.

The professor turned to me and said, "Milton, wouldn't you like to get your hands on that." I said, "No. I wouldn't." And he said, "Well, I *would*." And when we got back to the hospital, I called his wife and told her, "We were walking down the street behind a very obese woman, about five by five in dimensions, and your husband asked me if I wouldn't like to get my hands on that rear end. I told him I didn't have any desire to do so. And he told me he did."

His wife jumped up and said, "My husband said he would like to get his hands on a great big, fat behind?" I said, "That's what he said and he said it with great feeling." And she said, "And I have starved myself all these years to keep slim, boyish hips. No more starvation for me. He is going to get his hooks on a great, big, fat behind." (General laughter.)

A few weeks later, she came in to me and said, "You know my husband is too much of a gentleman. He is very prissy. He thinks he knows it all and I want you to tell him how to make love to me. He thinks that the only way you make love is if he lies on top of me. Some of the time I would like to lie on top of him."

I called her husband in and explained that lovemaking in any position that is enjoyed by both is correct. Anything that is not enjoyed by one is wrong. I went into great detail. That is all the psychotherapy I did.

(To group.) Now why didn't that professor in three years of psychoanalysis find out that his wife's boyish hips were wrong? Why didn't she in two years of psychoanalysis, five times a week, find out that her husband liked a large derrière?

So, I did all Freud's analysis and the other analyst's therapy in two short meetings. And now the professor is retired. They are grandparents, and she is five by five, and they are happy. (Erickson smiles.) And I think that is psychotherapy.

When I first came to Michigan, the first day, I saw a girl who

I soon found out was a medical technician. She was very pretty from the waist up and from the knees down. But she had the largest fanny I have ever seen on a woman. When she was walking down the hospital corridor and she would pass somebody, she swung her fanny at him and knocked him down. (Erickson gestures with his left arm.) I knew she didn't like her fanny. But she looked interesting to me.

I soon found out that she had a rather peculiar habit. On visiting days, she stood at the gates of the hospital grounds at a place that was visible from my office. Whenever a mother came in with a small child, I would see the girl asking three questions, the mother nodding each time. Then the mother came into the hospital to visit her relatives, while this medical technician took the small children of all the mothers, and babysat them on every pleasant day. Now for a girl to give up her day off to babysit the small children of other women, she must like children.

And then, after about a year, she suddenly developed hiccups, night and day. We had a staff of 169 physicians from Detroit. They all examined her and they all recommended a psychiatric consultation. The girl knew that I would be the one to do the psychiatric consultation. She knew my reputation—I could see things. And so, she flatly refused.

Her boss went to see her and said, "Now look here, June. You're getting free hospitalization here, free medical attention. Everybody is recommending a psychiatric consultation. You have refused. Your job is being kept open for you and you are collecting your pay even though you are a patient in bed. Now either you have the psychiatric consultation or use the telephone to call a private ambulance to take you to a private hospital. But you can keep your job if you will accept the psychiatric consultation."

She didn't like the prospect of paying a private hospital, a private ambulance, so she said, "All right, let him come."

I went over about two o'clock, and very carefully shut the door to her room. I held up my hand and said, "Keep your mouth shut, don't say anything (Erickson gestures with his left hand as if to stop traffic), until you have heard what I have to say.

Your trouble is that you haven't read the Song of Solomon. It's in the Bible beside your table, but you haven't read it. That is your problem. Now since you haven't read the Song of Solomon, I'll explain it to you. I've watched you for about a year, taking care of other women's little children, giving up your days off to do that. You always ask the mother if you can give them a stick of gum, some candy or a toy, if you can take care of them while they are visiting their sick relative. So I know you like children. And you think because you've got such a great big fanny, no man will ever look at you. You would know better if you had read the Song of Solomon." By that time I had her curiosity.

(To group.) I doubt if any of you ever read the Song of Solomon? (To one student.) You have? (Erickson nods.) Then I explained, "The man who will want to marry you, the man who will fall in love with you, will look at that great big, fat fanny of yours and see only a cradle for children. He will be a man who wants to father a lot of children. And he will see a beautiful cradle for children.

"Now, don't stop your hiccups now. Stop when it is 10:30 or 11:00 o'clock. That way everybody can think you had a spontaneous cure, and that I had nothing to do with it. Just keep on hiccupping and they will all know that I failed too. After I leave, read the Song of Solomon. It is in the Bible there beside your bed."

A few months later, after my secretary had gone to lunch, June came in and showed me her engagement ring. A few months after that, she waited until my secretary had gone to lunch, and she brought her fiancé in. He told me how he owned some land in a certain area, and he started telling me about the plans he and his fiancée had for building a home. They were going to have a lot of bedrooms and a great, big nursery. (Erickson smiles.)

I once asked my father why he married my mother. And he said, "Because her nose points west." (Laughter.) My mother had a deflected septum and she did have a crooked nose. I protested that she has to stand looking south to have her nose pointing west. My father said, "I came from Chicago. That's south of Wisconsin." I couldn't argue with that logic.

So I asked my mother, "Why did you marry dad?" And she said, "Because he had one blue eye and one white eye." I said, "Eyes are blue or brown or black." She said, "Your father had one blue eye. He was cross-eyed and only the white of the right eye showed at certain times." I said, "I've never seen his white eye." She said, "No, the day we got married, both eyes looked straight forward."

I said, "Did that eye ever turn back again?" She said, "Yes, once. He went to St. Louis and tried to enlist with Teddy Roosevelt's Rough Riders. They turned him down on vision. He came home with one blue eye and one white eye. But after he got home he started thinking. He had a wife and a daughter to support. He better do the right thing. So he had two blue eyes again." (Erickson smiles.) Ask and you shall learn. What time is it?

Jane: Four.

E: I can count to four. Stranger, will you come up here and sit in this chair, please? (Erickson addresses Sarah, who comes to the green chair.)

And did you happen to notice that I didn't ask her to leave that chair? (Erickson is talking about Anna.)

Now the others know this. How many fingers do you have?

Sarah: Five, uh, four.

E: Counting your thumbs as a finger.

Sarah: Five. Ten.

E: Which is it? Five or ten?

Sarah: Ten.

E: You sure?

Sarah: Yes. (Laughs.)

E: Now, put your hands on your thighs. Does it make any difference if you count them this way? (Erickson points right to left.) Or if you count them this way? (He points from left to right.) Do you get the correct count each way?

Sarah: Yes. (Smiles.)

E: You sure?

Sarah: Yes.

E: And if you add the fingers on one hand to the fingers on the other, will you get the correct answer?

Sarah: Yes.

E: I think you've got 11 fingers. . . . Do you really think I'm mistaken?

Sarah: Well, probably not in some way or another.

E: Well, you count as I point. (She counts as Erickson points to the fingers.)

Sarah: One, two, three, four, five, six, seven, eight, nine, ten.

E: That's the way you count them?

Sarah: Yes.

E: Well, I think you've got 11 fingers.

You said it didn't make any difference if you count this way or that way. (Erickson gestures.) And that the fingers from one hand added to the fingers of the other hand give the correct number. Correct?

Sarah: Right.

E: And you understood?

Sarah: Yes.

E: Ten, nine, eight, seven, six, and five is 11.

Sarah: (Smiles and laughs.) That's right.

E: Is this the first time you knew you had 11 fingers?

Sarah: (Nods yes and laughs.)

E: Don't you think you should have studied harder in school?

Sarah: Yes. (Smiling.)

E: I think so too. Do you know your right hand from your left hand?

Sarah: Yes, I do.

E: You are sure of that?

Sarah: Uh-huh.

E: Put that hand behind you. (Pointing to her left hand.) Now, which hand is left?

Sarah: (Smiles and laughs.)

E: So your right hand is your left hand? I think she ought to go back to school.

Sarah: I'm still there. That's the problem.

E: That's a nice technique in working with children.

I think I will do one more thing for the group. (To Stu.)
Can you get this card for me? (Erickson gets out a card and
gives it to Sarah.) Now read this carefully, but don't betray
your understanding of it. Pass it along without betraying your
understanding. (The card is passed around the room. On the
card is written: Read in every possible way the material enclosed in both sets of parentheses:

(7|0) (773H)

Erickson gets back the card.) Now what did you read? (Addresses
Sarah.)

Sarah: Do you want me to tell you the whole thing that is on the
card?

E: (Nods yes.)

Sarah: Do you want me to just read the numbers? I'm not sure.

E: Read it aloud. (Erickson shows the card to Sarah again.)

Sarah: The whole card . . . way?

E: Tell us what you read.

Sarah: Inside the parentheses? (Erickson nods.) 710. 7734.

E: Any of the rest of you read anything different? (To Siegfried.)
Repeat your answer.

Siegfried: I can mix the numbers.

E: Illustrate.

Siegfried: 017, or 107, or 3477, or 7347. . . .

E: The instructions were read in every possible way, the material
enclosed in the parenthesis. And I look at it and I see "OIL"
and "HELL." (Erickson takes the card, turns it over and passes
it to Sarah. She laughs. Erickson smiles. The card is passed
around the room.)

Now, why didn't you obey the instructions to read it every
possible way?

Christine: You know there is another, uh, reason that came out. . . .
Germans write sevens different. They wouldn't read them this
way. And I write my sevens different and he would too. (Indicating Siegfried.) And so for us, it wouldn't be the same thing.
If we turned it upside down, it would never come out this way.

E: But you both read English.

Christine: But we write our sevens like this. (She demonstrates.)

E: And when you listen to the patient, listen to what you hear, then get over in that chair and listen again, because there is another side to the story. And there is another side to this. (Erickson points to the card.)

I'll tell you of an experience I had. Mrs. Erickson and I were in Mexico City. A dentist invited us to have dinner in his home. The dentist was very proud of his wife and he told us what a great artist she was. And his wife said that wasn't so. She could do a little sketching and that was all, and it wasn't very good sketching. The dentist said it was marvelous sketching. And against her wishes he brought out a half a dozen of her sketches.

I looked at each one. She had added a frilly border of twisted lines around each picture. I looked at the picture. I looked at it this way, I looked at it this way, and this way, and back this way. (Erickson turns the card around.) And I was very puzzled because I looked at it and analyzed both ends.

I took a piece of paper and tore a hole in the paper about the size of my fingernail. I laid it on the ornamental border. The dentist looked and he saw a miniature face. I moved it along and he saw another miniature face. There were hundreds of tiny little faces concealed in that ornamental border.

I said, "Anybody who has enough talent to conceal hundreds of miniature faces with different expressions on them in a border and nobody can see them, and the artist not even know they are there, has to be a good artist." Now she is a well-known artist in Mexico City and she runs the city art gallery.

When you look at things, look at them. When you listen to patients, listen carefully and try to think what is the other side of the story. Because if you just hear the patient's story, you really don't know all of the story. When you turn the patient's story upside down, you read "OIL" and "HELL."

I think that is enough for you to try to digest until tomorrow. And those of you who haven't gone to Squaw Peak, do so. And those of you who haven't gone to the Botanical Gardens and the

Heard Museum, take advantage of it tomorrow morning. It is four o'clock now and the Heard Museum closes at five, so does the Botanical Gardens, so does the Zoo. Squaw Peak is always open. (Erickson smiles.)

Anna: Dr. Erickson, I am leaving tomorrow morning and I wanted to thank you very much.

E: Then this is the last time I'll see you, because I don't get out of bed until about 15 minutes to twelve tomorrow.

As for my fee, I haven't made it clear to you. My fee is very flexible. I tell my students to pay whatever you can do *comfortably*. My basic fee is $40.00 an hour. I couldn't in good conscience ask each of you to pay that. You know how many hours you have been here, and you can pay your proportionate share of that amount. If you feel awfully affluent, you can leave an even bigger check. I plan to keep on living no matter what I get. (Laughter.)

And should I take this innocent young creature in and show her what a genie is? (Erickson points to Sarah who laughs.)

Siegfried: May I decontaminate you?

E: If you please.

I'm going to take this innocent young creature in and show her Aladdin's Lamp. With a real genie.

Sarah: With a real genie—sounds pretty interesting.

Jeff: You are not getting older, you are getting stronger.

E: Tell it to me again!

THURSDAY

❖❖❖

(Five new people have entered the group today. In total 11 people are present. Erickson asks the new people to fill out data sheets. He looks around the room.)

E: Does anybody know how Pope John Paul was selected?

Christine: Like all other popes, by conclave.

E: No. The cardinals couldn't reach a decision; they took a recess and took a poll. (Erickson laughs.)

Siegfried: (Sitting in the green chair.) A lot of American jokes are with language and I seldom get them.

E: (Pauses.) Here is another American joke. A lady saw a short-tailed cat at the railroad station and she asked the station keeper, "Manx?" And he said, "No, from two to two to two two."

And most Americans don't get it. (Laughter.) The Manx cat out of Manx, England is naturally short-tailed. When the station master said, "Nope, from two to two to two two," he was

· referring to the train that arrived at two minutes to two and left at two minutes past two, and ran over the cat's tail and amputated it. (Erickson laughs.)

Siegfried: I got some words. (Laughter.)

E: And are there any Australians here? Because a New Zealander told me about Australians. He said Australians do not know the difference between a buffalo and a bison. Now do any of you know why?

An Australian knows what a buffalo is, but (in an Australian accent) he thinks that a bison is what he washes his face in. (Erickson pronounces face as "fice.")

(Erickson gets the data sheets from new people in the room. He puts his glasses on and reads the sheets.)

Is this a conspiracy against me? This week everybody (which is an inaccurate statement) wants me to figure out how old they are. They put down their date of birth, and give the ages of their siblings. Well, Bonnie, whoever you are. . . .

Bonnie: Right here.

E: You remind me of the good old days of teaching in the medical school. Please put the date on it. And, Ruth, have you an objection to the date?

Ruth: Today's date? (Erickson hands her paper back to her for correction.)

E: (Addresses Edie. He hands her back her paper.) The date. And you are also asking me to figure out how old you are.

And I'd tell my medical students the final examination will take place in Science Hall at 2:00 p.m. on Tuesday, the 12th. I said it very slowly, "Science Hall, Tuesday, at two o'clock in room 222." And I'd walk off and return for a look and here's everybody and they are saying, "What did he say? What did he say?"

Now, will you tell me your name again?

Linda: Linda.

E: How do you like sitting next to Count Dracula?

Linda: I met him before and I think he is friendly. (Laughs.)

E: You haven't met him at midnight.

Now, for some of you I will repeat: Our conscious life, our

conscious mind deals with our state of awareness which is a divided state of awareness. You came here to find out what I had to say. At the same time you are dividing your attention between me, the other people here, the bookcases on the walls, the pictures and everything else.

Now, the unconscious mind is a vast storehouse of your memories, your learnings. It has to be a storehouse because you cannot keep consciously in mind all the things you know. Your unconscious mind acts as a storehouse. Considering all the learnings you have acquired in a lifetime, you use the vast majority of them automatically in order to function.

Now, it was a long, hard job for you to learn how to talk. And now you can start in the morning and finish at night and you never bother about how do you say this syllable, how many syllables in each word, what are the right sounds, and so on. You never stop to think about that. But there was a time when you said, "Dink wa wa," and thought you were saying, "Drink of water." And now you use an adult vocabulary without that awful effort of infancy, of saying, "Dink wa wa." In infancy, you actually had to be consciously aware of exactly what you were saying and consciously remember to not say, "Dink dink wa wa," but "Dink wa wa."

I remember one of my daughters learning to talk would say, "Climb stairs, tip-tip, tip-tip, tip-tip . . ., Gonna put blank-blank on my doll-doll." And now she says, "I walk up the steps and I put the blanket on the doll." But she always repeated many of the words and she called her brother, "La la." His name is Lance.

Now in psychotherapy—if you want to do psychotherapy—you have to learn, first of all, that each of us has a different meaning to the words used in common. The word "running" has 142 meanings in English. You can say the word "run," and the girl who is conscious of the run in her stocking can become embarrassed. The fact is that you were talking about a run of luck in cards, or a run of fish, or the way the government is run, or how does a horse run, and how does a camel run in comparison to a horse. And so, your patients tell you many things and your tendency is to put your meaning upon the patient's words.

I told this the other day, but I will tell it again. (Erickson tells the story about "milk gravy." He ends the milk gravy story by stating:) So, we all have our special meanings.

How many of you can cook? Suppose you are on a camping trip, let us say in Northern Illinois or Wisconsin, and you decided to have fish for dinner. How would you cook them? (Erickson smiles.) And suppose you raided a farmer's cornfield and got a few ears of corn. How would you cook them?

Well, I'll tell you the most delicious way to do it. You catch a fish, and you eviscerate it. You don't scrape off the scales, you wrap it in plantain. That is a weed with wide leaves and it's nonpoisonous. Having wrapped the fish in plantain leaves, you take some nice mud from the river bottom and make a nice round ball, with the ends thinner than the rest of the ball. Then you drop it in the campfire, and when the ends of the ball blow out, you know the fish is cooked. You roll the ball out of the fire and you crack it and it splits apart. All the scales, and the fins, and the tail all stick to the plaintain leaves and you just have the fish cooked in its own juices. And they are delightful. Just add a little salt, and you have an Olympian feast ahead of you.

And if you happen to catch a quail, you eviscerate it. Wrap it very carefully in a ball of mud and drop it in the campfire. When the two ends blow out with steam, crack the ball, and all the feathers and skin stick to the dried mud. There you have the quail neatly roasted in its own juices. Add a pinch of salt and it is a wonderful meal.

There are other ways of cooking quail (laughter), but my preference is that.

And for roasting ears of corn: Encase them in mud and you put them in the fire for a reasonable length of time. Crack open the ball of mud which takes the husk away, and you have your corn nicely cooked. I know, I've done it.

All of you know that there are various ways of preparing

corn, and there are various ways for each individual to react to every situation.

Now here's a picture of which I am very fond. (Erickson takes the picture and passes it to Siegfried on his left.)

Siegfried: (Looks at picture.) I only get part of the meaning.

E: Let her see it. (Passes it to Bonnie.) Read it aloud.

Bonnie: "Award of honorary grandparent is to be bestowed on Dr. Milton Erickson, by Slade Nathan Cohn, son of Jim and Gracie Cohn, on our Slade's adoption anniversary, September 12, 1977, sealed and approved with this special 'stomp' of approval." (It has his footprint and "age two" on the picture. Bonnie holds it up for people to see.)

E: Pass it around.

All right. Jim was a high school graduate and a very idealistic young man. Gracie was a classmate, and also a very idealistic young woman.

Jim was drafted for the war in Viet Nam. He was serving in Viet Nam in noncombat duty. In a truck accident, he had his spinal column broken and his spinal cord severed.

He returned to the Veteran's Hospital in a wheelchair suffering from convulsive pain about every five minutes, night and day. The Veteran's Administration operated on Jim to relieve him of his pain, but that didn't work. In fact, that made his pain worse. And then they operated on him a second time, and that served no purpose at all. They were planning on doing a third operation to relieve him of that convulsive pain every five minutes.

And somewhere along the way, Jim or Gracie, or both, heard about me. They told the chief surgeon that they were going to see me for hypnosis about pain. So the surgeon took them into his office. For one whole hour, he told them that hypnosis was nonsense, and witchcraft, black magic, and sorcery. He described me as a charlatan, a faker, an ignoramus. In fact, he didn't like hypnosis, and he didn't like me. He considered it awfully wrong of them even to think about hypnosis.

And Jim still had his convulsions of pain every five minutes.

And Gracie was very sympathetic, and despite that hour-long lecture against hypnosis, they decided to come see me.

Gracie wheeled Jim's wheelchair into my office. The looks on the faces of both were the looks of fear, of unhappy expectation, the look of resentment, a faint look of hopefulness, a look of antagonism and a look of wariness. They were certainly not in good emotional state to listen to me. But they told me about the back injury and the two operations, and how the highly respectable chief surgeon at the Veteran's Hospital had said that hypnosis was black magic, witchcraft and the work of a charlatan.

So I told Gracie, "You stand over there on that rug. (Erickson points.) Stand up straight; look straight ahead, your hands beside you. And, Jim, here is a heavy oak cane. I used it when I walked. It's a heavy oak cane. You take it. If you see me doing anything you don't like, clobber me with it." (To Siegfried.) Clobber means "hit." (Everyone laughs.)

Siegfried: With the piece of wood?

E: An oak cane, a long stick that you use when you walk.

Jim took the cane and gripped it very tightly in his hand, and he watched me.

Then I told Gracie, "Gracie, I'm going to do something to you that you won't like—to which you will object very strenuously. I will stop doing it just as soon as you go into a hypnotic trance. Now you don't know what hypnosis is, nor what a hypnotic trance is, but in the back of your mind you *know* what it is. So you stand there and if I do something offensive to you, you can know that I'll stop just as soon as you are in a trance."

I lifted the point of my bamboo cane and began sliding it back and forth at the point of cleavage, trying to expose her breasts. And Gracie slowly closed her eyes and was in a deep trance. I put my cane down and Jim was watching me. He couldn't take his eyes off me. I said to Gracie, "Where is your hometown? What high school did you go to? Name some of your classmates. How do you like Arizona weather?" A few things like that. And Gracie answered with her eyes shut. I reached

THURSDAY   177

out and took hold of her arm and lifted it up and left it
cataleptic. (Erickson lifts his arm and leaves it cataleptic.)

I turned to Jim and said, "You heard Gracie speaking to me.
Now you talk to her." I reached out and put Gracie's hand
down. (Erickson puts his hand down.) And Jim said, "Gracie?
Gracie? Gracie?!" And he turned to me and said, "She doesn't
hear me." I said, "That's right, Jim. She is in a deep trance,
she can't hear you. Ask her any question you want to. She
won't hear you." So he asked a few more questions and got
never a quiver of movement.

Then I said, "Gracie, how many students were there in your
high school?" She told me. I reached out with one finger and
lifted her hand up again, and with one finger I put it down
again. (Erickson gestures with his left arm.) I told Jim, "Lift
Gracie's hand." He reached over and started to lift it, but I
had put Gracie's hand beside her and it was cataleptic. Jim
couldn't pull it away from her side. I reached out and lifted her
hand with one finger and told Jim to put it down and he tried.
Gracie's muscles contracted and she kept her hand where it was.
(Erickson demonstrates with his hand.)

I took my time doing all of this. And then I said, "Gracie,
stay in a deep trance, but open your eyes and walk from that
rug to over there to that chair." (Erickson points.) "And when
you sit down in the chair, close your eyes. Then awaken, open
your eyes and start wondering."

Gracie sat down, closed her eyes, opened them, and said,
"How did I get here? I was over there on that rug. How did
I get here?" Jim said, "You walked over there." Gracie said, "I
did not. I was standing over there on that rug. How did I get
here?" Jim tried to tell her, but Gracie disputed it. "I was
standing on the rug. How did I get here?" I let that argument
go on for a while.

Then I told Jim, "Look up at the clock. What time is it?"
He said, "It's twenty-five past nine." I said, "That's right. You
came in at nine o'clock and you had a convulsion of pain. You
haven't had any more convulsions." Jim said, "That's right,"
and went into a convulsion of pain. I said, "How did you like

that pain? You were free of it for 20 minutes." He said, "I didn't like it and I don't want it to happen again." I said, "I don't blame you. Now Jim, you look at Gracie. Gracie, you look at Jim. And, Gracie, as you look at Jim you will go slowly into a deep trance. And as you look at Gracie going into a deep trance, Jim, you will go into a trance." And within a minute's time, they were both in a deep trance.

I pointed out to him, "Jim, pain is a warning that the body gives. It is like an alarm clock that awakens you in the morning. You awaken, and you turn off the alarm. Then you proceed with preparing for the day's work." I said, "All right Jim, and you listen, Gracie. Jim, when you feel pain beginning, you just turn off the alarm, and let your body go about the day's work of comfort, and anything else that needs to be done. And listen well to me Gracie, because Jim doesn't have to see me all the time. Since you are his wife, when Jim feels pain coming on, he can ask you to sit down. He can look at you and you can look at him, and you both will go into a trance. After you are in a trance, Gracie, you can repeat some of the things I am going to teach you right *now*." And so I gave Gracie full instructions on how to talk to Jim.

So, I saw them a few more times to make certain that they had really learned. After the first meeting, they went back to the hospital and demanded to see the chief surgeon. For about an hour, they gave him a lecture about hypnosis. They told him how wrong he was, how very, very wrong. Jim said, "You don't see me having any pain convulsions, and you wanted to do a useless operation. You really ought to be ashamed of yourself. You should learn something about hypnosis." And at the next meeting of my class at Phoenix College, the surgeon came in and took notes.

A few days later, Jim and Gracie left the hospital and went to their home in Arizona. And the government, because Jim was disabled, furnished him with money to build a home. Jim, working in his wheelchair, helped build a great part of that home. The government furnished him with a tractor and 15 acres of land. Jim learned how to get out of his wheelchair and up onto the tractor seat, so he plows his own land.

At first, every two months, they would drive to Phoenix because Jim thought about hypnosis like he thought about antitetanus. He would ask me for a "booster shot." I would give him a booster shot. But pretty soon, Jim started showing up only every three months, then twice a year. Then they had a happy idea. They could telephone me. Jim would call me up and say, "Gracie is on the extension line. I think I need a booster." And so I would say, "Are you sitting down, Gracie?" She would say, "Yes." I would say, "All right, I'm going to hang up. You and Jim stay in a trance for 15 minutes. You say whatever is necessary to Jim, and Jim, you will listen to what Gracie says. At the end of 15 minutes, you can awaken."

Now Jim and Gracie wanted to have a baby. Gracie had six miscarriages, all within the first two years. She went to various doctors and they all recommended that she adopt a child instead of having one. So I sponsored the adoption of Slade Nathan Cohn.

When he was two years old, they brought him up to see me, and I like that little boy very much. He's almost as big as my four-year-old grandson and actually better behaved. Gracie and Jim were excellent parents. And just the other day, I sponsored the adoption of another child by Jim and Gracie.

Now what people don't *know* . . . it's infinite . . . things that they actually do know but believe that they don't know. Most of you think that you cannot induce anesthesia. Let me give you an example:

You go to college, and there is one professor who lectures in a monotonous tone of voice. You are not interested in the course and never will be. He drones on and on, and you wish the old buzzard would drop dead. You don't have any real hope that he will. He drones on and on. You are sitting in a hard wooden chair—your bottom aches and your back aches, your arms ache and you squirm around trying to find a comfortable position. The time on the clock seems to have stopped and the hour goes on and on forever. Finally, the old buzzard dries up. You stand up gratefully and shift around to get your body feeling comfortable.

The very next day, you sit in the same chair and you like that professor. He is talking about something that interests you. You lean forward and you listen, open-eyed and open-eared. That hard wooden chair doesn't hurt your bottom, doesn't make you ache. And that clock seems to be running too fast for you because the hour is too short. The lecture is over almost before it begins. And you've all had that experience. You produce your own anesthesia.

Now I will tell you about some cancer cases. A doctor in Mesa called me up and said, "I have a woman dying of cancer of the uterus. The story is rather sad. About a month ago, her husband suddenly dropped dead in the kitchen of heart failure. After the funeral, his widow came to me for a physical examination. By the time I completed the examination, I had to tell her that she had cancer of the uterus, and that it had spread to her hipbones and to her spinal column. I had to tell her that she had about three months to live. I told her to take it very easy; sooner or later she would have some pain, and I would give her narcotic drugs to ease the pain. And now this is September. She will be dead before December. And she suffers a great deal of pain. Large amounts of Demerol combined with morphine and other narcotic drugs have no effect on her. She is in constant pain. Would you use hypnosis on her?"

I agreed to. I went out to the home, because the woman wanted to die at home. As I came into the bedrom and introduced myself, the woman said, "I have a master's degree in English. I've published a volume of poetry, so I know something about the power of words. Do you really think that the power of your words will do things to my body that powerful chemicals cannot do?" I said, "Madam, you know the power of words. I know the power of words in *my* way. I would like to ask you a few questions. I understand that you are a Mormon. Are you a good Mormon?" She said, "I believe in my church. I was married in the Temple. I brought my children up the same way." I said, "How many children?" She said, "Two. I have a boy who will graduate from Arizona State University next June. I would like to see him in his cap and gown. But I will be long dead by then. My daughter is 18, and she is going to be married in the Temple next June. I would like to see her as a bride. Now, I will be long dead by then." I said, "Where is your daughter?" She said, "In the kitchen preparing my evening meal." I said, "May I call her into the bedroom?" The mother said, "Yes."

Then I asked the mother, "You are in very great pain right now?" She said, "Not only right now. I have been in pain all day and all last night. I will be in pain all night tonight." I said, "That is what you think. I don't have to think that way."

And the girl came into the bedroom—a very pretty 18-year-old girl. Mormons are very moral and very rigid in their code of morals. I asked the girl, "What are you willing to do for your mother?" And the girl had tears well up in her eyes and she said, "Anything, just anything." I said, "I'm glad to hear that. You can just sit down in this chair, because I need your help. Now you don't know how to go into a trance, but that is all right. As you sit here beside me, in the back of your mind, in your unconscious mind, or you may call it the back of your mind, you know how to go into a trance. So, to help your mother, just go into a trance, a very, very deep trance. So deep a trance that your mind will leave your body and float in outer space and you will sense only my voice which will accompany your mind in outer space. And you will sense *only* my voice."

I turned to the mother. The mother was staring at her daughter with an intense gaze, because her daughter's eyes were shut. She was not moving. Then I did something that I knew the mother would object to. The girl was wearing sandals and bobby socks, and her skirt came down to almost her ankles.

I said, "Now watch me carefully, Mother. You won't like what I am going to do. You will have serious objections. You won't understand why I'm doing it, but you just watch and you will find out." I began pulling the girl's skirt up over her legs, over her knees, up over her thighs. And Mother looked with absolute horror because that is something that you don't do to a Mormon maiden—expose the bare skin of her legs. And the mother was totally horrified.

When the thighs were uncovered two-thirds, I lifted my hand and brought it down with as hard a slap as I could give. (Erickson slaps his hand down on his own thigh.) Mother almost jumped out of her bed at the sound of that slap. She looked at her daughter, who hadn't moved, hadn't winced in any way. I moved my hand and mother could see the imprint of my hand on her skin. I lifted my hand again and brought it down on the other thigh just as hard. The girl didn't wince, didn't move. So far as I was concerned she was in outer space *sensing* only my voice.

And then I told the girl, "I'd like your mind to come back and be beside me. I want your eyes to open slowly, and I want you to see the junction of the walls and the ceiling on the other side of the room." I already had measured the width of the room with my eyes. I knew if she looked there, with peripheral vision she would see her bare thighs. She looked, and all of a sudden a deep flush appeared on her face. She began surreptitiously lowering her skirt. The mother saw that deep blush and surreptitious lowering of her skirt whereby she was apparently hoping nobody would notice.

I said to the girl, "There is one thing more I would like to have you do. You are sitting here beside me. I want you without moving your body to sit on the other side of the room." Then I began talking to her as if she were on the other side of the room. The girl answered my questions but she altered the intonation of her voice and she spoke as if she were over there. (Erickson looks across the room.) And the mother kept on looking back and forth. Mother detected the wrong intonation of her daughter's voice. I called the girl back and had her sit beside me. I said, "I want to thank you very much for helping me with your mother. You can wake up now, feeling fine, and go back to the kitchen and prepare your mother's evening meal." When she awakened, I thanked her again, because it is very important to thank the patient's unconscious mind as well as the conscious mind.

When the girl awakened, she went to the kitchen. I turned to the mother and said, "You don't know it yet, mother, but you are in a very deep trance and you are not feeling pain. Now, you know the power of words as you know words, and you also know the power of words in hypnosis. Now, mother, I can't be with you always, and it isn't really necessary, because I am going to tell you something that is very, very important.

"Now listen to me carefully. Your pain is going to return. There is nothing that I can do to stop that. Now when that pain comes, I want you to take your head and shoulders, put them in a wheelchair, and wheel out to the living room.

"I am going to leave a special TV there. You will see it in the far corner of the living room. Nobody else will be able to see that TV. You can turn on that TV mentally. It has wonderful poems and literature. You put your head and shoulders in the wheelchair and go out to the living room, turn on that TV; there will be no commercials on any of the programs." (Any woman who has written a volume of verse has an imagination —and can have a memory.) "And you watch the TV program. Every favorite program you have ever wanted to hear will be on the TV at your wish, and you will watch it for awhile. After awhile you will get tired and you will turn off the TV, and take your head and shoulders back into the bedroom and join your body. You will be tired and you will fall asleep. Have a nice restful sleep. After you awaken, you will be thirsty or hungry, or you will be lonesome for company. Your friends can come and visit you and any time pain threatens to come, you will take your head and shoulders, put them in a wheelchair, go out into the living room, and turn on the TV.

Six weeks later, I called upon her when I was making my usual Sunday morning drive on the desert. I dropped in at 6:00 a.m. The relief nurse was on duty, and apparently she had not been briefed fully. I had a bit of work persuading her that I was a doctor, and the doctor of that patient. I finally produced enough identification that she agreed that I *was* that patient's doctor, even if it was 6:00 a.m.

The nurse said, "She has been having a terrible night. She

keeps shushing me all night long. She thinks she is out in the living room. She is delirious. I keep trying to explain to her that she is in her bedroom, and my patient says, 'Shush.' "

I said to the patient, "It is all right. I'm going to turn off the TV. I'll explain things to your nurse so that she won't annoy you. When I leave, the TV program will come on at the exact point at which I turned it off." I explained things to the nurse. And mother shortly got tired. She shook her head and shoulders and went back to the bedroom, rejoined her body and fell asleep and awakened very hungry for her breakfast.

And her friends used to come in regularly to visit with her. They got used to her taking her head and shoulders and going out to listen to that TV that nobody else could see. She could go back, fall asleep, awaken thirsty or hungry, or ready for a bit of fruit or a drink of ice water. The friends got used to it.

The woman died suddenly, falling into a coma, the next August. She saw her son in cap and gown. She saw her daughter married in the Temple, coming back to let her mother see what she looked like as a bride. She lived 11 months in comfort. "Always take your head and shoulders out to watch that imaginary TV."

My sister had a mastectomy. When it came time to take the stitches out, my sister said, "Doctor, you know I am awfully chicken when it comes to taking out stitches. Do you mind if I take my head and feet and go into the solarium?" My sister explained, "When I was in the solarium, I kept looking through the door into my room. The doctor was always standing in a position that obscured my body. After awhile, I looked and he was gone, so I took my head and feet and went back and joined my body."

And one night my sister had returned from the hospital, and my father had returned from the hospital after a massive coronary. They were sitting there chatting socially and they both noticed that the other had a sudden attack of tachycardia. And my sister said, "Dad, you've got tachycardia, the same way I have. And I'll beat you to the cemetery. I have youth on my side which gives me an advantage over you." My father said, "No, child, I've got the advantage of age and experience and I'll beat you to the cemetery." They both had a hearty laugh. And my sister is still very much alive. My father died at 97½ years old.

The Erickson family, in large part, looks upon illness and misfortune as part of the roughage of life. And any soldier who ever lived on K-rations would tell you roughage is the best part of any diet. (Erickson laughs.)

Now I'll give you another cancer case. A doctor called me and said, "I have a 35-year-old mother of three children. She wants to die at home. She had a right mastectomy and it's too late. She already has metastases of the bones, her lungs and more scattered throughout the body. Drugs don't help her one bit. Will you try hypnosis on her?"

So I made a house call. As I opened the front door, I heard a chant coming from the bedroom. "Don't hurt me, don't hurt me, don't hurt me, don't scare me, don't scare me, don't scare me, don't hurt me, don't scare me, don't hurt me." I listened awhile to that steady chant.

I went into the bedroom and tried to introduce myself. The woman was lying on her right side curled up. I could yell and I could shout and I could repeat myself. And she chanted away constantly.

Then I thought, "Well, I'd better get her attention some way." So I joined in her chant, "I'm going to hurt you, I'm going to hurt you, I'm going to scare you, I'm going to scare you, I'm going to hurt you, I'm going to scare you, I'm going to hurt you." Finally she said, "Why?" But she didn't wait for my answer, so I continued with my chant only I altered it: "I want to help you, I want to help you, I want to help you, but I'll scare you, I'll scare you, I'll hurt you, but I want to help you, but I'll scare you, I want to help you." Suddenly, she interrupted and said, "How?" and went on with her chants. So I joined in the chant, "I'm going to help you, I'm going to help you, I'm going to scare you, I'm going to ask you to turn over mentally, just mentally, not physically, turn over mentally, not physically, turn over mentally, not physically, I'll hurt you, I'll scare you. I'll help you if you turn over mentally, not physically."

Finally, she said, "I've turned over mentally, not physically. Why do you want to scare me?" And then she started her usual chant. So I said, "I want to help you, I want to help you, I want to help you, I want to help you." And finally she interrupted herself by saying, "How?"

I said, "I want you to feel a mosquito bite on the sole of your right foot, biting, biting, it hurts, it itches, it's the worst mosquito bite you've ever had, it itches, it hurts, it's the worst mosquito bite you've ever had."

Finally she said, "Doctor, I'm sorry—my foot is numb. I can't feel that mosquito bite." I said, "That's all right, that's all right. That numbness is creeping up over your ankles, creeping up over your ankles; it's creeping up your leg, over your calf; it's creeping slowly up to your knee. Now it's creeping up your knees and up your thigh, almost halfway, now it is halfway, now it is halfway, now it is all the way up your hips and then it is going to cross over to your left hip and down your left thigh, slowly over your left knee and down, down, down to the sole of your left foot. And now you are numb from your hips down.

"And now that numbness is going to creep up your left side, slowly, slowly to your shoulder, to your neck and then down your arm, all the way to your fingertips. Then it will start creeping up your right side under your arm, and up over your shoulder, and down clear to your fingertips. And now I want the numbness to start creeping up your back, slowly up your back, higher and higher until it reaches the nape of your neck.

"And now we will have the numbness creeping up towards your umbilicus, still higher and I'm awfully sorry, I'm awfully sorry, I'm awfully sorry, but when it reaches the surgical wound where the right breast was, I can't make that numb . . . completely numb. That place where the surgery was done will feel like a very bad itchy, mosquito bite."

She said, "That's all right, it's so much better than the way it used to hurt, and I can stand the mosquito bite." I apologized because I couldn't take away the mosquito bite feeling. But she kept assuring me that she didn't mind that mosquito bite.

I went back to see her frequently. She began gaining weight and she ceased her chanting. So I told her, "You can distort time hypnotically so that each day would seem to be very short. It would seem to be a short time between my visits." I went to see her regularly every month.

In April she told me, "Doctor, just once more, I would like to walk through the house, through each room, and look at each room just once more before I die. And, just once more, I would like to use the bathroom."

I called her doctor and I said, "Give me the picture of her x-ray condition." He wanted to know why. I told him how she wanted to walk through the house. He said, "She has metastases of her hipbone, her pelvic bone and her spinal bone. I think the risk you are taking is two broken hips." I said, "All right, otherwise you think she can make it." He said, "Yes, I think she can."

I told the woman, "Now, I'm going to put a girdle on you, and you will feel a tighter and tighter and tighter girdle. It will hold your hips together very strongly." In other words, what I did was to contract her muscles to splint her bones. I said, "It would make it awkward for you to walk and you won't really be able to move your thighs very well. You will have to walk from the knee down."

So I walked beside her through all the rooms to see her three little boys' toys, their bedrooms, and their clothes. She used the bathroom. Then she awkwardly climbed upon the bed and I carefully took off the girdle.

In May, Mrs. Erickson and Betty Alice, my daughter, went with me. And the patient said, "Doctor, I have a new pain. It is in my stomach." I said, "All right, I will have to treat that pain."

I turned to my wife and daughter and said, "Go to sleep." And as they stood there, they went into deep trances. I told them to feel very bad pains in their stomach, feel very sick. They promptly began to feel very sick and to feel very severe pain. And my patient began feeling sympathetic towards them. Then I said, "Now, I am going to take their pain and your pain away." Carefully, I suggested the disappearance of the feeling of pain and of sickness. My wife and daughter awakened feeling fine and so did the patient.

And she died the last week of July while visiting with friends. She suddenly fell into a coma and never came out of it.

Now, there were two cases. I used the Mormon religion in one. I used the patient's symptoms in the other.

Now a third cancer case: A doctor called me up and said, "I have a patient at Good Samaritan Hospital. She is 52 years old. She has a master's degree. She is very intelligent, very well read, and she has a marvelous sense of humor. But she has got less than three months to live and she suffers pain constantly. I can give her a double shot of morphine and Demerol and percodan, all at the same time, plus nine grains of sodium amytal. It doesn't even make her drowsy, she suffers so much pain. But she can sit in a wheelchair and an ambulance can bring her out to your office. And the ambulance driver can push her into your office. Will you see what you can do with hypnosis?"

The ambulance driver pushed her in through this door and into my office there. (Erickson points to the side door of his office.) She came into the office. I was 70 years old, and my hair was essentially this color—it has been about this color for 15 years. She looked at me and said, "Sonny, do you really think that your hypnotic words will so alter my body when powerful chemicals have no effect on it?"

I said, "Madam, as I look at your eyes, the pupils are dilating and contracting steadily, and your facial muscles are quivering. So I *know* you are suffering constant pain—constant, stabbing, pulsating pain. I can see it with my eyes. Now tell me, Madam, if you saw a lean, hungry tiger in the next room, slowly walking into the room and eyeing you hungrily and licking its chops, how much pain would you feel?"

She said, "I wouldn't feel any under those circumstances. Well, my goodness. I don't feel any pain now. May I take that tiger back to the hospital with me?" I said, "Certainly, but I will have to tell your doctor." She said, "But don't tell the nurses. I want to have some fun with the nurses. Everytime they ask me

if I am having pain, I am going to tell them, 'Look under the
bed. If the tiger is still there, I haven't got a bit of pain.' "

Any 52-year-old woman who starts calling me "sonny" has
a sense of humor. So I made use of that.

In other words, whatever your patient has, make use of it. If
she has a chant, you could chant too. If she is a Mormon, even
though you aren't, you should know enough about Mormonism
so that you can make use of the Mormon religion. And Jim,
idealistic Jim and idealistic Gracie—when a strange man starts
to uncover her bra—you don't do that with highly idealistic
people—you get their attention immediately. (Erickson laughs.)

Christine: You said you gave specific instructions to Gracie as to what
to say to Jim in trance. Could you explain—be a little more
explicit?

E: I had Gracie literally memorize what I said about an alarm. You
awaken, you turn off the alarm, you alter your activities, and
do the right things for that day. If you are Catholic, you eat fish.
That is one of the right things to do. Since he was building a
house and helping cultivate a farm, that was the right thing to do.

Woman student: Are there limits to a degree to which the spasticity
of a paralysis can be controlled? Um, the pain from his spasticity
was controlled through the hypnosis?

E: Jim was very spastic. I didn't mention that. The spasticity disappeared when I started poking his wife's breasts. All the attention became spastic attention. (Erickson chuckles.) I didn't mind
that and he didn't.

Another woman: To what degree do you think that the cancer
patient has control over the cancer process in his own body?

E: There hasn't been enough experimental work done. But what I do
know is that Fred K. heard me lecture in Twin Falls, Idaho. Fred
K. was a leading surgeon there. He is a very progressive surgeon.
He decided Twin Falls needed a medical society. So he organized
a medical society. And then he decided that the city needed a
hospital, so he started a drive for a community hospital. Then
he decided that they should have a professional building for
offices. He is a moving power in Twin Falls.

After I lectured, Fred came up to me and said, "I listened to your lecture and I realized that the world could stand a shaky psychiatrist much better than it could stand a shaky surgeon. So he took a residency in psychiatry in Salt Lake City. Now he is a professor of psychiatry.

He refused to accept a professorship unless he was allowed to work with the surgical department. So, Fred would use hypnosis with every other patient he operated on to try to promote the healing of the surgical wound. And the patients on whom he used hypnosis to speed the healing process all healed their wounds faster than the other patients. That much I can tell you.

Jane: Dr. Erickson, I have Raynaud's Disease. Is there anything I can do in hypnosis with it.

E: Have you quit smoking?

Jane: Yeah, I don't smoke.

E: All right. In 1930, I saw Dr. Frank S. He had Raynaud's Disease. And he insisted on smoking. He liked inhaling cigarettes. He wanted to know what to do about his Raynaud's Disease. I said, "You are stuck with it." (Erickson looks at Jane.) "I don't think you should go to cold country." He was offered the superintendency of the State Hospital in Augusta, Maine. Frank said he wanted that job. I said, "Well, every time you feel your fingers cold, see if you can set, mentally, a little fire in your little fingertip." And Frank is a bit older than I am, and periodically he sets a little fire in his fingertips. There has been no advancement of the disease.

Jane: The only thing is, I'm toes.

E: So set a fire there every now and then, mentally.

Jane: Now?

E: If you could think *right now* of what I could think, it would make your face turn red. (Laughter.) Now, you know that you have capillary control in the face?

Jane: (Nods her head.)

E: In your arms? You have had goosebumps there before. (Jane looks at her arms.) When you go from warm weather to zero weather, you get goosebumps there and all over your body. I hope that you've had the experience of stepping into the bathtub when the water was too hot and discovering that you had a lot of goosebumps on your legs because there is an overflow from the heat receptors to the cold receptors.

Now you can blush with your feet as well as your face. (Erickson chuckles.) You have found out that you can set a fire in your face. (Erickson laughs.) And thanks for the demonstration. (Everybody laughs.)

Jane: It is very hot in here. (Laughter.)

E: Now, how deep a trance do you need for psychotherapy? You haven't been very attentive because I've been going in and out of a trance while I have been talking to you. I've learned how to go into a trance and I can discuss something with you and watch that rug rise up to this level. (Erickson gestures.) It is a much smaller rug. And I can talk to you about Jim and Gracie (Erickson is looking at the rug.), the hungry tiger or anything else, and all you notice is that I am a bit slower in my speech. (Erickson smiles and looks around.) I can go in and out of a trance without any of you knowing it.

Christine: Can you talk a bit more about self-hypnosis then?

E: All right. I was lecturing on hypnosis, I think somewhere in Indiana. And a man, six-feet, six-inches tall, all bone and muscle and very proud of it, came up to me to shake hands. I saw that bone-crusher hand approaching me, so I got hold of it first.

Then he told me his neckname was "Bulldog" and whenever he got an idea he held onto it and *nobody* could take it away from him. He said, "Not a single man in the whole world could put me in a trance." I said, "Would you like to find out the contrary?" He said, "There is not a single man—nobody can hypnotize me."

I said, "I would like to prove it to you, and have you meet the man who can hypnotize you." He said, "You are on. Bring him on." I said, "Now, tonight when you go to bed in your hotel room, take an hour at seven or eight o'clock. Get into your pajamas and sit down in a chair in front of your mirror, and look at the man who is going to put you into a trance."

The next day he said, "I awakened at eight o'clock this morning still sitting in that damn chair." (Laughter.) "I sat there all night long. I admit that I can put myself in a trance."

A patient I had in 1950 called me up and said, "I've been reading a book on autohypnosis for the past year. I spend two or three hours a day studying that book and following the directions completely. I can't put myself in a trance."

I said, "Joan, you were my patient in 1950. Your contact with me then should have told you to have enough sense to call me again. The book you have been reading is probably by (Erickson names a lay hypnotist)." She said, "That's right." I said, "All his books on self-hypnosis are nothing but trash. What you have been trying to do is consciously tell yourself what to do and how to do it. You are making the whole thing conscious. Now if you want to go into an autohypnotic trance, set your alarm clock to ring in 20 minutes. Set it on your dresser, and sit down and look at your image in the mirror."

I got a call the next day. She said, "I wound the alarm clock and set it. I sat down and looked at my image and the alarm rang. I thought I had made a mistake. This time, I very carefully set it to ring in 20 minutes. I put it on the dresser, sat down and looked at myself in the mirror and the alarm rang. And this time, the clock showed that 20 minutes had gone by."

In other words, you don't tell yourself what you are going to do in a trance state. Your unconscious mind knows an awful lot more than you do. If you *trust* your unconscious mind, it will do the autohypnosis that you want to do. And maybe it has a better idea than you have.

Incidentally, my nurse-daughter recently visited us from Dallas. She was talking about her work with patients. There is a lot of emergency work there, and it is very demanding and takes a lot of time. They specialize in automobile accidents and they can occur at any time in Dallas.

Her mother asked her about how she fell asleep after a devastating emergency room experience. And Roxanna said, "Oh, that's very simple. I've got a clock that you can read in the dark. When I get into bed, I take a look at that clock. I know that if I can read that clock in ten minutes time, I'll run up and down the stairs 20 times. I'm lazy and I haven't ever had to run up and down the stairs 20 times. But I know that *if* I read that clock 10 minutes later, I will get out of bed and really run up and down the stairs 20 times."

I published a paper on a man who lost his wife. He and his widowed son lived together. They did their own housework and ran their own real estate office. And they divided the housework.

The old man finally came to me and said, "I lie awake all night long, thrashing about and trying to go to sleep. I never get more than two hours of sleep. I usually fall to sleep about five o'clock and I wake up at seven."

I said, "All right, now you want correction of your insomnia. All you have to do is do what I say. You say you and your son divide up the housework. How do you divide it up?" He said, "My son does the things he likes to do and I do the things that I like to do." I said, "What do you hate doing most?" He said, "Waxing the floors. We've got hardwood floors. I like to keep them waxed. I'll do everything I have to do and what my son has to do if *he* will wax the floors. Because I can't stand waxing the floors."

I said, "All right, I have a remedy in mind for you. It will cost you eight hours of sleep. Do you think you can afford the loss of eight hours of sleep?" He said, "I've been losing that much sleep every night for a year. Of course, I can afford it."

I said, "Tonight when you go home, you take a jar of Johnson's Floor Wax and a rag, and you polish the floor all night long. You polish it until the time you usually get up in the morning. Then you go about the day's work. You will have only lost two hours sleep. And the next night, start waxing the floor at bedtime. Wax it all night long and go to the office on time. That will be a total of four hours sleep lost. The next night you polish the floors all night long and lose another two hours of sleep."

On the fourth night before he began polishing the floor, he told his son, "I think I will rest my eyes for a minute." He woke up at seven the next morning.

And now on his dresser is a can of Johnson's Floor Wax and a polishing rag. I told him, "You have an illuminated dial clock. If you can read the time of night on that clock 15 minutes after you go to bed, you polish the floor all night long." He hasn't missed a night's sleep since. (Erickson laughs.)

A doctor came to me and said, "I worked my way through college. I lost a lot of sleep. I found it hard to get through medical school. Before I got through medical school, I got married and started having a family. I had to lose a lot of sleep repaying my medical school fees and supporting my family.

"Ever since, I go to bed at 10:30 at night. I roll and toss and keep looking at the clock, hoping that it is morning, but it never is. And around five o'clock I go to sleep, but I have to get up at seven o'clock and go to the office. And you know, all the way through medical school, I promised myself that I would read all of Dickens, all of Sir Walter Scott, all of Dostoevski, because I like literature. I have never found time. I just roll and toss until five in the morning."

I said, "So you would like to sleep? And you are still bemoaning the fact that you have never read Dickens. Well, buy a set of Dickens.

"Now, I want to know the interior of your house. So you have a fireplace and a mantelpiece over the fireplace?" He said, "That's right." I told him, "You get an electric light and you put it on the mantelpiece and you put a volume of Dickens on the mantelpiece and you stand there from 10:30 until five in the morning and you read Dickens. That way you will catch up on all your literary aspirations."

Finally, he came to me and said, "Can I sit down to read Dickens?" I said, "All right." Then he came to me and said, "I am having trouble reading Dickens. I sit down and I start to read and before I have read a whole page, I am sound asleep. I wake up in the morning feeling cramped from sitting in that position."

I said, "All right, get a clock with an illuminated dial, and if you can read the time of night on that clock 15 minutes after you go to bed, you get up and stand at the mantelpiece and read Dickens. And now that you have read *some* of Dickens, you will discover lots of ways of finding time to read Dickens." He read all of Dickens, Scott, Flaubert, and Dostoyevski. And he dreads standing up at that mantelpiece and reading. He would rather sleep.

People come to you for help when they could furnish their own help. A woman wanted to quit smoking and lose weight. I told her she could do it with a great deal of satisfaction and not too much discomfort. She had told me, "I can't resist eating and I can't resist cigarettes, but I can resist exercise and I do."

I said, "You are a very religious woman, are you not?" She said, "Yes." I said, "Give me your absolute promise that you will do a few simple things I will ask of you." Then I said, "Keep your matches in the basement. You live in a two-story house with an attic. Do as much smoking as you wish. Keep your matches in the basement and your cigarettes in the attic. When you want to smoke, go down to the basement and take a match out of the box and leave it on top of the box. Run up to the attic and get a cigarette; go down to the basement and light it. That way you will get a lot of exercise.

"And you say you like to nibble. Now what would you like to do—run around the house, outside of it? Run so many laps and come in and eat whatever you want to?" She said, "That might be a good idea." I said, "All right. Of course, when you bake a cake you cut it into so many thin slices. For every slice you eat, you will run all the way around the house as fast as you can, and eat your thin slice of cake. If you want a second, you will run twice as many times around the house."

It's surprising how soon she wanted less and less of the cigarettes . . . down in the basement first to take out a match, leaving it there, and then running up to the attic and getting one cigarette, then going down to the basement and lighting it and enjoying the smoking. And running around the house so many times for the first piece of cake, and twice as many for the second piece, three times as many times (To group) for the third piece . . . and she reduced very nicely.

The important thing is not to do so much bookwork, following the rules you read in books. The important thing is to get the patient to do the things that are very, very good for him.

A Michigan man came to me and said, "I have an uncontrollable temper. When I lose my temper, I box the ears of the person nearest to me. I've boxed my wife's ears. I've knocked down my daughters and my sons many times. My temper is uncontrollable."

I said, "You live on a farm in Michigan. How do you heat the house? How do you do the cooking?" He said, "It's a farm and we have a wood burning range. We heat the house with that wood burning range in the winter. We do all of our cooking on that wood burning range." I said, "Where do you get your fuel?" He said, "I have a large wood lot." And I said, "What trees do you cut down?" He said, "Well, I cut down oak. I cut down ash. I don't cut down the elm trees because they are such hard work to split into fuel-sized wood."

I said, "From now on, you will cut down elm trees."

"When you cut down elm trees and saw them into blocks, to split them you drive your axe in and take it out, then drive it a little bit further. You have to drive it all the way, the full length of the block, before the block will separate into two parts. It is the most awful wood there is to split. And splitting one elm block is equal to splitting a dozen oak blocks.

"Now, when you lose your temper, take your axe and go split the hell out of that block of elm, and you will have all your energy drained from you." I know what splitting elm is—it is a most horrible task. And so he took out all of his explosive energy on splitting elm blocks of wood.

Siegfried: I have a question. You give examples of people who always do what you suggest, and they seem to be highly motivated, compared with my patients. (Laughter.) I think that they would often just not do it.

E: That is what my family says: "Why do your patients do the crazy things you tell them to do?" I say, "I tell it to them very seriously. They know I mean it. I am totally sincere. I am absolutely confident that they will do it. I never think, 'Will my patients do that ridicuolus thing?' No, I know that they will."

Now a woman came in, or rather she called me up, and asked me to see her husband to stop him from smoking by use of hypnosis. Her husband came in. He was a lawyer, earning

$35,000 a year. His wife had inherited a quarter of a million dollars before her marriage. She bought their house. She paid for the taxes and all the utilities. She paid for all the groceries. And she paid her husband's withholding tax, his income tax and her income tax. She didn't know what her husband did with his $35,000 a year.

I learned all this from the husband when I questioned him about smoking. I knew that he would *not* quit smoking. I told him so at the end of the hour—that he had no intention of quitting, and could I call his wife up and tell his wife that he was a born loser. Maybe if I did that she would get off his back and stop nagging him about quitting smoking.

So he agreed that I could call up his wife in his presence and tell his wife that he was a born loser and also tell her to get off his back and stop nagging him. I felt justified in doing that. He is a lawyer, he ought to know the ordinary words of the English language. He should know the use of words.

I called her up and said, "I'm sorry to tell you that your husband is a born loser. So would you please keep off his back and quit nagging him. He doesn't want to quit smoking and he isn't going to quit."

Two days later she came storming into my office without an appointment. The tears were running down her cheeks in a steady stream. She said, "I cry every time I go to a doctor's office. I make a puddle on the floor with my tears just as I am doing right now. And tomorrow I've got to take my children to see the pediatrician. I'll cry all the way there and all the way back. Can you do anything to help me?" I said, "Yes, crying is a very childish thing. How often do you cry?" She said, "Every time I start to do something. I graduated from college and got a teacher's certificate and I cried steadily for one week when I got a job teaching school. So I had to quit because I cried so much."

I said, "All right, tomorrow you have got to take your children to the pediatrician. You are going to cry all the way there and all the way back. I suggest that crying is a childish thing, so replace it with another childish thing that is not noticeable. Get hold of a cucumber pickle about that size (Erickson demonstrates) and nurse it all the way to the doctor's and all the way back."

The day after the appointment, she came in the office extremely angry, but not crying. She said, "Why didn't you tell me to nurse the pickle *while* I was there?" (Erickson smiles.) I said, "That was your responsibility, not mine. Now I will give you another task to do. This afternoon, I want you to climb Squaw Peak and come in tomorrow and report."

She came in the next day and said, "I climbed Squaw Peak and believe it or not I lost the trail 50 feet from the top. I climbed over a lot of jagged rocks where I had no business to be. When I got to the top I felt my first sense of personal accomplishment— of achievement. And I'm going to climb Squaw Peak tomorrow and not lose the trail. I will come in and report to you. All the way down, I wondered how I could have lost that trail. It is impossible to lose."

She came in the next day and told me she had climbed Squaw Peak successfully and had that same feeling of accomplishment.

Sometime later she came in unexpectedly and said, "I think my husband is married more to his mother than he is to me. My husband can't do anything around the home—fix a leaky faucet or do the simplest kind of a task. His mother can call him up at 1:00 a.m. He will dress and go across town and fix a leaky faucet for her or hang a picture for her. But my husband can't do that at home. I either have to hire a plumber or a carpenter or do it myself."

I said, "Well, your husband ought to be your husband, and not the husband of his mother."

She said, "I don't like my mother-in-law. She will show up on my porch at four in the afternoon. Sometimes she will bring guests and she will demand of me a very fancy dinner. I may have to go out shopping to get the necessary things. And I make a wonderful dinner for her and her guests. But I gag and feel sick to my stomach when I join them at the meal."

I said, "I don't think that is very courteous on the part of your mother-in-law to show up at your front porch at four in the afternoon and demand a dinner. So the next time she shows up, prepare the dinner. When it comes time to sit down, don't. Explain that you have an urgent appointment that evening. I don't care where you go—it can be to the parking lot of a movie. And don't come home until eleven o'clock."

A few days later she came in and said, "My mother-in-law and my husband showed up with the guest at four o'clock and demanded a very big dinner. So I followed your advice. I made them a wonderful dinner. When it came time for us to sit down, I told them that I had a very important engagement that evening and I left. I didn't return home until eleven o'clock. I found my husband and my mother-in-law had played their usual trick on their guest. They had made him sick-drunk and he had vomited all over the dining room carpet, and I had that to clean up."

I said, "Well, dinner guests who vomit on the dining room carpet, or help others to do it, should not be given a special dinner *any* time." She said, "That's what I think."

She came in later and said, "I pay all the utility bills, taxes, my husband's income tax and my own. My husband once in a while brings home a sack of groceries. That's because he wants some special dish made. He is going to take me over to San Diego to a law convention. I don't want to go." I said, "Your husband wants to take you there. Let him do so. When you come back, tell me how you enjoyed it."

She came back and said, "I wanted to stay in a hotel that had a swimming pool. My husband told me that the hotel on the other side of the street had much more atmosphere. So we stayed there with no swimming pool. I couldn't tell any difference in the atmosphere. I paid a thousand dollars for one week in that room. And all the meals were extra.

"When we went down to the dining room, our 18-month-old child pounded on the highchair tray and gurgled and made a noise. My husband slapped her face, making a scene in the dining room." I said, "Your husband is a lawyer and he ought to know the law about child abuse. I think that is child abuse and I think that the law would hold you responsible also for any further child abuse." She said, "That's what I thought. He is not going to slap the children anymore."

Some weeks later she came in and said, "Two, three, four times a year my husband gets two, three, four or five thousand dollars in debt. Then he asks me to sell some of my securities and to get him out of debt." I said, "A man with a $35,000 a year salary, whose wife pays all the living expenses and the income taxes, ought to pay his own debts out of his salary." She said, "I think so too. I am not going to sell any more securities." I said, "If you do, even a quarter of a million dollars won't last very long."

A few weeks later she came in and said, "Two or three times a year my husband comes to me and asks for a separation. But it isn't really a separation. I don't know where he goes or stays. Always on Thursday evening he shows up and he wants a very special dinner. And on Sundays, he plays with the kids after the meals and goes away. I don't know where." I said, "Well, I think you ought to be *honest* with him. If he asks you for a separation, be honest about it, and give him one. Tell him, 'All right, you can have your separation as long as you want it and this time it will be real. There will be no Thursday dinners, no Sunday dinners. I will change the locks on all the doors and windows.'"

About six months later she came in the office and said, "Do I have grounds for a divorce?" I told her, "I'm a psychiatrist, not a lawyer. But I can refer you to an honest lawyer." So she took his name and she got her divorce in a hurry.

About six months later she came to the office without an appointment and said, "You lied to me by implication." I said, "How did I lie by implication?" She said, "I came in and asked you if I had grounds for a divorce and you said you were a psychiatrist, not a lawyer. You sent me to a lawyer who got me a divorce on legal grounds. Every time I think of being married to that creep for seven years, I get sick to my stomach. I got a divorce for *personal* reasons."

I said, "If I had told you to get a divorce for personal reasons, what would you have done?" She said, "I would have defended him and stayed married to him." I said, "That's right. Now, what have you been doing the last six months?" She said, "Well, as soon as I got a divorce, I got a job teaching school. I like it. I don't cry anymore."

Nurse a cucumber pickle, and tell her that her husband is a born loser. And he, a lawyer, should have known better than to have me call him a born loser. And she gradually realized it . . . every time she came in to make a complaint.

Siegfried: Please repeat the last sentence. I didn't get it.

E: Every time she came in to make a complaint about her husband, she realized the truth and meaning of my calling her husband a born loser. That is why I called her up the first time, to tell her that her husband was a born loser.

Siegfried: Is that what you think. That he is a born loser?

E: Well, don't you think so? He lost his wife, his family. He has to spend his own money to support himself. He had to pay money to support his children. He has to pay his own income tax.

Siegfried: But I think he can change also.

E: You think so? Any young married man who will impose upon his wife in the first seven years in that fashion is not going to change. And he is still his Mama's boy. He takes his mother out to dinner, and she can call him at 1:00 a.m. to have him fix a leaky faucet.

Siegfried: Yeah, but I think he can learn to do a good separation from his mother. Do you think he is bound forever?

E: Yes, because he isn't going to see anybody untie him.

Siegfried: So you think that he is not yet ready to make that change?

E: I don't think he will ever be ready.

Siegfried: Uh-huh.

E: And now, Christine, you go in my office—somewhere there—and find an envelope with case histories. It's a manila envelope. It is probably in the stationery stand beside the desk. (Christine goes into the back office and gets Erickson the case folder he requested.) A 30-year-old man ought not to go across town at 1:00 a.m. to fix a leaky faucet for his mother.

Siegfried: Yes, I agree with that.

E: And he should pay for his own income tax.

Now, who has a good reading voice in English? Don't shout all at once.

Jane: I do.

E: (Erickson hands her the transcript.) Read that letter aloud.

Jane: "February 29th. Dear Dr. Erickson. I am writing in response to your request during our phone conversation of some weeks ago that I write you. I would have written sooner, but I wanted to check with Dr. L. to see if she was interested in accompanying me to Phoenix (if it is possible to see you). She was out of town for a few weeks, and hence the delay. It was she who highly recommended you to me. She also indicated that she is interested in coming to Phoenix with me if it can possibly fit into her already overloaded schedule.

"Concerning my problem, I began to stutter somewhere between the ages of four to four-and-a-half. I began to speak in the twelfth month of life. The onset of the stutter was pretty nearly coincident with the birth of my sister (my first sibling), and a tonsillectomy sometime early in my fifth year. As to how these events related to my stutter, I have never quite pieced them together. I have made many attempts to unravel childhood traumas, including conventional psychotherapy, unsuccessful attempts at hypnosis (Dr. L. thinks I can be hypnotized), "scream" therapy with C. D., the Fisher-Hoffman Process. I have tried various "body" therapies, i.e., Rolfing, Lomi body work, polarity therapy, acupuncture, bioenergetics, and breathing techniques. I have tried mechanical devices. I have done EST, as well as many meditative, spiritual, and yogic practices. My stutter still remains. Some of the things I have tried have helped me in varying amounts, but I have the feeling that there still remains some highly charged material from the past which I am mortally afraid to face.

"Several Bay Area psychic friends of mine have told me that my relationship with my mother is still unresolved. I am also aware that I have difficulty dealing with anger. Although I am 30 years old, people tell me that I am childlike (many people find it hard to believe that I am over 20), and many still regard me as a child. I want to grow up and get on with my life. I am tired of living my life in this emotional soup.

"The pattern of my life has heretofore been as follows: In all of my undertakings, initially there is the promise of dazzling success. Things go well until the going gets a little rough. This is when I usually give up and fail.

"I am particularly hopeful to give up the pattern of stuttering, because it really has prevented me from flowing freely with other people and sometimes even being with them. I have also allowed it to prevent my expansive movement in the world. Since it is a childhood trait, to an extent it keeps me feeling like a child.

"My life right now is entering upon a period of change, but at present I am still unable to manifest my skills in the world and earn my living. My current situation is wracked with existential guilt. The only jobs presently available to me are semiskilled or unskilled labor jobs. This is painfully unsatisfactory to me in light of my past. I sailed through graduate school (in operations research and theoretical statistics) dropping out before I got a Ph.D. in order to pursue music. I did music for awhile—things went well. I was liking to hear what I played and was receiving some recognition for my music. Then I stopped playing for awhile, and when I resumed I felt that there was less consciousness and more rigidity in my left side. From that point on my music has been deteriorating, and I no longer consider myself a serious professional musician. With my diminished ability to play music, my self-hate has increased, as did my consumption of drugs. It has only been in the last two years that I have been tapering off drugs (I was taking them pretty regularly for seven years).

"I feel like I am in a stronger place now and have an ardent desire to make my life work. I am hopeful about the prospect of working with you, although I am consciously aware of a strong resistance to being healthy, which still continues to haunt me. This resistance is part of my ego-pattern too. Perhaps out of fear or mistrust, I subtly resist cooperating with people.

"I hope to hear from you soon. I look forward to working with you if you will take me on. I will be available at your convenience after the first of April (except Tuesday evenings through April). Respectfully yours, George Leckie."

E: Here is a patient who called me up several weeks previously. I said,

"Hello." And he said, "Ba—ba, ba, ba, ba, ba, ba." I said, "Write to me," and hung up.

Now, several weeks later, he writes this long story about his neurosis and seven years' devotion to drugs. I thought immediately, getting a late letter in reply to my telephone request, "Here is one of those professional patients who *never* is going to get well, and who will play me for a sucker to get all my time and energy and have it result in a failure." So I read that letter and wrote back a letter that I thought would appeal to him and induce him to write another letter that I could use in teaching. (To Jane.) All right.

Jane: (Continues by reading the letter of response that Erickson wrote.)

"March 7th. Dear Mr. Leckie. Since your telephone call to me to ask for help when you were unable to ask for help and had to be told how to communicate with me which you should have done without being told to do so, I will summarize your problem for you, perhaps hoping in vain that it may serve some purpose for you advantageously.

"Usually such phone calls as you made are not followed by the requested letter. If a letter is sent, there is a delay attributed to someone else—Dr. L. in your case.

"Next, there is an account of a long career in seeking help and not accepting it, but occasionally offering a brief token acceptance.

"Invariably there is a listing of probable and possible causes of the problem, thus insuring the possibility for the therapist to look in the wrong direction, thereby making more certain the continuance of the long career of diligent search without results. Only by remaining unaware of the cause can a problem be successfully retained.

"To demonstrate a consistency in patterns of behavior, other types of failures must be mentioned—for you, music, maturing, making a living, not getting a Ph.D.

"The letter would be incomplete without some neatly worded subtle threats. In your case a promise to mistrust and not cooperate, among others.

"Most vital of all is the placing of a restriction, however small, upon therapy. It need not even be rational, just some kind of restriction, even an irrelevant one as was your restriction of Tuesday evenings through April. By what stretch of imagination did you manage to think that you could have any of my evenings?

"If you have read this letter to this point, surely the question must arise, 'Do you want to be my patient?' Does it not suggest that I might deal with your highly treasured problem, as attested by your seven years of devotion to drugs which at best can only impede speech?

"Do I expect a reply to this letter???? Yours, with what you may consider abominable sincerity, Milton H. Erickson, M.D."

E: Then you know what you would do if you got a letter like that. But listen to his reply.

Jane: "March 11th. Dear Dr. Erickson. So direct of you to do away with needless formalities with a mere flick of the pen. I was totally unprepared for the ensuing onslaught. I hadn't previously been aware of all those games (except for my procrastination game—as evidenced by my excuse concerning Dr. L.) which you so accurately perceived from my letter. Your perspicacity overwhelms me.

"There was an understandable tone of indignation (as well as compassion) in your letter. To arouse your ire was never my intent. Apparently you credit me with guile in trying to mislead you, which again, I never intended.

"My problem does not seem unfamiliar to you. In fact, I get that you read my letter as somewhat of a 'form letter' with the filled-in blanks from my particular history.

"Yes, I still do want to be your patient. Yes, my failure neurosis *is* highly treasured—aren't they all? I offer my apology for being so presumptuous as to try to place a restriction upon therapy.

"I await your response. Yours, humbly, George Leckie.

P.S. I don't usually stutter as severely as I did on the phone with you that day. I was especially nervous and fearful. I still am fearful of you."

(Jane looks to Erickson before reading the next letter. He nods, indicating that she should proceed.)

"March 24th. Dear Mr. Leckie. A few corrections are in order. 1) Ugly realities are never brushed away by 'a mere flick of the pen.' They remain until the patient develops sufficient honesty to abandon them. 2) A simplified statement of the truth is not an 'ensuing onslaught.' 3) For one to be 'not aware of all those games,' your skill in all those games I mentioned as well as those games I did not mention betokened long and diligent practice to become unaware of 'those games.' 4) You are overwhelmed by my 'perspicacity.' Actually, you are in no position to attempt to offer a compliment to anybody. 5) As for 'an understandable tone of indignation,' you are, as is customary for you, mistaken. It was a tone of amusement sufficiently great to gamble that you would be induced to write a letter of reply. 6) With slightly more effort you could have come up with a far better understatement than 'my problem does not seem unfamiliar to you.' 7) The availability of a large container nearly full of salt made it almost possible to accept your statement, 'Yes, I do want to be your patient.' Even if the container had been full I doubt that the outcome could have been otherwise. 8) '. . . my failure neurosis is highly treasured—aren't they all?' is so ridiculously absurd that, looked at freely, it conceivably could embarrass even you. 9) An 'apology' for a pretentious restriction is actually an irrelevancy and does not bear upon the actual issue. 10) You state that you 'treasure' your neurosis 'highly' and then append the word 'humbly' thus affording a contrast serving no end but that of amusement. 11) You write 'I still am fearful of you' when really you have a 'highly treasured' 'failure neurosis' much more deserving of your fear. 12) I do appreciate your voluntary efforts to amuse me. With the same sincerity as before, Milton H. Erickson, M.D." (Laughter.) (Jane continues with next letter.)

"April 9th. Dear Mr. Leckie. I suggest that you write to me around April 19-20, expressing your wishes and purposes in asking for an appointment with me. Sincerely, Milton H. Erickson, M.D."

(Next letter).

"April 19th. Dear Dr. Erickson. Concerning my 'wishes and purposes in asking for an appointment' with you—

"My wish is based on a discussion I had with Dr. L. a few months back. She recounted how, through hypnosis, you quickly and ruthlessly dissolved the long-standing emotional hangups of a champion skater. Dr. L. was truly in awe of your expertise, and felt that you could be of help to me.

"My wish (although perhaps only my fantasy) is that, through hypnosis, we could get in touch with and resolve my early child-hood family situation which is most likely responsible for my never really growing up. I want to get to the place of being able to consciously take full responsibility for my life. I want to abandon my nearly lifelong patterns of failure and stuttering. I want to resolve the sibling rivalry with one of my brothers. I want to be able to love, instead of dislike and fear, others. *I want to love myself!* (Presently, I don't.) I need to reprogram myself with a positive outlook.

"If, with the aid of your efforts, this tall order of wishes could be realized, I would then be free to create and serve—as I desire to do. Presently, this is not the case for me, for my endeavors invariably end in failure and frustration.

"Dr. L. feels I can be hypnotized. I foresee some possible difficulty in this, because previous attempts have proven unsuccessful. My fear is that my condition is a spiritual one, and that no one other than myself can help me. However, I still hope for the best and look forward to meeting you and working with you.

"I will call you Thursday, April 22, at 9:00 a.m. Hopefully and sincerely, George Leckie."

E: He did call me, hopefully and sincerely. Of course, Mrs. Erickson took the phone call and said, "Dr. Erickson is not receiving phone calls."

Jane: (Next letter.)

"April 23rd. Dear Mr. Leckie. Your special delivery letter arrived with 20 cents postage due and terminated with an insistence on a telephone conversation despite my earlier request for written communication rather than an attempted verbal communication.

"You expressed a wish, which you qualified as a possible fantasy, to get in 'touch with and resolve my early childhood family situation.' This is merely a request for insight into an unchangeable past, not therapy.

"You express a want but not an intention to resolve a childhood sibling rivalry but you make no mention of wanting to meet the simplest needs of adulthood.

"You base your request for therapy on the beliefs and hopes of Dr. L., which are positive in contrast to your wealth of negative expectations and dubious desires.

"To accept you as a patient I would require evidence of a capacity to accept responsibility for a substandard minimal self-sufficiency. Yours truly, Milton H. Erickson, M.D."

(Next letter.)
"April 28th. Dear Dr. Erickson. 'To accept you as a patient, I would require evidence of a capacity to accept responsibility for a substandard minimal self-sufficiency.'

"Please pardon my ignorance, but I don't know exactly what you mean. What, specifically and simply stated, would constitute the satisfaction of your aforestated requirement?

"At this point I can only offer guesses, but here goes:

"I worked and supported myself as a groundskeeper last year for five months. I got laid off due to change in managerial policy requiring a cut in personnel. I have been collecting federal unemployment insurance ever since, while continuing to job-hunt and earn a few scarce dollars here and there playing music. I am currently playing with a band which is recording an album. Is that satisfactory? Relevant?

"My only other guess is that you might possibly be concerned as to whether or not I can raise money to pay you for a consultation. The answer is 'Yes, I can.'

"I hope and trust that I have not misinterpreted your requirement. Furthermore, I hope I have demonstrated evidence of its satisfaction for you. I have read the requirement to a few of my erudite friends, both of whom corroborated my interpretations.

"If your requirement has been satisfactorily fulfilled, I will accept an appointment at your convenience. I await your response. Yours truly, George Leckie. (P.S. Enclosed is a 20-cent stamp.)"

Jane: (Next letter.)

"May 8th. Dear Mr. Leckie. The object of psychotherapy is an alteration for the better of all behaviors resulting in the patient's neurotic maladjustments. In all of your letters you have consistently and insistently upheld your understandings, emphasized the importance of your failures, hinted, sometimes quite subtly, at your intention to keep your present plight unchanged while making a pretense of cooperating in seeking therapy, and at the same time contending that I meet your demands and accept your interpretations.

"An amusing and highly illustrative quotation from your last letter is: 'I have read the requirements to a few of my erudite friends, both of whom corroborated my interpretations.' (The underlinings are mine.)

"I know of nothing more to write to you with any certainty that would be of value or interest to you. Sincerely yours, Milton H. Erickson, M.D."

E: If I wanted to, I could write to him and get the same correspondence.

I got a letter from a woman once who said, "I've been in active psychoanalysis for 30 years. I am now completing four years of Gestalt therapy. After that, may I be your patient?" There is no hope for those people—they are professional patients. That is their sole goal in life.

And that lawyer . . . he did a good job on a salary basis. When he spends his money, he gets nothing of value. He owes for his car. He is behind in payment of his rent. He is behind in his child support. Yet, he gets $35,000 a year. He doesn't even own his car. He had been married for seven years and he is no better off than he was the first day he got a job. In fact, he is worse off. He was married to a quarter of a million dollars. Now, he hasn't even got that. He is a born loser. Born to lose. Born to be a failure.

My first lesson in that was when I was in medical school. I was assigned two patients to examine and do a history on. I went to the nearest patient. He was a man, 73 years old. His parents had been on welfare. He grew up living on welfare. He became a juvenile delinquent. He never did an honest day's work in his life. He did petty thieving; he spent a lot of time in jail. He spent time in jail because he was vagrant with no means of support. He had been sent to the State General Hospitals for the best medical care. It didn't cost him anything. He always went back to petty thievery, bumming and doing nothing. Here he was, 73 years old. He had a mild physical disorder that would heal in a few days. Then he could go back and live at public expense. My thought was, "Why should a man who had been a bum all his life live to be 73 years old when men who had contributed to society died in their forties, fifties and sixties?"

I went to see my next patient. She was about the most beautiful girl I ever saw. Eighteen years old and had a very charming personality. I engaged her in conversation, and she talked freely and intelligently about the old masters, about Cellini, ancient history, all the good literature of the past. She was very highly intelligent, beautiful, charming, likeable and she was talented. She could write poetry, stories, she could paint, she was a good musician.

I started my physical examination with the scalp, the ears. Then I looked into her eyes. I put down my ophthalmoscope and explained to her that I had forgotten to do a certain errand. I would be back shortly.

I went to the doctor's lounge and sat down and said, "Erickson, you better face life as it really is. That old bum is going to get well and live. He has been a social burden all his life. He will never contribute an honest day's work. And here you have this beautiful, charming, highly intelligent, talented girl, and the retinas of her eyes show that she is going to die of Bright's disease within three months. You better face it, Erickson. All your life, you are going to be confronted with the unfairness of life.

Beauty, talent, brains, ability—wasted. And a worthless old bum, preserved. He was a born loser. And she was born to be a casualty."

There was a commercial on TV for cat food. It shows a cat playing with a ball of yarn and that reminded me I ought to show you something. Would you hand me that wood?

The head of the department of art at a state university came in to see me. He saw this carving. He picked it up and examined it and said, "I've been a professor of art at the state university. I make my living carving. I've had my carvings recognized all over Europe, Asia, South America and the United States." (And he is a famous wood carver.) "This is a carving that is art. Art expresses human life, human thinking, human behavior, human experience. I don't understand this, but it is art. It is very meaningful art. But I don't understand it." So, pass it around for everybody to look at. (Erickson hands it to Siegfried.)

(Note: The carving is an aboriginal carving of a manatee.)

In other words, it tells you a story of a people. The story of how they lived; a story of what is important in life and why it is important in life; how all the people are governed in that particular ethnic group.

Siegfried: May I ask another question? I am a transactional analyst and one of the major focuses of the theory is that the life plan is based on a very early decision, that might be a decision, not in mind, but more basically. And mostly it can be changed.

We would look at that person that you talked about—thinking that, in principle, his decision about being a loser can be changed when he can regress to that stage where the decision to lose had been made. It can change his life when he finds the support that makes better options and a better decision for him available. What do you think about that?

E: It can be, but how?

I will tell you the story of Joe. I was ten years old at the time and living on a farm in Wisconsin. One summer morning my father sent me to the nearby village on an errand. As I approached the village, some of my schoolmates saw me and came and told me, "Joe is back." I didn't know who Joe was. They told me what their parents had told them.

And the story of Joe was not very good. He had been expelled from every school because he was combative, aggressive and destructive. He would soak a cat or dog with kerosene and set it on fire. He tried to burn down his father's barn and home twice. He had stabbed the pigs, the calves, the cows and horses with pitchforks.

His father and mother, when he was 12 years old, acknowledged that they couldn't handle their son. They went to court and had him committed to the Boy's Industrial School, which is a permanent home for delinquent children who cannot be handled in an ordinary home for delinquents. After three years of school, they paroled him to visit his parents. He committed some felonies on the way home. The police arrested him and returned him to the industrial school, where he had to stay until he was 21 years old.

At age 21, he had to be discharged by law. He had a prison-made suit and prison-made shoes and a $10 bill when he was discharged. His parents were dead. Their property had otherwise been disposed of, so that was all he had—$10.00, a prison suit and prison shoes.

He went to Milwaukee and promptly committed armed robbery and burglary. He was arrested by the police and sent to the young men's reformatory. At the reformatory, they tried to treat him like the other inmates. But Joe preferred to fight everybody. He would have riots and fights in the dining room, smash up the tables and that sort of thing. So they locked him in a cell and fed him in the cell. Once or twice a week, two or three guards as large as he was took him for a walk as exercise, after dark. And Joe spent the entire term at the young men's reformatory in Green Bay without any time off for good behavior.

When he was discharged, he went into the town of Green Bay and committed burglaries and other felonies and was promptly sent to the state prison. At the state prison they tried to treat him like the other convicts and Joe would have nothing of that. He just wanted to beat up the other convicts and break windows and cause trouble. So they sent him to the dungeon.

The dungeon is in the basement—eight feet by eight feet and the floor was concrete and sloped toward a gutter in front of the dungeon. No sanitation provisions were made. He was locked in that dungeon, with or without clothes. I've been in that dungeon and it is lightproof and soundproof. And once a day, usually 1:00 or 2:00 a.m., a tray of food is slipped through a hole in the doorway. The tray might be bread and water or the usual prison fare. And two prison guards his size (he was 6' 3"), one standing ten feet to his right and the other ten feet to his left, took him out for exercise after dark so he wouldn't beat up on any of the inmates.

He spent the term in prison in the dungeon. One term in the dungeon is usually enough to tame anybody—lightproof, soundproof and no sanitation. After his first term of 30 days he came out fighting mad, so he went back. In fact, he spent his entire first term in the state prison in that dungeon. Usually two stays in that dungeon are likely to cause you to become psychotic or stir bugs. And Joe spent a couple of years there.

When he was released, he went into a local village and committed some more felonies. He was promptly arrested and sent back to the state prison for another sentence which he also spent in that dungeon.

After completing his second sentence in the state prison, he was discharged. He returned to the village of Lowell, where his parents used to shop. There were three stores in that village. He spent his first three days standing beside the cash registers mentally adding up the day's income.

All three stores were burglarized. A motorboat on the river that passed through the village disappeared. Everybody knew that Joe burglarized the stores and stole the motorboat.

I came into the village on the fourth day. Joe was sitting on a bench unwaveringly staring into space. My playmates and I formed a semi-circle around him, staring bug-eyed at a real live convict. Joe paid no attention to us.

A little over two miles from the village was a farmer, his wife and daughter. He had two hundred acres of rich Dodge County farmland all paid for. In other words, he was a very rich farmer.

To work two hundred acres you need at least two men. He had a hired man who on that morning had quit because of a death in the family. He was returning to Milwaukee and he stated to the farmer that he would not be back.

Well, the farmer had a daughter, age 23, and a very attractive girl. She had what was considered an excellent education. She was an eighth grade graduate. She was 5'10", very strong. She could butcher a hog alone, plow a field, pitch hay, cultivate corn and do any work that a hired man could do. She was also an excellent dressmaker. She usually made the bridal dresses for the young girls that got married, and the baby dresses. She was an excellent cook and was recognized as the best cook, the best pie maker and the best cake maker in the community.

On that morning when I went to the village at 8:10 a.m., Edye, the farmer's daughter, was sent to town on an errand by her father. Edye tied up her horse and buggy and came walking down the street. Joe stood up and barred her way. Joe looked her up and down very thoroughly, and Edye stood her ground and looked up and down Joe. Finally, Joe said, "Can I take you to the Friday night dance?" In that community, the village of Lowell, a Friday night dance was held in the town hall and everybody attended. Edye said, "You can, if you are a gentleman." Joe stepped aside and Edye went on her errand.

On Friday night, Edye came in to attend the dance, tied up her horse and buggy, and then went into town hall. There was Joe, waiting. They danced every dance that evening, even though it made the other young men very envious and resentful.

Now, Joe was 6' 3", a very powerfully built young man and good looking. The next morning, all three merchants found their stolen goods returned and the powerboat was returned to the owner's pier. Joe was seen walking down the road toward Edye's father's farm. It was learned later that Joe asked Edye's father for the job as a hired man. Edye's father said, "Being a hired man is hard work. It begins at sunrise and you work until long after sundown. You go to church on Sunday morning but you work the rest of the day. There are no holidays, no days free

of work and the pay is $15 a month. I'll fix you up a room in the
barn; you can eat with the family." Joe took the job.

Within three months every farmer wished that he had a hired
man like Joe, because Joe was, in country talk, "a working fool."
He just worked and worked and worked. After a day's work for
his boss, he would go help out the neighbor with the broken leg
and did the neighbor's work too. Joe became very popular and
all the other farmers wished they had a hired man like Joe. Joe
was not very talkative, but he was friendly.

After a year, a wave of gossip went over the community. Joe
was seen taking Edye out for a ride in the horse and buggy on
Saturday night. That was standard procedure for courting a girl
or "sparking" as it was called.

The next morning there was another wave of gossip because
Joe took Edye to church. That meant only one thing. A few
months later Joe and Edye were married. Joe moved out of the
barn into the main house. He became her father's permanent
hired man, very much respected by everyone. Joe and Edye
had no children. And Joe became interested in the community.

When the Erickson kid announced that he was going to high
school, the entire community felt very bad because the Erickson
kid seemed to be a promising young farmer. They all knew that
a high school education ruined a man. Joe looked me up and
encouraged me to go to high school and encouraged a lot of
others to go to high school. When I announced my desire to go
to the university, Joe encouraged me and he encouraged a lot
of others.

So someone, as a joke, put his name on the ballot for the school
board. Everybody voted for Joe, which gave him the largest number of votes, and that automatically made him president of the
school board. Everybody attended that first meeting of the school
board. Every parent, in fact every citizen, was there to see what
Joe would say.

Joe said, "You folks elected me president of the school board
by giving me the most votes. Now I don't know nothin' about
schooling. I know all you folks want your kids to grow up and
be decent and the best way to do that is to send them to school.

You hire the best teachers and you buy the best stuff for the schools, and you don't yell about taxes." Joe was reelected many times to the school board.

Eventually, Edye's parents died and she inherited the farm and Joe looked for a hired man. He went to the reformatory and asked for the names of promising ex-convicts. Some lasted a day, some a week, some a month, some worked a considerable period of time before they felt ready to go out and make good in society.

Joe died in his seventies and Edye died a few months later. The entire neighborhood was interested in the will. The will provided that the farm could be sold in small farms and the additional land sold to anybody interested. All the money was to go into a trust fund administered by a bank and the superintendent of the reformatory to aid promising young ex-convicts.

Now all the psychotherapy he had was, "You can, if you are a gentleman."

When I got the job as state psychologist, I had to examine all the inmates of the correctional and penal institutions. Joe congratulated me and said, "There is an old record at Waukesha you ought to read. There is an old record at Green Bay and an old record at (E. names another penal institution)." I knew he meant *his* record. So I read them. It was the blackest kind of record. He was a troublemaker for the first 29 years of his life. Then a pretty girl said, "You can take me to the dance if you are a gentleman." No other change was made in Joe. He made the changes. The therapist doesn't do it, the patient does.

I had a similar patient named Pete. By the age of 32 years, he had served 20 years locked up. And when Pete got out of the Arizona State Prison, he came to Phoenix; he got drunk, picked up a girl—a divorcée with two children. He went home with her.

She had a job and he lived on her for seven months. He worked in taverns as a bouncer, for drinks. He always got drunk and always got in fights. And tavern after tavern discharged him. After seven months, the girl got tired of his fault-finding and his hangovers the next morning. So she told him, "Get out and stay out."

He went to all the taverns and begged them for a job and
they said, "No, you will do too much damage." He went back
to his girlfriend and asked her for a second chance. She said,
"No." So that July, in a temperature of 109 degrees, he walked
six miles from his girlfriend's home to my office.

He had been to see me twice before. Shortly after he got out
of prison, the halfway house for prison rehabilitation sent him
to me for psychotherapy. He visited with me for an hour and
said, "You know where you can stuff that," and walked out. His
girlfriend brought him back. He listened politely for an hour
and said politely, "You know where you can stuff that," and
walked out.

His girlfriend came to see me for psychotherapy. We talked
about things. She mentioned how impatient she was for her
ten-year-old and eleven-year-old daughters to grow up and earn
their own living, on the streets. I asked her if she wanted her
daughters to become prostitutes or streetwalkers. She said, "If it's
good enough for me, it's good enough for them." She realized
I didn't agree with her, so she walked out on me.

After she kicked Pete out, he walked all the way from her
home six miles to my office and said, "What was that you tried
to tell me?" I told him for another hour and politely he said,
"You know where you can stuff that," and walked out.

He went back to his girlfriend and begged again to be allowed
to live with her and she said, "No." He went to all the taverns
and they again said, "No." So Pete walked back here. That was
a total of 18 miles at a temperature of 109 degrees and Pete
had a bad hangover.

Pete came in and said, "What was that you tried to tell me?" I
said, "I'm sorry, Pete, but I've stuffed it. Now all I can say to
you is this: I've got a big backyard that is fenced in. There is an
old mattress out there that you can sleep on. If it rains, you can
drag it under the eaves, but I don't think it is going to rain. If
you get cold during the night, I'll furnish you with a blanket,
but I don't think it will get cold. There is an outdoor faucet
for your drink, and in the morning, you rap at the kitchen door
and my wife will give you a can of baked beans and pork."

We went to the side gate and I said, "And, Pete, if you want me to confiscate your boots so you won't run away, you will have to beg me to." He didn't beg me to, so I didn't confiscate his boots.

That afternoon, my youngest daughter and my granddaughter from Michigan drove into the carport. My daughter came out and said, "Who's that man nude to the waist and looking awfully sick, sitting in our backyard?" I said, "That's Pete, an alcoholic patient of mine. He is thinking things over." She said, "He has got a big scar on his chest. I am interested in medicine. I want to go out and talk with him and find out where he got that scar." I said, "It's all right for you girls to go out and talk to him."

Pete was sitting there in the lawn chair feeling very sorry for himself and very lonesome. He was glad to talk to the girls. He gave them his history. I don't know it. He talked and talked to the girls.

My daughter found out that he was shot in the heart during a burglary and rushed to the emergency ward. He had undergone open heart surgery. The blood was extracted from his heart and his heart was sewn up again. He had served time in prison after that.

The girls talked to him until evening time and my daughter said, "What would you like for dinner tonight, Pete?" And Pete said, "I would like a pint but I am sure I won't get that." My daughter laughed and said, "No, you won't get that. I'll fix up a dinner for you." She is a gourmet cook and she fixed up a dinner for Pete. The kind of a dinner he had never before eaten. He really enjoyed that dinner.

The next morning, she fixed a gourmet breakfast for him and the girls talked to him all the next day. They got well acquainted with Pete.

After four days and four nights in my backyard, Pete asked me for permission to go to his girlfriend's home. He said that he had an old car parked in her driveway. He thought that he could fix it up and sell it for $25.00. Well, I had no legal right to keep Pete in my backyard. He wanted to go out. He had that right. I told him to go ahead. He returned with $25.00 in his pocket.

He said that he wanted to think things over. He spent the night. The next morning, he asked to go out and look for work. He came back with two job offers, one that paid well and was easy work, but of uncertain duration, and the other job was hard work—a factory job with good pay and long hours and steady work.

Pete said that he wanted to think over which job he would take. He spent another night in my backyard. In the morning, he said that he had made up his mind to take the factory job. He explained that the $25 he had would pay for a cheap room and hamburgers and hot dogs until his first paycheck came in.

The first Thursday he was out, he called his girlfriend and said, "Put on your hat, I'm taking you out." She said, "You are not. You're not taking me anywhere." And Pete said, "I'm taking you even if I have to carry you." She said, "Where do you think you are going to take me?" He said, "To Alcoholics Anonymous. We both need to go to Alcoholics Anonymous."

He went there regularly with his girlfriend. And when Pete made his maiden speech after two weeks, his introduction was, "Any drunk, no matter how worthless a bum he is, can get sober and stay sober. All he needs is a backyard launching pad." (Laughter.)

And his girlfriend, after attending Alcoholics Anonymous for a while with Pete, came to me for psychotherapy. She had decided that her daughters should go to high school, and then to business school to learn shorthand and typing, and earn an honest living, because they deserved a better life than she had.

To my knowledge, Pete has been sober and hardworking for four years, going on five. And all the psychotherapy I really did to him was that through the gate. I said, "If you want me to confiscate your boots so you won't run away, you will have to beg me to." My work in the state prison taught me about convict honor and that was an appeal to his sense of convict honor.

I don't think the therapist does anything except provide the opportunity to think about your problem in a favorable climate.

And all the rules of Gestalt therapy, psychoanalysis and transactional analysis . . . many theorists write them down in books as if every person was like every other person. And so far as I've found in 50 years, every person is a different individual. I always meet every person as an individual, emphasizing his or her own individual qualities.

With Pete, I appealed to his convict honor, and thereby kept him in the backyard where he had to think. And Pete has told me, my daughter and my granddaughter don't belong on this planet. They are unlike any other woman he has ever seen. They don't belong to this planet. (Erickson smiles.)

A couple of years later my daughter came home from medical school and said, "I want to examine Pete's heart." We called up Pete and he came over. She did the most thorough examination of his heart and blood pressure and told him, "It's normal, Pete." He said, "I could have told you that in the first place." (E. smiles.)

The past can't be changed. Insight into the past can be educational. Now, patients are living *today*. Each day brings change in your life.

Just think of the changes in this century. In 1900 you traveled by horse or train. Anybody who thought about going to the moon had to be locked up in the State Hospital. They told Henry Ford to get a horse. They told him, "that gas buggy will never, never replace a horse."

There were a lot of riots about the development of railroads in this country. I read a lot of anti-railroad propaganda in the library in Boston. But, we got the railroad. And we have got cars. When the Greyhound Bus first started, there was a lot of prejudice against buses. Now there are a lot of bus lines.

In the 1920s, they knew that Dr. Goddard should be locked up in an insane asylum because he talked about a rocket to the moon. In 1930 I read a scientific article written by a physicist proving that if a plane flew faster than the speed of sound, it would disintegrate into molecules and so would the pilot. Now we have jet planes that break the sound barrier and the pilot lives and the planes continue undamaged.

Just recently, I found out that it may take a week or two to
get your car repaired at the garage on the next block. But if you
wanted to repair a very complicated machine on the planet Mars,
it takes a weekend. (Erickson smiles.)

Siegfried: (Looks questioningly.)

E: On the planet Mars, a very complicated machine can be repaired
in a weekend.

Siegfried: What kind of machine is that?

E: The Mariner that landed on Mars.

Siegfried: I got it.

E: And in the garage in the next block you wait a week.

Jane: Are you saying then that when you are dealing with patients
that you would prefer not to look at the past; you just take them
from where they are now?

E: Yes, take them from where they are now. That's where they are
going to live today. Tomorrow, they live in tomorrow . . . next
week, next month and next year. You might as well forget your
past. Just as you forgot how you learned how to stand up, how
you learned to walk, how you learned to talk. You have forgotten all of that.

There was a time when you said (spells out the letters), "B-o-
t-h-er, b . . . ba . . . ba . . . bother." Now you read page after page
aloud and you never think about identifying the syllables or the
letters or the pronunciation. When she read the letter (indicating Jane), she gave the quotation marks this way. (Erickson
gestures with his hand, making the sign for quotation marks with
his fingers.) It took a long time to remember how to punctuate
correctly. Now you . . . (Erickson again gives the gesture for
quotes.)

Jane: So you think that is true of a person's emotional development
as well as their physiological and linguistic development?

E: Joe had a bad emotional development for 29 years, and Edye said,
"You can, if you are a gentleman."

Jane: So, he made a decision just like that.

E: How many decisions do you make like that in your life?

Siegfried: Just a couple.

E: A couple? An awful lot. And you don't need to know how you learned to stand up and how to walk across the street. You don't even know how you cross the street. You don't know whether you walk a straight line, or how you are going to pause and look at this or that. You just walk along, automatically.

I hear my students asking about hypnotic automatic writing. All of you have done automatic writing. I know that, even though you are strangers to me. I can tell *you*, for example, that you did some automatic writing. (Erickson looks at Jane.) And you know that I am right.

Last January, you wrote 1978. Every January, you automatically write the last year. And you do it automatically. I get many checks dated with the wrong year, every January.

And now and then I might be talking to a student or thinking about a student and putting an autograph in his book, and I put in the date, "1953," for others, "1967." Because when I talked to that person, something about 1953 or 1967 would come up. When I was autographing his book, I gave that date because I was thinking about that person. And thinking about that person, I thought about the year that had been important to him.

You all do a lot of things automatically.

Now, some people learn to do automatic writing right away. And some think that it is something that you have to learn. So I tell them to put your pencil on the paper and watch your hand begin to move. There will be up and down movements and curved movements. Pretty soon there is a hand levitation—you get the hand levitated. Some people, a lot of people, think that they must go through the same learning processes in automatic writing by which they learned ordinary writing. So they show their belief.

Most neurotic ills come from people feeling inadequate, incompetent. And have they really measured their competence?

I think that every one of you can have the experience of working to get your first trance. You will be wondering, "Am I doing this right? Is he responding right? What is the next thing I should do?"

Now, let's take somebody I really don't know. (Erickson

looks at a woman, then addresses Siegfried.) Suppose you change seats with her. (Erickson is looking down and says.) Have you ever been in a trance?

Woman: Yes, you put me in one. (She touches E. on the arm.)

E: Well, you pick out somebody I've never put in a trance.

Woman: You can put Bonnie in one. (Bonnie is a therapist from Phoenix.)

E: (To the woman.) You change seats with her. (Bonnie sits down.) Now, first of all you notice that I didn't ask her to sit in this chair. (Erickson points to the chair. Bonnie nods "yes.") I just asked *her* to sit in *that* chair. You are over here, but I didn't ask you to come here, did I?

Bonnie: No.

E: Are you in a trance? (Bonnie smiles.) Are you?

Bonnie: I feel like I am in a slight one. (Nods yes.) I feel very calm and relaxed. (She nods her head yes.)

E: Will you say you are in a trance? (Bonnie nods her head yes.) She is agreeable people. (Erickson lifts her right hand and leaves it there cataleptically.) Today is the first day that you met me, isn't it?

Bonnie: Uh-hum.

E: Are you in the habit of letting strange men pick up your arm and leave it in midair?

Bonnie: No. (Smiles.)

E: You can't prove it by me. (Erickson laughs.) How long before you think you can close your eyes?

Bonnie: (Blinks her eyes.) I think I will close them now.

E: Go ahead. You will also go into a trance . . . and feel very comfortable. Go very deeply . . . (Bonnie lowers her hand) . . . and easily. And the more comfortable you feel, the deeper in a trance you will go. And you won't be alone. There will be others in a trance.

The rest of you can look around, and see how many of the rest of you have arrested your motor mobility that goes with the waking state—all of you show reduced psychomotor activity. You look at their eyes. They don't show the usual normal eye blink. There is a different . . . eye blink.

(Erickson addresses Siegfried.) And you are finding it hard to keep your eyes open. (Erickson nods his head slowly and perseveringly.) So you might as well as close them *now,* and keep them closed. (Erickson continues to nod his head.) All the way closed and feel very comfortable. Comfortable all over. (Siegfried has his eyes closed.) And you learn faster in a trance than you will in a waking state. You can't learn your unconscious by using your conscious mind.

Now, all of the things I've said to you will come back translated into your own language, into your own ways of understanding. And, in the future, you will discover sudden insights, sudden understanding, a sudden thought that you hadn't thought of before. It will only be your unconscious mind, feeding to your conscious mind things that you already knew, but you didn't know you knew. Because we all do our own learning in our own way.

Joe learned that just looking at Edye completely changed everything in his life, and Pete found out sitting in a backyard. He didn't even know why he even continued to sit in a backyard. (Bonnie opens her eyes.) He didn't recognize how thoroughly *I* understood convict honor, but he was caught up in it. And *he* changed *his* mind from a lifetime of social destructibility.

Now, I will tell you a story. Big Louise was a bouncer in the speakeasies of Providence, Rhode Island, in 1930. Big Louise was 6'6", all muscle and bone. She worked as a bouncer in the speakeasies. She had a little hobby. She would go out walking at night. If she happened to come across a policeman alone, she would beat him up and send him to the hospital. That was her little hobby.

The Chief of Police of Providence got tired of Big Louise putting his policemen in the hospital. So he went to court and had her committed to the insane asylum as dangerous to others.

At the state hospital—she had been there six months—she didn't like it. She knew that she wasn't insane. She didn't see anything wrong with her little hobby. It was only policemen that she beat up. So she got even with the hospital by doing $500 worth of damage every month on the ward. The Superintendent was very much distressed by that, because the hospital budget didn't provide funds for Big Louise's temper tantrums.

He mentioned it to me one morning—told me all about Big Louise. I asked if I could treat her and what restrictions would be placed on me. He said, "You can do anything to her you want to, except don't kill her."

I went to the ward—I had been assigned to the male ward—I introduced myself to Big Louise and told her that before she went on another rampage I'd like to have her sit down on the bench and talk to me. She said, "You mean you want to hold me still while about 20 male attendants gather to rush in and overpower me." I said, "No, Louise, I'll only talk to you." After the 15 minutes is up, you can do anything you wish, and nobody will interfere with you."

One day, the nurse called me and said, "Big Louise wants to see you." Big Louise was pacing back and forth in front of the bed. I said, "Sit down, Louise, and talk to me." She said, "Are you having the male attendants gather to rush in and overpower me?" I said, "Nobody is going to rush in and overpower you. In fact, nobody is going to interfere with *you*. Just sit down and talk to me about wintertime in New England." So Louise sat down suspiciously.

After about ten minutes, I signaled the nurse (Erickson moves his hand up and down), but Louise couldn't see it. The nurse made a phone call and about a dozen or twenty student nurses rushed into the ward. One grabbed the chair and started smashing windows on the east side. Four of the giggling student nurses rushed to a table. Each one took hold of a leg of the table and ripped it off. Another one broke the telephone off the wall. They really started smashing things up. I told them, thoroughly, what to do, and they were all giggling and laughing.

Big Louise jumped up and said, "Don't, girls. Don't, girls. Please don't." The girls kept right on. Louise kept on begging them to stop, because Louise didn't like to see her *own* behavior. That was the last time Louise ever did any damage.

Two months later, Big Louise called for me. She said, "Dr. Erickson, I can't stand *living* on the ward with all these crazy women. Can you give me a job in the hospital laundry?" Well, Louise had been tried in the laundry, but she had damaged a lot of things there. She had been barred from the laundry. I said, "Yes, Louise, I will get you a job in the laundry." We had a perfectly good understanding. Louise worked so well in the laundry that she was made the manager of it. She was discharged as a patient and hired as an employee.

Now, a 6'6" carpenter on the hospital maintenance staff came and looked at Big Louise and found her good to look upon, so they got married. For 15 years, to my knowledge, Louise managed the laundry doing very good work. The carpenter got along all right. Of course, Louise and the carpenter, on weekends, always had their beer drinking episodes and ordinary family arguments. They had their little family fights, but no fights with anybody else. They were good employees.

Now I don't know what happened in Louise's past that made her grow up that way. I didn't let her look at her *past* behavior.

She did as is advised in Corinthians 12: "When I was a child, I spoke as a child, I did as a child. Now that I have become a man, I've put aside childish things. I speak as a man, I do as a man."

I gave Louise one nice look at her childish behavior. That was enough. I had her see her childish behavior in the behavior of other people who should know better. That was all the therapy that was needed.

I think the textbooks on therapy try to impress upon you a great number of concepts. Concepts that you should take from your patients, not from books, because books teach you you should do things in a certain way: "E" comes after "I," except after "C," as in "neighborhood," as in "weigh," as in "neigh." For every rule, there is an exception. I think that true psychotherapy (Erickson looks at Bonnie) is knowing that each patient is an individual, unique and different.

E: (Addressing Bonnie.) How did you like your trance?

Bonnie: Fine.

E: Now, I didn't awaken you, because I wanted to illustrate a point. You stayed in a trance as long as you wanted to. Why should you stay any longer unless there is a purpose? I made it purposeless for you to stay in a trance.

(Erickson looks down.) Once I hypnotized a dentist's assistant in San Francisco to demonstrate hypnotic phenomena. I told her to wake up. She presented every appearance of being wide awake. Everybody thought she was awake. For the next two weeks, she remained in a trance night and day.

Then on a later trip to San Francisco, I met her again. She was then awake. I said, "You didn't wake up when I told you to. If it is all right for me to know, I'd like to know why you stayed in a trance."

She said, "I am glad to tell you. I've been carrying on an affair with my employer. His wife had been refusing to give him a divorce. I thought if he wanted to have an affair with me, he should either get a divorce or be faithful to his wife. I went into a trance. I knew in the trance I could tell him exactly how I felt. But, by that time, his wife had decided that she didn't want to remain married to him. So she got a divorce—on her own, and on her own terms. My employer came and told me. Then, I knew that it would be all right to come out of the trance. Now we are married. His wife is happy, I am happy, and the dentist is happy."

Another time, I hypnotized two dental assistants in L.A. I noticed they didn't come out of a trance when I told them to, but they appeared to be out of the trance to everybody else. So I knew they had some reason for staying in a trance.

Two weeks later I lectured at the same place. The two dental assistants were there. So I had a talk with them privately and asked them, "Why have you nurses been in a trance for two whole weeks?" They said, "We are doing an experiment. We wanted to know if we could work as well in a trance state as we did in a waking state. And if you think that two weeks of doing that is enough to prove a point, we will wake up now." I told them any hypnotic subject can work as well in a trance state as he can in a waking state, and probably do it much better because there are fewer distractions.

If I were having my chauffeur drive me in dangerous traffic, I would put him in a deep trance. I would want my chauffeur to pay attention to the traffic problem. I wouldn't want him, on a windy day, to see that girl whose skirt was blown up by the wind. I would want my chauffeur to see all the traffic problems, and nothing else. I wouldn't want him paying attention to the conversation in the car. I wouldn't want any things outside the car to distract him—anything, outside of driving problems, to distract him.

One of my daughters-in-law agonized for two years about taking her M.A. essay examination. She was so sure she couldn't pass the essay examination. Her husband told her she could pass it easily. I told her, "Now, why should my daughter-in-law believe her husband? He doesn't know everything. Now, why should my daughter-in-law believe her father-in-law? He doesn't know everything." She knew how hard her master's examination was.

But she did come to me for help, so I told her, "Go into a trance and now forget about your master's examination, because someday in the future you will wander into a certain room at Arizona State University. You will see some mimeographed questions and some blue books. Find a comfortable seat. Pay no attention to anybody else, and have a nice time daydreaming about your vacation trip to New England, your vacation trip to South Carolina, your vacation trips elsewhere. But now and then you can notice that your hand has been writing and you are not really interested in that."

She came home that day from the university, not remembering that she had been there. And two weeks later, she was checking over the mail and she told her husband, "There's something awfully wrong here. Here's a letter from the registrar saying that I passed my master's examination and I haven't taken it yet." My son said, "Wait a few more days, maybe the registrar will send you your master's diploma." She said, "How could that be? I haven't written my master's examination yet." But she didn't have to know that she had written it. The registrar had to know. What time is it?

Christine: It's twenty past four.

E: The sum of kindness in the heart is the torment of working too long. There are newcomers here today. (To one woman.) Do you believe in Aladdin's lamp? (General laughter. To another person.) Do you? (Erickson takes the newcomers inside his home to see the collection.)

FRIDAY

❖❖

Note: Sid Rosen, a psychiatrist from New York and a longtime colleague of Dr. Erickson, is in attendance at today's session. He is sitting in the green chair.

E: My wife and I were talking about a problem this morning—about the orientation that we get in our early life. We were commenting on the difference between a city child's orientation to life and the country child's orientation to life.

The country child is oriented to getting up at sunrise and working all summer long until after sundown and always working with a view toward the future. You plant things; you wait for them to grow; and you harvest them. Everything you do on the farm is oriented toward the future.

The city child is oriented to the things going on *now*. And in

231

the drug-use society, the "now" orientation is extremely common. It is a very limited "now" orientation.

Whenever you see patients, you really ought to consider, "What type of orientation do they have?" Are they actually looking forward to something in the future, and really looking forward? A country boy just naturally looks forward to the future.

I will give you an example from my own experience. I spent one summer grubbing up brush from ten acres of land. My father plowed it that fall, and replowed it the next spring and planted it to oats. The oats grew very well and we hoped to get an excellent crop. Late that summer, on a Thursday evening, we went over to see how that crop was getting along, and when we could harvest it. My father examined the individual oat stalks and said, "Boy, this is not going to be a bumper crop of 33 bushels an acre. It will be at least 100 bushels an acre, and they will be ready to harvest next Monday."

As we were walking home happily thinking about a thousand bushels of oats, and what it meant to us financially, it started to sprinkle. It rained all night Thursday, all day Friday, all night Friday, all day Saturday, all night Saturday, all day Sunday. In the early morning on Monday, the rain ceased. When we finally were able to wade through the water to that back field, the field was totally flat. There weren't any upright oats. My father said, "I hope that enough of the oats were ripe enough so that they will sprout. That way we will have some green feed for the cattle this fall. And next year is another year."

And that is really orientation to the future, and very, very necessary in farming.

Now the city boy has a "now" orientation. A city boy usually gets his orientation to the future a bit earlier than the farm boy. The farm boy has one that is consistent all along. He still has to plant his wild oats, and he usually plants them a little bit later than the city boy. The city boy does it *now*, and the farm boy waits.

In the drug cultures, they don't seem to have any orientation to the future. They know that somebody died of an overdose, but that means only that the pusher gave him too high a grade of heroin. And then they all want to find the same pusher so they can get a bigger shot, a better effect. And those who have had a psychosis, a psychotic break, from Angel's Dust, will nevertheless take a second dose of Angel's Dust and have a second psychosis, even a third psychosis. It takes a long time for them to get a future orientation.

Now, the request has been made that I undertake to outline, at least in part, the growth and development of the sex life of the individual. (Note: Prior to the session, I requested that E. include this discussion in Friday's lecture.)

Now, sex is a biological phenomenon. It is a local matter for the male. He doesn't even grow a single whisker in addition. It is just a local experience for him.

For a woman, biologically, the sexual experience, to be complete, means: impregnation, a nine-month period of pregnancy, delivery, nursing the baby for six to nine months, and then caring for that child for 16 to 18 years in our culture.

When a woman begins an active sexual life, the first thing that happens is that there is a change in her endocrine system. The calcium in her skeleton changes. Her hairline is likely to change very, very slightly. Eyebrow ridges become slightly more prominent. Her nose lengthens by perhaps a millimeter or a fraction of a millimeter in length. Her lips become a little bit fuller. The angle of the jaw changes. The chin becomes a little bit heavier. The fat pads of the chest and the hips either enlarge or become more dense, and the center of gravity changes.

As a result, she carries her body differently. Her walk is different. The way she swings her arm as she walks, and the way she carries her body is completely altered. And if you learn to observe, you can learn to recognize those changes almost immediately. Because biologically, her entire body enters into it. You watch the growth of pregnancy and see how her body enlarges. It changes all through pregnancy, all through lactation.

I had a sister who tried desperately for 13 years to get pregnant. Because I was her brother, she didn't think I knew anything about medicine, which is not an uncommon thing between siblings. So, she had tried to be a foster mother for newly born infants, always giving them a home until they were adopted. She didn't want to adopt a child. Finally, after 10 years of being a foster mother for newly born infants up to the end of their first year, she asked me for advice.

I told her very simply, "You've been trying to get pregnant. There is something lacking in you. But if you will adopt a child so that you can really feel a sense of physical ownership and endow that child with physical meaning for you—a special physical meaning—I don't know how to describe it any other way— you adopt a child, and within three months you will be pregnant. She adopted a son in March and in June she was pregnant. She had several other pregnancies.

I mentioned earlier this week when I went to Worcester State Hospital, Dr. A. took me on rounds and invited me into his office and said "Sit down, Erickson." And then said, "Erickson, if you are interested in psychiatry, you've got it made. You have got a bad limp. I don't know how you got your bad limp, but I got mine in World War I. Now your limp is of infinite value to you in psychiatry, because your limp will evoke the maternal urge in women, and they will confide in you very readily. As for male patients, as a psychiatrist you won't evoke their fear, hostility or anger, because you are just a cripple. And they are superior to you so there will be no competition. There will be no recognition of you as a man. You are just a cripple, and therefore a very safe person in whom to confide. And so, walk around with a blank face, your mouth shut, your eyes open and your ears open, and you wait to form your judgment until you have some actual evidence to support your inferences and your judgments."

Now, when it comes to the sexual growth and development of the individual, a newly born baby is extremely ignorant. It has a sucking reflex and it can cry. But it is a meaningless cry. It is, I expect, the discomfort with the new environment.

After a while the baby becomes aware of the fact that now and then a warm wet feeling occurs. And it is a pleasant warm wet feeling. It takes baby quite some time to discover, always after that warm wet feeling, there comes a cold wet feeling which is unpleasant. Eventually, the child learns to associate one with the other.

You can pick up a very young infant who is hungry and you can pat him on the tummy and lay him back in bed. If he could think, he would be thinking, "That was a wonderful meal, very stimulating." Then he would start to go to sleep until the next hunger pang hits him. Then he could think, "That meal didn't stick to my ribs very long." So you pick him up a second time and this time you pat him on the back and he feels stimulated and comfortable. You put him back in bed and he starts to go to sleep until the next hunger pang hits him. Then he starts yelling for food, because that patting on the back was not a meal that stuck to his ribs very long.

After a while, mother begins to notice that the meaningless cries acquire a meaning that say, "I'm hungry," "I'm cold," "I'm wet," "I'm lonesome," "I want petting," "I want cuddling," "I want attention." Each cry is altered as the child begins to comprehend various things.

Too many mothers try to train their children to the potty chair, but they start too soon. If they start too soon, they can actually condition the child to use the potty chair. But, if they start too soon the training soon breaks down, and the mother can't understand it.

Usually the child is lying on a blanket on the floor or in the playpen, and all of a sudden the child sits up and looks all around the room (Erickson demonstrates). He is very curious. And mother says, "Johnny is going to wet." She rushes to pick him up and put him on the potty chair. Johnny has discovered the third element that warns about urination—pelvic pressure. He doesn't know where to locate that pelvic pressures; he just looks around the room. So when the child recognizes pelvic pressure and knows that there is going to be a warm wet feeling followed by a cold wet feeling, he announces it.

Now, one thing about a child is that he is unacquainted with his body. He doesn't know that his hands are his. He doesn't know that he is moving them. He doesn't recognize his knees or his feet. They are just objects. So he has to feel them over and over again. And learning to recognize your body is really a very difficult thing.

I know how difficult it is. At 17, when I was paralyzed completely and able to move only my eyes—nothing was wrong with my hearing or with my thinking—the practical nurse that looked after me would put a towel over my face so I couldn't see. She would touch me on the hand and ask me to tell her where I was touched. I would have to guess the left leg, the right leg, my abdomen, my hand, my right hand, my left hand or even my face. It took a long, long time for me to learn where my toes were or where my feet were, and to recognize the individual parts of my body. I had to do a great deal of blindfolded experiences before I could recognize it. And so I learned to sympathize and understand what goes on in the infant's mind.

Now, an infant can reach the stage of development in which he can pick up a rattle and shake it or handle a toy. He still doesn't really know where his hands are. One day, he sees a funny looking object so he tries to pick it up. It's a very bewildering experience because the rattle doesn't go away. It doesn't suddenly move to one side. Finally, one day, he touches the contralateral hand and the bewildered look on the infant's face is marvelous to behold. Because he touches this. . . . (Erickson touches his right hand with his left.) He gets dorsal stimulation and palmar hand stimulation and they seem to be connected in some way. The child learns to reach the other hand (Erickson demonstrates) with the other hand much more rapidly once one has been located. Then you find the child very curiously examining each finger and learning that they are all part of this and part of this . . . (Erickson touches his right wrist, forearm and elbow) and related to this and on up the shoulder.

With my eight children, I've watched each one of them discover their own physical identity. They all follow the same general pattern. Some learn their hands before they learn their legs.

Another thing about the infant at birth—the head is one-seventh of the length of the body. The child's body keeps on getting longer and longer and the infant can lift his hand so high (Erickson demonstrates by touching his head). But, in the future, it is going to lift its hand way above the head. That is a curious thing in the child's experience.

Now, father and mother take great pride in teaching baby, "Show me your hair, your forehead, your eyes, your nose, your mouth, your chin and your ear." They think that baby knows where his hair is, or where his eyes are. The parents are usually careful to have the child do the learning with the right hand, so the child becomes right-handed.

Johnny doesn't really know where his ears are, because all he learned from his parents was "up and front and down the same side as his hand." (Erickson touches the left side of his face with his left hand.) Contralateral learning is really a very different thing. (Erickson touches his right ear with his left hand.) Then he has to do the other contralateral learning. (Erickson touches his left ear with his right hand.) His parents think he really knows where his ears are. And you watch the baby and then see if the baby will get his hand up here, and have him touch his ear. (Erickson demonstrates by putting his left hand over the top of his head and touching his right ear.) And the amazed look on his face as he says to himself, "So that's where my ear is." And he has to learn the contralateral ear with the other hand. (Erickson demonstrates.) And it is a very interesting thing to watch the baby feel over and over from the top of his head to the tip of his ear, contralaterally. He still doesn't know where his ears are until he can put his hand behind his head and touch the contralateral ear (Erickson demonstrates). And with sudden surprise he says, "So that's where my ear is." He has to know it from the front, from below, from above and from in back. Then he is secure in his knowledge.

There are many other things to learn. The baby is lying in the crib and the father and mother tower above him and all the movement is up there. (Erickson demonstrates.)

My son Robert came home from some months in the hospital after a traffic accident. When his cast was finally taken off, he was lying on the couch at home. He rolled over and looked at the floor. He said, "Daddy, the floor is as far away as the ceiling and I'm afraid to try to stand up." I said, "You learned how far away the ceiling is. Now you have got to learn how far away the floor is." It took several days for him to measure the distance. (Erickson demonstrates, looking up and looking down and measuring the distance from the floor to the ceiling.)

And, with a growing infant, his head is this high (Erickson demonstrates) and they keep growing longer and longer. His hands reach down here and then further and further (Erickson starts with his head and then moves his left hand down towards his knee.) So the relative distance to various parts of the body differs almost from day to day—at least from week to week.

I can remember one son saying, "Mother, stand back to back with me. I want to see how tall I am." He was a half-inch shorter than his mother. Two weeks later, he again measured himself. He was a half-inch taller than his mother. He was at what we call "the awkward stage." His muscles are the same, but the bones are longer. He is using the muscle at the same strength with longer levers. Parents call that "the awkward stage." It is an age of growth.

And little Johnny has to locate and identify every part of his body. It comes as a surprise to him that he urinates through his penis. Before, it was just a warm wet feeling.

As soon as he walks, he wants to use the bathroom standing up, like daddy. And he sprays the entire bathroom and he is puzzled about that. He gets an elementary lesson. "When you use your penis, direct its use." He learns to use the commode to urinate in. That's part of the struggle.

Then he has to learn time in relation to urination. He discovers that it is easy to go into the bathroom from the hall, harder to get to the bathroom on time from the livingroom, still harder to get there from the kitchen, much harder to get there from the front porch, the back porch, and the backyard. Eventually, he learns to make a full allowance for the time requirements to get to the bathroom.

Then he gets his second tremendously important lesson for the future. He arrives at the bathroom on time but some adult is occupying the place. So he wets his pants. (Erickson laughs.) Mother thinks that he did it out of anger. He did it because he didn't know the importance of urination in relationship to the general population. (Erickson laughs.)

Now all these learnings take place in segmental fashion. He learns there is a social aspect to urination.

Then another thing: When Johnny is fully toilet-trained, mother puts a brand new suit on him and tells him, "Sit still in the chair; don't move; don't get dirty. We are going to church." Johnny wets his pants. Why? Well, he has got a new suit on and where in hell is his penis located in relationship to those new clothes. Mother should have taken him to the bathroom and had him locate his penis in relationship to that new suit. Instead, mother thinks that Johnny is getting even with her in some way. She knows that he is fully trained, but she overlooked the fact that he is wearing a new suit. And where in hell is his penis in relationship to that new suit?

I'll give you a nice story to illustrate that. A general was reviewing a core of women in the army, and he told them, "Suck up your gut and don't wear your handkerchiefs in your blouse pockets." (Erickson laughs.) Someone had to tell him that those weren't handkerchiefs. (Erickson laughs.) Because we forget . . . so many things when we grow up.

Now, Johnny has learned to come in to the bathroom on time. He learned to direct a stream of urine. He learned to make social provisions for urination; that urination is not confined to the home "john." Yet, some people try to make it so.

I'll give you a case history. Two families lived side by side, across the street from the grade school. One family had a boy and the other a girl. The two families had a family business. When the two children graduated from grade school, the parents sold their homes and bought homes across the street from the high school. Son and daughter graduated from high school and didn't go to college. Eventually, they were absorbed in the family business and fell in love to the delight of both sets of parents. One evening, their parents gave them a very nice wedding and **wedding reception.**

The two sets of parents had rented an apartment for the youthful couple about a mile and a half away. At 10:30 p.m., the youthful couple went to their new apartment and undressed to go to bed, and all hell broke loose. That "john" was a strange one. Each of them had been trained to come home from school and use the family bathroom. Here was a strange bathroom. They had never used a strange bathroom in their life. They always used the bathroom at home. So they had to dress, go back home, and use the family bathroom.

They consummated the marriage all right, but the next morning, they had to go home and use the family bathroom.

Then they came to see me to learn "how do you use a strange 'john'?" So I had to teach them that you can urinate wherever it is possible and with the privacy that you want. It doesn't have to be a familiar "john." Their parents didn't want them using school lavatories . . . under any circumstances.

Now, as a young boy grows up. . . .

Sid Rosen: How did you teach them? Did you tell them stories about it?

E: I took them in my bathroom and showed them the bathroom. I told them that eight children and two parents used it, some of the patients used it. I discussed it openly.

My daughter went to a social banquet with a young man who invited her to go. The father came to me and said, "Now, Dr. Erickson, my son wants to take your daughter to the banquet. I don't want to insult you, but you are aware that we belong to two different levels of society." I said, "Yes, I know you inherited your millions from your grandfather, and your wife inherited her millions from her grandfather. Therefore, you are on a different social level." He said, "All right, now that we understand that. I hope you will let your daughter realize that she could have no aspirations." He was being very courteous. (Erickson smiles.)

After the banquet, he came and apologized. He said, "My son took your daughter to the banquet and I was ashamed of all the adults that were there. There were a half-dozen forks and spoons. All the adults were looking sideways to see which spoon to use.

Your daughter looked around to see. She looked around openly
and honestly. She wasn't trying to hide her ignorance at all."

And he said, "My wife wants to know where your daughter got
that beautiful evening gown." I called my 12-year-old daughter
in and said, "Mr. X wants to know where you got your evening
gown. He has already apologized to me for putting me to the
expense of buying such an elaborate evening gown." My daughter said, "I made it. I went downtown, bought the cloth, and I
made it." (Erickson smiles.) And then he apologized a lot more
(Erickson laughs) because his wife wanted to know in what store
my daughter bought such a beautiful evening gown. It was in-
conceivable to him that an individual could make an evening
gown.

Now a penis is not limited in its use. (Erickson and group
laugh.) A boy has to learn how to pee on the cat, dog, the flower
bed, the lawn mower, into bottles and cans, through knotholes
in the fence. He has to climb a tree to see if the urine will reach
all the way to the ground. In other words, there is a rather blind
recognition that the penis is used in the outside world. But
nobody tells you how you use it in the outside world. He has to
do it experimentally.

I remember in Michigan that the head housekeeper, a registered nurse, used to get so angry at finding bottles and cans
of urine my sons had secreted here and there. I couldn't tell her
why because she was so prissy that you couldn't speak the truth
to her. All boys go through that stage.

I have seven sisters and four daughters. They all went through
the same stage. After dark, they tried urinating in the corner of
the backyard. They went on picnics and experimented. They
had to learn the same thing—that the genital-urinary tract had
an outside world use. They had to experiment to find out what
it was.

A boy can be born with an erection. It is a bladder distension
phenomenon. One of the tasks a boy has to learn is that the penis
has three different types of enervation. The flaccid penis has a
set of nerves in the skin, a set of nerves (this is simplified) in the
shaft of the penis, another set of nerves in the head of the penis.

The boy has to learn what the feelings are when the penis is flaccid. When it is partway erect there is another type of feeling; halfway erect, another type of feeling; three-quarters erect, another type of feeling; and fully erect, still another kind of feeling. (Erickson demonstrates by raising his left hand halfway up from the armrest; three-quarters of the way, etc.)

And the boy has to play with his penis. People call it masturbation. I call it "the baby talk of penile orientation." He has to learn all the feelings of his penis at every stage of erection. He has got to enjoy the feelings. He has got to learn how to lose his erection, and how to get it back.

In my psychiatric experience, I've encountered men who didn't know how to get an erection. I've encountered men who suffered from premature ejaculation, men who suffered great fear about the entrance of the penis into the vagina. They hadn't learned a lot of things. So, the boy practices his masturbation to learn how to get an erection, how to enjoy it, how to lose it, and how to get it back.

Then he is confronted with another problem. He has been, up to that time, competing with his fellows, "See how strong I am. Feel my muscles. Let me feel your muscles." (Erickson demonstrates with his left arm.) "See if it is as hard as my muscle." So he has to go through a stage where he identifies with other males. Because he has to know that his penis is as hard as the other boys' penis. So there is a lot of experimentation and feeling. Some people call it the homosexual stage. I call it the "group orientation stage," "sex orientation stage," "the same-sex orientation stage."

Then he has to learn to ejaculate. For simplification, ejaculation consists of urethral secretions, prostatic secretions and sperm. And the first ejaculation is likely to be urethal, or partly urethral and prostatic.

Having an ejaculation is like eating food. When you start feeding semisolid food to a baby, he can swallow it. Time can pass and it will get through the stomach and through the pylorus and into the intestine before the baby's salivary glands begin to secrete saliva for that food. The child has to learn to digest each food, have that digestion begin in the mouth, and have added to it esophageal secretions of the stomach, in the stomach, lower end of the stomach, and the upper end of the small intestine. Secretions from A to Z. They learn to digest different foods at different ages.

Now, the boy has to masturbate until he gets his ejaculate into three—urethral, prostatic and seminiferous—and get them almost simultaneously, but in the correct order.

I had a doctor come to me and say, "I've been married for 13 years. I've got an 11-year-old boy. Neither my wife nor I enjoy intercourse. It is an unpleasant labor." I said, "How much masturbating did you do as a child?" He said, "I masturbated twice and both times, thank goodness, my father caught me. I didn't complete it."

I told him, "All right, take a condom specimen to your office and have it analyzed. In all, he took eleven condom specimens to his office and had the pathologist analyze it. In some there was prostatic secretion and urethral; in some, prostatic and seminiferous. Seminiferous was the least frequent part of the ejaculation.

He came back and said, "I may have gone to medical school, but I didn't learn anything." I said, "You should have masturbated so that you could get those three types of secretions in the proper physiological order. You can't get full physiological satisfaction unless those secretions occur in the proper order." So I told him to lock himself in the bathroom everyday and masturbate.

I think on about the 28th day he encountered his wife in the hallway on the way to the bathroom. He picked her up. He took her to the bedroom and had intercourse with her. They both told me that they enjoyed intercourse for the first time. He learned to get the proper ejaculation.

Now, some boys learn that very rapidly. Some boys may have to masturbate a thousand times before they catch on. It is like other learning.

Then there is another learning that has to take place. That is that masturbation with ejaculation is not intended by nature to be a manual procedure. So the boy, in his sleep, begins connecting emotional reactions and ideation to ejaculation. And so he has wet dreams. Mother thinks he has been playing with himself. He ought to be ashamed of himself; he is a big boy now. Actually, that is a biological way in which a male finds out that he can separate sexual activity from hand activity.

Then, he begins to notice girls. I'll give you a story about one of my sons.

He was in high school and he said, "Dad, I want to do my homework at Eve's. She is a whiz on math and on history. And I would like to do my homework with Eve." He started doing that.

Then he began taking Eve to the roller skating rink. At first, they skated separately, and pretty soon they began holding hands and skating together—engaging in rhythmical, physical activity. After leaving the rink, they went to Pat's or Mike's or Dairy Queen, and got mucous membrane stimulation. And that really became the important part of the skating.

The next summer, he took her swimming. He came back from the first time swimming with Eve and said, "Dad, do you realize how much skin a girl has?" I told him, "The same amount of skin that a boy has."

Every morning when I shaved, my children like to watch me shave because I used a barber's razor. I always explained, "When little girls grow up, they don't get whiskers. They get bumps on their chests. When boys grow up, they get whiskers. That is the difference between a boy and a girl."

And my son inquired about those little bumps that Eve was developing. I said, "How much have you noticed them?" He said, "Well, all boys like to accidentally bump a girl's breasts." I said, "Yes, that's right, and what else?" He said, "Well, their fanny is bigger than a boy's fanny, and the boys always like to bump up against the girls." (Erickson laughs.) I said, "That's right. That's part of growing up."

Finally, my son began calling Eve "his girl." He took her swimming and dancing. Of course, they always had hamburgers and hot dogs with all the relishes, and ice cream, all flavors.

One winter day, about ten below zero on Friday morning, my older son said, "The Boy Scouts are going to have a nighttime camp-out for the weekend. Will you take us?" I said, "Certainly." I was ready to take them after they came home from school. Then my son broke the news: "We don't start until 10:30. This camp-out is supposed to begin at midnight." I said, "All right." I had given my word that I would take them. It didn't look very sensible to me as an adult to go out to camp in the snow at ten degrees below zero.

After we got in the car, my son broke the news to me. "I promised the other boys that you would pick them up." The other boys were waiting in the village of Wayne. They all packed their gear in the trunk and climbed in the car.

On the way to the camp-out place, one of the boys asked my second son, "Lance, what did you do this evening?" Lance said, "I went to the box social at school." And all the gibbering he got. The idea of a sensible boy going to a box social at school. Finally, after gibbering him thoroughly for wasting his money and buying a girl's box lunch and paying good money for it, one of the boys asked, "Who's box did you buy?" He said, "I bought Karen's." All the gibbering turned to admiration. "Boy, I wish I had thought of that." "Are you cool!" "Are you neat!" And all the other slang expressions of admiration of that day.

I listened and I wondered why buying Karen's box was so right an idea. I kept silent.

At the camping spot, they climbed over a ten-foot snowdrift to set up camp, and they slept in sleeping bags. They had breakfast Saturday morning. They all had a midnight snack over the campfire. And Sunday evening I picked them up.

After I got the boys home, I took Lance into a separate room and said, "Lance, you told the other boys that you went to the box social. They jeered you; they called you a fool, an idiot, a chump and a blockhead. They really ridiculed you. But then one of them asked you whose box you bought and you said, 'Karen's.' Then they all started wishing they had done the same thing. Now I am going to ask a few questions, and I want you to answer the questions exactly. Is Karen a pretty girl?" "No,

homely as a mud fence." "Is she a good athlete? Play ball?"
"Nope, clumsiest girl in school." "Has she got a nice personality?" "Nope, nobody likes her." "Is she a very bright girl?"
"Uh-uh, the dumbest girl in school." I had exhausted my knowledge of why Karen's box was so desirable. I said, "Now tell me
why did you buy Karen's box?" "She is the fattest girl in school.
She had four oranges, four bananas, four pieces of cake, four
pieces of pie, eight sandwiches of peanut butter and jelly. And I
can eat faster than she can." (Erickson laughs. Group laughs.)

Nice proof that a way to a man's heart is through his stomach.

Bert (Erickson's oldest son) enlisted in the Marines at the age
of 17. After his enlistment expired, he returned home.

One day, he said, "Dad, what do you think about Rhonda?"
I said, "Practically nothing." He said, "Dad, you know what I
mean. What do you think of Rhonda?" I said, "I practically
never think of her. I do think she is a pretty girl, a bright girl."
And he said disgustedly, "Listen, Dad, you know what I mean.
Why don't you answer my question?" I said, "Since you know
what you mean, why don't you ask me the question so I will
know what you mean."

He said, "Dad, when Rhonda gets married, will she have a
mess of kids as fast as possible? Will she wear her hair in curlers
all day, and will she slop around in carpet slippers and a bathrobe? When her husband comes home from work, will she com-
plain that she couldn't do a thing with the kids, or the washing
machine, or something like that?" I said, "Bert, you know her
mother, and I know her mother. I think that Rhonda has had a
good teacher. I think she will probably put into practice the
teaching she has had throughout her lifetime."

Ten years later, Bert was visiting in Michigan and ran into his
boy scout friend who said, "Welcome, Bert." He said, "By the
way, Bert, I married your high school flame, Rhonda. Now why
don't you take dinner with us tonight?" Bert said, "I would like
to, Bob, but don't you think we ought to call up Rhonda and
tell her?" Bob said, "No, let's surprise her."

They entered the house that evening. Rhonda said, "Hello,
Bert. Bob, the kids have been half-sick all day, and there isn't a

thing to eat in the refrigerator." Bob said, "That's all right, Rhonda. I'll take Bert out for hamburgers instead." He was used to that. (Erickson looks around and smiles.)

One day, I took my two boys out swimming. They changed into their swimming suits in the bedroom. When they were both in the nude, Lance happened to look at Bert and he said, "My goodness, Bert, you are growing older." And Bert modestly admitted he was. He had two pubic hairs. (Erickson laughs.) A sign of growing *older*.

Bert wanted to get married. When he thought he was old enough to get married, he got an old truck with a rusty roof. He began dating girls from everywhere—University of Michigan and elsewhere. As they drove along in that truck, the rust would drift down from the rusty roof into the girl's hair. He would tell her how pretty it looked. The girls seldom gave him a second date. They wanted something better than an old truck with a rusty roof.

One day he saw a girl across the street from the home he purchased. He had purchased a home in Garden City, saying to himself, "I'm young and strong. I can hold down two jobs and I can pay for that house now while I am young and strong. If my bride likes it, we will have it. If she doesn't like it, it can be a down payment for another place that she likes.

One day he looked across the street and saw a blonde girl there looking after her younger siblings. He watched the girl very carefully. He liked the way she handled her younger siblings. He admired her. She really had a nice way of dealing with children.

So, he hired a horse and plow and he plowed up his front lawn and made it into a garden, which he hoed and kept as neat as could be. He let the radishes go to seed; the beans get ripe on the vine; tomatoes got rotten on the vines.

One day, that girl came timidly over to the garden and said, "Mr. Erickson, I know you are working two different jobs. You have a very nice garden, and all the produce is going to waste. Would you mind if I can it and share it?" Bert said, "No, that would be very nice." So she started canning all the garden produce. He had a big garden.

Then he began neglecting the hoeing. One day, the girl said, "Mr. Erickson, I know you are very busy and I hope you don't mind that I hoed that place you didn't get to hoe." Bert said it was very nice of her. Bert knew that he wanted a wife who would want to live on a farm, who would like to work in the garden and who would like to can fruits and vegetables.

And now they live on a farm in western Arkansas. They have six field hands and a kitchen helper. Lillian still looks as good as she looked when she was a young girl.

When her first child was born, she was pleased it was a boy. When the second, third, fourth and fifth turned out to be boys, she felt very disappointed. When the doctor told her that the sixth child was a girl, she burst into tears and said, "Why do you tell me a lie like that? I can't have a girl baby." Well, the doctor proved it to her.

The sixth boy was born after his sister. Now the oldest boy is a college graduate. Bert said *he* wouldn't go to college because in class he had to listen to all the other students making mistakes. He could read stuff at home and learn. He has always been interested in growing plants. He has filing cabinets full of agricultural information.

When he was in the Marines, he took a thoughtful look towards the future. He knew about the Depression and the Depression years. So while he was in the Marines, on his leaves of absence, he learned to repair shoes. Because in times of depression, a shoe repairman is overloaded with work. He is sure of employment all day long, all night long. So he learned to do that. He also learned to be a tree surgeon, mostly in the Marines on his days off.

After he was discharged from the Marines, he said, "I'll have to go down to Detroit and get a job." I said, "You're aware of the unemployment situation—all the returned veterans looking for jobs." Bert said, "I know. I'll come home with a job."

He went downtown. There had been a windstorm, and a lot of

limbs had broken off the trees. The city horticultural crew was
out trimming the broken branches.

Bert called the foreman on one such job and said, "Do you
mind if I pile up the brush?" The foreman said, "Go ahead,
you can't make it any worse than it is now." Bert did a strictly
professional job of piling the brush. The foreman looked at him
and said, "You seem to have a talent for this. Here is some gear,
put it on. I'll take you up a tree and see if you know how to cut
off broken limbs." He took Bert up and pointed out a broken
limb, easily sawed off. And Bert did a strictly professional job.

The foreman said, "You seem to have real talent. Just try this
other limb." Bert looked it over. It was a very difficult limb. He
sized it up carefully and then he did an expert job. The foreman
said, "I'm shorthanded for tree trimming crew and experienced
men. You have got natural talent. You take over my job here as
foreman, and I'll go and work as a foreman on another crew I
have out trimming trees." So Bert got a job.

Sid Rosen: I'm getting a little irritated and realize why. I had a feeling you were insulting city people. You started with two groups,
the city and the country. Most of these stories today have been
about country people who plan and reap the benefits of their
planning and so on. I wonder if these stories would be helpful for telling to city patients too? Patients who live in cities?

E: With less emphasis.

Sid Rosen: With less emphasis.

E: Uh-hmm.

Sid Rosen: I know about the man who started to work in a restaurant
and worked his way up and so on. That kind of story would be
more applicable to somebody trying to get into business.

E: I haven't told the others that.

Sid: Uh-hm.

E: A grade school graduate, a Mexican boy, came to me and said, "A
Chicano has no chance of getting a job. I've only got a grade
school education. I've looked for work, but nobody wants to hire
a Chicano."

I said, "Juan, do you really want to work?" He said, "I sure
do." I said, "I'll tell you how to get a job and you will do exactly

as I say. There is a certain restaurant in Phoenix that I know. You go there and ask permission to mop up the kitchen twice a day. Say you want to do it for free. You want to learn how to mop out a kitchen. Don't accept any pay. Don't accept any food. Eat only at home on food your mother supplies."

I said, "Now as you mop up the kitchen twice a day neatly and carefully, they will start to take advantage of you. They will ask you to peel potatoes and to cut up vegetables. They won't offer you pay. But they will overwork you and they will get to depend on you. In about a year's time you will be having a job. But you will have to work for it."

Juan did his part nobly. Pretty soon they thought he was wasted just helping the cook. In rushes on the restaurant, they had him as a busboy. The chef liked Juan because Juan was so competent preparing vegetables and helping with the cooking.

Then they knew a convention was coming to town and that most of those attending the convention would eat at that restaurant. So I told Juan, "A convention is coming to town next Monday. You tell the manager that you *think* you can get a job for pay in Tucson, and you hope that he doesn't mind if you apply for that job in Tucson."

I don't know what the wages were then. I don't remember. I told Juan to tell the manager that the wage was much smaller than the usual one. The manager said, "I can do better than that for you." He offered Juan a dollar more a week." So Juan became a full-time employee.

A year later, they were depending on Juan a great deal in the kitchen. The chef had taught him and he learned well. Then another convention was coming to town and so I told Juan, "Tell the manager that you think you can get a much higher paying job in Tucson." The manager said, "I can pay more than the Tucson restaurant can. You've got a job with me permanently."

Juan became one of the highest paid chefs in Phoenix. He now owns his own restaurant which now seats 270 people. He is building a second one that will seat at least 300 people. (To Sid Rosen.) Is that it?

Sid: I like that. Balance. Do you find that city people can also get something from stories about flowers and gardens and so on, even though they might not have had much experience with those things?

E: I've sent more than one depressed man to go and dig and plant a flower garden for someone. I sent one man to his sister-in-law's home. She and her husband worked. There were no kids and I knew that she wanted a flower garden. I talked it over with her. Then I told my depressed patient from Yuma, "Your sister-in-law in Phoenix would like a flower garden. So you get the tools and make her a nice, big flower garden."

By the time he had it finished, I had located another couple, a working couple, that wanted a flower garden. The patient became enthusiastic about that. Then he went home, and cleaned up his own backyard. He built some shelves for his wife in his new home—the new home is what caused him to get depressed. It had a big mortgage on it. But he recovered from his depression. And whenever he came to Phoenix, he went to see the flower gardens he had constructed.

Sid: I'm trying to find the New York equivalent of climbing Squaw Peak. I've got a couple of people walking over the Brooklyn Bridge. That helps. (Erickson nods.) A couple more are jogging. I gave them specific instructions about how they were to start jogging. It's a marvelous antidepressant.

E: The George Washington Bridge.

Sid: The George Washington Bridge would be good.

E: The Holland Tunnel.

Sid: Holland Tunnel. Empire State Building.

E: (Nods.)

Sid: I wouldn't send anybody through the Holland Tunnel walking. They would suffocate.

E: I've been through it.

Sid: On foot?

E: Driving—very slowly. I think I could have walked faster.

Sid: (Laughs.) That's true.

E: For the young people who are depressed, if they have any artistic skill, draw a picture of the Empire State Building; draw the outline of the New York skyline. (Sid nods.) Draw a picture of the Hudson River with sailboats on it.

Sid: Central Park pond.

E: (Nods.) Find a tree and . . .

Sid: They love to be given these assignments . . .

E: And find a nice crooked tree in Central Park with a squirrel in it.

Sid: (Sid smiles.) Boojum?

E: Boojum tree.

Sid: Boojum tree—we don't have those.

E: Now, concerning the sexual revolution of the '60s: In the sexual revolution of the '60s, men and women started living together and enjoying sexual freedom. If anybody wants my opinion about that, it's this: All I can say is that I agree with Dr. Margaret Mead, that the family situation, either narrow or extended, has been in existence for about three million years. I don't think the revolution of the '60s will really seriously affect three million years of practice. How do you feel about that, Sidney?

Sid: I tend to agree. I like your emphasis on patterns and things that one can count on to be repeated . . . children and one generation to another and so on. That is very, very comforting for anybody to listen to, and it's also inspiring.

E: And now to illustrate that from a totally different point of view. If I were on a train traveling from San Francisco to New York and I got very lonesome and I desperately wanted to find somebody to talk to and everybody else was a total stranger to me, would I try to start a conversation with that pretty young girl reading a movie magazine, or *True Confessions?* No. Would I try to talk to that pretty girl in her twenties who's reading some novel? No. Would I talk to that old lady who was knitting a stocking? No. Would I talk to the man reading a law book? No. Would I talk to a man who had a stethoscope? No, because all he could do was shop-talk.

    The person I would start a conversation with immediately would be either male or female of any age so long as they wore a University of Wisconsin lapel button. They would know all about Picnic Point, the Science Hall, and State Street, and basketball and Observatory Hill. They would speak the language of my youth, the language of my emotions, the language of my memories. We would have a language in common.

Of course, if I saw someone doing some carving, I'd stop and talk to him or her. If I saw a woman working on a patchwork quilt, I'd think of my mother and all the patchwork quilts she made for her children, her grandchildren, her great-grandchildren and me. That would be part of my language.

And so when you look at a patient, when you listen to a patient, find out what his orientation is. Then try to give him some idea of how to orient himself. (Note: Here Erickson intentionally repeats the story of the purple cow made by a retarded girl.)

Also concerning sexual development: The girls go through it similarly but differently in many regards. You can see four high school girls walking, arms around each other, four abreast, using up the entire sidewalk. I think it's a pleasure to step in the gutter so that they can have the sidewalk. What are the girls learning? The pressure around the body.

And at the induction board, married men and men with sweethearts were being inducted for active duty, combat duty. I heard the wives say, "Kiss me so hard on the lips that they bleed, because you may never again kiss me. Hug me so tight that you will break my ribs. I want to remember that hug." And yet the gentlest kiss by a rapist burns like fire, because it is literally unforgettable and ruins the lives of girls. It's the emotional background.

When you have a patient with some senseless phobia, sympathize with it, and somehow or the other, get them to violate that phobia.

I was lecturing in Memphis, Tennessee, and my host and hostess attended. At the end of the lecture, the hostess remarked, "The lecture lasted rather long, so let's eat at a restaurant. We know a very nice French restaurant. My husband and I have dined there twice a week for 25 years."

I looked upon that statement as entirely pathological. To eat at the same restaurant in Memphis, where there are a lot of restaurants . . . to eat at the same one twice a week for 25 years . . . so I agreed.

Of course, having my suspicions, I ordered escargots. And the way they looked at me as I ate my snails. (Erickson pulls away and grimaces.) When I was down to one snail, I persuaded my host to taste it. He ate it and said, "That's good." So then I persuaded his wife to taste it and she found it good. So I ordered my second order of escargots. They ordered their first order, and they enjoyed it.

Six months later, I was in Memphis lecturing and they were again my hosts. The lecture lasted late and my hostess said, "Instead of having dinner at home, let's go to a restaurant. We know a very nice German restaurant, or would you prefer some other type? There is a catfish restaurant that is very nice." She offered me several other choices. Since they mentioned the German restaurant, I went there with them. Halfway through the meal, I turned to my host and said, "By the way, when was the last time you went to that French restaurant?" He said, I don't know, six weeks, two months. Honey, when did we go last to that French restaurant?" She said, "Oh, I think about two months ago."

After 25 years, twice a week . . . (Erickson laughs) . . . that was pathological.

Sid: Did they always usually order the same food at the restaurant, too?

E: I didn't ask. I knew what they avoided. Once they ate escargots, they could go to any other restaurant in Memphis.

You sit around the pool at a motel and watch the people who plunge in, and the people who dip one toe and then another toe and then another toe, and finally can get all of their body wet.

When I first joined the staff at Worcester, Tom and Martha, a young couple there, junior psychiatrists, were very friendly toward me. They invited me to go swimming at the lake which was adjacent to the hospital farm. I got into my bathing suit, put on a bathrobe, and got into their car. And Martha was very sullen and silent and unresponsive in the car during the half-mile drive to the lake. Tom was charming, sociable and talkative. I wondered.

When we reached the beach, Martha leapt out of the car, threw her bathrobe in the back of the car. She strolled down to the lakeshore and plunged into the water and started swimming away. Never a word to us.

Tom got out of the car cheerfully, casually. He put his bathrobe in the backseat. So did I. He walked down to the water, and when Tom's big toe touched the wet sand, he said, "I think I will go swimming tomorrow."

So I plunged into the lake and had my swim with Martha. On the way back to the hospital, I asked Martha, "How much water does Tom put into the bathtub." She said, "A lousy one inch."

Tom was offered a promotion to the senior psychiatrist that week. He told the superintendent, "I don't think I'm ready." The superintendent said, "I wouldn't have offered it to you if I didn't think you were ready. Now you are either going to take the promotion or you leave and find a job elsewhere."

Tom and Martha left. By that time, I knew Martha well enough to know that she was very much in love with Tom and he with her. Martha was looking forward to a nice home and children.

Twenty-five years later, I was lecturing in Pennsylvania, when an old grey-haired man and a haggard old woman approached me and said, "Do you recognize us?" I said, "No, but your question implies that I should." He said, "I'm Tom." And she said, "I'm Martha." I said, "When are you going swimming, Tom?" He said, "Tomorrow." I turned to Martha and said, "How much water does Tom put in the bathtub?" She said, "The same lousy, stinking one inch." I said, "What are you doing now, Tom?" He said, "I'm retired." "At what rank?" "Junior psychiatrist." If I had had time, I would have somehow or other managed to shove Tom into the lake.

Sid: What about Martha?

E: And Martha could have had some children.

Because once you break that restrictive, phobic pattern, the person will venture into other things. And our patients tend to restrict themselves and really cheat themselves out of a lot of things.

I got a phone call from a friend in California last night. He said, "I finally found out the cure for the idiocies of teenagers. Put them in a deep freeze and let them thaw out when they are 21." (Erickson laughs.)

My son Lance was very seriously troubled because he was disgusted by my lack of intelligence. He was very frank in telling me I was rather stupid. Then he went to Michigan to go to the University. Later he told me, "You know Dad, it only took two years for me to find out that you had suddenly jumped from idiocy to intelligence." Not long ago he called from Michigan and said, "Dad, you've got your revenge. My oldest child has at last discovered I have some brains. There are three more yet to find that out."

Man: My father used to tell me those stories. (Erickson nods.)

E: Now I will tell you a case history. It is rather complicated and yet rather simple.

Robert Dean had graduated from the Naval Academy and had been commissioned as a second lieutenant. It was war time, and he had been given a month's leave of absence and assigned to a destroyer.

He went to Francis Brakeland, head of Naval psychiatry, and explained his neurosis to Brakeland. Brakeland recognized his problem and said, "Second Lieutenant, there is nothing I can do for you. I can't change your orders. There is no way I can get you a land-based job. You've got your orders to go aboard a destroyer. All I can do for you is order a court martial. The court martial will send you to Walter Reed Hospital. Your condition will get worse, you will be transferred to St. Elizabeth's Hospital. There you can live and become psychotic, and live your life out as a psychotic man. But you could, on your leave of absence, go to the Johns Hopkins Clinic and see if they can give you some private help.

Robert went there and told them his problem. They questioned him for some time and told him, "We can't help you.

But, there is a man named Erickson in Michigan who might be able to help you."

So Robert called his father in New York. His father called me and asked me if I would see his son. I said I would be in Philadelphia next week. He could come to Philadelphia and tell me about his son, and I would consider it.

The father came to my hotel room—it was a very interesting and charming time for me. He came in and introduced himself to me and said, "I am only five feet tall. I had a hell-of-a-time stretching myself so I could get into the Army for the First World War. I had to eat a lot of bananas and drink milk to make the weight requirements. And the damned Army kept me a buck-private all through World War I. I swore when I got out of the Army that if I ever got married and had a son I'd have him grow up to be a military officer, preferably in the Navy. Because I've got no use for the U.S. Army.

I said, "All right, now what's Robert's problem?" He said, "He has got what you call a bashful bladder. He can't urinate in the presence of other people. He is a damn fool. He says he's had that bashful bladder ever since he was a little kid. He had one hell of a time in the Academy.

"By the way, I thought you shrinks charged a lot of money. Why do you have such a cheap room? Can't you afford anything better? Or are you just plain stingy?" I said, "What else can you tell me about Robert?" He said, "Well, he had his troubles in camp. Why don't you buy some decent clothes? Can't you afford a better suit than that?" I said, "Let's hear about Robert." "Well, Robert would come home for vacation. The public accommodations in a gas station weren't good enough for him. He would rent a hotel room, lock the door, and go to the bathroom and relieve himself. In fact, he did that sort of thing all through high school . . . and are you too cheap to buy a decent tie?" I said, "Tell me about Robert."

He said, "It's getting close to noon. Do you suppose you could haul that gimpy, awkward carcass of yours down to the hotel dining room?" I told him that I thought I could.

On the way down to the dining room he asked me if it didn't

embarrass me to be so clumsy with my limp. "How many old ladies do you knock over when you walk down the street? How many kids do you fall over? Old men do you knock down?" I said, "I manage to get along all right."

We arrived at the dining room and he said, "This hotel has lousy food. I know a good restaurant in the middle of the next block. Do you suppose you could haul that gimpy carcass down the street without knocking down old men and old women and falling over kids, or will I have to hire a taxi?" I told him I thought I could haul my carcass all right.

In the middle of the next block, he apologized. He was mistaken. The restaurant was in the next block. And he insulted my walk, my appearance, everything imaginable he could think of to insult me.

He told me he was a real estate broker. He sold real estate. And he made it a point to roll every client over the barrel and squeeze every last cent out of him.

Finally, we arrived at the restaurant, twelve blocks away. He said, "Of course, we could dine on the ground floor. I prefer dining in the balcony. Can you drag that carcass of yours upstairs or will I have to help drag it?" I said, "I think I can drag it up." So he picked out a table in the balcony.

Before the waitress came, he told me, "This restaurant has marvelous cooks. They really know how to prepare beef. But their fish is half-rotten and half-cooked, their mashed potatoes are watery and only half-done. They make their ice tea out of river water and try to cover it up with ice. It's terrible."

The waitress appeared and he indicated to her that I was to examine the menu first. I ordered roast prime rib of beef, baked potato and hot coffee. I've forgotten what else. Then she turned and gave the menu to him, and he said, "Cancel his order. Bring him fish, mashed potatoes and ice tea." And he gave an order similar to mine: Roast rib of beef, baked potato, hot coffee and the same dessert I had ordered. The waitress kept on looking at me and I kept my face blank because I was really having a good time.

When the waitress finally came and arrived with two trays,

looking very uneasy and unhappy, I said, "Give the fish and mashed potatoes to the gentleman who ordered it. Give me the roast rib of beef." She did, and scuttled away as fast as she could. He looked at me and said, "That is the first time anybody has ever done that to *me*." I said, "There is always a first time for everything."

He ate his fish and his mashed potatoes and drank his ice tea. I enjoyed my roast prime rib.

After we finished dinner, he said, "Well, I brought you here to a good restaurant. How about you paying the bill?" I said, "You invited me. I am your guest. You will pay the bill." He said, "How about you picking up the tip?" I said, "That is the responsibility of the host."

Then he took out a Texas wallet. A Texas wallet is filled with bills and you usually try to have a thousand dollar bill, a few five hundred dollar bills, hundred dollar bills, fifty dollar bills, twenties, tens, fives and ones.

He took out that overstuffed wallet and peeled off the amount and reached in his pocket for the odd-cents change. He left a nickel tip. Without his knowing it, I slipped a nice tip for the waitress. In the anixety state she was in, she needed a tip. (Laughter.) He asked me if he'd have to drag my carcass down the stairway. I told him I could at least fall down. I wouldn't need his help. When we reached the door, he said, "Can you haul that awkward carcass of yours back to the hotel or do I have to hire a cab?" I said, "I think I can make it to the hotel." He said, "Well, for heaven's sake be careful and don't knock down any old ladies or old men or stumble over kids. And don't fall in the street." He pulled the most uncomplimentary remarks all the way back to the hotel.

Back at the hotel, I said, "There are a few more things I would like to know about your son." So he came up and we entered my room. He asked me if I could afford a better suitcase. He told me what a cheap grade briefcase I had. I was taking notes, noting what he was saying. He said, "What in hell is the matter with you? Are you one of those shrinks who can't even furnish his own pen? You have to use the hotel pen and the hotel stationery to take notes?" I said, "I want to know more about Robert." So he told me a few more things, and wanted to know if I would take Robert as a patient. I said, "Tell Robert to show up at my office in Michigan at 6:00 p.m."

Robert arrived, a second lieutenant in the Navy, in uniform. He looked in the office from the corridor and he said, "So you're the big shot that is going to cure me." I said, "I'm the psychiatrist who is going to work with you."

Robert entered the office and took a long, careful look at a 6'6" medical student in uniform—the medical students were inducted in the Army but allowed to go to medical school in return for so many years of service. He said, "What's that long drink of nothing doing here?" I said, "Jerry is a medical student of mine." He said, "What kind of shrink are you that you have a medical student help you?" I said, "A very competent one."

And he then saw the professor of art at the University of Michigan in the room. He said, "What's that bozo with a soup strainer on his face doing here?" I said, "He is a professor of art at the University of Michigan. He, too, is going to assist me in your therapy."

Robert said, "I thought medical consultations were private." I said, "They are. And I've got a lot of help to keep it strictly private. Now come in and sit down."

So he sat down. Jerry closed the door. Then I said, "Jerry, go into a nice deep trance." Jerry did and I demonstrated every hypnotic phenomenon I could, and Jerry was an excellent subject.

While Jerry was still in a trance I turned to the art professor and said, "Now you go into a trance. Jerry went in knowing that you were in a waking state. In the trance state you present every appearance of being awake. You will talk to Robert and to me and you will not be able to hear or see Jerry." So the art professor went into a trance.

Then I awakened Jerry and started a social conversation. I made a few casual remarks to the art professor. He answered them. He made a remark to Robert, and Jerry turned to speak to the art professor. The art professor said, "Listen, Robert." He asked me a question. Jerry looked bewildered at that discourteous behavior. He started to ask the professor another question. The professor spoke to Robert, ignoring Jerry, and Jerry's eyes widened and he smiled and remarked to me, "So you put him into a trance while I was in a trance." I said, "That's right."

Then I put Jerry back into a trance, and awakened the professor. I awakened Jerry with an amnesia for his second trance. Jerry was still under the apprehension that the professor was still in a trance. He looked very startled when the professor spoke to him.

Robert looked confused, so I played around with Jerry and the professor demonstrating phenomenon after phenomenon. Robert was very, very interested. He lost his hostility to me.

Finally, I said, "Well, good night, Robert. I'll see you tomorrow at 6:00 p.m." Then I told the professor that he need not come again. He had served his purpose. I told Jerry, "You show up every evening."

The next evening when Robert came in, I said, "Robert, last night I showed you hypnosis. Tonight, I am going to induce a light trance in you. It can be light; it can be medium; it can be deep. All I want is for you, in the trance, to do anything or everything that Jerry demonstrated, that the professor demonstrated." Robert said, "I'll do my best.

So Robert went into a trance. I explained to him that he had seen Jerry do automatic drawing and automatic writing and carry out various post-hypnotic suggestions. I told him, "After you awaken, your right hand will find its way to the desk top. It will pick up a pencil and you will draw a picture. You won't know you are doing it because you will be so interested in talking to Jerry."

So Robert awakened and started talking to Jerry. He and Jerry had a nice conversation. His right hand picked up a pencil and drew a picture of a man on a pad of paper at hand. The picture of the man was a circle for the head, a straight line for the neck, a straight line for the body, two straight lines for the arms and for the legs, two circles for the hands, and two circles for the feet.

Under it he printed the word, "Father." To my surprise, he absentmindedly tore off the sheet, folded it and folded it until it was a small wad of paper. Then he absentmindedly slipped it into his blouse pocket. Jerry and I watched that performance with peripheral vision while we talked about various things.

The next night when Robert showed up, he flushed as he came into the office. Jerry and I both noticed his flush. I asked, "How did you enjoy your sleep last night?" Robert said, "Fine. I slept very well." I said, "Did anything unusual happen last night?" Robert said, "No," and flushed again. I said, "Robert, I don't think you are telling the truth. What unusual thing happened last night?" He said, "Well, when I went to bed I found a wad of paper in my blouse pocket. I don't know how it got there because I didn't put it there. Sure enough it was there. I threw it in the wastebasket. He flushed again. I said, Robert, I think you are lying to me. What did you do with that wad of paper?" He said, "I unfolded it." I said, "What did you see?" He said, "On one side was a very childish picture of a man and under it was printed the word, 'Father.' " I said, "What did you do with the paper?" He said, "I threw it in the wastepaper basket." He flushed again. I said, "Robert, I want the truth. What did you do with that piece of paper?" He said, "Well, if I must tell you, all right. I put it in the commode and urinated on it and flushed it down the toilet." I said, "Thanks for telling me the truth, Robert." So, Jerry and Robert had a nice social conversation. Then I dismissed him and told Jerry what to expect.

Jerry was a very bright young medical student. When Robert came in the next day, they greeted each other. They started discussing everything except his problem.

The first evening I met him, Robert had told me the nature of his problem. Ever since he could remember, he always had to find some secluded spot to urinate. He didn't know when it first began. He didn't know why it began. He said living in the Academy was just plain hell. He had to violate dormitory rules because he couldn't use the dormitory lavatory for fear someone else might come in. He had catalogued all lavatories at the Academy. He had catalogued them chronologically. There were three lavatories that were certain to be vacant at 1:00, at 2:00 and 3:00 a.m. He always had to sneak out of the dormitory and use one of those lavatories. He had succeeded in getting through the Academy without being caught.

Then he said, "Another hellish part of the years at the Academy was that it was good public relations for the members of the Academy to accept invitations for a weekend at some private home." Robert said, "They picked us up on Friday evening and the hostess would ask you if you wanted coffee, tea, milk, soft drinks, wine, or apple cider. All those hostesses could think of was passing out some ice water, tea, coffee, milk and soft drinks. I had to be courteous and drink. At breakfast, a glass of milk or any soft drink I wanted. All day Sunday, drink, drink, drink. You had to be polite, and I had to wait until Monday morning back at the Academy to see if I could find one of the three lavatories to relieve myself. I went through hell with a stretched out bladder Friday night, all day Saturday and all day Sunday. It was just plain hell.

"Whenever I would hear footsteps outside the lavatory, there would be an awful clap of thunder in my head, and I would *freeze* stiff. Sometimes, it would take me over an hour to get over freezing stiff.

"It has been awfully difficult all the years in the Academy. I had no other choice. My father wanted me to be a Naval officer and I just had to stick it out. And my father, every vacation, made fun of me because I used a hotel room. He got mad at me all through high school because I always went to a hotel.

"I don't like my father. He drinks beer everyday. He likes to get drunk every Saturday and Sunday. He calls my mother a sniveling woman because she goes to church, because she belongs to the Women's Christian Temperance Union. I don't like that. I can't say I had a really happy time growing up. My father likes to extract everything he can from his clients, and he does. He drinks that beer, and I can't stand the thought of drinking beer. And my father finds fault with me for siding with my mother."

While we continued talking about social things that evening, Robert suddenly looked out the window and said, "Is it raining

out there? Is that a drop of water running down the windowpane?" There wasn't a cloud in the sky. There was no water on
the window. I made note of that as a symbolic remark. I knew
that it had something very important in it, but the only deduc-
tion I could draw was: Rain is falling water; urine is falling
water. Robert in his symbolic way was mentioning that to me.

Then I said to Jerry, "Any particular plans, Jerry?" Jerry said,
"Well, if you will let me go, I think I will spend the weekend,
this week, canoeing down the Ausable River in northern Michigan. It is a nice river to take a canoe trip down. I've done it
before. The rapids make it exciting."

I turned to Robert and said, "Since Jerry isn't going to be
here, what would you like to do for the weekend?" He said,
"Well, I'd like to go home and visit my mother." I said, "Well,
what will you do?" He said, "Well, if it doesn't rain, I'll mow
the lawn."

For a man about to go to war—combat duty—to mow the lawn
if it doesn't rain sounded very symbolic to me.

I said, "All right. I'll see you again on Monday at 6:00 p.m." I
asked Robert what train he would take back to Syracuse and he
told me. So I told him, "Be sure you catch that train."

I made a telephone call to Robert's father, Mr. Dean, and told
him what train to catch to come to Detroit to see me. I told him
to be sure to catch the train I specified. He grumbled. I didn't
want him to see Robert, or Robert to see him.

When he came in the office at 6:00 p.m. the next day after he
arrived, Robert's father looked at my secretary. He said, "What's
that grey-haired bitch doing here?" I said, "Miss X is my secretary. She is working overtime on my work on your son. She is at
present taking down in shorthand everything you say, everything
I say, everything anybody else says." He said, "Can't we get rid
of that old bitch?" I said, "No. I need her here to take down
whatever is said in this office."

He said, "What is that long drink of water doing here?" I said,
"He is a medical student. He is helping me work with your
son, doing therapy." Then he said, "What kind of shrink are you

that you need a medical student?" I said, "A very competent one."

Then he noticed the art professor and he said, "What is that bozo doing here?" I said, "He is a professor of art at the University of Michigan. He, too, is helping me do therapy on your son."

He said, "Good God. I thought medical interviews are confidential." I said, "We are all keeping them confidential. I hope you will."

He said, "Can't you get rid of that old grey-haired bitch?" I said, "She is not old; she is just prematurely grey and she is working overtime. She is going to work overtime until she is paid." He said, "She is your secretary. I've got nothing to do with paying her." Then I said, "She is working overtime in the therapy for your son. So you will pay her." He said, "She is your secretary." I said, "She is doing work for your son. Pay her." He said, "Do I have to?" I said, "You certainly do."

I had seen his wallet at the restaurant. He hauled it out and said, "How about a dollar?" I said, "Don't be ridiculous." He said, "You mean I have to pay that grey-haired bitch five dollars?" I said, "Certainly not. I told you not to be ridiculous." He said, "Ten dollars?" I said, "You are just barely approaching the sum." He said, "Not fifteen dollars?" I said, "You're right. Not fifteen dollars, but thirty dollars." He said, "Are you crazy?" I said, "No, I just like to see people properly paid." He peeled off thirty dollars and handed it to her. She wrote a receipt, thanked him, and bid him good night.

Then Mr. Dean looked around and said, "What are these bozos standing around here for? Do you want me to pay them?" I said, "Of course." He said, "Thirty dollars?" I said, "Don't be ridiculous. Seventy-five dollars apiece for them." He said, "I think I can take lessons from you about rolling clients over the barrel and extracting their last cent." I said, "All right, pay them." And they each got their seventy-five dollars and wrote him a receipt and bid him good night.

Then Mr. Dean said, "I suppose you want to be paid. I suppose a hundred dollars." I said, "Don't be ridiculous." He said, "You are not going to charge me five hundred dollars, are you?" I said, "Of course not. I am charging you $1,500 cash *now*." He said, "I *can* take lessons from you about rolling clients for their last cent." So he peeled off three five hundred dollar bills and handed them to me. I gave him a receipt.

He said, "Now, do you have anything more in mind?" I said, "Oh yes. You like to drink beer. Your wife likes to go to church. She belongs to the Women's Christian Temperance Union. She doesn't like to have you get drunk on weekends. She doesn't like your beer breath everyday of the week. Now I am going to limit you to four glasses of beer." He said, "Hell, that's all right." I said, "Not the way you're thinking. They will be eight-ounce glasses—not the kind of glass you had in mind to have made for you. Now write me a pay-on-demand note for $1,000. It will be my privilege to cash that note the first time you get drunk. And, otherwise, for your beer drinking, you can have four eight-ounce glasses a day and no more."

He wrote out the pay-on-demand note and said, "I know I can take lessons from you in extracting money." I said, "All right. Robert is at home visiting his mother. I don't want you to meet Robert. You will not return to Syracuse until such-and-such a train leaves." And I gave him the hour.

So Robert returned on Monday morning. He flushed as he came in. I said, "How did you enjoy the weekend, Robert?" He said, "Fine." I said, "What did you do?" He said, "I mowed the lawn. It didn't rain." He flushed very deeply when he said that.

I had asked Jerry to coach me in military language. Robert was standing facing me. I said, "Attention. Close ranks. About face. March. Left face. March. Halt. Take a deep drink at the water fountain and march to the lavatory and take a piss. About face. March. Stop at the water fountain. Take a deep drink, straighten up. March. Right face. Enter the office and stand at attention." Jerry leapt to his feet when I said, "Attention," and closed ranks with Robert who stood at attention. They did as I told them.

And then I said, "Now, Robert, at ease." I said, "Last week you mentioned, 'Is it raining? Is there a drop of water running down the windowpane?' Those were symbolic remarks. The only meaning I could deduce then was that rain is falling water and falling urine is falling water. You went home. You mowed the lawn and you said, 'It didn't rain.' Now, Robert, I want to know the whole truth."

Robert said, "It's rather embarrassing. I mowed the lawn. I didn't know why. I took the lawn mower and put it back in the garage. The front of the garage is a door. It opens upward. The neighbors across the street can look into the garage and see everything that is going on there. After I brought the lawn mower into the garage, I urinated on it. Then I knew!

"When I was a little boy and was out in the garage, I saw a brand new lawn mower so I peed on it. I didn't hear my mother enter the garage. She boxed both of my ears, clamped her hand over my mouth and dragged me into the house. She gave me a fearful lecture. It was a long and horrified lecture.

"After that, I couldn't urinate in the house unless my mother was busy in the kitchen, and my father was away at the office. Then when I went to camp or school, I had to run away and find some secluded spot to urinate. If anybody approached, I heard that same thunder clap. I didn't recognize it as my ears being boxed."

I said, "So that's your problem, Robert. Attention. Close ranks. About face. March. About face. Halt. Drink deeply. March. Take a piss. About face. March back. Stop at the water fountain. Take a deep drink and march into the office. At ease, gentlemen." I said, "Now, Robert, do you think you will have any more trouble?" Robert laughed and said, "No."

Rain is falling water. New lawn mowers, for little boys, need to be baptized.

Now, this was in July. On New Year's Day in New York, I got a call from Mr. Dean. He said, "I'm drunk as a hoot owl, so cash that damned pay-on-demand note." I said, "Mr. Dean, when you gave me that pay-on-demand note for $1,000, I told you I have the privilege of cashing it the first time you got drunk. I do not wish to cash it now." He swore off the beer and began attending church with his wife.

Twenty-five years later, I happened to be caught in Syracuse because of a blizzard. I called him up from my hotel and said, "Good evening, Mr. Dean. How are you?" I identified myself. He said, "Will you come visit us?" I said, "No, my plane leaves at 4:00 a.m. tomorrow morning. It would be too inconvenient for you." He said, "Mrs. Dean will be very sorry to have missed you." I said, "Have her call me when she gets back from church." He said, "I will." We had a long pleasant talk.

Robert went aboard a destroyer all throughout the war. He was aboard the ship upon which Japan surrendered. He watched the whole ceremony. After the war, he joined the Naval Air Force and was killed in an air accident in about 1949.

Mr. Dean and I talked on the phone—I received a Christmas card every year since that famous New York City "I'm-drunker-than-a-hoot-owl" call. Mr. Dean said, "I've not had a drink of beer since then. I've had good church attendance." When Mrs. Dean came in from church that evening, she called me up at the hotel. Mrs. Dean asked me, "Whatever happened to that $1,000 pay-on-demand note?" I said, " I gave it to Robert. I told him why I had Mr. Dean sign it, and the conditions. Robert told me that he would keep it for awhile to see if Mr. Dean intended to stay sober and then he would burn it. So if it wasn't in his effects you received from the Navy, he undoubtedly burned it."

Now, Mr. and Mrs. Dean are dead and Robert is dead. Robert had 28 days to get over his bashful bladder. I took a little bit over a week. I worked blindly, but not too blindly. I knew a bullying father when I saw him. I subdued him and made him a nice human being. (Erickson looks at Sid and waits for a reaction.)

Sid: Beautiful story.

E: I wish Robert were still alive. Jerry, and the professor, and "the grey-haired bitch" are still alive.

I think that you should take a patient as he is. He is only going to live today, tomorrow, next week, next month, next year. His living conditions are those of today.

Insight into the past may be somewhat educational. But insight into the past isn't going to change the past. If you were jealous of your mother, it is always going to be a fact that you *were* jealous of her. If you were unduly fixated on your mother, it is always going to be the fact. You may have insight, but it doesn't change the fact. Your patient has to live in accord with things of today. So you orient your therapy to the patient living today and tomorrow, and hopefully next week and next year.

And you have been hoping that I would continue to live for some years, now, haven't you? (To Sid.)

Sid: Absolutely. Your father lived to 97 years, you said.

E: Um-hmm. On PBS, I saw a sad and disgusting story, about an old woman living in a nursing home. She told about her woes of living in a nursing home. She lived on welfare for 40 years. Now, at 90, she was still living on welfare in a nursing home. She said, "I haven't had a decent moment of life for the last six years because I've been dreading that I would be dead the next day. And I worried and worried and worried about being dead for the past six years and I haven't had a single, happy moment." My thought was, "Why in hell don't you crochet an afghan and hope to hell you get it done before you croak." (Erickson smiles.)

Because we all start dying when we are born. Some of us are faster than others. Why not live and enjoy, because you can wake up dead. You won't know about it. But somebody else will worry then. Until that time—enjoy life.

Do you know a good recipe for longevity? (Addresses Sid.)

Sid: No. Tell us.

E: Always be sure to get up in the morning. (Laughter.) And you can insure that by drinking a lot of water before you go to bed. (Laughter.)

Sid: You get up too early in the morning.

E: It is absolutely guaranteed. What time is it?

Siegfried: Ten to three.

E: I'll give you another case history. I will have to tell you some extra background information. In medical school, one of my classmates was rather shy and retiring—a good student, but very timid. I liked him.

One day in our physiology class, we were divided into groups of four. Each group was given a rabbit on which we were to do certain procedures. We were told by Dr. Mead, the professor, "If your rabbit dies, boys, you get a zero. So be careful."

Unfortunately, the rabbit in my group died. Dr. Mead said, "Sorry, boys, you get a zero." I said, "Sorry, Dr. Mead, but the autopsy has not yet been done." He said, "All right. For being smart enough to know that an autopsy should be done, I'll give you a grade of 50." We did the autopsy and asked him to look. He saw that the rabbit had really died of a massive pericarditis. He said, "That rabbit had no right to be alive when it came into the laboratory. So you boys get an A for your grade."

One summer day, this classmate entered my office and said, "I always remembered what you did about that rabbit. I hated the thought of a zero, and I've never forgotten how you got a grade of 50, and then a grade of A, by just talking up to Dr. Mead.

"I have been in the practice of medicine in a suburb of Milwaukee for 20 years, and now I've been forced to retire because I am too neurotic. You see, when I was a little boy, my father was very rich and my mother was equally rich. We had a very big house, and a very big lawn in Milwaukee.

"Every spring I had to dig out the dandelions and they paid me a nickel for every bushel of dandelions. When I got the basket full of dandelions, I called my father to come out and trample down the dandelions so that the basket was only half full. And then I would tell them when I had a full basket. Then usually my father or mother would come and trample down the dandelions. It was a long hard time to fill that basket. They paid me a nickel for all that work.

"When I was in medical school, I met a girl living in Milwaukee. She had the same kind of parents that I had. We fell in love and got secretly married. She didn't dare tell her folks and I didn't dare tell my folks. Her father and mother died and my father died. My father left me independently wealthy and mother is independently wealthy. My wife is independently wealthy, but that hasn't helped at all.

"I got through my internship, and Mother notified me that I was to practice in a certain suburb. She rented the office, and she hired a very competent nurse to run the office. She ran that office. All I did was do the physical examinations, medical histories and write prescriptions. She would take the prescriptions. She explained them to the patient and she would give them a second appointment. I just did the work. She ran the office; she ran me.

"I always wet my pants several times a day. I always had to keep extra work pants in my office. But, I like medicine.

"My wife is quite social. I've never learned to be social. My wife likes to entertain. If I happen to come home when there is a houseful of guests, I just walk straight through the room and down to the basement. My hobby is growing orchids. I will stay there until I am sure that the last guest has left.

"I eat breakfast at home; sometimes in a restaurant. I am very neurotic about that. I can't stand staying in a restaurant very long. I can't stand to go to a restaurant where there are waitresses. I have to have male waiters. To be sure that I don't stay too long in a restaurant, I order mashed potatoes in one restaurant, and eat them in a hurry. Then I go to another restaurant and order a pork chop, and eat it as fast as I can. Then I go to another restaurant and order a vegetable, bread and milk, and eat fast and leave. If I want dessert, I go to another place with a male waiter.

"We never celebrate Thanksgiving Day or Christmas. To avoid Christmas, I take my family to Sun Valley, Idaho. My wife and my daughter like to ski where the other people ski. I get out early in the morning and I ski where nobody else skis. I come home after dark. There are some places that you can eat where there are only male waiters.

"My mother has a summer cabin on the lake. She bought one for me and my wife and daughter. She always calls the office and tells me when to take my vacation. She always takes her vacation at the same time.

"Every morning, my mother comes over and tells my wife what to have for breakfast, lunch and dinner. She tells me what days I can go swimming, what days I can go sailing, what days I can go canoeing, and what days I can go fishing. And I haven't got the courage to stand up against my mother, and neither has my wife, because her parents treated her the same way. But, they are dead. Now, she is living the kind of life she likes more, except for the handicap that I am.

"I like to play the cello and I am really very good at it. But the only way I can play the cello is to go to my bedroom and lock the door and play. My wife and daughter listen outside the door.

"Everyday my mother calls up and talks to me for an hour about the daily events. I have to write her a ten-page letter twice a week. She runs me, and I just can't stand it anymore.

"I came to Phoenix, bought a house and lot. I told my wife I was retiring from medical practice and that we were going to live in Phoenix. She felt quite bad because I didn't let her choose the house and lot. I was afraid to tell her about it. I've been afraid all my life."

I said, "Well, Ralph, before I take you on as a patient, I'll have to talk with your wife and to your daughter. How old is your daughter?" He said, "Twenty-one." I said, "All right, send in your wife tomorrow, and your daughter the next day."

I interviewed them and the wife confirmed all that her husband said. She added that he always took his daughter out to a restaurant for Thanksgiving dinner because Ralph couldn't stand the social drain of Thanksgiving dinner. She confirmed that they never had a Christmas, nor a Christmas tree, nor a Christmas present.

The daughter came in and said, "I love my daddy. He is very soft and gentle—a kind man. But he has never given me a kiss or a hug or told me that he loved me. He has never given me a birthday present, or a Christmas present, or a Valentine's card, or an Easter card. He is just a soft, gentle, kind man who seems to be afraid of everything except his patients. His patients like him. He does good medical work. I wish I had a daddy."

I saw Ralph. I said, "Your wife and your daughter corroborated your story and gave a few more details." So I told Ralph, "I'm going to handle you the way I handled Dr. Mead. I told him he couldn't give us a zero because the autopsy wasn't done.

I watched him give us a grade of 50 because the autopsy had not yet been done. Fortunately, he gave us a grade of A after the autopsy was done. I'm going to treat you the same way, Ralph.

"Now the first thing I'm going to do to you, Ralph, is stop you wetting your pants. Now this is an early summer. I've looked over your home and your lot. There are plenty of dandelions on it. I explained to your wife to get a trowel and a bushel basket. You put on an old pair of black trousers. You go out at 8:00 and sit down on the lawn and start digging up dandelions. There are lots of them there, Ralph. You will sit on the lawn from eight in the morning until six at night. Your wife will furnish you with two gallons of good lemonade and salt pills. Now you know how many salt pills you will have to take, and you are going to drink the full two gallons of lemonade. Everything you need to urinate you just sit there and urinate on the ground. Now, Phoenix is a small town (at that time it was), and people are friendly. The passersby will want to stop and talk with you and watch you dig out the dandelions. And you will be drinking lemonade and urinating, and you are going to sit there all day."

Ralph did as he was told. He wore a big straw hat to protect himself from the sun. He dug dandelions. His wife dumped the basket for him. That night he took a bath and went to bed. The next morning he put on a pair of trousers. He went to the neighbors and took out their dandelions all day, getting up and going to his own bathroom and relieving himself.

So, he stopped having any more wet trousers from just that one utterly penal condition. He got his fill of wet pants. He learned to *live*, wearing wet pants and talking to strangers. So he knew he could *live*.

Then Ralph came to see me regularly and discuss things. One day I told Ralph, "You have a peculiar way of shopping. You buy your own shirts, suits and shoes. You do it by walking in the store and saying, 'I'll take that shirt (Erickson points and looks away from where he is pointing), and send it C.O.D.' When you get home, you look at the neckband to see if it is the right size. If it isn't you send it back. You walk in and say, 'I'll take that shirt,' (Erickson points and looks away) until you get a shirt that fits you. You buy your suits by walking in and saying, 'I'll take that suit. Send it C.O.D.' " He bought his shoes the same way.

I said, "Now, you really don't know how to shop. So I am going to take you shopping. Either you appear at my office or I will pick you up at your home. We are going to go shopping on Tuesday."

Ralph came over and said, "Are you sure you want to do this today?" I said, "Yes. We are going to take plenty of time and we will have plenty of opportunity to do the shopping."

Ralph shuddered when he saw what store I stopped at. As we entered the store, a very beautiful clerk approached us and said, "Good morning, Dr. Erickson, and you must be Dr. Stevenson. I am sure that you will want to buy some underthings for your wife." And she offered to model panties, bras, slips, stockings, and she put on a big sales pitch.

Ralph acted undecided about the panties he was about to buy his wife and daughter. She said, "Doctor, black lace panties are really very beautiful. All women like to wear black lace panties. See, I like to wear them." She hauled up her dress. Ralph tried to look away. He caught my eye and saw that I was looking with pleasure on those black lace panties, so Ralph looked.

She drew back her blouse and showed her bra and offered to model bras, slips and stockings. She showed him how nicely her stockings fit. Poor Ralph knew that the only way he could get out of the store was by looking at and feeling the goods, and making a choice.

Ralph didn't think about the size. He had made all his purchases. In 1950, $200 worth of underthings was quite a pile of underthings. He had all of them gift wrapped and sent to his home. His wife and daughter looked them over and found practically nothing of their size. So, they gave the underthings to the Salvation Army or the Goodwill. They went downtown and bought duplicates that did fit them.

Then I hold Ralph, "There is another big step that you have got to make. I don't think that you have ever taken your wife out to see the sunrise." Ralph admitted that he hadn't. I said, "On

Sunday, I will take you and your wife out to see the sunrise."
I called at 3:00 a.m. I drove here and there until finally I found
a place at which to watch the sunrise. His wife enjoyed it, and
we both saw to it that Ralph made comments on the colors of the
sunrise. That night Ralph took his wife out to see the sunset. He
wasn't going to let me handle *that*.

Then I told him one day, "You know, Ralph, your peculiar
behavior about restaurants is distressing. You haven't taken your
family out to a restaurant. Unfortunately, next Tuesday, you and
your wife are going to take me and my wife out for prime ribs
for an evening dinner. I assure you, Ralph, that Betty and I will
enjoy being your guests."

On the way to the restaurant, I said, "There are two ways into
the restaurant, Ralph. The front way or the back way. What is
your choice?" And I guessed correctly—Ralph chose the back
way.

As we entered the back way, a very pretty waitress said, "Good
evening, Dr. Erickson, and you must be Dr. Stevenson." She
fastened herself to him to help him off with his coat and hat.
She led him to the table. I picked out the side of the table. She
wanted to know if Ralph felt comfortable in that chair or should
she get another chair. She was a most solicitous waitress—all was
done with good manners and with good taste. She was very, very
solicitous. Ralph didn't know which way to look.

The waitress left us, and Ralph suddenly found that there was
a clock on the wall that he could see. We waited and waited.
Half an hour later the waitress showed up with four trays of
salads. His wife, my wife and I had no difficulty in choosing a
salad. The waitress was very concerned. Ralph looked away and
said, "I'll take that one." (Erickson looks away and points.)

She said, "You haven't even looked at it." She used the tongs
and she picked up each constituent of the salad and explained
what it was. Ralph said, "I'll take it." She said, "But you haven't
looked at the other three salads." So she had him examine all
four salads twice before she let him choose his salad.

Then she said, "I have four different dressings." She explained
them very carefully to Ralph and she made him choose his salad

dressing. But she went through the list to make sure that he knew what choice he had. She said, "Now, how about this, how about this, how about that?" She waltzed through the choice of salad dressings twice before she let him make his choice. Then she served the salad; they were excellent salads.

Then another hour passed and Ralph kept looking at that clock the whole hour, until finally she brought the menu around. The three of us had no trouble selecting our dinner. But that waitress made certain that Ralph thought about every item on the menu. She discussed the merits of each possible dish and finally she let him choose the roast prime rib of beef. Ralph heaved a sigh of relief. Then the waitress pointed out, "How do you want it done? Well done, very well done, medium well done, rare, medium rare or very rare? Do you want much fat or just a little?"

Poor Ralph—it was a long ordeal selecting exactly what kind of roast beef. Then she came to potatoes. She offered him I don't know how many different choices of potatoes. Finally he agreed on baked potatoes. George found out about the butter, sour cream and chives. He changed his mind several times. The same on every other dish. The meal was served. The other three of us enjoyed our dinner.

The waitress stood at Ralph's side and she kept asking him if he enjoyed this and if he enjoyed that. She said, "Now look at me, please, when you answer." And she told jokes. She was an old family friend. Poor Ralph. Finally, she had to tell him, "You haven't cleaned up your plate." And she made him clean up the plate.

Then when he finished she said, "Did you like your dinner very much, Dr. Stevenson?" He said, "Yes." She said, "Well, say so." He said, "I liked my dinner very much." She said, "Did you like it very, very much?" Ralph saw me staring and he knew he had no choice so he told her he had enjoyed it very, very much. Then she said, "Did you enjoy it very, very, very much?" And Ralph told her he enjoyed it very, very, very much.

She heaved a sigh of relief and said, "I'm so glad you enjoyed it very, very, very much. This restaurant has a rule. When a patron enjoys his dinner very, very, very much, he has to kiss the chef. She's very fat. There are two ways of going to the kitchen: You can go the front way, but there is a little tunnel that we call going the back way. I can lead you either way. Now, do you want to go the front way or the back way? If we go the back way we don't have to go all the way to the kitchen."

Ralph looked at me and looked away and said, "I'll go the back way." She said, "Thank you, Dr. Stevenson. Your willingness to go the back way is enough reward. Now let me help you on with your hat and coat and come back and see us again."

The next night Ralph took his wife and daughter to the same restaurant. And the same waitress waited on them with absolutely correct professional waitress behavior. I had coached that waitress very well. After that, Ralph would take his family to the restaurant and feel very comfortable.

Then I said, "Ralph, you know your wife and daughter find it very tiresome living in Phoenix with all this heat and nothing to do. And your wife likes to dance." Ralph said, "I don't know how." I said, "I was afraid of that, Ralph. I made arrangements with some very beautiful young girls to teach you how to dance. Of course, your wife has volunteered, but I think maybe you would prefer the beautiful young girls." He said, "I'll let my wife teach me."

Ralph found out that he liked square dancing. He went square dancing with his wife every night. He joined all the square dancing clubs then in Phoenix. He even sent me through the mail a postcard, a picture postcard. It was a very daring thing for him to do. The picture on the postcard was two outdoor privies—one labeled "Cowboys" and the other labeled "Cowbelles."

Ralph came to me and said, "You know, I've always had an ambition to call a square dance. Do you think it would be all right for me to call a square dance?" I said, "Yes, Ralph. It is an excellent ambition. I think that you would enjoy it. While you are enjoying that, I think, in return, for their very special enjoyment, you will play your cello for your wife and daughter so that they don't have to stand outside your locked bedroom door to hear you play the cello." Ralph agreed to give a public concert for his wife and daughter, and he called many a square dance. He even took part in a play given by a square dance club.

Then I told Ralph, "There is still another big hurdle for you to make in your recovery. You are doing well so far. Now, while you have been in Phoenix, your mother has called you twice a week and you've explained for an hour on each call everything that is going on. And your mother writes you from two to four long letters each week. You have to answer her letters in addition to the phone calls and write at least ten pages to her per week."

Now we have got to change that. I am going to cut the umbilical cord for you. So you buy a picnic table, set it up in your front yard. Get an empty whiskey bottle with the label showing and another whiskey bottle, half-full, with a colorful label on it. You buy a straw hat and you will sit in your front yard, your bare feet on the table, one whiskey bottle lying on its side, label apparent, another whiskey bottle, label apparent, upright and half-full. You will wear your hat tipped to one side. You'll be lolling in the chair, your eyes half-closed. Your wife will color your nose red with rouge and your cheeks with rouge. We will take a nice color photograph of that, and mail it to your mother." He never got another phone call from his mother, never a letter.

One summer, Ralph wrote to his mother, "Laura, Carol and I are going to take our vacation in the cabin on the lake at such-and-such dates." They went, and mother didn't show up. They had a nice vacation.

One day the daughter came to me and said, "You know, it is getting pretty close to Christmas. Daddy has never given me a Christmas gift, or a birthday gift or a birthday card, a birthday kiss or anything. I would like to see a Christmas tree at my home."

I told his wife, "I'm too busy to purchase a Christmas tree with Ralph. I am too busy to help him decorate it. Now you go ahead and get a Christmas tree and decorate it and buy all the presents you want for yourself and what you want for your daughter and what you want for Ralph. Ralph won't ask you any questions

when he sees that Christmas tree. He will just shudder when
he sees the packages under it because he will know that I am
behind it in some way."

On Christmas Eve, Mrs. Erickson, my oldest son and I went
over. I said, "Ralph, some people have a tradition of opening
their Christmas gifts on Christmas Eve. The Ericksons have the
tradition of opening gifts on Christmas day. So, let's start your
tradition on Christmas Eve. Now, Ralph, there is only one way
to give a present at Christmas time. You pick it up from under
the tree (Erickson gestures) and you hand it to the recipient.
You call the recipient by name; you wish the recipient a Merry
Christmas and give her a kiss."

Ralph reluctantly approached the tree. I had the gifts arranged properly. He picked up the package and he walked over
to his daughter. He looked at the floor and said, "Merry Christmas, Carol," and gave her a kiss on the cheek.

I said, "Carol, is that the right way?" She said, "It isn't. He
gave me a peck on the cheek and you could barely hear him say
'Merry Christmas' or call me by name." I said, "What are you
going to do about it?" Carol said, "Let's give him a demonstration." I said, "I was afraid we would have to do that. That is
why I brought my son. He is your age, he is reasonably good
looking, so you can make your choice between my son and me."
She said, "I choose you, Dr. Erickson."

So she returned the gift that I had picked out, to under the
tree. I walked over to her and said, "Merry Christmas, Carol."
She threw her arms around me and gave me a ten-minute clinger.
Then she said, "Daddy, you weren't watching. Now I will have
to do it all over again." Ralph watched that time.

He picked up the second gift. I had arranged it for his wife.
He looked at his wife. His wife was looking at my son and me.
Ralph walked over to her and said, "Merry Christmas, Laura."
He kissed her on the mouth. The rest of the presents were given
properly. (Erickson laughs.)

And then Carol came to me and said, "I'm going to get married. Daddy used to go to every wedding of his patients. At
every wedding, he always starts out crying. He bawls so loud

that you can hear him all through the church. I want to be married in church. I don't want my daddy bawling his head off like a calf and disturbing everybody with his crying. Can you stop it?"

I said, "Yes, I can. Just tell your mother to sit on the aisle side of the pew in the church. Ralph is to sit to her left. I will sit to the left of your father."

Ralph looked surprised when I joined him and his wife and family in the pew. I got hold of Ralph's hand, his finger, and I put the Chinese lock on his fingers. I made it a very painful experience. (Erickson demonstrates holding the knuckles of the first two digits of his forefinger and pressing tightly.) Then as the wedding proceeded, as soon as Ralph's face began to become distorted with signs of crying, I squeezed his fingers and his crying look was replaced by an angry look. The wedding went off very quietly.

I said, "Now, Carol is having her wedding reception in the church yard. And, Ralph, you and I can walk hand-in-hand, or do you think you can make it on your own?" Ralph said, "I'll make it on my own." And he did.

Ralph planned a house for his wife in Apache Junction where she picked the place. He had a telephone line put in, and the house built according to his wife's specifications.

Before the house was completed, Ralph came to see me and he said, "The past two months I have had a bladder pain." I said, "Ralph, at your age, with a bladder pain for two months—you know you should have come to see me before." He said, "Yes, I know I should have come. I knew that you would tell me to see a doctor. I don't want to see one." I said, "Give me a description of that pain." Ralph gave me an absolutely perfect description of the pain. I said, "Ralph, I hope that it is a benign tumor. I think that you have a malignancy of the prostate. I want you to see a urologist." Ralph said, "I am not going to see a urologist. And you can't make me." I said, "I will take it up with your wife and daughter." He said, "That's all right. I am not going to see a urologist."

After sufficient pleading by his wife and daughter for some

weeks, he consented to see a urologist. Then he said, "But not in Phoenix." I said, "Where are you willing to go?" He said, "Well, I might go to Mayo." I said, "How will you travel?" He said, "I don't like air travel." I said, "That means a train or a bus. A bus has too many stops and you can change your mind, so I suggest you use a train. Now, Ralph, do I have to send some pretty nurses with you to make sure you get to Mayo, or will you give me your word you will go there alone?" Ralph sighed and said, "I will give you my word to go alone."

Actually he took a plane from Chicago to Rochester, Minnesota, and he called me from Mayo to tell me he was there. So I called back to find out from Mayo if he was really there. He was.

They examined him and operated on him. They told him, "If you had only come to us two months earlier, we could have saved your life. Our best guess is that you have about two more years to live—so live happily, as much as you can."

Ralph came back and told me, "I should have told you in the first place, because I knew that you would make me go. I've got two more years of life left. Have you any suggestions?" I said, "Hurry up in building that house. At least you can see it completed. And be sure you have every social pleasure that is possible, go out to dinner, go to dances."

Ralph was sick enough in the last months of his life to go to bed. It took about a month for him to die then. I came over to see him on his deathbed. A practical nurse was taking care of him. As I entered the room, she turned and looked and said, "Oh, it is you, Dr. Erickson. I am not going to stay in this room with *you*." She turned and walked out.

Ralph said, "Why does she treat you that way?" I said, "She has good reason. Don't worry about it. I will handle the situation." We conversed for awhile and I said goodbye to Ralph. He said goodbye to me. He thanked me for giving him several very nice years of life which he really enjoyed living. He added honestly, "I didn't like the way you did some of the things."

As for that practical nurse, about two months later she called me and said, "Dr. Erickson, I was the practical nurse with Dr. Stevenson. I saw you come in the room and said I wouldn't stay in the room with you. Do you remember why?" I said, "Yes. A long time ago, I told you, 'Your husband makes a good living as a machinist. You teach school all year and in the summers you work as a practical nurse. All your earnings are spent paying your income tax, all the living expenses and your husband's income tax, and you pay his withholding tax. And you do all that on your own earnings.' You had a three-year-old son, when I first saw you.

"You told me how your husband had bought a car and was dissatisfied with it. And because he was a machinist, he undertook to build the super, super car of the future. I told you then your husband spends every spare hour, every evening, every holiday, every Sunday, working on that super, super car and spending all of his income, buying new parts and discarding them; buying more and more, and getting dissatisfied with them; buying a license for that car each year so he can drive it around the block occasionally if the engine is in good condition. He bought new bodies, new frames, new hoods, new engines, new everything.

"I told you years ago, when I first saw you, that your son, growing up in that kind of home where mother was hard put to support the family, and who allowed her husband to waste all his money building a super, super car, spending every spare minute of his waking hours on that car . . . that your three-year-old boy would grow up and be arrested for a crime relating to automobiles before he was 15 years old."

She said, "Yes, that is the story. I was so angry that I refused to pay your fee. I burned with anger all these years. My son will be 15 years old next month. He has been arrested for joyriding. He was put on probation. Now he has stolen a car and broken probation. He won't be 15 until next month. I will put a check in the mail to pay for what I owe you."

I said, "Don't bother. You have paid for your lesson very dearly. I would like to give you some more advice. When does your husband have to renew his driver's license?" She said, "This month." I said, "I thought so. I noted that in your record. Now this time, let him drive his super, super car of the future to the auto licensing building to take his driver's examination. Don't loan him your car."

So her husband went to get his driver's license renewed. He passed the written test. The inspector took him outside to give him his road test. When they walked toward his car, the inspector said, "You drove that thing here?" He walked all around it, lifted the hood and looked at it. He thoroughly looked and examined the car. He opened the trunk door and called another inspector. They really examined the appearance of that super car.

They had a conference and they approached him and said, "If we had seen you drive that car to this parking lot, we would have given you a ticket. But we didn't see you do it. But you are not going to drive that car on the streets. We are going to notify the city police. The only thing you can do is call a towing company. We recommend that you have them tow it to the city dump or sell it to them for salvage." The man persuaded the towing company to buy the car for salvage.

After being taken to his home, he told his wife, "I'm sorry." He explained the situation and added again, "I'm sorry. From now on I'm going to give you my paycheck and I will let you buy a car for me to go to work in. I am going to give up my ambition."

She said bitterly, "Along with your super car that you are giving up, you are giving up our son. I'll buy you a car and I'll take your paycheck weekly."

(Erickson addresses group.) Isn't that a horrible story?

Sid: What was there about the super car that made it so obnoxious?

E: The chassis didn't fit the frame. The engine was much too large for a car of that type. The carburetor wasn't right. The inspectors were furious. They said it was a hazard. They asked how many miles he had driven it. It wasn't very far—two miles. They said it would probably last until the towing company got it to the dumping grounds.

Sid: You have seen the car? You guessed that they would feel that way?

E: That is what the inspector told him and he told his wife. She told me.

Sid: But, you told his wife to have him drive his car down for the test.

E: Yes.

Sid: You knew something was going to happen.

E: Because she told me how many different sets of fenders he had bought and they never fit the hood. So he purchased new hoods which didn't fit the fenders. Then he purchased a chassis that didn't fit the fenders or the hood. A new trunk door that didn't fit the trunk.

Sid: I see.

E: I never saw her again except that one very bitter conversation which summarized what the inspector said, what they advised, and what had ensued.

There are some people you can't help. You can try.

The shock technique I tried on her was wrong. I told her the consequences of what she was doing. She should have known that when her husband had a salary that was larger than hers, he should pay his own withholding tax, his own income tax. But she paid that, and that seemed to me to be a situation requiring shock therapy. Obviously, she couldn't even see that paying his withholding tax and his income tax was wrong.

Sid: What would have been a better kind of therapy do you suppose?

E: I know that I couldn't have approched that man. He was obsessed with the idea of a super, super car of the future. He was proud of his ability as a machinist. There was no way of taking that from him, and she wouldn't respond to the bald truth. He should be supporting her. She shouldn't be paying his withholding tax and income tax and paying for the state license on his car and loaning him her car to take his driving test over the years.

How blind can a woman be? They can be awfully, awfully blind.

Sid: And a man too. In other words, there was nothing that you could do to open her eyes.

E: I couldn't find any way. I tried—first by being very gentle and then by telling her the straight truth. But, I think that she called me up just because I had been gentle at first with her. When I saw that gentleness had failed, I presented her with the harsh truth. She couldn't take that either.

Oh yes, I had one other call from her a couple of years later. She said, "I'm not working this summer. I'm taking a vacation."

Now I'll tell you another story. Ralph told me, "My mother's sister lives in Milwaukee. She's 52 years old. She never got married. She's independently wealthy. My aunt has only one interest in life. She goes to the Episcopalian Church on every possible occasion. She has no friends there. She never speaks to anybody. She slips out at the end of the sermon very carefully. She likes me and I like her, but for the last nine months she's been horribly depressed. She has a housekeeper come in every morning and a maid that comes in every morning. They stay all day and do the cooking, the housekeeping and the shopping. She pays the yardman for keeping up the lawn and for shoveling the sidewalk in the wintertime. The housekeeper manages everything.

"My aunt sits around reading her Bible and going to church. She has no friends. She and my mother have quarreled, and they won't speak to each other. I feel too incompetent to visit her very often. I have always been fond of her and now I know she has been profoundly despondent for nine months. On your next trip to Milwaukee to lecture, will you call on her and see what you can do for her?"

I called one evening. The housekeeper and maid had left for the day. I identified myself very carefully. She was very passive, and I demanded a tour of her home. She was sufficiently passive to permit me to have a guided tour. She led me from room to room.

I looked around very carefully for everything. In the sun room I saw three adult African violets of different colors in full bloom, and a potting pot in which she was propagating another African violet.

Now, you know, African violets are very delicate plants. They are very easily killed by the slightest amount of neglect.

When I saw those three African violets of different colors I said, "I'm going to give you some medical orders, and I want them carried out. Now you understand that. Will you agree that you will carry them out?" She passively agreed. Then I said, "Tomorrow you send your housekeeper to a nursery or a florist and you get African violets of all different hues." I think at that time there were 13 different hues of African violets. I said, "Those will be *your* African violets and you are going to take good care of them. That's a medical order.

"Then you tell your housekeeper also to purchase 200 gift flower pots and 50 potting pots and potting soil. I want you to break off a leaf from each of your African violets and plant it in potting pots and grow additional mature African violets." They propagate by planting the leaf.

I said, "And when you have an adequate supply of African violets, I want you to send one to every baby that's born in any family in your church. I want you to send an African violet to the family of every baby christened in your church. I want you to send a gift adult African violet to everyone who is sick in your church. When a girl announces her engagement, I want you to send her an African violet. When they get married, I want you to send African violets. In case of death, you send a condolence card with an African violet. And the church bazaars—contribute a dozen or a score of African violets for sale." I knew at one time she had 200 adult African violets in her home.

Anybody that takes care of 200 African violets is too busy to be depressed. (General laughter.) She died in her seventies with the title of "The African Violet Queen of Milwaukee." I saw her only once. (Erickson laughs.)

Sid: With a lot of friends too, I'm sure.

E: Yes, she certainly had friends of all ages. When a child gets sick and gets a beautiful flowerpot with a beautiful plant in it, she's made a friend of that child. The parents are going to be so pleased, they're going to have the child thank her. So she was kept busy over 20 years. I think that was the important thing— not insight into her past, or insight into her single state.

Sid: Doing.

E: Doing. And doing something that was social. But she didn't realize how much of a social thing it was. She just got caught up. That was another thing for which Ralph was very grateful.

A rancher brought his wife in to see me. He said, "She's been depressed and suicidal for nine whole months. She's got arthritis. We haven't been married very long. She developed severe arthritis and she has gone to the orthopedic surgeon for therapy. I've taken her to psychiatrists for psychotherapy. They all recommended electric shock or insulin shock when she's in her fifties.

"She wants to have a baby and the orthopedist told her, 'Getting pregnant may make your arthritis worse and I would advise against it since you are already sufficiently handicapped.' She went to an obstetrician who said, 'I wouldn't advise a pregnancy. You are very greatly handicapped and the arthritis may get worse. You may be unable to deliver the baby.' "

Her husband brought her in to see me, carrying her. I let her tell me her story. She said pregnancy was worth more to her than life. The husband said, "I have to keep every sharp knife out of her reach." Because a suicidal patient will commit suicide despite your care—because there are many delays that can occur before suicide happens.

I said, "Now madam, you say that a pregnancy is more important to you than your life. The obstetrician advises against it. The orthopedic surgeon advises against it. Your psychiatrists have, also. My advice is: Get pregnant as soon as you can. If your arthritis gets worse, you stay in bed and you can enjoy your pregnancy. Now when it comes time to deliver, you can have a caesarean section. There is no law against it. It's the sensible thing to do."

So she promptly got pregnant and her arthritis improved. She lost her depression. It was a very happy nine-month pregnancy. She delivered the baby without incident and she really enjoyed Cynthia, the name she gave the baby. Her husband was very happy.

Unfortunately, at the age of six months, Cynthia died of crib death. After some months, her husband brought her in and said, "She's worse than ever." I asked the woman about it. She said,

"I just want to die. I've got no reason for living." Very harshly and meticulously I said, "Woman, how can you be so stupid? For nine long months you had the happiest time of your life. You want to kill yourself and destroy those memories? That's wrong. For six long delightful months you enjoyed Cynthia. Are you going to destroy those memories? I think it's criminally wrong.

"So your husband will take you home and get you an eucalyptus sapling. You tell him where to plant it. Eucalyptus trees grow very rapidly in Arizona. I want you to name that eucalyptus sapling, 'Cynthia.' I want you to watch Cynthia grow. I want you to look forward to the day when you can sit in the shade of Cynthia."

I went out a year later to see her. The sapling had grown very rapidly. (I had one at least 60 feet tall in my backyard, and it was only six years old.) She welcomed me. She was no longer confined to bed or a chair. She was walking around greatly improved in her arthritis. She had flower beds that occupied more space than this entire building does. She showed me all around her flower beds. She showed me all different kinds of flowers. She gave me an armful of sweetpeas to bring home.

Patients often can't think for themselves. You can start them thinking in some good reality way. Every flower she grew reminded her of Cynthia, as did the eucalyptus tree that I named Cynthia.

I've used that program in a lot of cases. I had a man who worked for Reynolds Aluminum, who worked and suffered a severe backache. I got him to discuss his pain, his family life, the hardness of the job, the fact that he looked forward to having his own home, a dream home. He built a house according to his dream plans to please his wife, but that house took every cent he ever managed to save and the mortgage on it was a terrible burden on him. He told me the thing he felt worst about was that since boyhood he had dreamed of a house of his own with a white picket fence around it. He said, "I can't afford to buy another piece of lumber and my back aches too much to put in time building a picket fence, and I can't afford it. I wanted it to be painted white and that dream house isn't satisfying to me. I come home from work and sitting in my rocking chair, I lean back and that's the only relief I get. If I sit at the table, my back begins to hurt."

I said, "I'll have to see you another time but first I want you to see a friend of mine, a rheumatologist. The rheumatologist owes me a lot of money and I'll tell him not to charge you. We'll put it against the account he owes me."

The rheumatologist was a very capable man. He examined the man very carefully and said, "There is no real organic pathology. I think the man feels the burden of life too heavy on his back." He sent the man back to me.

I said, "You can't afford to buy enough lumber for a picket fence around your house and the big lot that you have. And you've dreamed of that for many long years. Now I think you could enjoy going to Beacon's Storage Warehouse. They have a lot of crated furniture in there and they uncrate it and throw a lot of secondhand lumber into the backyard. There are various other places in town, furniture places, where things come in that are crated or in big boxes. I think you'll enjoy going through those backyards and finding the lumber you need for your picket fence. And whitewash is very cheap. You can have a white picket fence all around your yard, and you can enjoy that picket fence. And you could enjoy whitewashing it. Whitewash won't cost you very much. Of course, you'll have to renew it, but you'll be working steadily saving money. Then you'll have your dream house with the white picket fence." He found a lot of second-hand lumber in Beacon's warehouse and various furniture stores and he got his picket fence. Well, why not?

My son Bert, when he lived in Phoenix, said he wanted to earn some money to help buy machinery for his farm. One firm he worked for got in material by the truckload that was always crated in birch lumber. He assured his employer he would stack that waste lumber or do whatever the man wanted him to do with it. Then his employer said, "It will save money if you take it to the dumping ground." Bert said, "I'll try to find a use for it myself." So he built a house with birch lumber. And he built a camper that he put on his truck, and he took his family for a tour of the Rocky Mountain States. I believe that people should work.

Here's another example: A man advertised that he had 12,000 adult orange trees that he had allowed to die. They had been dead for a number of years. A realtor came along and offered to buy all that acreage of orange trees. He advertised 12,000 adult orange trees to anybody who would come and cut them down. It was broadcast over the TV news stations, but nobody showed up.

Now if trees die out and don't crack, then you've got cured lumber there. And orange wood is very desirable in the furniture industry. Twelve thousand trunks of adult orange trees could have been a fortune to anybody who really wanted to get some money. Because you could take a chain saw—it's hard work —but you could take a chain saw and you could cut about a 1,000 trees in a day, or maybe 500. Cut off the tops and cut them off at ground level, and stack those logs. Then you'd have a valuable bit of lumber to sell to a furniture factory. In spite of six months' advertising, he finally had to set fire to the dead orange trees.

If my son had been available, I would have sent him down with a chain saw and had him rent a truck.

As soon as the depression began to make itself felt thoroughly, quite a number of people would comb the alleys to get tin cans, bottles and cast-off lumber. Some would make as much as a few hundred dollars a week where formerly they had been on welfare.

Sid: Do you have anyway that works in getting people away from collecting insurance? I have a back injury patient like the one that you mentioned. I used hypnosis to get the reason for his pain. He finally came up with "the smell of paint." And then he got into a whole anger rap against his former bosses who had mistreated him for many, many years, and finally fired him when he was in the hospital after an injury. He said, "The insurance company treats me very well. It's a wonderful insurance company." It looks now as if he's ready to stay on that insurance for the rest of his life.

E: I know, I had a lot of those patients.

Sid: Is there any way of getting them off?

E: You question them very carefully about boyhood dreams, boyhood desires, and what they really like to do. Just as with the man with the backache. It was an old-burden backache. He wanted a dream house with a white picket fence.

Sid: OK. Good.

E: I have a friend in Portland, Oregon, named Don. I spent several days in his home while on a lecture trip. He's a plastic surgeon and he had a gift for using hypnosis. One night he was called out on an emergency. Some speeder had been thrown out of his car and slid on his face for about 20 feet on a gravel road. His face was a horrible mess. He came to the hospital suffering a great deal of pain.

Don said, "You know, before I can give you an anesthetic, I've got to wash your face and have you ever heard of violins?" The patient said, "I'm hurting. I don't want to hear about violins."

Don said, "The way to make a violin is this. You're out driving your car and you look around and you see an old dead tree, a stump, or some cast-off lumber. You examine it curiously. Then you take sandpaper and planes. You then sit down and sandpaper it and you stain it. You may make violins and cellos." Don went into great, elaborate detail.

The patient kept on saying, "I don't want to hear about violins. Why don't you get to work on my face." Don cheerfully went on talking about violins. He told how he won a national championship as a country music violinist; how he entered fiddling contests all over the United States and won championships. He spoke about myrtlewood, other kinds of wood, the grain of wood, how it takes the strain.

The patient said, "When are you going to get to work on my face?" Don said, "Well, first I've got to wash your face and pick out some of the gravel. Do you know this tune of music?" And he kept on boring his patient, boring his pain. Finally Don said to the nurse, "How do you like my work?" The patient said, "Well, you've got my face all sewed up."

Sid: Boring his pain. That's great.

E: He said, "That patient was so surprised." The patient said, "What can I do to repay you?" Don said, "You can remember me."

Sid: What?

E: "You can remember me." Sometime later, my friend got a block of wood out of which he made some cellos and violins. (When you seem to be doing damn fool things, it takes your patient's mind off his pain.) And Don is very perfect at that. (To group.) What time is it, please.

Sid: 4:22.

E: Shame on you—you let me overwork again. My speech is getting thicker and thicker. But, you know, a tape recorder never pays any attention to my speech defect. It records my speech and plays it back very well. It doesn't record defects. I seem to have a good voice on a tape recorder.

Sid: Excellent.

Woman: Thank you.

Siegfried: Tomorrow there is no session. Tomorrow is Saturday.

E: That is rest time for me. It takes about two days to recover. (General laughter.) And, Sidney?

Sid: Yes?

E: As we looked over the group, I hope that you were attentive. Because when you watch a group of students when you are lecturing to them, you see evidence of subliminal speech.

Sid: Oh, yes. I saw many of them. I felt some in myself too. You mean actual subliminal speech and not just movements?

E: Subliminal speech and movements.

Sid: Yes. I am more aware of the movements.

E: And it is surprising how many girls are cowards.

Sid: Cowards? In what sense?

E: When you look at your students from time to time, you see a certain facial expression. My long experience tells me what those facial expressions mean. They are usually too cowardly to vocalize them or to act upon them.

Sid: Um-hmm.

E: (To one woman.) I read your face.

Woman: You did? (Laughter.)

People say their "Thank you's" to Dr. Erickson and ask him to autograph books, and then they leave.

APPENDIX:
COMMENTARY ON THE INDUCTIONS
WITH SALLY AND ROSA

❖❖❖

This appendix contains a record of a discussion between Erickson and myself of the inductions that Erickson did with Sally and Rosa on Tuesday. Erickson and I watched the inductions on videotape and turned off the tape frequently to discuss aspects of Erickson's work.

The discussion occurred on two separate days—January 30 and February 3, 1980. The actual inductions were performed six months earlier.

For those interested in hypnosis, it would be a valuable exercise to study the inductions that appear in the text and infer what Erickson was actually doing in the inductions. Then the reader can compare his inferences with the discussion that appears in the following Appendix. As mentioned in the introduction, it would take an astute observer to get more than 50% of the subtle communication forms that Erickson used to influence Sally and Rosa.

Z: *It's Tuesday, the second day of the workshop and Sally was not there the first day. It's about 15 minutes into the session when she comes in the office door. You're telling the story of the bed-wetter who gave you the gift of the purple yarn octopus. Sally comes in late and you immediately use her for a subject. It's an excellent induction. Very, very nice.*

E: Why are you hiding back there? (E. turns and addresses Sally.)

S: I was waiting for a good time to interrupt. Let's see if I can find a seat.

E: I can pick up at any point; so come in and find a seat.

S: Is there a seat back there?

E: Can't that seat be shoved over? (E. indicates that Rosa, who is sitting in the green chair next to E., is to move her seat over to her left to make room for Sally.) You can put another chair right here. (E. points to a place directly to his left.) Hand her a chair. (A male sets up a folding chair just to the left of E. Sally sits down next to E. and crosses her legs toward him.)

E: You don't need to cross your legs.

S: (Uncrosses her legs and laughs.) I thought you might comment on that.

E: Our foreign visitors may not know, "A dillar, a dollar, a ten o'clock scholar," but you know that rhyme, don't you?

S: No.

E: *Did you get the significance of "A dillar, a dollar?"*

Z: *Yes, I did. It's excellent. "A dillar, a dollar, a ten o'clock scholar, what makes you comes so soon. You used to come at ten o'clock and now you come at noon."*

E: *Uh-huh. It evokes childhood memories.*

Z: *Yes, that was lovely. Now you had decided immediately that you were going to use her for a subject.*

E: *Uh-huh.*

Z: *And was that a sort of a punishment for her being late?*

E: *No, I had embarrassed her.*

Z: Yes.

E: And I gave her happy childhood memories when she sat down next to me.

Z: Yes, you sat her there.

E: Uh-huh, and what child in school doesn't want to sit beside the teacher? (E. laughs.)

Z: Well, there are four things about her personality that stand out and you use every one of them very nicely. One, she expresses multiple contradictions. For example, she doesn't want to be seen, and yet she comes in late. She makes herself very obvious by coming in late. A second personality characteristic is that she's a more "one-up" personality. A third characteristic is her need to be very precise and unerring. Thereby, she is noncommittal in her speech. She is noncommittal in a very particular way; you'll realize that immediately. A fourth characteristic is that she is stubborn.

After coming in she points to the back of the room and you have her sit up front. Then she crosses her legs and you say, "You don't need to cross your legs." She laughs and uncrosses her legs, saying, "I thought you might comment on that." It's another expression of contradiction because she doesn't allow herself to be in a "one-down" role verbally, but her body language and the rest of her behavior are more cooperative.

E: She said, "I thought you might comment on that." That's inside her.

Z: I don't follow.

E: "You uncross your legs." That's from outside in. When you uncross them and you comment on them, that's you inside, commenting on your internal behavior.

Z: So she was already internally oriented and was commenting on her own internal behavior. I see.

E: She was expressing her own individual hopes.

Z: (Laughs.) That you would comment on her crossing her legs.

E: Uh-huh.

E: (Incredulous.) You never learned about, "A dillar, a dollar, a ten o'clock scholar?"

S: I don't know the rest of it.
E: Frankly, I don't either. (Sally laughs.)

Z: Now that wasn't true. You did know the rest of it.
E: Uh-huh.
Z: Did you do that to keep your indirect comment on her lateness
unconscious?
E: I quickly agreed with her.
Z: Thereby establishing a commonality.
E: Uh-huh.

E: Are you feeling comfortable?
S: No, actually I walked in in the middle of things and I'm, ... I uh.
E: And I never met you before.
S: Mmm . . . I did see you one time last summer. I came with a
group.
E: Did you go into a trance?
S: I believe so, yeah. (Nods her head.)
E: You don't know.
S: I believe so. (S. nods head "yes.")
E: Just a belief?
S: Uh-huh.
E: A belief, and not a reality?
S: It's sort of the same.
E: (Incredulous.) A belief is a reality?
S: Sometimes.
E: Sometimes. Is this belief of yours, that you went into a trance, a
reality or a belief? (Sally laughs, and clears her throat. She seems
embarrassed and self-conscious.)

E: That's an inner struggle with her.
Z: Yes. You asked her if she was in a trance before. On the verbal
level she says she "believes so," but on the nonverbal level she
nods her head, indicating agreement.
E: That's inner response. Let me give you a gross example.
When I was working on the Psychiatric Ward, I got word that
two disturbed patients had come in. I hadn't seen them yet. So
when my medical students arrived, I said, "There are two new

*disturbed patients on Wards C and D. Let's go up and see them."
I kept my cane out of sight. I was wearing white clothes. I opened
the door just a little bit. The patient looked up and said, "I see
you have a white coat. The White House is in Washington, D.C.
Mexico City is the capital of Mexico." You know that. I know
that. Every Tom, Dick and Harry knows that. Those are external
things.*

*The next patient said, "You've got a white coat on. Cripple
Creek is in Colorado." (She couldn't see my cane.) "Yesterday
I saw a snake in the road." Those are internal. Now I had to get
a book and I had to go to where her brother showed me where
the snake had been. I could see the trail of the snake. It took me
16 hours of work.*

*Now that patient had been reading a book on the early days of
Cripple Creek in Colorado. There were miners in Cripple Creek.
The book emphasized that the miners didn't make their fortunes.
They gambled it away. The Chinese laundrymen worked and
slaved and made fortunes.*

*And that was the second day I had my coat on. It was a laundry
problem. That's an internal appraisal.*

*Now what was meant by the track of the snake in the road? I
got a book and read it. The road to Cripple Creek was like a
snake's trail. That's all internal.*

I use external and internal all the time with subjects.

Z: *You mean you focus them external and then internal, external and
then internal?*

E: *Not alternately. I change from time to time.*

Z: *Which disrupts their conscious pattern.*

E: *Yes. And it starts a new pattern.*

Z: *Let's go back to the beginning for a moment. You ask her if she
has been in a trance before. When you ask her that question, she
has to have an internal association. She has to think back to the
time that she was here before. She says, "I believe so, yeah," and
she nods her head. Then you pick up on her style of being noncommittal. On a verbal level she says, "I believe so," and she
nods her head again. Next you play on the words "belief" and
"reality."*

> *She's not willing to be committal on any verbal level. On a verbal level she is not allowing herself to be in a student position. She is not allowing herself to be "one-down" at all verbally. But on a nonverbal level she is more responsive.*

E: *She is, yes. Look. (E. takes a coaster from the top of the desk and holds it next to his chest for a moment. Then he places it down on the edge of the desk.) I suppose you would say I put it there.*

Z: *I suppose so. (Laughs.)*

E: *You see, I'm not committing myself, but I have committed myself.*

Z: *Yes.*

E: *And that's what she did.*

Z: *Yes. Then she has to have some internal association to the meaning of the words "belief" and "reality."*

E: *She is drawing back to let you think she has equated them.*

Z: *Yes. You'll notice that she stays very consistent with her non-committedness.*

E: *Uh-huh.*

S: Does it matter? (Group laughter.)

E: That's another question. My question is, is your belief a belief or a reality?

S: I think that it is probably both.

E: Now a belief may be an unreality and it can be a reality. And your belief is both, an unreality and a reality?

S: No. It's both a belief and reality. (Sally shakes and holds her head.)

E: You mean it is both a belief which could be a reality . . . or an unreality and it is also a reality? Now which is it? (Sally laughs.)

S: I really don't know right now.

E: Well, why did you take so long to tell me that? (Sally laughs.)

Z: *That was the first definite statement that she made. Then when she made that definite statement, you released some of the tension.*

E: *She has her head down.*

Z: *Yes, she has her head down. So, you built up her uncomfortableness by using confusion.*

E: *So she had to escape from it.*

Z: *And the only way she could escape from it was to be definite. You*

*helped create a situation where she would be committal on a
verbal level.*

E: Yes, and in a subdued way.

Z: So that she woud be "one-down."

E: Uh-hum.

S: I don't know that either.

E: Are you feeling comfortable?

S: Oh, I'm feeling better, yeah. (Speaking softly.) I hope that people
here are not bothered by my interruption.

E: You're not feeling self-conscious?

S: Mmm ... I probably would feel better sitting in the back, but ...

E: Out of sight?

S: Out of sight? Well, maybe.

*Z: Here she says, "I hope that people are not bothered by my inter-
ruption." That's the second time that she's made a reference to
her hope that people are not bothered by her coming in late.
Incidentally, the next day, Wednesday, she comes in late. She is
very stubborn.*

E: She justifies it.

*Z: Yes. I see. By coming in late the second day she justifies being late
the first day.*

E: Uh-huh.

*Z: In this interchange she is again talking about her hope that people
are not bothered by her interruption. And yet she makes a point
of bothering people with her interruption by coming in late. It's
another contradiction.*

*Also, there are other contradictions she expresses. Here's Sally
who speaks very softly, almost as if she did not want attention directed towards her, yet on the other hand she comes in late
and directs attention towards her. There are contradictions also
apparent in the way she dresses. She wears a tube top that is
sexy and revealing, but she covers it up by wearing a blouse over
the tube top.*

*And then there's another contradiction I would like to clarify
and get your opinion on. What about this possible contradiction
between being a grownup and being a little girl?*

E: "A dillar, a dollar" made her a little girl.

*Z: You forced her to have an internal association about growing up.
OK.*

*E: Where do little children feel better sitting? In the back of the
room.*

Z: Emphasizing little girl qualities?

E: And she's emphasizing it.

E: What's that?

S: Inconspicious.

E: So you don't like being conspicious?

S: Oh, jeez. (Sally laughs and again seems self-conscious. She puts her
left hand over her mouth as she clears her throat.) No . . . no
. . . uh . . .

E: What does inconspicious mean?

Z: Not being noticed.

E: What else?

Z: I don't know.

E: There is something conspicuous on my desk.

Z: Yes, stands out.

E: Name it.

*Z: Oh, I was looking at the wood carving of the bird and then the
apple doll. (There is a sculptured apple doll of Erickson dressed
in a purple suit that sits on his desk.)*

*E: This pencil is awfully inconspicuous. It's in front too. (He points
to one of a number of pencils that are lying on the top of his
desk.)*

E: Being small.

Z: Being small is being inconspicuous.

*E: Being big is being conspicuous. She was "little girl" after the men-
tion of "A dillar, a dollar," when she interrupted. This is the
second mention of interrupting.*

Z: Right.

*E: That brings back "A dillar, a dollar' which puts her in the school-
girl role where she is little. She comes back the next day and
gets right back into that "little" role again.*

E: And you don't like what I'm doing to you right now.

S: Umm, no, well, I have mixed feelings. I'm flattered by the attention, and I'm curious about what you are saying.

E: (Overlapping.) And you wish to *hell* I would stop. (General laughter.)

S: Umm, mixed feelings. (Nods her head "yes.") If I were just talking to you and hadn't interrupted, that would be one thing, but . . .

E: *And when you speak to a little child and say, "hell," you are emphasizing that you're a grownup, and she is little.*

Z: *I see. It's very nice, because what you do shortly is that you do the formal induction and you elicit associations and develop the idea of being regressed. You build the induction around the idea of being a little girl and thinking about being a big girl. Therefore, things just flow very nicely.*

E: So you're concerned about these people?

S: Well, yes. I, their time here . . .

E: Um-hum.

S: And I walked in on their time.

Z: *This is her third reference to interrupting people. You challenged that in the way you said, "Um-hum." It was suggestive that you had some doubt about her concern for these people.*

E: *Um-hum.*

E: (Looking to the floor.) Now let's lay to rest another firm belief that, in doing psychotherapy, you should make your patients feel at ease and comfortable.

Z: *Here you broke your attention from her for the first time by looking at the floor. You mention the words "rest" and "comfort" so that she has to have association to the idea of rest and comfort.*

E: *Um-hum. And it is said in such a way that there is no way of disputing it.*

Z: *There is absolutely no way of disputing it.*

E: I've done my best to make her feel ill at ease, conspicuous and embarrassed. And (to the group) that's hardly a way to begin a good therapeutic relationship, is it? (E. looks at Sally, takes hold of her right hand at the wrist and lifts it up slowly.) Close your eyes. (She looks at him,' smiles, then looks down at her right hand, and closes her eyes.)

Z: *You focused away from her, and then she defocused. She went off because you weren't talking directly to her anymore. So she went internal.*

E: *Rest and comfort.*

Z: *Yes, you mentioned rest and comfort.*

E: *So a disruption was created which she followed with rest and comfort, because they were internal. I could separate myself from her. But what was she going to do with the "rest and comfort?" She would continue it.*

E: And keep them closed. (E. takes his hand off her wrist, leaving her right hand suspended cataleptically.) Go deeply into a trance. (E. has his fingers around her wrist. Sally's arm drops slightly. E. pushes her arm down in a stepwise manner. E. continues speaking slowly and methodically.)

Z: *Now, she let her hand remain up. But, it looked as if you felt her hand falling. So you took control and you put her hand down, reemphasizing your control.*

E: *Yes. When I put it down, I used the same touch that I used when I lifted it up. (E. demonstrates by lifting Z's arm.) There's an uncertainty in my touch.*

Z: *So that she has to go internal again and focus her attention on figuring out ...*

E: *The internal side.*

E: And feel very comfortable, very much at ease, and really enjoy feeling very comfortable . . . so comfortable . . . you can forget about everything except that wonderful feeling of comfort.

E: *You can forget everything, except comfort.*

Z: *Yes, she came in and you made her feel very uncomfortable. You increased the tension. Then you started seeding ideas about com-*

*fort. Then, you could come back more directly to the idea of
comfort, thereby releasing tension.*

    *Now, there's another thing you start doing here. You move
away from her physically. Then, shortly, you start leaning very
close to her, so close that you would be uncomfortably close to
her. You'll see how close you do come to her. Then here she is,
with her body comfortable, due to the hypnotic suggestions. You
are really leaning in close, yet she has to get some sense of being
comfortable.*

E: *And that's an internal reaction.*

Z: *Yes. There's a tension when you move close, but when she goes
into the trance, her body is comfortable. So are you doing that
so she does not feel that normal internal reaction of discomfort?*

E: *No. I altered the intonation of my voice there and I leaned toward
her and that attracted her attention to my voice.*

Z: *Because of her internal reaction?*

E: *Yes. So no matter where I was, she could go deeper and deeper and
further and further away from me and yet be close to me.*

Z: *Do you mean that she would go further away to get away from that
uncomfortable feeling when you move close?*

E: *No. She would go deeper into trance and then move away from me.
An external reality. So I get myself very close to her and she can
leave reality and still be close to me.*

Z: *Yes, I see. I thought that what you were doing was dealing with
some reaction in her about being uncomfortable being close to
people. Because you move uncomfortably close and then you
suggest feelings of comfort in her body. Thereby you leave her
in a position where she is close to people, and yet her body is
comfortably relaxed.*

E: *But I wanted her to go further away from the others.*

Z: *I see. And close to you.*

E: And after a while, it will seem as if your mind leaves your body
and floats through space and goes back in time. (Pause.)

E: *I removed reality and got her back in time.*

Z: *Yes.*

E: It's no longer 1979, or even '78. And 1975 is in the future. (E. leans close to Sally.) And so is 1970. And time is rolling back.

E: '*And so is nineteen* seventy-five."

Z: *You marked that with your voice and then you moved very close as you said it.*

E: *Yes.*

Z: *Again reinforcing her relationship with you no matter where she is in time and space.*

E: *And so she has an association to my voice.*

Z: *First, you seeded the idea of being a little girl with the nursery rhyme. Then you come back to that by using various hypnotic communication forms so that, again, she would experience herself as a little girl. Now you start doing the induction which is based on what you've already established. So you are slowly revivifying being a little girl and you are doing it in small progressive steps.*

E: Soon it will be 1960, soon 1955 . . . and then you will know it's 1953, and you will know that you are a little girl.

E: *You are going down in years, '60, '55, '53. (E. gestures by slowly moving his head down as he names the years.)*

Z: *And you were moving down as you mentioned the years.*

E: *Now, that's altered locus of voice.*

Z: *And she has some additional association and response to that minimal cue of changing your voice.*

E: *Where do you naturally locate the future? Ahead and beyond.*

Z: *I see. Then the past is below and back.*

E: *That's common learning. Unrecognized learning. Forward and upward for the future. Backwards and downwards for the past.*

E: It's nice being a little girl.

Z: *One additional thing here. You say to her, "You will know that you are a little girl. It's nice being a little girl." You're making statements there that she could construe on two levels. On one level, she could think internally, "Well, have I been 'little girlish' in the way that I normally am in the world?" The other association that she could have is that of being a little girl in the sense of the hypnotic sequence of time that you are talking about.*

E: *I'm talking about time and she isn't going to have time to think about other things such as, "How do I appear in the world?" I am continuing to guide her along.*

E: And maybe you are looking forward to your birthday party, or going somewhere . . . going to visit Grandma . . . or going to visit school.

E: *"Going" is a very powerful word. The goal is not the important thing. It's the feeling—the sense of going, and it makes the goal real.*

Z: *Also, here, you start to use the word "maybe." "Maybe you are looking forward to your birthday." Sally is one-up, so you present her with her possibilities.*

E: *And she takes over the control.*

Z: *Within your hypnotic frame though.*

E: *Yes, within the framework that has been given her. Only she can't analyze that framework.*

Z: *It goes by too fast.*

E: And maybe right *now* you are sitting in the school, watching your teacher.

E: *"Maybe right* now-w-w-w *you are sitting in school." "Now" is present, and I draw it out. It is a long present. "And* now-w-w-w *. . ." There is time for lots of thinking in that "now," but it is limited to now.*

Z: *So, she's going back to the past and then the past becomes "now."*

E: *Yes. An elongated now. So it's a continuous now. You think of today as "now" and it is all day. You don't think of any part of today as past. And so I give that continuation of "now" by saying, "Now-w-w-w . . ."*

Z: *Thereby drawing it out in time. This is very funny because when I do presentations on you and explain your inductions, I explain to people that if they are really good observers and good listeners, they'll only miss about 50% of what is going on. So here I am, and I'm only missing another 50%.*

E: Or maybe you are playing in the yard, in the schoolyard, or maybe it is vacation time. (E. sits back.) And you're really having a good time.

Z: *And that's definite. "And you're really having a good time."*

E: *"Having a good time" means what?*

Z: *She's having a good time back then, which is "now" for her.*

E: *"You're having a good time" doesn't define the time. Whether it's playing jacks, or jumping rope or teeter-tottering. But it is "now-w-w's ..." good time.*

Z: *Which she has to define.*

E: *She has to define it, but she has to define it in the terms of "now."*

Z: *Which is the hypnosis.*

E: *Yes, and school time.*

E: I want you to enjoy being a little girl who is someday going to grow up. (E. leans close to Sally.) And maybe you might like to wonder what you will be when you grow up. Maybe you would like to wonder about what you will be doing when you are a big girl. I wonder if you will like high school, and you can wonder the same thing.

E: *"When you are a big girl." (E. uses a lilting voice.)*

Z: *So you use your voice to create additional pressure that she's "down" and that she is wondering "up" into the future. Your melodic voice is one that you might use talking to a little girl, thereby providing additional suggestions with your intonation.*

E: *Yes.*

Z: *Also, you create some relatedness. "I wonder if you will like high school, and you can wonder the same thing."*

E: And my voice goes everywhere with you and changes into the voices of your parents, your teachers, your playmates and the voices of the wind and of the rain.

Z: *That was elegant. "Your parents, your teachers, your playmates, and the wind and the rain." It's so comforting and it covers everything. It covers so many possibilities—the grownups and the adults, the superego, playmates, the ego, the people that are*

*important to a little girl—and then the wind and the rain, like
the id, the primitive emotions.*

E: *It's very comprehensive. One thing you don't know about me,
Jeff. My father was very poor. I learned to read very rapidly, and
I read an unabridged dictionary. I spent hours and hours reading
that. In grade school, they took intelligence tests on me, and the
teachers were so astonished at my vocabulary.*

*Once in Montana, I walked into a doctor's home for an eve-
ning and I picked up an object and looked at it curiously. He
said, "Do you know what that is?" I said, "Yes, a narwhal tusk."
He said, "How on earth did you know? My grandfather owned
it and I've never found a person who could recognize it."*

*I was seeing the picture of the narwhal in the dictionary and
that tusk all at the same time. And reading the unabridged dictionary, which I read from beginning to end before I was
through with the third grade, gave me a tremendous knowledge
of the meanings of words.*

Z: *All right. Now in this last statement to her, in psychoanalytic
terms, you mention superego functions—parents and teachers.
Then you mention ego—playmates, and then id—the wind and
the rain. And you did that sequentially. You went from the top
to the bottom with some intent of creating an all-inclusiveness,
but it was more than an all-inclusiveness. On other occasions I
have heard you say that phrase that your voice could change, but
I have never heard you say it and add the idea of wind and rain.*

E: *I often do. What does wind sound like to you when you are little?*

Z: *Oh, I don't know. A whistle.*

E: *(E. knocks on the desk slowly and repeatedly a number of times.)
You can recognize this as making sound on this. Wind makes
sound and you can't see the source of the sound anywhere. It's a
very wonderful thing. The sound of the wind.*

Z: *It's there, and yet it is not there.*

E: *It's there but it is coming from nowhere, yet it is there.*

Z: *And so she could have the same association to your voice.*

E: *Yes. And raindrops. You hear them on the leaves of the tree that
you are standing under close by. You hear the sound off the*

leaves on top of the tree. You hear it on top of the roof. They're everywhere. And you've been used to locating sounds because that's awfully important in childhood.

Z: *Coming from nowhere and yet being everywhere.*

E: *And all the childhood wonderment. You watch a two-year-old listening to the wind—the absolute wonderment on his face. His conscious learning is that it takes an object to make a noise. Now here is a noise without an object.*

Z: *And can you say anything about the sequence of going from parents, teachers, playmates to the wind and the rain?*

E: *You're making it all-inclusive. You're using emotional associations to parents, teachers, which is related to going down, down, down.*

Z: *To more primitive or basic emotions.*

E: *Yes, and your subject will use that basic emotion.*

Z: *All right, you broke the chain we were talking about where you were suggesting possibilities such as 'Maybe it's vacation time.'' She could choose internal associations around being a little girl. Then you switch and suggest that your voice could be everywhere with her. Next, you'll see that you come back to those little girl associations where she can make the choices. So it really makes that phrase "My voice goes everywhere with you," stand out.*

E: *Um-hum.*

E: Maybe you are out in the garden, picking flowers, and sometime when you are a great big girl, you are going to meet a lot of people and you will tell them some happy things about when you were a little girl. And the more comfortable you feel, the more like a little girl you feel, because you are a little girl.

E: *I keep lowering my head as I emphasize, "You are a little girl."*

Z: *Again, you emphasize a suggestion by changing the locus of your voice.*

E: *(Lilting voice.) "And sometime you are going to meet a lot of people."*

Z: *When you're grown up. So, you are suggesting . . .*

E: *That she is going to grow up and that she can do it then.*

Z: *And you are suggesting that with your inflection. Also, when you say, "And some time," then you're sitting up tall, and that's associated with the conscious awake state, and again you are emphasizing a suggestion by directing the locus of your voice.*

E: *Um-hum.*

E: Now I don't know where you live, but you might like to go barefoot. You might like to sit in your swimming pool and dangle your feet in the water and you wish you could swim. (Sally smiles a little bit.) And would you like your favorite candy to eat right now? (Sally smiles and nods slowly.) Here it is and now you *feel* it in your mouth and enjoy it. (E. touches her hand as if he had given her something. Long pause. E. sits back.)

Z: *Now this was wonderful. Here you give her some alternatives that she can reject. "You might like to go barefoot. You might like to sit in your swimming pool, and wish you could swim." Then you come back to this idea, "Would you like your favorite candy to eat right now?"*

And then what does every little girl learn about candy? Every little girl learns that you don't take candy from strangers. And here you are, asking her if she would like candy, and she says, "Yes." Then, you are not a stranger anymore.

E: *Um-hum.*

Z: *Did you have that symbolism in mind when you gave her the candy?*

E: *Yes. There is one other thing. Little girls like candy. I want to be sure of my transference. Dangling legs in the pool or going barefoot, that's permissible. I got two permissibles leading up to something that might not be permissible, but is delicious. So I weighted the reply.*

Z: *So, then again you chained the ideas. It's like a "yes" set. One permissible idea, then another permissible idea and then she's ready to accept the third idea as being more permissible. That's excellent.*

Then, there's that idea of trust. How do you establish trust in a trance? You give her a piece of candy and she takes it. The issue of trust is dealt with when she decides to take the candy.

E: *Um-humm. And Freud said it takes three months to establish transference.*

Z: *That was excellent. And then you emphasize by inflection that she feel it in her mouth.*

E: *And another thing—dangling her legs in the pool can occur at any age. Going barefoot defines the age. And they are all related to childhood. Dangling legs is an adult thing, too. And so she translates her dangling legs as an adult. Going barefoot is also part of her translation and she internally makes dangling legs childhood, because of the mention of going barefoot. And then the candy . . .*

Z: *Which makes it more internal and more child.*

E: *Um-hum. Because I can't always be certain just exactly where I am. But, I know how to play it. There are multiple meanings of words. That was a nice learning for you to learn that "forward and upward" is the future and "backwards" is the past. And yet you have known that for how long?*

E: Now sometime, when you are a big girl, you will tell a lot of strangers about your favorite candy when you were a little girl.

E: *You just took that picture of Roxie (Erickson's daughter) and me holding Laurel (Roxie's infant daughter who is nicknamed "Screech" because of her powerful cry) and the screech owl. (E. is holding a small ironwood owl that he had given to Laurel as a gift.) Now, how real will it be when I am long dead and she looks at that picture? The screech owl adds tremendous meaning to that picture. It gives you the sense of humanity and kindness and thoughtfulness, and tremendously so. And it is a very simple thing. And it is a little screech owl and yet she was a big girl, relatively speaking. The screech owl was down here. She was up here. (E. gestures to indicate that he was supporting the child with his left arm while holding the ironwood owl in his left hand, below Laurel.)*

E: *Now, at age 16, when she looks at that, she is going to see the smallness of the screech owl, and the bigness of the little baby. That will reunite with all her own feelings of bigness in high school and the warm memories of being a little baby and that little screech owl. So you see how all of those memories are put together, unnoticeably.*

Z: *That's very nice symbolism. And so, when she thinks back about the candy . . .*

E: *She will remember that. She will think of that candy and when I'm in sight she will think about candy and me.*

Z: *Which are the issues of trust and comfort, and not being a stranger.*

Es *A long continuance. That picture is a long continuance . . . the screech owl and Laurel.*

Z: *You are very kind with Sally, too. You take the extra effort to be thoughtful.*

E: *How did Lance's (Erickson's son) wife react? She told him she would like a picture of him when they became engaged. Lance gave her a picture I had taken of him lying on the floor in the nude.*

Z: *As an infant?*

E: *As an infant. And her love encompassed Lance from that time forward.*

Z: *This next symbol here that you do with Sally is also very nice.*

E: And there's a lot of things to learn. A great many things to learn. I'm going to show you one of them right now. I am going to take hold of your hand. (E. lifts Sally's left hand.) I'm going to lift it up. I'm going to put it on your shoulder, right there. (E. slowly lifts up Sally's hand by the wrist and then puts it on her lower right shoulder.) And I want your arm to be paralyzed, so you *can't* move it. You can't move it until I tell you to move it. Not even when you are a big girl, not even when you are grown up. You can't move your left hand and arm until I tell you so.

E: *What am I doing there?*

Z: *My association to that is this. You didn't put her arm on the top of her shoulder where it would weigh her down. It was on the side of her arm. It was comforting because that was a more comforting position. She is holding herself together. In a moment you are going to wake her up from the head up, and she will stay in that position.*

E: *I'm paralyzing her body. Now in her vocabulary, paralysis is bad.*

*And it will remain until I say otherwise. Whatever is bad, I can
remove. And I am a doctor.*

Z: *So the symbol goes one level deeper. There was that symbol of
comfort. Then there is also an association to discomfort—a negative feeling to the paralysis but it will be removed when you
remove it. I see.*

E: *Some of the bad I am removing.*

Z: *And if you remove one bad thing . . .*

E: *If I type one key on the typewriter, I'll type two.*

Z: *Also, "paralyzed" is more of an adult word. It is not a child word.*

E: *No.*

    *I was listening to someone on TV today, and I said, "That's a
Michigan accent." You see, you are never given a course in accent learning, yet you pick up those accents. You don't know
you are picking them up, but you are learning them and you
learn how to recognize them. We do learn that and, like paralysis, it spreads. From Michigan to Wisconsin to New York. What
does the knowledge of accents do?*

Z: *The knowledge of accents spreads, and so her paralysis spreads.*

E: *(Overlapping.) Have you noticed how much your own recognition
of accents has improved since you have been abroad?*

Z: *Oh yes, it is very interesting to hear the German accent.*

E: *Yes, to* hear *it. And know consciously that you are hearing it.*

Z: *Yes.*

E: *And you have no idea when you started to learn . . .*

Z: *The hearing of accents. All right. So when you put Sally's arm up
and she has that arm paralyzed, she spreads it to her body.*

E: *Yes. And we all want the body to be good and confident when
used. Confidence is very general; it involves the whole body. And
paralysis is bad and it can be disowned.*

Z: *But the comfort can stay.*

E: Now, first of all, I want you to awaken from the neck up while
your body goes sounder and sounder asleep . . . You'll wake up
from the neck up.

E: *From the neck up. (E. raises his head.)*

Z: *And you inflected "up," reinforcing the verbal suggestion with the
intonation.*

E: It's hard, but you can do it. (Pause.) And it's a nice feeling to have
your body sound asleep, your arm paralyzed, and be awake from
the neck up. And how old are you? (Pause. Sally smiles.)

E: How old are you? . . . How old are you? (E. leans close to Sally.)

S: (Softly.) Uh—34.

E: (Nods.) All right. (E. sits back.) You are 35 and why are you keeping your eyes shut?

E: *She didn't want to say 35. That's why she smiled. She slowly got
around her ordinary pattern of being noncommittal.*

Z: *She delayed her response and she got around her pattern of being
noncommittal. She awoke from the head up and she was going to
be her adult self.*

E: *Um-hum.*

Z: *And then she hesitates and says "34." You come back and you say
35. What was going on there?*

E: *She was slowly coming around her unwillingness to be committal.*

Z: *Because you forced her to make a statement where she had to
make a definite statement of her age. Why did you say 35, after
she said 34?*

E: *I think I misunderstood. I see no purpose in misunderstanding.*

Z: *You come back to her age later and then it is as if you give her a
chance to correct you. She spoke very softly, and it is very possible that you just did not hear her correctly. But when you come
back to it later, she has a chance to correct you, and to correct
you by making a definite statement. Even if you mishear her, it
works out very nicely.*

E: *Your errors should be used. And one thing you should have
noticed . . . I'm very slow.*

Z: *You're very slow in your speech, which is very different from
your voice tempo when you were telling an anecdote. You are
much more measured in the way you are speaking when you
are doing the induction.*

E: *Because a person in a trance does things automatically and very
rapidly—too rapidly to vocalize.*

Z: *To have those associations inside their own head or to say their associations externally?*

E: *Your thinking goes on much more rapidly than your tongue. And you are depending on the unconscious which moves like lightning. You carefully alter time by your slowness. You have been taught from childhood on, "Look at me when you are speaking to me. Look at me when I speak to you. When I ask you a question, you answer right away." But you don't want the last part of the answer. You want the whole answer. If they answer right away they would give just the last part of the answer. So you induce, first of all, an elasticity of time. Then they can talk to you freely, fully. And when I asked her her age, she had to do an awful lot of thinking.*

Z: *Yes.*

E: *And that thinking was to get around her noncommittal pattern.*

Z: *She was resisting the idea of saying a definite statement at an unconscious level?*

E: *No. Her waking pattern would be quick and noncommittal. And when I asked her her age, she was not quick.*

Z: *Right.*

E: *She took her time and was committal. And it takes time to get out of one pattern and into another because her head was awake.*

Z: *So the solution for getting over the noncommittedness, is to take time.*

E: *Take time.*

S: It feels nice.

E: Well, I *think* your eyes are going to open. (Sally smiles and keeps her eyes shut. Pause.)

E: *There I'm giving her all the time in the world to doubt.*

E: They are, aren't they? (Sally clears her throat.)

E: *Now she is beginning to realize that when I said her eyes are going to open, they will open. She's slowly learning that her eyes are going to open and so they are blinking. And that's her process of accepting the absolute truth of what you say.*

Z: *She has to process it and doubt.*

E: *No. She has to process it as a new behavior, different from her ordinary conscious behavior. It's responsive behavior. And in her usual waking, noncommittal state, she would say, "Yes, they are going to open—no, they're not." This allowed her gently to get the "yes" without there being any conflict.*

E: They are going to open and stay open. (Sally smiles, moistens her lips with her tongue, opens her eyes and blinks.)

E: *You can see the struggle there.*

Z: *There was a struggle.*

E: *The opening was associated with a smile. She practiced that smile several times first.*

Z: *Before she allowed it to come out.*

E: *Yes. She smiled several times before she opened her eyes. And then when she opened her eyes, she was smiling. But she smiled before, indicating that her eyes would open.*

Z: *I'm confused. Her smiling was an indicator that her eyes were going to open?*

E: *And she was adding a smile.*

Z: *A pleasant feeling.*

E: *A pleasant feeling to the beginning of the opening of her eyes. So, that means, in medical terms, the patient feels pleased when they see the doctor coming with pills. The patient feels pleased when the doctor or the nurse or medical technician comes with the syringe.*

Z: *Because they know they are getting treated.*

E: *Um-hum. And I made her demonstrate that she was going to open her eyes. I was taking charge of her eyes and she added my taking charge of her eyes, a pleasant feeling.*

Z: *Her smile.*

E: *Um-hum.*

Z: *And then she carried that over when she did open her eyes.*

E: *So the opening of her eyes in response to me was a pleasure, and not a duty.*

Z: *And that would allow for more commitment too, because it wasn't a duty.*

E: *Yes, that's right. When you are duty bound, you don't like it.*

Z: *Especially Sally, with her style of not being committed.*
E: *Um-hum.*

E: I was right. (Sally keeps staring ahead.) Where are you?
S: Umm? I think I'm here.
E: You're here?
S: Um-hum.
E: And what are some of your memories when you were a little girl?
    (E. leans towards Sally.) Something that you can tell to strangers.
S: Um. Well . . .
E: Louder.
S: (Clears throat.) I, uh, I remember . . . uh . . . a tree, and backyard,
    and . . . um . . .
E: Did you climb some of those trees?
S: (Speaking softly.) No. They were small plants . . . um . . . and an
    alleyway.
E: Where?
S: In an alleyway between the rows of houses and all the kids played
    in the backyard and the back alley. They played, um . . .
E: Who were those kids?
S: Their names? You mean their names?
E: Um-hum.
S: Oh, well . . . um . . . (Sally continues to stare to her right or look at
    E. E. is leaning close to her. Her hand is still on her shoulder
    and she is not making any visual contact with people in the
    room.) Well, I remember Maria, and Eileen, and David and
    Guiseppe.
E: Becky?
S: (Speaking louder.) Guiseppe.
E: And what did you think, when you were a little girl, that you
    would grow up to be when you are a big girl?
S: I thought, uh . . . an astronomer or a writer. (Sally grimaces.)
E: Do you think that will happen?
S: I think one of them will happen. (Pause.)

E: *What do you make of the behavior of that one fellow? (Indicating
    one of the participants.)*
Z: *He was leaning forward and looking?*

E: Leaning forward and listening.

Z: Oh. He's left-eared. (His head is tilted so that his left ear faces E.)

E: And I told him, "You have better hearing in one ear than the other." And he knew that. He was surprised when I knew it.

    And here she is, trying to deal with her unconscious memories as a girl in the alley, and she is demonstrating the time it takes to get from the conscious to the unconscious. She is very slow in answering. Because it takes time to get from the "now" to the remote past. It took a long time to get from the remote past to the present.

Z: Then when you asked her what did she think she would grow up to be, she said she thought an astronomer or writer, and she grimaces after she says "writer."

E: How did you learn to write?

Z: Practice, I guess.

E: You learned to write this way. (E. gestures, grimacing and twisting.)

Z: Yes. Grimacing.

E: You are using your body.

Z: Yes, twisting your body and feet. You learn to write with your whole body.

E: Um-hum. And when she bit her lip on the term of "writing," she was calling up that experience of the painfulness of writing. I remember how difficult it was to write "t" and lift your pencil up and cross it. And how difficult it was when you wrote "i" and picked your pencil up and dotted it.

Z: She's still dissociated, then.

E:Um-hum. And the word "writing" threw her way back. "Astronnomy"—that's an adult word and her head is awake.

Z: I see, and then it had no meaning for her body.

E: Um-hum.

S: I'm . . . my left hand didn't move. (She smiles.) I'm real surprised about that. (She laughs.)

E: You are a little bit surprised about your left hand.

E: Did you notice there that I moved my left hand first?

Z: I didn't notice that.

E: *Play it back.*

Z: *So she saw that out of her peripheral vision? Which is what caused her attention to go to her arm?*

E: *See for yourself. (The tape is played back and, in fact, E. did move his left hand just before Sally made the statement about her left hand being paralyzed.)*

    The movement of my left hand guided her thinking, and nobody usually realizes that.

Z: *Well, unless you pointed it out here, nobody would have. There are also some things happening on the verbal level. She says, "My left hand didn't move. I'm* real *surprised about that." That's an exaggeration. She exaggerates a statement which is different from her style. And you come back and say, "You are* a *little bit* surprised." *You took away some of the feeling. You play the other side of her polarity.*

E: *Um-hum.*

Z: *That could allow her to be more definite.*

E: *And you don't want your patient to say "no, my hand is not moving." You say, "You may think your hand is not moving." And you've done the saying of the "not."*

Z: *And then that allows her to be more affirmative.*

E: *Yes.*

Z: *And so you did a reversal after her exaggeration, and you corrected her exaggeration.*

E: *I didn't want her to remain up there exaggerated. I wanted her to get down to her real self.*

S: I recall that you said that it wouldn't move and, uh . . .

E: Did you believe me?

S: I guess I did. (Smiles.)

E: You are just guessing. (Sally laughs.)

Z: *You played with her noncommittedness before, over the ideas of "belief" and "reality." Here you say, "just guessing," and she laughs. She catches on to the game. She never says that she does, but her body again indicates that she catches on.*

E: *Um-hum.*

S: It seems I, uh . . . it seems like it didn't move to me.

E: It's more than a guess then. (Sally laughs.)

S: Umm . . . yes. (Softly.) I . . . it's very surprising too that you can wake up from the neck up and not the neck down.

E: It's surprising that you what?

S: That you can . . . um . . . that your body can be asleep from the neck down and you can be talking . . . you know . . . and be awake. And your body can feel so numb. (Laughs.)

E: In other words, you can't walk?

S: Well, not right this minute. (Sally shakes her head "no.")

E: Not just now.

S: (Sighs.) Um-umm, not just now.

E: *And there she shook her head and immediately committed to the idea that she can't walk. So she came around to an immediate commitment.*

Z: *It was easier for her to make a negative commitment than it was to make a positive commitment. But making a negative commitment is one step to making a positive commitment.*

E: *Um-hum.*

Z: *Also, all of this time, she is just focused on you. She is not glancing around.*

E: *We were alone.*

E: Any obstetrician in this group now knows how to produce anesthesia . . . of the body. (E. looks expectantly towards Sally. Sally nods her head "yes" and then shakes her head "no." She continues to stare blankly to her right.) (Sally clears her throat.) How does it feel to be 35 years old and be unable to walk?

S: 34.

E: 34. (E. smiles.)

Z: *She corrected you and you were very gracious. You weren't off balance in any way.*

E: *Well, why should I be?*

Z: *Also, she becomes one-up. She struggled against you to try to be one-up before.*

E: *And I gave her one-up.*

Z: *Yes. She corrected you on her age. But, she had to make a definite statement to do so.*

E: *You can always yield and come out on top.*

S: Um . . . it feels . . . right now it feels pleasant.

E: Very pleasant.

S: Uh-huh.

Z: *And then you exaggerate with a positive emotion. She says "pleasant," and you say "very pleasant."*

E: Now, when you first came in, did you like the joking attitude that I took toward you?

S: I probably did.

Z: *First you underline the pleasant feeling and then you went back to the joking feeling. However, it wasn't joking. Actually, you made her feel very uncomfortable. And so, by pairing the two ideas in time, her attitude about that unpleasantness becomes more positive.*

E: *Yes.*

E: You probably did? (Sally laughs.) Or you probably didn't?

E: Yes, it's probably so.

Z: *She again answers in her equivocal way, and you emphasize "you probably did" with your inflection.*

E: *A rising inflection on the "did." "You probably* did."

Z: *Emphasizing the positive side with your inflection.*

E: *Um-hum.*

E: (Smiling). Now is the moment for truth.

S: Huh? (Sally laughs.)

E: Now is the moment for truth.

S: Well, yeah, I had mixed feelings. (Laughs.)

Z: *She stayed equivocal. She didn't verbally take "the moment for truth." So next you start to exaggerate it.*

E: You say "mixed feelings." Very mixed feelings?

S: Well, yeah, I liked it and I didn't.

E: Very, very mixed feelings?

S: Uh . . . I don't know if I can make that distinction.

Z: *So you play it out now from the other side. You exaggerate her noncommittedness by making the distinction so absurd that she couldn't be noncommittal. The distinctions became too absurd: "very mixed; very, very mixed."*

E: *You use them as a foil.*

Z: *So you hoist her on her own petard.*

E: *You hoist her on her own petard, yes. And then she'll reject the petard and not you.*

Z: *You give her a chance to see some of the effects of noncommitted- ness—"Very mixed; very, very mixed." You're playful, and the rejecting of the behavior has to come from her.*

E: Did you wish to hell that you hadn't come?

S: Oh, no. I'm very glad I came. (Sally bites her bottom lip.)

E: And, so far, in coming here, you've learned how not to walk.

S: (Laughs.) Yeah. Not to move from my neck down. (Sally nods.)

E: How did that candy taste?

S: (Softly.) Oh, real good, but . . . uh . . . I had . . . uh . . . there were several different kinds.

E: (Smiles.) So you've been eating candy?

S: (Smiles.) Uh-huh.

E: Who gave it to you?

S: You did.

E: (Nods.) Generous of me, wasn't it?

E: *She has been very noncommittal. And she said that it tasted very good emphatically, or words to that effect.*

Z: *Yes.*

E: *And that was directly committal. I'm giving her a chance to be noncommittal and committal.*

Z: *Another positive step.*

S: Yes. It was really nice. (Smiling.)

E: Did you enjoy that candy?

S: Uh, yes.

Z: *She's committing herself definitely.*

E: She's learning a pattern—a new pattern.

E: And all philosophers say reality is in the head. (Smiles.) Who are all these people? (Sally looks around. E. leans close to her.)

S: I have no idea.

E: She had no idea "Who are all these people?" She did have an idea. I said, "Who are all these people?" And it required her to give a negative response.

Z: Then you force her here to make contact with people.

E: Um·hum.

Z: And your next statement is, "Tell me your frank opinion of them," which is very difficult. You really put her on the spot by the way you force her to make contact with people.

E: Yes.

Z: To what end?

E: Her arm is still paralyzed.

Z: Yes, and she's comfortable in her body.

E: And some people love their illness and keep their illness, so you force them to do something to be frank. And then she is frank. She can take orders.

Z: Although you know that she is going to be noncommittal in her direct response, but she still has to make a more committal response.

E: That's right. And you give her a safe situation in which to make a committed answer. You see, in a noncommittal pattern, if you can force her to make a committed response, although very general, then you can force her to make it specific. You go from a very general to a specific, and a specific is removing her paralysis.

Z: Do you remember how she removes her paralysis?

E: No.

Z: It's excellent. You will really enjoy the way that it happens.

E: Now, tell me your frank opinion of them.

S: Well, they all . . . look different.

E: They look different.

S: Yeah, they all look different. (She clears her throat.) They all look nice; they all look different . . . from each other.

E: All people are different from each other. (Sally laughs self-consciously, clears her throat, and sighs.)

Z: *Here you forced her to make contact with people and that can bring up some negative feeling. Here you are forcing her to make contact with people and you forced her to give a frank opinion, which is something very difficult. She's not going to be committal, but she is committed to your direction and so you've got a partial commitment there because she is committed to the direction that you set.*

Then her association may also be to have some negative feeling towards people. She must have some negative feelings toward people because she comes in late and she disrupts people. Therefore, you can infer some negative feelings towards people. But here she is—she is sitting there in hypnosis and she has got her arm crossed over her body—and you are saying, "Tell me your frank opinion of these people." If she thinks anything negative, she can't say it, and also she's insulated from some negative feeling by the hypnosis and by the comforting position.

E: *Um-hum.*

Z: *And you definitely broke her focus on you by forcing contact with others. Why?*

E: Because it has to go to her. Because the doctor does leave the waiting room or the patient's room and the focus goes back to the patient. You make it a reality situation.

Z: *It's also an interesting way to integrate her into the group. She has to look around. She has to make contact with people.*

E: *And to think frankly. So I gave her permission.*

Z: *To have negative thoughts?*

E: *Yes. If I give you something, that implies I can take it away from you. Right?*

Z: *Right.*

E: *So I gave her permission.*

E: Where's Eileen now?

S: Oh, I don't know . . . um . . .

E: How long has it been since you thought about Eileen?

S: Oh, well, hmm . . . a fairly long time. Uh, her, uh . . . Maria was her sister. She was closer to my age and, uh, she was the younger sister, uh, and I recall them—you know—they are people I remember in my youth, but I seldom think about them.

E: Where was your home?

S: Oh, in Philadelphia.

E: And you were in the backyard?

S: Uh-huh.

E: In Philadelphia?

S: Uh-huh.

E: How did you get here?

S: (Laughs.) Oh, maybe I just, um, thought about being here.

E: Just notice. . . . He is moving his leg. He is moving his feet and toes, and she is moving hers. (E. is pointing to people in the room.) How come you are sitting so still?

Z: *Is this an attempt to get her to be more committal?*

E: *And to force her to recognize fine details around her.*

Z: *Thereby ratifying the trance.*

E: *We are alone in the backyard in Philadelphia. "How did you get here?" "Here" is very specific. The backyard in Philadelphia is awfully unspecific. How many backyards are there in Philadelphia?*

Z: *Yes, and how many times and dates.*

E: *And the "here" is awfully specific. You see, I'm getting general ideas and specific ideas all mixed up.*

Z: *With the idea of giving her the opportunity to be more specific.*

E: *Yes.*

S: Well, I recall that you said something about that . . . um . . .

E: (Interrupting.) Do you always do what I say?

S: (Shaking her head.) It is very unusual that I take directions.

E: (Interrupting.) And would you say that you are an unusual girl?

S: No. It's unusual for me to follow directions.

Z: *You've reframed that "unusual." She is saying unusual with a negative feeling attached to it—"It's unusual to follow directions." Then you say, "unusual"—"You are an unusual girl," and there's a positive feeling attached to it. She rejects it verbally by saying, "It's unusual for me to follow directions."*

E: *"You are an unusual girl" is remembered.*

Z: *I see. It is remembered on the unconscious level.*

E: *Yes, and it's emotionally satisfying.*

S: I never follow directions.

E: You never do?

S: I can't say never—seldom. (Smiles.)

E: You're sure you never follow directions?

S: No, I think I just did. (Sally laughs and clears her throat.)

E: You follow ridiculous suggestions?

S: (Laughs.) Um . . . well, I could probably move.

E: *"Follows directions"—notice her reply.*

Z: *She starts thinking about her arm, and that was a very specific internal thought on her part. You were just very general. She could have responded to any previous suggestion.*

E: *She was trapped. She was forced to think internally, specifically, in regard to her paralysis.*

Z: *And your generalness led to her specifying.*

S: I could probably move.

E: Huh?

S: I could probably move if I really decided to.

E: *She said, "I could probably move."*

E: As you look around at each person, *who* is the next one you *think* will go into a trance? Look at every one of them.

Z: *This is interesting. Why do you make her make contact with every-one in the room and decide who she thinks the next one to go into a trance will be?*

E: *She has to think about "x, y, and w" and she's part of the alphabet.*

Z: *It puts her in the group and makes her a part.*

S: (Sally looks around the room.) Umm . . . maybe this woman down here with the ring on her finger. (Pointing to Anna.)

E: Which one?

S: (Softly.) The woman facing us with the ring on her left finger, with the glasses on her head. (E. leans very close.)

E: And what else?

S: What else? I think she is probably the next person who will be in a trance.

E: You're sure you didn't overlook somebody?

S: Well, there are a couple of people that I had the feeling . . . the man next to her.

E: *"I have a feeling." That was a more committed response.*

E: Anybody else?

S: Uh . . . yes, anybody else.

E: Huh?

S: Anybody else. (Smiles.)

E: How about the girl sitting to your left? (Indicating Rosa.)

S: Yeah.

Z: *This is a very nice part here. Look at Rosa. She's leaning away from you, and her arms are crossed and her legs are crossed. Yet you suggest to Sally that she pick Rosa even though her body posture indicates resistance.*

E: How long do you think it would take *her* to uncross her legs and close her eyes? (Rosa has her arms and legs crossed; she's sitting on the far left side of the green chair, away from Erickson.)

S: Not very long.

E: Well, watch her. (Rosa does not uncross her legs. She looks back at E. Then, she looks down and looks up and smiles and looks around.)

R: (Shrugging her shoulders and smiling.) I don't feel like uncrossing them.

E: *She committed herself to "Not very long" and Rosa resists carefully and thoroughly. Yet Sally's committed herself to "not very long."*

Z: *She's living through an error?*

E: *Yes. Some people can't bear to make a mistake. She made a mistake and she's bearing up very well under it.*

Z: Yes, she made a mistake by saying "not very long," and so she'll have to live through the mistake.

E: Yes, and that's very educational.

E: I didn't tell you to be uncomfortable; nobody told you to be uncomfortable. (Rosa nods her head.)

E: I just asked this girl how long is it going to take you to uncross your legs . . . and close your eyes and go into a trance. (Rosa nods her head.) (Pause, during which time E. looks expectantly at Rosa.)

Z: So you shift the focus and you go past Sally to Rosa. Then Sally drops out of attention. You had been giving a lot of attention to Sally and now you're withdrawing that attention. She can't get that attention again when you start working with Rosa.

E: Yes, but she committed herself and she made a mistake and she lives through that mistake.

E: (Speaking to Sally to his immediate left.) Watch her. (Pause.) (Rosa distinctly closes and opens her eyes.) And she closed her eyes and she opened them. How long will it be before you closes [sic] them and keep them closed? (Pause. E. looks at Rosa.)

Z: That was a nice piece of being ungrammatical. "How long will it be before you closes them and keeps them closed?" It should be "she closes them" or "you close them" and you said "you closes them." That creates some confusion and focuses her on the word "close."

E: Yes, but she's been out of the situation. I've got to drag her in some way.

Z: Rosa?

E: No, Sally. Sally's been out.

Z: Yes. So Sally had to watch Rosa and that brought her back into the situation.

E: And then Sally's original commitment was, "It wouldn't be long before Rosa closed her eyes." So I brought her back.

Z: That's very nice. So she'll have to realize the time factor, and have to realize her mistake and thereby learn that she could live through making the mistake. Her noncommittedness is to avoid making mistakes. So, basically the pattern of working with Sally's personality is to expand her pattern of being flexible and to allow her to be committal, and to allow her to make mistakes and feel OK.

E: *I did an offensive thing in medical school. When a patient was going to die, all of the class was serially assigned to do a physical. Then the patient had an autopsy. All of the rest of the class would go down to the autopsy praying they had made the right diagnosis. They were offended that I always hoped that I made the wrong diagnosis.*

Z: *I lost you.*

E: *I hoped I'd make the wrong diagnosis because, if I had, I had more to learn. If I had made the right diagnosis, I had no more to learn and the class didn't understand that. So I've had her learn to commit herself and* learn more. *Then I bring her back into the situation.*

Z: *OK. Then, just a bit more on this. You push at Rosa and eventually she does close her eyes. It takes a long time because Rosa shows from the beginning that she is going to be resistant. You knew from the beginning that she was going to be resistant. You knew she was going to be resistant so then you just took your time.*

E: *I took my time and played one against the other.*

Z: *Yes.*

E: *Sally would learn positively, and Rosa would learn, "Don't try to resist."*

DAY TWO OF THE DISCUSSION (2/3/80)

Z: *The last thing you were doing was that you had brought Sally out of the trance and then you were doing an induction with Rosa. You explained that you were having Sally live out a mistake. She could make a mistake and still survive. Sally had said that Rosa would be the next person to go into a trance and that she could do that very easily but actually Rosa would be very resistant. Let's review a little bit of that last section.*

R: I don't feel like uncrossing them. (Rosa shrugs her shoulders.)

E: I didn't tell you to be uncomfortable. Nobody told you to be uncomfortable. (Rosa nods her head.) I just asked this girl how
long is it going to take you to uncross your legs . . . and close
your eyes and go into a trance. (Rosa nods her head "yes." Pause.
E. looks expectantly at Rosa. Speaking to Sally who is to his
immediate left.) Watch her. (Pause. Rosa distinctly closes and
opens her eyes.)

Z: *You were putting a lot of indirect pressure on Rosa to conform.
When you did that, Sally, who was in the middle, dropped out
of awareness. Then you forced Sally to come back and observe
Rosa for two reasons: One, Sally has to see her mistake and she
has to really notice it, and two, that puts extra pressure on Rosa
to respond.*

E: *Yes.*

Z: *But Rosa is still "crossed" in her posture. It's an interesting
struggle of wills here because you are not going to be denied.
Rosa is going to close her eyes, but she's very resistant to closing
her eyes and uncrossing her legs. It almost becomes a battle, and
she's going to conform to what your expectations and your suggestions are.*

E: *But the important thing is that while it is a battle, how much does
Rosa realize that it is a battle?*

Z: *How much does she realize? I think she realizes it as a battle.*

E: *Yes, but how much battle am I putting up?*

Z: *You're not putting up any battle. It's all indirect. You're just talking to Sally. But, you're looking at Rosa and your attitude
towards her is very expectant.*

E: *I'm directing my voice to Rosa.*

E: She closed her eyes and she opened them. How long will it be
before you closes [sic] them and keeps them closed? (Pause. E.
looks at Rosa.)

Z: *The other day we mentioned that you use an ungrammatical sentence here to focus her attention on "closes."*

E: *That's right. Because if I say "you close them," that's contestable,* but "closes"—how can you contest that? She's got to go through a lot of psychological maneuvers to define that as a grammatical error.

Z: Yes. Then the contesting would be more difficult because some of the energy would be absorbed by figuring out the grammatical error.

E: All right. When you are lecturing to an audience on a controversial subject, you're very careful. If you look at a hostile member of the audience, you mispronounce a word and he says, "I can do better than that." And so he has a feeling of superiority. But he doesn't know that it's limited to a word.

Z: And he contests the form, not the substance.

E: Um-hum.

Z: It's a variation of that idea of giving the symbol to absorb feelings. For example, there's the case where you have the woman plant a tree when she lost her child. The symbol absorbs the feeling. Here you say something ungrammatical and that absorbs and deflects some of the feeling.

E: You get the hostility on the word only, and you give them a happy feeling.

Z: A feeling of superiority.

E: Um-hum. It's happiness recognized as happiness but not defined as to what kind of happiness it is.

Z: Not defined as a superior feeling?

E: Not defined in relationship to the topic. They're just happy with you.

Z: For making a mistake.

E: Now an Adlerian who taught in Chicago debated me once. I didn't want to. I protested. He thought I was afraid. I used all sorts of diversion techniques including mispronunciations and he'd get so happy over correcting my mispronunciations, he found his happiness radiating to what I said.

    He had dominated the Chicago school for so long. He knew more about Adler than I did. I kept pulling that ploy on him, and finally he broke down crying.

Z: And the crying was due to?

E: He kept on getting happy about what I was saying but he was not *able to attach it to the fact that he was correcting my words and mispronunciations. He found he was agreeing with me on my points. He didn't want to agree with me. He was debating against me.*

E: (Rosa blinks.) She's having harder work opening her eyes. (Rosa closes her eyes, bites her lips and then opens her eyes. Pause. Sally closes her eyes.)

E: *She's struggling hopelessly.*

Z: *When I've shown this to people they've gotten concerned because you put so much pressure on her. Yet she's also indicating her cooperation very early on a nonverbal level. She closes her eyes and opens them.*

E: *Yes, the audience gets upset because they would want to withdraw and they can't identify with her. She doesn't want to withdraw from me.*

Z: *No, she doesn't.*

E: *She hopes for a win but she's not defined that win as mine or hers. She wants somebody to win, and she's not been allowed yet to say, "I want to win," because her eyes shut and she moves her hand. And she keeps looking at me. She's hoping for success but it's undefined success. But I know it's my success. She wants to stick in there until a success is achieved.*

E: She's trying hard to play a game with me but she's losing. (Pause.) And she doesn't know how close she is to being in a trance. (To Rosa.) So close your eyes, *now.*

E: *There's another thing to be borne in mind. Patients come to you for help. They may resist help, but they hope desperately you'll win. She's seeking information but she knows the only way she can get it is by my winning. So she's trapped between her desire to win herself and her even greater desire to learn.*

Z: *Yes. And it's very nice that you're willing to keep on going with the struggle. There's a nice kindness there. You supply some limits so she ultimately will win by losing.*

E: *That's right.*

Z: *And now here you have been making indirect comments, like:*

"She's trying to play a game with me. She's having harder work opening her eyes." But now you look at her and you say directly to her, "So close your eyes now, and keep them closed now," though you know that she's not going to just close her eyes immediately. However, you still give her the opportunity . . .

E: *To choose her time. So it doesn't become a choice of closing her eyes. It becomes a choice of time. I can afford time.*

Z: *Yes. Besides that she may get scared at this point that you might not win. That might give her more impetus to come around to your side later.*

E: *Um-hmm.*

E: And keep them closed *now.* (Rosa blinks her eyes once and then blinks them again for a longer period of time.) That's all right. You can take your time . . . (Rosa blinks again.) But you'll close them (Rosa blinks again) and keep them closed . . . longer. (Rosa blinks her eyes again and opens them.) Keep them closed longer. (Pause. Rosa blinks.)

E: And the next time they close, let them stay closed. (Pause. Rosa closes her eyes and opens them. Then she closes and opens them again. There is a deliberateness to the way she closes her eyes.) And you're beginning to know that they will close. You're fighting hard to keep them open, and you don't know why I'm picking on you. (Rosa closes and opens her eyes twice.) That's right. (Rosa closes her eyes and they stay shut.) *That's* right.

Z: *And then they stay closed.*

E: "That's right." (Softly.) "That's *right.*"

Z: *I see, there's a comforting tone in the way you say, "That's right."*

E: *The comforting tone.*

Z: *Also, all of this time her eyes have just been focused on you. She can't be really caring very much about what's happening in her peripheral vision. She's just focused on you.*

E: *And my comforting tone is not one of triumph.*

Z: *I see. It's one of comfort for her.*

E: *If I said "close" triumphantly, she would have opened them.*

Z: *Yes.*

E: *I said it comfortingly.*

Z: So she ultimately wins anyway.

E: And she wins comfort. She's got a new goal entirely—one of comfort.

Z: Yes, so actually we can say it's another one of those cases where Erickson wins and the patient gets the prize. Also, she closes her eyes and she keeps them closed finally when you say, "You don't know why I'm picking on you." That seems to relax some of the tension. Why?

E: "You don't know why I'm picking on you." Then she can spread her resistance over a wide area.

Z: She has to have an association to why you're picking on her and she can have many associations?

E: And none of them are right.

Z: Why were you picking on her?

E: To lessen the depth of her resistance. I spread it all out.

Z: What an excellent way of working with resistance! You just spread it out so thin. . . .

E: That it's useless.

Z: Now, she has been staring at you and her attention has been very focused. She moves a lot. She's not fixed in her behavior, but in terms of defining hypnosis as a state of focused attention, she's been in a trance.

E: That moving is to convince her that she is not in a trance. Knowing that you have to convince yourself with each movement you make, that tells you "That previous movement didn't convince me. This one doesn't; this one doesn't."

Z: So she keeps on struggling to make orienting movements that will convince herself.

E: And losing every time. Jeff, you're the first person I've met who's willing to try to understand what's going on in the subject and me at the same time. You're willing to see the word "comfort" and you're willing to see the lack of comfort in her movements. How her movements are not to convince herself. They're only to unconvince her.

Z: When I do workshops on Ericksonian therapy, in the first part I teach Ericksonian diagnosis. It's a different kind of diagnosis— for example: How you diagnose the person's style of being atten-

tive? How you diagnose his style of being responsive? How you diagnose his communication style, and linguistic style? Not a psychiatric diagnosis, but a diagnosis that involves understanding intra- and interpersonal factors, such as one's style of controlling the relationship.

Then, from that diagnosis, I build into another section about how you give suggestions to fit the diagnosis of the persons. For example, I use the idea of taking out the garbage. If the person is an internally preoccupied person, the suggestion to take out the garbage can be given differently than if one is external in his orientation. If one is a more "one-up" person or a more "one-down" person, the way that you would give your suggestion would be different in each case. I think it's helpful for people because some people emphasize your technique, and not the fact that what you're doing stems from a diagnosis of the individual.

E: *The effect on the subject.*

Z: *And the way that you give your suggestions depends on your diagnosis of what's going on inside the subject. You use a different kind of diagnosis.*

E: *There's another thing to be taken into consideration: how all of us learn to talk. There's a long, long experience of making errors. "I seed [sic] him. I sawed [sic] him." We've all got that history of making mistakes in grammar and pronunciation. There's a wealth of learning you get from making mistakes. You can deliberately make a mistake and make a direct appeal to their actual possession of the history of mistakes, and their wanting to be corrected and you offer the correction.*

Zs *And also by doing that you revivify that old ...*

E: *Receptive mood.*

Z: *When they were younger.*

E: *Yes. "Mama, I seed [sic] somebody." And Mama says, "You saw somebody." And the child is grateful. So when I mispronounce a word and they correct me, the old frame of reference comes back. It gives them a feeling of being pacified and grateful, only they can't define it. Then you move on to something else.*

Now, for example, on our honeymoon, Betty couldn't drive

the car. We were on a lonesome country road. A bee flew in the
car and stung her on the knee. She slapped it. She picked it up
and dumped it out the window. I drove the car off on the
shoulder of the road and stopped it, and said, with profound
feeling, "I'm so glad it stung you instead of me."

Z: *I don't understand.*

E: *I meant it. And the look of absolute horror on her face. Because I*
had been stung by a bee once before. I was unconscious for three
days. When she got that bit of information, the horror of her
bridegroom being glad that she got stung was transformed into
the utter and glorious satisfaction that she'd *been stung.*

Z: *She'd been protective.*

E: *Um-hum. And there was her bridegroom wishing her harm, and*
she being grateful. When a bee comes around, she is terrified
on my behalf. And of course there was that tremendous horror
when I said that. It was overwhelming. And then there was some-
thing that was even more overwhelming immediately following.
Both were overwhelming emotions side by side.

Z: *It's a nice sequence of arousing the negative feeling, and then*
an immediate transformation into the positive feeling.

E: *I can be sound asleep and if a mosquito bites me I'd wake up with*
diarrhea and a horrible allergic reaction all over my body. I'd
have to take a hot bath for about an hour. So if she sees a mos-
quito in the bedroom, she knows what that mosquito will do to
me, and she's up in arms with the spray and the swatter.

Z: *So you can get an association to the protective feeling from the*
patient or from the subject, and then have the subject oriented
towards protecting you.

E: *That's right. She didn't want to be stung by that bee but it*
amounted to no more than an ordinary mosquito bite to an
ordinary person.

Z: *Then any feeling she would have about being stung by the bee*
would be gone with the other emotions that were elicited.

E: *By the horrible feeling of my being glad she was stung, and then*
that tremendously greater feeling because where would she have
been on a lonesome country road unable to drive a car, not

*understanding my unconsciousness. It would have been an un-
believably difficult situation.*

Z: *And so when you said that, you had in mind a protectiveness to
Betty. She didn't need to worry about getting the bee sting.*

E: *No. I was tremendously relieved. Then I realized how it looked
to her. Then, I could relieve her feeling. First, there was an awful
negative feeling and then overwhelming positive feeling.*

Z: *Now, back to the induction.*

E: *Rosa's losing and I've given her comfort.*

Z: *Yes. So at first there was a negative feeling and then the comfort
and there's the resistance . . .*

E: *And because she was losing and had all those negative feelings
about losing, and then my very impressive comfort.*

Z: *Which you accomplished by the way you said, "That's right." Anything more that you can say about diagnosing her particular personality and her particular style of resisting?*

E: *In general teaching about hypnosis, they tell you to avoid resistance.*

Z: *Yes.*

E: *Use it.*

Z: *Yes. I love this idea now of defusing the resistance and spreading
it so thin that there's nothing there. It's a new concept to me, and
I like that idea.*

    *There's a stubbornness that Rosa has. It's a different kind of
stubbornness than Sally's stubbornness. Can you make a statement about the difference between Rosa's style of resistance and
Sally's style of resistance?*

E: *She resists referring to person, while Sally makes it "my idea and
your idea" resistance.*

Z: *So Rosa's is more a direct conflict, and Sally is in conflict about
something.*

E: *Yes, about something. Now, Rosa is defending herself against
me as a person.*

Z: *That's very nice. I like that distinction.*

E: Now what I wanted you to see was her cooperation. Now then, a patient can resist, and they will resist. And I thought she would resist.

E: I said, "A patient can resist" and so she had resisted again.

Z: When she moved her body?

E: Uh-huh. Yes. That was to improve her comfort.

Z: It also moves her closer to you. She moves closer to you and she makes herself more comfortable when she leans her arm on the chair. And she did that when you said the word "resistance."

E: Yes.

Z: So you can resist in a positive direction.

E: The word "resistance" has a new meaning. It has a meaning of comfort, and I approve that she can resist.

Z: Before you were talking directly to her or indirectly about her, but when she closed her eyes, you broke away and you changed the locus of your voice and went back to the group. Why?

E: Let her enjoy her comfort. It's her comfort, let her enjoy it. I moved away. I respected her comfort.

E: And illustrate resistance very nicely.

E: There she moved away from me, and she's testing the comfort of resistance. She's still enjoying comfort. In other words, her comfort is hers.

Z: And then you also tagged the word "resistance" again. You say she'll "illustrate resistance very nicely," so that there's another positive feeling attached to the word "resistance."

E: She doesn't know it yet but she *is* going to uncross her legs. But she wants to show she doesn't have to. That's all right. When you deal with patients, they always want to hang on to something. And, as a therapist, you should let them. (Pause. Rosa leans forward in her chair but still has her legs crossed.)

E: "They always want to hang on to something." She's going to hang on to her crossed legs with my permission. Because you always want to hang on to something. For example, there's that marble, that dolly and that truck. Those are yours, but this is mine.

Z: This attitude is also found in childhood.

E: You're told in childhood to share your toys, but this is mine. Kim, being Oriental (Kim is Dr. Erickson's adopted granddaughter), has a heritage of thousands of generations of Vietnamese thinking. It took Kim one year to teach Betty Alice something that Betty Alice thought was remarkable. (Kim was adopted by Betty Alice when Kim was nine months old.) Two-year-old Kim taught her, "These are David's toys, only David can play with them. These are Michael's toys, only Michael can play with them. These are my toys, only I play with them. These are our toys and we all play with them." In the Vietnamese, for thousands of generations, "This plot of land is mine." They cultivate the same plot of land generation after generation in the same old way.

Z: You make a case for a racial kind of consciousness?

E: We have billions of brain cells that have the capacity to respond to billions of different stimuli, and the brain cells are very specialized. When you come from people who generation after generation only use certain brain cells, every signal that you get as an infant centers you around that. Now take the Jews for example. They have been persecuted for thousands of years. And Jews can fight among themselves. When Jews fight they are very bitter in their fighting unless some other nationality intrudes, and then that other nationality fights unified Jews. The quarreling Jews unite against the common enemy.

Z: Yes.

E: Isn't that right?

Z: Yes.

E: And Norwegians have been sailors for countless generations, and they were explorers, then they disseminated. And Greeks have been Greeks for generations and when they come to America, they form a big colony. Even fourth generation Greeks still talk in Greek. They don't split up. They stick together. A Lebanese colony is a Lebanese colony. A Syrian colony is a Syrian colony. But the Norwegians spread everywhere.

The Americans spread everywhere. You see, while we're born with similar brain cells, there's a pattern of response that's inherent in our behavior.

*I talked to a Polish Jew yesterday, a very highly intelligent
man. He was in absolute agony. He talked to me for about two
hours yesterday. He said, "What did I do wrong that my children
born in the United States did not respect the old Polish ways?"
The old Polish ways were the only thing that he could understand. He's a meat cutter and his son is a nuclear physicist. The
old man's heart is broken. His son should have been a meat
cutter. Their mother is a good housewife. The daughter wants a
career. He said, "What have I done wrong that has made my
children go wrong?"*

*In some cultures a plot of land was given to a family—let's say
a thousand years ago, and they're still growing their crops on
that one plot and facing starvation.*

Z: *Cultural differences have become very rigidly ingrained.*

E: *Ingrained so that you indirectly warn the child away from their
natural response.*

Z: *Can you make a connection back to the transcript?*

E: *Now with Rosa, she's got her own personal concept of male-female
relationships.*

Z: *You mean being Italian.*

E: *That's right.*

*Now a close friend of mine had a good practice in Milwaukee.
One of his patients was an Italian man who finally broke down
and told my friend, "I came from the old country with my wife.
Every time I come home, she's been gossiping all day. I have to
fix my own dinner. I have to do the laundry. I have to do all the
housework." My friend asked, "From what part of Italy do you
come?" He said a certain part. "Where does your wife come
from?" He said a certain part. My friend said, "You come from
a part of Italy where you're taught to treat your wife with kindness. Your wife comes from a part of Italy where if a husband
loves her, he shows it by beating up on her. When you go home,
if there's no dinner, you spank your wife hard and tell her, "I
want my dinner when I come home." It turned out to be the best
response because she had learned from infancy on that a man
beats his wife because that's the way of showing love.*

With Rosa, she's got her own individuality that she holds apart from men. It's a learning that has to do with defiance, making men prove that they're stronger. So you've got to prove it.

Z: *I think it was Carl Whitaker who said that any kind of therapy has to start with a fight, and the therapist has to be up for the fight or no psychotherapy is going to happen. And so the patient comes in and tests your strength.*

E: *He wants to know if you have the right kind of strength and that means a fight. Are you meek and mild as you should be, or are you strong and combative as you should be?*

A young Greek doctor had been married, I think, three times. He married an American girl each time. He came from a matri-archal part of Greece. His mother told him each time he got married, "After you've been with that girl for a few months, I'll get you a divorce, then you'll get engaged to another girl." He told me about it. I listened to both of them. I listened to his mother. I let his mother tell me what a good bridegroom should do. He should go on the honeymoon with his mother and leave his bride at home. And his bride should be his mother's slave. I led her out on a limb and then told her, her son was an Amer-ican. He had the right to marry the kind of girl he wanted, and that she was living in America and she could not make a slave out of his wife. The son was standing there looking, and his mother broke into Greek. It horrified him because he didn't know his mother knew that kind of language.

There was another girl I knew who came from a patriarchal area in Spain where the bridegroom stays home and the girl goes on the honeymoon with her father.

She was much more accessible. I went to visit them after they got married. I was introduced to the girl's father. He said, "So you're the man who told my daughter to go on the honeymoon with her husband, who tells me I have no rights at all." I said, "That's right."

And the Greek mother-in-law came over every day to tell the bride what to cook and what to do, and how to arrange her furni-ture. I told the mother, "I'm telling your daughter-in-law that when she gets tired of you in the house she should say, 'Do you want me to call Dr. Erickson?' "

Z: *Appeal to a higher authority.*

E: *And mother-in-law always left immediately. And Beatrice's mother (Beatrice is a patient E. referred to Z.) is an absolute dictator. And Beatrice's mother came over to tell me what Beatrice should do. I said, "You've been with Beatrice too long so you leave for home today." And Beatrice came in the same day and said, "My mother was so mad, she walked home." It was six miles from here to there. "She just about walked down to the airport. She wouldn't let me take her."*

Z: *Your willingness to take control of those situations is impressive. You're very incisive about your interventions.*

E: *In doing your therapy you deal with all kinds of patterns. You have to learn to recognize which kind of incisive intervention they need.*

Z: *Let's go back to the induction. The last thing with Rosa was that you were talking about resistance. You talk about resistance and then you talk about the fact that she's going to uncross her legs. Also, you talk about the fact that she can hang on to something. Therefore, what she can hang on to is keeping her legs crossed. She can make that pairing in her associations.*

E: Because the patient is not your slave. You're trying to help him. You're asking him to do things and we all grow up with the feeling "I'm nobody's slave, I don't have to . . . do things." And you use hypnosis for the patient to discover they can do things (Rosa opens her eyes.), even things that they think are against their wishes. (Sally coughs. Addressing Rosa). Now how do you feel about me picking on you?

R: I just wanted to see if I could resist what you were saying.

E: Yes. (Sally coughs.)

Z: *Now here is Sally and she starts this coughing which is really interesting because you'll see what happens in a moment from her coughing. You had the attention off of Sally for a long time. You ask Rosa the question, "Now how do you feel about me picking on you?" And that takes her one step away from any possible negative feeling that she might have because it's weighted in a positive direction. Therefore she'll have the idea in her mind that it was okay for you to pick on her.*

E: *Play it back again. Watch Rosa turn her palm towards me. Her hand is open towards me. (The tape is replayed.)*

Z: *She moved back away and then she moved forward.*

E: *With open hand.*

Z: *Yes, with an expectation of receiving.*

E: *Uh-huh.*

R: I mean, I could uncross my legs. (Rosa uncrosses them and then crosses them again. Meanwhile, Sally is coughing and laughing. E. pauses.)

E: (To Rosa.) And I told you that you would uncross your legs.

R: Hmmm?

E: I told you that you *would* uncross your legs.

R: Yes, I can.

(Sally is coughing and the coughing caused her to move her arms in order to cover her mouth. A man in the group then gives her a cough drop and Sally puts that in her mouth. Then, she opens her arms and shrugs at E.)

S: (To E.) Did you tell me I was going to cough? (Sally laughs and touches E., and coughs again.)

E: *She uses that cough which belongs to her.*

Z: *Yes. Then, there's her way of showing you that. She takes the cough drop and then shrugs to you and with open arms. She used that cough to free the paralyzed arm. She knew that she was developing a symptom. She's a bright woman and she perceived that. She knew that she was developing a symptom to free her arm.*

E: *It was illustrated so beautifully.*

Z: *Yes, beautifully illustrated.*

E: Now, wasn't that a nice *devious* way (Sally coughs and covers her mouth), a nice intelligent *devious* way to get control . . . of her left hand.

Z: *That was very nice. You phrased it, "A nice devious way, a nice intelligent devious way to get control," and then you paused slightly.*

E: *I approved.*

Z: *You approved.*

E: *I gave her a sense of approval.*

S: (Laughs, coughs and shakes her head "yes.") Develop a symptom.

E: You got rid of that paralyzed arm.

S: Um-hum.

E: And you did it by coughing (Sally nods and coughs), and it worked too, didn't it? (Sally laughs and coughs.) You're not really a slave.

S: Guess not.

E: Because you got tired of keeping your left hand up there so how could you get it down? Just cough enough . . . (Sally laughs) and you get it down.

S: (Sighs and laughs.)

Christine: Could I ask a question about this getting tired of having her arm up? I thought that in a trance one usually doesn't get tired, no matter what awkward position one is in. Is that a misconception? (To Sally.) Did your arm really get tired . . . of being up there or were you so awake that you felt awkward sitting in that position?

S: Um, I felt, um, I experienced it as kind of um . . . maybe . . . just a different feeling, an awareness of tension. But, um . . . I could have sat there a lot longer.

C: You could have?

S: I felt as if I could have, yeah, sat there a lot longer . . . um, it was kind of strange you know, I . . .

E: *She could have sat there a lot longer.*

Z: *Yes, she could have. You had withdrawn the attention from Sally. Sally had that contradiction, she wanted your attention but she wanted to sit in the back. Then you withdrew the attention when you were dealing with Rosa so Sally was stuck there with her arm paralyzed. She developed a symptom to get her arm free and she also developed an excellent way of getting your attention back to her.*

E: *She also demonstrated that she was right-handed.*

Z: *I didn't notice. What did she do?*

E: *After she freed her left hand, she kept putting her right up to cover her mouth.*

Z: *Uh-huh.*

E: *So it was definitely a freeing of her left hand because it was more natural for her to do it (cover her mouth) with her right hand. (E. demonstrates with his arms.)*

Z: *So she freed her left hand to cover her mouth when actually she was right-handed and all she needed to do was to cover her mouth with her right hand anyway.*

E: *That's a fine analysis that Sally shows.*

Z: *And she knew it. Sally knew that she was developing that symptom but it didn't matter. Her conscious awareness didn't matter.*

E: *That's right.*

Z: *And then the next thing that happens is that Christine asks a question. Sally starts talking to Christine describing what she was feeling. So they sort of take over, but you don't let that happen. You interrupt Sally from answering Christine and you focus attention back on you.*

E: (Interrupting and addressing Rosa.) Your name is Carol, isn't it?

R: What's that?

E: Your name is Carol.

R: My name? No.

E: What is it?

R: Do you want to know my name? (E. nods.) Rosa. (E. looks quizzically.)

E: Rosa?

R: Like Rose.

Z: *Now you go back to focusing on Rosa so you really don't let Sally get away with getting attention with the symptom. You go back on your direction which was to be working with Rosa.*

E: *And I'm in charge of the situation. Sally and Christine want to take charge. I do it so that Christine doesn't know I'm taking charge.*

E: All right, now I had Rosa show resistance.

Z: And she moved closer.

E: Yes.

Z: She's interested in what you're going to say.

E: "Resistance" has a different meaning to her.

Z: She has the same position that she took when she was making herself comfortable when you mentioned "resistance" before. A confirmation.

E: And Rose did a beautiful job of showing resistance. Rose showed resistance and also showed an acquiescence because her eyes did close. What's your name? (Addressing Sally.)

S: Sally.

E: Sally (Sally nods "yes.") Now I was having Rose show resistance and yet yielding. (Sally smiles.) Sally here developed a cough so she could free herself and show resistance *too.*

E: She moves forward.

Z: When you said the word "resistance" again. (The induction is replayed to demonstrate that Rosa does move when the word resistance is mentioned.)

Z: When you said "resistance" she moved forward and made herself comfortable. That's marvelous.

E: She had time to digest the word.

Z: Yes, and make that totally unconscious response. She's conditioned. You said "resistance" and then she moves to become more comfortable.

E: (To Rosa.) And you set the example for Sally to get her arm free.

R: Well, I closed my eyes because I thought it was easier at that point to close them. Otherwise you were going on telling me just to close them. So, I said, "Okay, I'll just close them so that you would stop asking me to close them."

Z: Now there, you congratuate Rosa. You say, "And you set the example for Sally to get her arm free." Why congratulate Rosa on paving the way?

E: Give credit wherever you can. I said "resistance" to Rosa and Sally took advantage of it. I congratulated Rosa and Sally took a share of it.

Z: *And Sally took a share of it. Very nice. It establishes a bond between them.*

E: Um-hum. But you closed them and Sally followed your example of the resistance. She did it indirectly by coughing. (Sally smiles.) Clever girl. (Sally coughs and clears her throat. To Sally.) Now, how are you going to get your legs free?

S: (Laughs.) Uh . . . I'll just make them. (E. waits expectantly. Sally laughs.) Okay, watch. Uh . . . (Sally looks around and down at her legs before she moves them. E. looks at her legs and waits.)

E: *That's an amusing situation, not a childish one.*

Z: *Yes, it becomes play.*

E: *With me.*

Z: *She's playing with you.*

E: *Yes. It's an amusing thing that she's sharing with me. We're both sharing it.*

Z: *And so then, are you putting a positive feeling tone on her resistance?*

E: *Putting a positive feeling tone on sharing with me.*

Z: *Yes, but before she moved, and because of that she could have some negative feeling. But you didn't let her have any negative feeling tone because of her symptom. You congratulated her on being intelligent and being clever. Now you ask her how she's going to move her legs, so you are again ratifying the trance, ratifying your control, but it's playful.*

E: *And we both enjoy it. It's all right to enjoy it.*

Z: *Any other thing you were teaching by doing that?*

E: *I'm maintaining positive rapport.*

E: And what did she do? She first made use of visual clues. She looked for a different place to put her foot.

Z: *She had to look before she moved her legs. She went through another sensory process.*

E: *Yes, her sensory process. It was my word "visual" and her action was visual.*

Z: *She looked before she moved her legs and so you were again pointing out a dissociation.*

E: Um-hum and keeping that dissociation under my control. It was under my control and in our cooperation. She was assisting in keeping it under my control.

E: She went through another sensory process in order to get a muscle response. (To Sally.) Now, *how* are you going to stand up?
S: Well, I'll just stand up. (She looks down first, laughs, then pushes herself forward and stands up. E. laughs.)
E: Does it ordinarily take that much effort? (Sally laughs and clears her throat.)

E: She reorients herself to her muscles.
Z: Yes, and it's a slow process so, again, she's ratifying the trance.
    The next thing you do is you come back to the candy. You hypnotically gave her some candy before when she was a little girl in the trance. It was symbolic of establishing rapport and establishing trust.

E: You're sure you ate some candy?
S: Just now? . . . Yeah . . . Or before?
E: Before.
S: Well, yeah, but I remembered that it was a suggestion.
E: (Moves forward and closer to Sally.) Do you think you're wide awake now?

Z: "Do you think you're wide awake now?" That's the introduction to the next trance. You talked about the candy, that reorients her to the previous trance and so there's the set-up to go to the next trance. This is very nice because, remember, she had a doubt. She's very noncommittal and now you play to allow her to have her doubts in a positive direction.

S: (Laughs.) Yeah, I think I'm pretty much awake.
E: Pretty much awake. *Are* you awake?

E: She got a bit closer to me.
Z: Sally moved closer to you then. Then she says, "pretty much awake." You confront her and ask her to specify directly, "Are you awake?" Then she says "yes" and you say, "Are you sure?"

Her habitual reply is to doubt but you set things up so she will doubt in a positive direction.

S: Yes, I'm awake.

E: You're sure of it?

S: (Laughs.) Yeah.

E: (Lifts Sally's right hand slowly. Her hands were clasped and he slowly separates them and lifts her left arm by the wrist.)

S: It doesn't look like it belongs to me.

E: What?

S: It doesn't look like it belongs to me . . . when you do that. (E. leaves Sally's arm suspended cataleptically. E. laughs and Sally laughs.)

E: You are less sure about being awake.

E: *"It doesn't look like it belongs to me." I kept in contact; she had time to think. "It doesn't belong to me."*

(E. points to the videotape deck and suggests to Z.) That belongs to you.

Z: *I wish it did. It doesn't.*

E: *See what happens; a contrary thought came in.*

Z: *Yes. (Laughs.) And what if it did belong to me?*

E: *What were you doing during that delay?*

Z: *(Laughing.) Going back and forth. I couldn't help but think about it. All right. First you make her specify that she's awake and there's a little harshness in your voice and it makes her be specific. Then you lift up her arm as you did to indicate the first trance, and you say, "You're less sure about being awake." Habitually, she's been making those noncommittal qualifying statements. You say, "less sure" and she has to agree that she's less sure about being awake.*

S: (Smiles.) Less sure, yes. I don't experience any, uh, sense of weight in my right arm; my right arm having no sense of weight.

E: Experiences no sense of weight. (Addressing Christine.) That answers your question, doesn't it?

E: *There's Rosa lifting her left hand to her face.*

Z: *Modeling.*

E: Rosa lifted her hand up to her face.

Z: Rosa was modeling Sally?

E: Um-hum. And making certain she could put her hand down.

Z: So, she was modeling and resisting at the same time. She wanted to have the experience. She wanted to explore and know what the experience was like on an unconscious level.

E: But, at first, she lifts her hand really without feeling the lifting. She felt it putting it down. Play it back and watch it. (The tape is replayed.)

E: (To Sally.) Can you *keep it there* or will it lift up to your face? (E. gestures "up" with his left hand.)

Z: I think that you inflected on the first clause, "Can you keep it there?" You model movement with your left arm, but I think it's the inflection that she responded to. But she had a choice. She was more verbally oriented than visually oriented so she responded to the intonation.

E: That's why it's so necessary to observe subjects over and over and over again.

Z: Keep reminding me.

E: Because you missed that movement of the right arm of Rosa lifting up one way and coming down another way.

S: Um, I can probably keep it there.

E: Watch it. I think it's going to move up.

S: Uh-uh . . . no. (Shakes head no.)

Z: You suggest it's going to move up. You again establish control and direction.

E: It'll move up in little jerks. (Pause.) (Sally looks blankly forward, then looks at E. Sally shakes her head no.)

E: Maybe you felt that jerk. It's coming up. (Sally looks at her hand.) See that jerk?

Z: Now that's a double-barreled word, the word "jerk." You remember Sally came in late. There were a number of times that she said she was concerned about interrupting all the people. Then out of her peripheral vision she has to see people and you're

saying "jerk" and watching the jerks. Are you making a double-barreled association to defuse feelings or confront her?
E: *I was not.*

S: When you mention it, I do feel it.
E: Hmmm?
S: When you mention a jerk, I do feel it.
E: You don't feel all the jerks.
S: Ummmmm. (E. pushes her hand down in slow stepwise movements by resting his fingers on her wrist. Then, he takes his hand away.)

E: *I pushed her hand down very gently, continuously.*
Z: *Yes and she resisted.*
E: *I pushed her hand down and then stopped pushing. She was maintaining the upright position and only lowering it in exact accord with my downward movement.*
Z: *Again emphasizing that she was allowing your control especially on a nonverbal level.*

E: You resisted having it lowered, didn't you?

Z: *She resisted having it lowered and that puts another feeling to the word "resistance." She resisted having it lowered.*
E: *But she was maintaining her relationship with me.*
Z: *As you define it. Under your definition.*

S: Um-hum.
E: Why?
S: I was okay with it the way that it was. (Laughing.)
E: (Smiles.) It was okay . . . the way it was.

Z: *You end the trance with her, the second trance, and you start telling the Golden Drumstick story. The theme of that story is you can live through very difficult circumstances and come out a winner. You put Sally on the spot and you had her live through some very difficult experiences in the beginning of the day by making her feel ill at ease and conspicuous. Then you told an anecdote that had the same general theme in accord with what had happened with Sally, but with a positive ending, i.e., there was more flexibility and expansion and a more efficient way of being in the world.*

Okay, why this second trance with Sally with the jerks in her arm?

E: *I had multiple purposes there. I had a whole group and I used Sally to illustrate and I might as well illustrate with a story that fit Sally personally and would satisfy the group.*

Z: *Yes, you could teach the group at the same time. You do that elegantly. You describe a principle and then illustrate it with a story and then do it at the same time in the room. But why this second trance with the arm movements?*

E: *I can tell you a story. A young man went into an old men's club in England. He started a conversation with one of the old gentlemen there. The young man said, "Have you ever done any mountain climbing?" The old man said, "Yes, once." They went on to another subject. The young man asked, "Have you ever traveled abroad?" The old man said, "Yes, once." Then the old man's son entered the room. The old man introduced him to his questioner and said, "Here's my son." The young man said, "Your only son?"*

I didn't want it to be a one time thing because that closes it off. When you have a second trance you can have a third, a fourth, a fifth, and that knowledge allows a continuation of the thought, "I can have a trance ten years from now."

Z: *Into the future. All right.*

Now, there's one more thing I want to ask you for some clarification: Here you work with Sally and with Rosa with consummate precision. You are not missing anything that's going on. You're very much with the person and very precise. Then, when you tell your stories and your teaching anecdotes, people don't usually realize that precision. It's like an O. Henry short story that comes up to the denouement, and all of a sudden the solution is apparent. But they don't get to realize all of the precision that went along before that decisive intervention. You don't emphasize that in your teaching either. If people pick it up, they pick it up, and if they don't, they don't.

E: *People can be lazy. If I started teaching by precision, I'd bore them.*

Now, how many people looking at this teaching analysis realize how much they overlooked. Because they feel they saw everything.

I know Dr. R. came back a month later with a transcript. I interpreted a certain word on page, let's say eight. Then on page 16, I interpreted another word there as an extension of the word on page eight. He said, "Are you making that up?" I said, "No. Let's go back to the old transcript." Then I told him that special interpretation of the word in such a slight way allowed for a major interpretation eight pages later.

After that, about two months later, he came in with the original manuscript and had me interpret it again. He had a secretary transcribe it and then he matched it with my first interpretation. He found that I gave him the same interpretation both times. Now Dr. R. had been trained well to take a history in detail but he didn't know that I could pay attention to detail much better than he could.

People assume so much. The first time Dr. R. and his wife came to see me, his wife was wearing sandals, that's all, no stockings. He introduced me to her and I sent her out of the room. I asked him, "How long have you been married?" He said, "Fifteen years." I said, "And you've come to me to learn about observations?" He said, "Yes." I said, "Now you've been married 15 years. Does your wife have webbed toes?" He said, "No." I said, "She has. Now don't you look at her feet when I call her back. I'll ask her the same question." When she came back I asked her some questions, then I asked her if she had webbed toes. She said, "No." I said, "Are you sure?" She said, "Yes." I said, "Your husband is sure of it too. Now let's look and see." The second and third toe of both feet were webbed. People assume so much.

Z: *Overlooking the obvious.*

(Next E. tells some additional anecdotes that are directed to Z. The anecdotes have to do with enhancing visual perceptiveness and trusting one's unconscious.)